Patent Ethics

Patent Ethics

Prosecution

David Hricik and Mercedes Meyer

Oxford University Press, Inc., publishes works that further Oxford University's objective of excellence in research, scholarship, and education.

Oxford   New York
Auckland   Cape Town   Dar es Salaam   Hong Kong   Karachi   Kuala Lumpur   Madrid   Melbourne
Mexico City   Nairobi   New Delhi   Shanghai   Taipei   Toronto

With offices in
Argentina   Austria   Brazil   Chile   Czech Republic   France   Greece   Guatemala   Hungary   Italy
Japan   Poland   Portugal   Singapore   South Korea   Switzerland   Thailand   Turkey   Ukraine
Vietnam

Library of Congress Cataloging-in-Publication Data
Hricik, David Charles.
  Patent ethics : prosecution / David Hricik, Mercedes Meyer.
     p. cm.
  Includes bibliographical references and index.
  ISBN 978-0-19-533835-5 ((pbk.) : alk. paper)
  1. Patent lawyers—United States. 2. Legal ethics—United States.
  3. Patent suits—United States. 4. Attorney and client—United States.
     I. Meyer, Mercedes. II. Title.
  KF3165.H75 2009
  346.7304'86—dc22   2009005446

1 2 3 4 5 6 7 8 9

Printed in the United States of America on acid-free paper

Note to Readers
This publication is designed to provide accurate and authoritative information in regard to the subject matter covered. It is based upon sources believed to be accurate and reliable and is intended to be current as of the time it was written. It is sold with the understanding that the publisher is not engaged in rendering legal, accounting, or other professional services. If legal advice or other expert assistance is required, the services of a competent professional person should be sought. Also, to confirm that the information has not been affected or changed by recent developments, traditional legal research techniques should be used, including checking primary sources where appropriate.

(Based on the Declaration of Principles jointly adopted by a Committee of the American Bar Association and a Committee of Publishers and Associations.)

You may order this or any other Oxford University Press publication by
visiting the Oxford University Press website at www.oup.com

David dedicates this book to his mother and father, to Joella, Abby, Alex, Houston, and Julian, and to those who taught him what little he knows about writing well.

Mercedes dedicates this book to her husband, Stephen, and daughter, Merrill, for their patience while she wrote the book, often on family vacations; to her parents, Dan and Gunda Meyer (the 2nd Meyer textbook, but with all words and no pictures); and to David Hricik for taking her along on this great quest.

Contents

ABOUT THE AUTHORS   xiii

CHAPTER 1 **Introduction to the Subject Matter**   1

CHAPTER 2 **Registration and the Unauthorized Practice of Law**   5

    A. The Basic Grant of Authority   5
    B. The Limitations and the Unauthorized Practice of Law   6
        1. Patent Attorneys   6
        2. Patent Agents   7
        3. Validity, Infringement, and Other Opinions
           and Evaluations   9

CHAPTER 3 **Choice of Law: Identifying the Applicable Standards**   11

    A. Basic Choice of Law   11
    B. Standards Applicable During Prosecution   14
        1. Office of Enrollment and Discipline   15
        2. U.S. Patent and Trademark Office Disqualification   16
    C. Preemption by the Patent and Trademark Office Code
       of Professional Conduct   17
    D. Federal Circuit Choice of Law   19
    E. Conclusion on Choice of Law   21
    F. Special Choice of Law Issues Facing Patent Agents   22

CHAPTER 4 **Client Identity, Matter Scope, Ending Matters,
and Prospective Consent**   25

    A. Client Identity   25
        1. Inventors   26
           A. The Law   26
           B. What to Do   30
        2. Business Entities   31
           A. The Law   31
           B. What to Do   37

B. Representation Ending Dates in Patent Matters 37
1. The Law 37
2. What to Do 39
C. Scope of the Representation 39
D. Prospective Consent 40
1. Standards Governing Prospective Consent 40

CHAPTER 5 **Loyalty and Current Client Conflicts of Interest** 45

A. The Patent and Trademark Office Code of Professional
Conduct and Analogous State Law 47
B. The Meaning of "Adversity" and "Differing Interests" 48
C. The Meaning of "Material Limitations" 51
D. Adversity and Material Limitations Created by the
Property Right 52
1. Problems Created by Priority 52
A. Narrowing Claims to Disfavor One Client
Over Another 52
B. Office Action Responses and Rule 131 Antedating 54
E. The Conflict Created by the Right to Exclude 59
F. Information: Liability and Conflict 60
G. Additional Possible Prosecution Conflicts 61
H. What to Do 62
1. Prosecution Problems 62
2. Corporate Affiliate Intellectual Property 63
3. Lateral Hires 63
I. Conclusion 64

CHAPTER 6 **Former Client Conflicts** 65

A. The Three Principal Prohibitions 65
1. The Substantial Relationship Test 66
2. Disqualification for Possession of Confidences 69
3. Challenging or Interpreting Work Product 70
B. Examples of Former Client Conflicts 71

CHAPTER 7 **Competency in Patent Prosecution** 73

A. Introduction 74
B. Selecting the Proper Form of Protection 75
1. Patent, Trade Secret, Copyright, Trademark,
or a Combination 75
C. Which Type of Patent or Other Form of Protection to Use? 77
D. Which Type of Claim: Process, Product,
or Product-by-Process? 78
E. Which Form(s) of Claim? 79
F. Definiteness 80

G. Drafting Claims as Broadly as Practicable   81
H. Drafting Claims to Avoid Unnecessary Amendment   83
I.   Appealing Improper Rejections   84
J. Being Clear and Precise in Claims and Specification   85
K. Drafting Specifications That Comply with the Patent Act 87
    1. Best Mode   87
    2. Written Description   88
    3. Enabling Disclosure   89
L. Including All, but Only, True Inventors   90
    1. The Basic Requirement   90
    2. Special Issues Concerning Joint Inventors   92
        A. Who Is a Joint Inventor?   92
        B. What Does Joint Inventorship Convey by
            Way of a Property Right?   94
        C. What to Do   94
        D. Problems Lawyers Face When Representing
            Joint Inventors   97
        E. Conclusion   98
M. Responding to Office Actions   98
N. Meeting Deadlines and Prosecuting Diligently   99
O. Handing-Off or Giving Notice of the Maintenance
    Fee Obligation   100
P. Using Continuation-in-Part Applications to Obtain
    Earlier Filing Dates When Proper   101

CHAPTER 8 **The Duty of Candor and Inequitable Conduct**   103

A. Background   105
    1. Preemption of State Law   105
    2. First Principles of Inequitable Conduct   111
    3. Materiality Is Not Limited to the Circumstances
        Specified in Rule 1.56   112
B. Knowledge of the Information Is Not Necessarily Required:
    The Duty to Investigate May Exist, but Imputation
    Should Not Apply   116
C. Knowledge That the Information Is Material
    Is Not Necessarily Required   123
D. Intent to Deceive May Be Inferred   125
    1. *Whose* Knowledge Counts?   127
    2. *When* Must Information Be Disclosed?   128
E. Recurrent Fact Patterns Constituting Inequitable
    Conduct   129
    1. Nondisclosure of Prior Art   129
    2. Submitted but Buried Material Information   131
    3. Submitted but Mischaracterized References   133

4. Misleading Translations of Foreign-Language
   Prior Art References   135
   A. Withholding Full or Partial Translations the
      Applicant Possesses   135
   B. Submitting a Partial Translation That Omits
      the Most Material Aspects of the Reference   136
   C. Characterizing the Whole Reference on a
      Partial Translation   138
5. Withholding Information That Contradicts Statements
   to the U.S. Patent and Trademark Office   139
6. Test Data   139
7. Relationships between Declarants and Applicants   143
8. Section 112 Requirements   144
   A. Enablement   144
   B. Best Mode   146
9. Prior Sales   146
10. Co-Pending Applications   148
   A. Of Same Client of Same Lawyer   148
   B. Of Different Clients of Same Lawyer   149
   C. Of Different Clients of Other Firm Lawyers   149
11. Rejection of Substantially Similar Claims by
    Another Examiner   150
12. *McKesson* Disclosure Statements   151
13. Existence of and Information Gleaned from
    Ongoing Litigation   153
14. Misrepresentations of Information Relating
    to Inventorship   155
15. Misclaiming Priority of Disclosure   157
16. Maintenance Fees, Small Entity Status,
    and Inequitable Conduct   158
17. Petitions to Reinstate   159
18. Petitions to Make Special   160
19. Reexamination   160

CHAPTER 9 **Maintenance Fees and Annuities**   163

A. Maintenance Fees   164
B. Other Issues   166

CHAPTER 10 **Combining Prosecution with Other Forms
of Representation**   167

A. Identifying the Applicable Standards   168
B. Combining Prosecution and Litigation   169
   1. The Possibility of Misuse of Discovery Materials
      While Prosecuting Applications   169
      A. Is Prosecution of Patents by Itself Sufficient to Bar
         Access to Highly Confidential Information?   170
   2. *In re Sibia*   172

3. The Majority View   176
4. A Suggested Analysis   180
C. A Proposed Prosecution Bar Raises Potential
    Conflicts and Liability   182
D. Issues to Consider in Crafting Protective Orders   186
    1. Liability and Disqualification of Prosecuting
        Litigators   190
E. Inequitable Conduct as a Conflict   191
F. Depositions of Prosecuting Litigators   192
    1. Advocate-as-Witness Disqualification   194
G. Combining Opinion and Trial Representations   197
    1. Advocate-as-Witness Disqualification   197
        A. The Courts Split on Advocate-as-
            Witness Disqualification   198
        B. What to Do   200
    2. Enhanced Risk of Waiver of Work Product   201
        A. What to Do   209
H. Conclusion   209

APPENDIX 1 Annotated Patent and Trademark Office Code of
            Professional Conduct   211

APPENDIX 2 Forms and Checklists   283

APPENDIX 3 U.S. Patent and Trademark Office—Office of
            Enrollment and Discipline Decisions   307

APPENDIX 4 Correlation Tables   333

TABLE OF CASES   345

INDEX   361

About the Authors

David Hricik is a Professor of Law at Mercer University School of Law in Macon, Georgia, where he has taught patent law and legal ethics, among other courses, since 2002. He represented clients in patent litigation, legal malpractice, and general commercial litigation for 14 years before becoming a full-time faculty member. He continues to represent clients in patent litigation, and to consult with law firms, insurance companies, and brokers on risk management, conflicts of interest, and best practices in patent prosecution and litigation. He also serves as an expert witness in cases involving ethical issues in patent practice. He has written and spoken extensively on ethical issues in intellectual property practice, civil procedure, and patent law.

Mercedes Meyer is a Partner with the law firm of Drinker Biddle & Reath LLP in Washington, D.C. For 12 years, her practice has focused on assisting clients, primarily in the biotechnology and pharmaceutical sectors, to develop and maintain their patent portfolios worldwide. She is an active member of the American Intellectual Property Law Association (AIPLA), where she is the current Vice Chairperson of the Biotechnology Committee. She has a doctorate in virology from the University of Texas M.D. Anderson Cancer Center and University of Texas Health Science Center-Houston Health Science Center; a law degree from the University of Houston Law Center; and undergraduate degree in chemistry from Bryn Mawr College. Mercedes has prepared and prosecuted numerous patent applications, prepared a variety of opinions on patents and patent applications, and has appeared before the Board of Patent Appeals and Interferences in several patent interference proceedings. Mercedes is a registered patent attorney before the U.S. Patent and Trademark Office, as well as being licensed in Texas and the District of Columbia.

CHAPTER
1

Introduction to the Subject Matter

This book addresses ethical issues that face lawyers, patent agents, companies, and firms that prosecute, litigate, and opine about patents. It begins by discussing choice of law, which is an issue pertinent to all intellectual property (IP) lawyers, and then addresses several issues of concern specific to patent practitioners.

Although some of the authority we rely on was decided under other standards, our focus is the ethical standards promulgated by the U.S. Patent and Trademark Office (USPTO) and contained in the Patent and Trademark Office Code of Professional Conduct (PTO Code),[1] an annotated copy of which is in Appendix 1.

The PTO Code is largely based on the American Bar Association (ABA) Model Code of Professional Responsibility (Model Code).[2] Thus, it is a comprehensive ethical code that covers everything found in codes governing lawyers.[3] The PTO Code applies to lawyers who become registered to prosecute patents, as well as to patent agents.[4] The PTO Code today must be balanced with the fact that most states follow the 1983 version of ABA Model Rules of Professional Responsibility (Model Rules), and that other states follow a version of the Model Rules amended soon after 2000 and often referred to as the "Ethics 2000" version of the Model Rules. No state still follows the Model Code. Thus, differences between the PTO Code and rules in effect in the 50 states are likely to remain into the future. The need to understand these differences will increase if the current trend of heightened Office of Enrollment and Discipline oversight continues.

Congress authorized the USPTO to establish disciplinary rules and to discipline practitioners who violate them.[5] In accordance with that authority,

---

1. *See* 37 C.F.R. §§ 10.01–170 *et seq.*
2. *See generally* David S. D'Ascenzo, *Federal Objective or Common Law Champerty?—Ethical Issues Regarding Lawyers Acquiring an Interest in a Patent*, 3 TEX. INTELL. PROP. L.J. 255, 258–59, 270 (1995).
3. *See generally* William Jacob, *Professional Ethics Before the USPTO: A Discussion for Beginners*, 16 PROF. L. 22 (2005) (describing scope of PTO Code).
4. *See* 37 C.F.R. § 10.1(r).
5. 35 U.S.C. §§ 2(b)(2)(D), 32 (2006).

the USPTO established the Office of Enrollment and Discipline (OED).[6] The OED reviews complaints, conducts investigations, and enforces the PTO Code.[7] Over the years, the OED has written numerous opinions interpreting and applying the PTO Code.[8] Over the last 20 years, the number of disciplinary actions for practitioners has increased. The OED has indicated that it will pursue violations of the PTO Code and has recently provided a more expansive view of the scope of practitioners' duties. Consequently, practitioners can expect investigations by the OED will continue to increase.

Malpractice claims based on alleged errors in patent prosecution are also increasing, both in terms of their frequency and their severity.[9] It is important to recognize what may not be obvious: If liability is clear—such as if a deadline was missed through negligence—then the issues will be causation and damages. Under such circumstances, the law in some states almost presumes that the negligence that causes the loss of patent rights causes the damage, with the only question being the amount.[10]

The consequences to aggrieved clients of malpractice or a conflict of interest have grown as the value of patents and other intellectual property has grown. Judgments in favor of patentees in the tens- and hundreds of millions of dollars are no longer unheard of. The fact that judgments and settlements in intellectual property (IP) infringement litigation have grown significantly over the past twenty years also means that the liability for a mistake during prosecution has also increased.

These trends have not gone unnoticed. Twenty years ago, patent law did not garner the highest cost for malpractice insurance, rather the practice of securities law did. Today, the highest malpractice insurance cost rests with those firms practicing intellectual property law and especially those involved in complex worldwide filings. Mistakes or conflicts of interest that affect prosecution can, therefore, lead to substantial claims against lawyers.[11]

The practice of patent law also presents problems that do not occur in other types of law such as real estate, bankruptcy, or even environmental practice.

---

6. *See id.*; 37 C.F.R. § 10.2(a).
7. *See, e.g., Weiffenbach v. Logan,* 27 U.S.P.Q.2d 1870 (Comm'r Pat. 1993); *McCandlish v. Doe,* 22 U.S.P.Q.2d 1223 (Comm'r Pat. 1992); *Weiffenbach v. Frank,* 18 U.S.P.Q.2d 1397 (Comm'r Pat. 1991); *Weiffenbach v. Gould,* 14 U.S.P.Q.2d 1331 (Comm'r Pat. 1989); *Small v. Weiffenbach,* 10 U.S.P.Q.2d 1898 (Comm'r Pat. 1989).
8. *See, e.g.,* cases cited in the Appendices.
9. *See generally* A. Samuel Oddi, *Patent Attorney Malpractice: An Oxymoron No More,* 2004 U. Ill. J.L. Tech. & Pol'y 1 (2004).
10. *See Kairos Scientific Inc. v. Fish & Richardson, P.C.,* 2006 Cal. App. Unpub. LEXIS 667 (2006) (mostly upholding award of $30 million in case where firm admitted missing a PCT application deadline).
11. *E.g., Jazz Photo Corp. v. Dreier,* 2005 WL 3542468 (D.N.J. Dec. 23, 2005) (client who had filed for bankruptcy after judgment for $30 million was entered against it sued its patent litigation counsel for negligence in the underlying suit).

The scenarios common to patent practice require vigilance to spot conflicts of interest, both when the matter is taken in by the firm and in some cases during years of prosecution and maintenance. The practice requires review of new matters based on the parties and any adverse parties or affiliates, and also the subject matter must be analyzed to determine whether conflicts exist. For example, issues can arise when rebutting a rejection that cites as a reference a patent owned by another patent client. Other issues related to the unique nature of patent practice also arise. Because patent prosecution can be conducted by nonlawyer patent agents, questions of the unauthorized practice of law arise, such as when a patent agent assists in obtaining an executed assignment.[12] Likewise, complex issues concerning the role of state law in governing practice before the office can arise. Those issues implicate common prosecution issues, such as the duty or candor.

The book is organized in five parts. In the first part, we provide a thorough, topical discussion of ethical issues arising in prosecution. Appendix 1 includes the PTO Code, annotated with case law and further commentary. Appendix 2 includes forms, referenced in the first part of the book, for adaption to your particular practice, and which are designed to reduce liability in patent practice. Appendix 3 includes a summary of OED decisions. Finally, Appendix 4 reprints a table comparing the PTO Code with other likely pertinent ethical codes.

---

12. Effective September 15, 2008, patent agents may prepare an assignment but only in limited circumstances: specifically, only if it relates to an application in which the agent represents the owner "and when drafting the assignment the practitioner does not more than replicate the terms of a previously existing oral or written obligation of assignment from one person or party to another person or party." 37 C.F.R. § 11.5(b)(1)(ii).

CHAPTER

2

Registration and the Unauthorized Practice of Law

A. The Basic Grant of Authority   5

B. The Limitations and the Unauthorized Practice of Law   6

   1. Patent Attorneys   6

   2. Patent Agents   7

   3. Validity, Infringement, and Other Opinions and Evaluations   9

A. The Basic Grant of Authority

The U.S. Patent and Trademark Office (USPTO) does not have the power to grant licenses to lawyers or nonlawyers to practice law generally.[1] Thus, registration as a patent attorney or patent agent does not permit a person to, for example, litigate a tort case for an injured plaintiff. Instead, registration only empowers the person "to represent applicants having prospective or immediate business before the USPTO in the preparation and prosecution of patent applications."[2]

In late 2008, the USPTO for the first time defined more precisely what the phrase "preparation and prosecution of patent applications" means. The USPTO wrote that:

> Practice before the Office in patent matters includes, but is not limited to, pre-paring and prosecuting any patent application, consulting with or giving advice to a client in contemplation of filing a patent application or other document with the Office, drafting the specification or claims of a patent application; drafting an amendment or reply to a communication from the Office that may require written argument to establish the patentability of a claimed invention; drafting a reply to a communication from the Office regarding a patent appli-cation; and drafting a communication for a public use, interference, reexami-nation proceeding, petition, appeal to or any other proceeding before the Board

---

1. *Sperry v. Florida ex rel.* Florida Bar, 373 U.S. 379, 402 (1963).
2. 37 C.F.R. § 11.5(a).

of Patent Appeals and Interferences, or other proceeding. Registration to practice before the Office in patent cases sanctions the performance of those services which are reasonably necessary and incident to the preparation and prosecution of patent applications or other proceeding before the Office involving a patent application or patent in which the practitioner is authorized to participate. The services include:

    (i) Considering the advisability of relying upon alternative forms of protection which may be available under state law, and

    (ii) Drafting an assignment or causing an assignment to be executed for the patent owner in contemplation of filing or prosecution of a patent application for the patent owner, where the practitioner represents the patent owner after a patent issues in a proceeding before the Office, and when drafting the assignment the practitioner does no more than replicate the terms of a previously existing oral or written obligation of assignment from one person or party to another person or party.[3]

The basic grant of power is quite broad, because it permits a practitioner (patent agent or patent attorney) to engage in all activities listed in the paragraph, as well as other unlisted activities in preparing or prosecuting applications.

More important than the grant, however, are the limitations implicit in the language to advise about alternative forms of protection and to prepare assignments. Those limitations, however, are not obvious or intuitive.

B. The Limitations and the Unauthorized Practice of Law

There are limitations inherent in this grant, and significant differences in the limitations with respect to patent attorneys as compared to patent agents. Some of those limitations are specific, although others are implicit in the grant.

1. Patent Attorneys

With respect to patent attorneys, the grant makes it clear that a patent attorney can advise a client contemplating the filing of a patent application to consider relying on alternative forms of intellectual property protection available under state law. However, whether the patent attorney could actually advise about the scope and content of those protections would depend on

---

3. 37 C.F.R. § 11.5(b)(1).

whether that advice constitutes the unauthorized practice of law. In other words, the authority to advise the client to consider alternative forms does not constitute a grant of power by the USPTO to advise as to the substance, as the commentary to the rules makes clear. Specifically, after explaining that a patent agent should advise a client to consult "with an attorney of the client's choice [the state statute providing an alternative form of protection has been adopted] regarding state law based alternative forms of protection available under statute law," the USPTO wrote:

> The same would obtain for a registered patent attorney who is not licensed in the state where the attorney is practicing unless the state where the attorney is practicing has authorized the attorney to provide legal services. For example, if the attorney is "corporate counsel" or "in-house counsel" and is licensed to practice law in another state, the attorney may provide legal advice about the state's statutes to the attorney's corporate employer if the state where the attorney is practicing has authorized the attorney to provide legal services for the attorney's employer in the state where the attorney is practicing.[4]

Thus, patent attorneys must consult the state law regarding the unauthorized practice of law to determine whether they can advise about the substance of state law. The power to advise a client to consider alternative forms does not authorize advising about the substance.

With respect to drafting assignments, the same analysis holds true: The lawyer cannot undertake to draft an assignment for a client, other than in the limited form authorized by the rule, without determining whether doing so is authorized by state law. If not, the lawyer may be engaging in the unauthorized practice of law.

Beyond that, and as is more fully shown below, a lawyer cannot rely on his USPTO registration to justify activities that do not relate to patent applications or patents. For example, whether a patent attorney can provide an opinion of counsel to a client turns on whether the opinion relates to patent prosecution; if the opinion does not, then state law must authorize the patent attorney to act, as registration will not.

2. Patent Agents

With respect to patent agents, the agent is severely restricted in both advising about state law and providing assignments.

A patent agent, not being licensed to practice law, cannot advise about the substance of state law concerning alternative forms of protection. Thus,

---

4. 73 Fed. Reg. 47,650 (Aug. 14, 2008).

although a patent attorney can, when authorized by state law, advise an applicant or prospective applicant about alternative forms, a patent agent can only advise the client to consider alternative forms, but he or she cannot advise about the substance.

The authority of an agent to draft an assignment is, for similar reasons, limited solely to the authority granted by the rule: To draft an assignment beyond the scope of the rule is to engage in the unauthorized practice of law, at least where the drafting of an assignment constitutes the practice of law in the state where the patent agent is acting. For example, the USPTO in its commentary to the 2008 amendments wrote:

> There is no statute or rule requiring training in contract law as a condition to be registered as a patent agent. No comment suggested any means whereby patent agents could receive adequate training and the competence to provide legal advice could be confirmed. Absent adequate training, a person drafting an assignment could overlook issues for which lawyers have received training. For example, in addition to preparing an assignment form, it may be necessary to advise whether the inventor is obligated to assign the invention, and if so, to whom. It may be necessary to resolve ownership questions, for example, to file a terminal disclaimer where there is no previously existing employment agreement or where an employment agreement contains no obligation to assign patent rights. In some situations, assignments lead to serious complexities, which can impact title and prevent patent enforcement. Patent agents are not empowered by their registration to provide advice about title and enforcement of patents. Accordingly, it is appropriate to set forth authority of practitioners to prepare an assignment or cause an assignment to be executed by virtue of their registration.
>
> Preparing an assignment or causing an assignment to be executed is appropriate only when they are reasonably necessary and incidental to the preparation and prosecution of a patent application, or other proceeding before the Office involving a patent application or patent in which the practitioner is authorized to participate. The patent application may be, for example, a provisional, nonprovisional or reissue application. Other proceedings include, for example, an interference or reexamination proceeding. A practitioner, by virtue of being registered, may prepare an assignment or cause it to be signed in the foregoing circumstances if in drafting the assignment the practitioner does no more than replicate the terms of a previously existing oral or written obligation of assignment from one person or party to another person or party. Registration does not authorize a registered practitioner to recommend or determine the terms to be included in an assignment. The practitioner is not authorized to select or recommend a particular form assignment from among standard form assignments. Registration does not authorize a practitioner to draft an assignment or other document in circumstances that do not contemplate a proceeding before the Office involving a patent application or patent. For example, where an assignment is prepared in contemplation of selling a patent or in contemplation of litigation, there is no proceeding before the Office. When, after a patent issues, there is no proceeding before the Office in

which the patent agent may represent the patent owner, drafting an assignment or causing the assignment to be signed are not activities reasonably necessary and incidental to representing a patent owner before the Office.

Section 11.5(b)(1) provides circumstances in which a registered practitioner may prepare an assignment or cause an assignment to be executed. The assignment must be reasonably necessary and incidental to filing and prosecuting a patent application for the patent owner or the practitioner represents the patent owner after the patent issues in a proceeding before the Office. In drafting the assignment the practitioner must not do more than replicate the terms of a previously existing oral or written obligation of assignment from one person or party to another person or party. Thus, where a previously existing written employment agreement between an inventor and the employing corporation contains one or more clauses obligating an inventor to assign to the company inventions made in the course of employment, a practitioner may draft an assignment wherein the provisions replicate those of the employment agreement.[5]

Thus, unless the assignment is authorized by the rule, or its preparation does not constitute the practice of law under applicable state law, then the patent agent may not draft it.

3. Validity, Infringement, and Other Opinions and Evaluations

Other limitations on patent agents and patent attorneys relate to opinions. The grant of authority is limited to that necessary to prosecute patents. Consequently, an opinion for use in litigation is not an opinion for use in prosecution. Thus, if giving an opinion would constitute the practice of law, then a patent agent may not provide it; and if it would constitute the unauthorized practice of law, then the patent attorney may not provide it.

The USPTO made both these points clear and attempted to provide better guidance as to when an opinion would, and would not, relate to prosecution in its 2008 commentary to the new rules:

> Whether a validity opinion involves practice before the Office depends on the circumstances in which the opinion is sought and furnished. For example, an opinion of the validity of another party's patent when the client is contemplating litigation and not seeking reexamination of the other party's patent could not be reasonably necessary and incident to the preparation and prosecution of patent applications or other proceedings before the Office involving a patent application or patent. In such situations, the opinion may constitute

---

5. *Id.*

unauthorized practice of law. Similarly, a validity opinion for the sale or purchase of the patent is neither the preparation nor the prosecution of a patent application. Likewise, the opinion is not a proceeding before the Office involving a patent application or patent. Registration to practice before the Office in patent cases does not authorize a person to provide a validity opinion that is not reasonably necessary and incident to representing parties before the Office. In contrast, a validity opinion issued in contemplation of filing a request for reexamination would be in contemplation of a proceeding before the Office involving a patent. Due to registration to practice before the Office in patent cases, a practitioner may issue a validity opinion in contemplation of filing a request for reexamination.

In no circumstance would practice before the Office include the rendering of opinions on infringement. Under the law, the Office has no authority to resolve infringement cases. Thus, registration to practice before the Office in patent cases does not include authority to render infringement opinions.[6]

These limitations on opinion practice might not be apparent to patent attorneys or patent agents. They were the subject of significant criticism during the notice and comment period, and might yet be challenged. However, for the time being, they are the boundaries noted by the USPTO.

---

6. *Id.*, citing *Mahoning Cty. Bar Assn. v. Harpman*, 608 N.E.2d 872 (Ohio Bd.Unauth. Prac. 1993). In that case, the state held that various documents created for a reexamination were within the grant of authority from the Patent Office, but the provision of legal services to the patentee after the reexamination had ended constituted the unauthorized practice of law.

3

Choice of Law
Identifying the Applicable Standards

A. Basic Choice of Law   11

B. Standards Applicable During Prosecution   14
    1. Office of Enrollment and Discipline   15
    2. U.S. Patent and Trademark Office Disqualification   16

C. Preemption by the Patent and Trademark Office
    Code of Professional Conduct   17

D. Federal Circuit Choice of Law   19

E. Conclusion on Choice of Law   21

F. Special Choice of Law Issues Facing Patent Agents   22

A. Basic Choice of Law

This section addresses a fundamental question that confronts patent practitioners: Which ethical rules will apply during either prosecution or federal court litigation? By itself, the question of choice of law can be complicated and is an inquiry that lawyers must undertake with little guidance.[1]

Four sets of ethical rules and the authorities interpreting them can be relevant to determining the ethical, disciplinary, and malpractice issues[2] that arise during patent prosecution or litigation: the Model Code of Professional Responsibility (Model Code),[3] the Model Rules of Professional Conduct

---

1. Judith A. McMorrow, *The (F)utility of Rules: Regulating Attorney Conduct in Federal Court*, S F 13 ALJ-ABA 317 (2000).
2. As explained below, ethical rules are applied by the PTO in disciplinary matters and in deciding disqualification motions, and in some states ethical rules inform the standard of care applicable in malpractice suits.
3. Model Code of Professional Responsibility (1980), *available at* http://www.abanet.org/cpr/mrpc/mcpr.pdf [hereinafter Model code]. Note that links to all of the ethics opinions and

(Model Rules),[4] the disciplinary rules of the state in which the practitioner is also licensed (for example, for practitioners licensed in Washington, D.C., the Washington Rules of Professional Conduct, known as the "Washington Rules,"[5] and the code developed by the U.S. Patent and Trademark Office (USPTO) entitled *Representation of Others Before the Patent and Trademark Office* (Patent and Trademark Office Code of Professional Conduct [PTO Code]).[6]

The Model Code was promulgated by the American Bar Association (ABA) in 1969 and was widely adopted by the states as their disciplinary rules.[7] The PTO Code is based on the Model Code, but it was not adopted by the USPTO until 1985.[8] Both the Model Code and the PTO Code are all-encompassing codes of professional conduct, covering issues ranging from the amount of fees,[9] to lawyer advertising,[10] to protection of confidential information of a client.[11] However, the USPTO modified the language in the Model Code, so the wording of a particular rule in the PTO Code is not necessarily identical to the wording in the Model Code.[12]

The ABA promulgated the Model Rules in 1983.[13] Most states soon thereafter replaced their versions of the Model Code with their own versions of the Model Rules,[14] making changes to the Model Rules before adopting them.[15] As a result, the wording of a state rule can differ from its Model Rules counterpart.

---

other rules cited here (as well as every other set on the web) are available on www.legalethics.com or www.Hricik.com.

4. Model Rules of Professional Conduct (2003), *available at* http://www.abanet.org/cpr/mrpc/mrpc_home.html [hereinafter Model Rules].

5. Washington Rules of Professional Conduct, *available at* http://www.law.uh.edu/libraries/ethics/RulesofDisciplinaryProcedure/033107.pdf (effective Mar. 31, 2007).

6. PTO Definitions, 37 C.F.R. § 10.1 (2005).

7. "The Model Code was adopted by the [ABA] House of Delegates on August 12, 1969, and subsequently by the vast majority of state and federal jurisdictions." Annotated Model Rules of Prof. Conduct vii (5th ed. 2003) [hereinafter Ann. Model Rules].

8. The PTO Code was first proposed in 1984. Practice Before the Patent and Trademark Office, 49 Fed. Reg. 10012–01 (proposed Mar. 16, 1984) (to be codified at pts. 1, 2, and 10). It went through extensive notice and comment periods and was adopted as a final rule on February 6, 1985. Practice Before the Patent and Trademark Office, 50 Fed. Reg. 5158–01 (Feb. 6, 1985).

9. *E.g.*, 37 C.F.R. § 10.36 (2005).

10. *E.g.*, *id.* § 10.32.

11. *E.g.*, *id.* § 10.57.

12. For a fairly extensive list of the variations among states, *see* ABA/BNA Lawyers' Manual on Professional Conduct §§ 01:11–66 (2004).

13. *See* Ann. Model Rules, at viii–ix.

14. *Id.* at viii.

15. The ABA also made more than thirty amendments to the Model Rules. *See* Ann. Model Rules, at vii.

Other federal statutes,[16] cases applying them,[17] internal USPTO practice guidelines (principally the Manual of Patent Examining Procedure [MPEP]),[18] and cases applying the MPEP,[19] can also have an impact on a practitioner's responsibilities. Finally, state substantive law—the law of agency, of fiduciaries, and the like—and state case law can inform either the standard of care or other aspects of a representation.[20]

When a question as to the propriety of lawyer conduct arises during federal court litigation, a lawyer must analyze which ethical rules and whose interpretation of them applies.[21] Furthermore, the propriety of some conduct turns on whether a district court must follow the Federal Circuit's interpretation of the Federal Rules of Civil Procedure, or that of the regional circuit in which the district court hearing a patent infringement suit sits. Importantly, when deciding whether a prosecuting litigator may have access to an opponent's proprietary information, the issue of which circuit's interpretation of the rules of procedure matters greatly. Thus, practitioners must also be aware of the body of case law addressing when an issue is "unique to patent law" and so is governed by Federal Circuit law, and when it is not and is governed by regional circuit law.

The fact that the rules differ in wording is important because both the USPTO and federal courts hearing patent infringement suits rely on decisions interpreting the Model Code and Model Rules as well as state versions of the Model Rules in deciding ethical matters even though those rules are worded differently. In addition, tribunals have frequently given differing interpretations even to identically worded rules.[22] Nonetheless, the following shows that all of these ethical rules, and decisions interpreting them, can bear on matters arising during patent prosecution and litigation.

---

16. *E.g.*, 35 U.S.C. § 33 (2005).
17. *E.g.*, *Galarowicz v. Comm'r of Patents & Trademarks*, 848 F.2d 1245 (Fed. Cir. 1988) (unpublished).
18. The MPEP is the Manual of Patent Examining Procedure, and comprises the PTO's internal guidelines. "While the MPEP does not have the force of law, it is entitled to judicial notice as an official interpretation of statutes or regulations as long as it is not in conflict therewith." *Bristol-Myers Squibb Co. v. Ben Venue Labs.*, 90 F. Supp. 2d 522, 537 n.7 (D.N.J. 2000).
19. *E.g.*, *Molins PLC v. Textron, Inc.*, 48 F.3d 1172 (Fed. Cir. 1995) (duty of disclosure under MPEP).
20. *See, e.g., Monco v. Janus*, 583 N.E.2d 575, 581 (Ill. App. 1991) (a transaction between patent practitioner and client must be "closely scrutinized").
21. *See* McMorrow, *supra* note 1.
22. Most notorious is the variation courts have given to the scope of whether and if so which current and former employees are "represented by counsel" in terms of Model Rule 4.2. *See generally Messing, Rudavsky & Weliky, P.C. v. President & Fellows of Harvard Coll.*, 764 N.E.2d 825 (Mass. 2002) (discussing the numerous interpretations of this rule).

B. Standards Applicable During Prosecution

The problem that practitioners face when seeking to identify the controlling standard during prosecution is twofold: First, during representation of a client before the USPTO, different ethical standards may be applied even within the USPTO, and second, there is insufficient judicial or administrative guidance on the question of whether the PTO Code preempts application of state law. This lack of guidance leaves it unclear, for example, whether a lawyer complying with the USPTO's standards can nevertheless be disciplined under a conflicting state standard. As shown below, commentators have taken positions at odds with the USPTO and with each other on both of these issues.

These two questions are fundamental, because the issue of which rules apply can determine the propriety of a particular set of standards. A simple and common question demonstrates the impact of choice of law: May a practitioner who is also a licensed attorney be adverse to a current client in a USPTO proceeding by, for example, representing the opposing party in an interference proceeding? The answer can depend on whether state rules or the PTO Code applies. Under the Model Rules (which most states have adopted as disciplinary rules), a lawyer generally may not be adverse to a current client;[23] but in the only case directly on point, the USPTO interpreted the PTO Code to generally permit such representations.[24] If the client against whose interests the lawyer is acting in the interference proceeding moves to disqualify the lawyer, but the motion is denied, can the client nonetheless rely on state law either to enjoin the lawyer from appearing in that interference proceeding, or later sue the lawyer and argue that the representation violated state law? The following sheds the available light on those questions.

---

23. *See generally* Thomas D. Morgan, *Suing a Current Client*, 9 GEO. J. LEGAL ETHICS 1157 (1996) (discussing origins of the general rule prohibiting concurrent adverse representations).

24. Section 10.66 of the PTO Code prohibits a lawyer from accepting employment in a matter "if the exercise of the practitioner's independent professional judgment in behalf of a client will be or is likely to be adversely affected . . . or if it would be likely to involve the practitioner in representing differing interests" unless the clients consent and "it is obvious that the practitioner can adequately represent the interest of each" client. 37 C.F.R. § 10.66 (2005). "Differing interests" are defined to "include every interest that may adversely affect either the judgment or the loyalty of a practitioner to a client, whether it be a conflicting, inconsistent, diverse, or other interest." *Id.* § 10.1(f). Despite that broad prohibition, being adverse to a current client is not "a strict liability offense" in disqualification petitions decided under the PTO Code. *Univ. of New Mexico v. Fordham Univ.*, No. 104,761, 2002 WL 529661, at *3 (Bd. Pat. App. & Inter. Apr. 2, 2002).

1. Office of Enrollment and Discipline

Congress gave the USPTO authority to establish disciplinary rules and to discipline lawyers who violate them.[25] In accordance with that authority, the USPTO established the Office of Enrollment and Discipline (OED).[26] The OED reviews complaints, conducts investigations, and enforces the PTO Code.[27] Over the years, the OED has written numerous opinions interpreting and applying the PTO Code in disciplinary matters.[28]

The USPTO has authority to reprimand, suspend or exclude practitioners, either generally or from a particular matter, but only if it proves that the practitioner has violated a disciplinary rule in the PTO Code.[29] Thus, a practitioner can be disciplined by the OED only for violations of the PTO Code. As a result, the PTO Code controls the question of whether the OED can bring a disciplinary proceeding.[30]

Returning to the illustrative question of whether a practitioner may be adverse to a current client in an interference proceeding: There is no authority from the OED interpreting the conflicts provision of the PTO Code. However, the PTO Code is based on, and its conflicts provision is identical to, the Model Code.[31] The Model Code's conflict provisions have been generally interpreted to preclude any adverse representations.[32] Thus, the OED could discipline lawyers for appearing adverse to a current client in an interference proceeding. As next shown, however, the practitioner would not necessarily be disqualified by Board of Patent Appeals and Interferences (the Board).

25. 35 U.S.C. §§ 2(b)(2)(D), 32 (2005).
26. *See id.*; 37 C.F.R. § 1011.2(a) (2005).
27. *See, e.g., Weiffenbach v. Logan,* 1993 Comm'r. Pat. LEXIS 2, 27 U.S.P.Q.2d 1870 (Comm'r Pat. & Trademarks 1993); *McCandlish v. Doe,* 1992 Comm'r. Pat. LEXIS 1, 22 U.S.P.Q.2d 1223 (Comm'r Pat. & Trademarks 1992); *Weiffenbach v. Frank,* 1992 Comm'r. Pat. LEXIS 1, 18 U.S.P.Q.2d 1397 (Comm'r. Pat. & Trademarks 1991); *Weiffenbach v. Gould,* 1989 Comm'r. Pat. LEXIS 10, 14 U.S.P.Q.2d 1331 (Comm'r. Pat. & Trademarks 1989); *Small v. Weiffenbach,* 1989 Comm'r. Pat. LEXIS 3, 10 U.S.P.Q.2d 1898 (Comm'r. Pat. & Trademarks 1989); 37 C.F.R. § 11.2 (2004).
28. These opinions are *available at* http://www.uspto.gov/web/offices/com/sol/foia/oed/ oed.htm.
29. *See* 35 U.S.C. §§ 2(b)(2)(D), 32; 37 C.F.R. § 10.130(a).
30. In *Kansas v. Mayes,* 531 P.2d 102, 185 U.S.P.Q. 624 (Kan. 1975), the court affirmed disbarment of a practitioner by applying state disciplinary rules, but the PTO Code had not, then, been adopted.
31. *Compare* 37 C.F.R. § 10.66, *with* MODEL Code DR 5-105.
32. *See* Samuel R. Miller, Richard E. Rochman, & Ray Cannon, *Conflicts of Interest in Corporate Litigation,* 48 BUS. LAW. 141, 171 (1992) (recognizing that the *Model Code* had widely been interpreted as creating a per se prohibition against concurrent adverse representations).

2. U.S. Patent and Trademark Office Disqualification

Ethical issues can be raised by various USPTO personnel and entities in both *ex parte* prosecution and *inter partes* proceedings and also by the participants to *inter partes* proceedings. The USPTO regulations authorize third parties and USPTO personnel to bring motions (called "petitions") to disqualify counsel.[33] However, the USPTO is not required to apply the PTO Code to the adjudication of disqualification petitions. Instead, USPTO regulations specifically provide that the PTO Code does not control in that context. Rather, disqualification must "be handled on a case-by-case basis under such conditions as the Commissioner deems appropriate."[34]

Yet, the PTO Code applies to practitioners during prosecution as well as during *inter partes* opposition or interference proceedings.[35] Violations of the PTO Code will render practitioners subject to *discipline* by the OED. However, because of this "case-by-case" approach in *disqualification* petitions, the USPTO is not required to follow the PTO Code in deciding such petitions. Obviously concerned about notice and due process, however, the USPTO has clearly been guided by the PTO Code in deciding petitions to disqualify.[36] Although that seems to give some certainty—the PTO Code will likely be at least a guide to disqualification—the USPTO has stated that when deciding disqualification petitions, its interpretation of the PTO Code can be "aided by decisions of federal courts."[37] Decisions of federal courts, however,

---

33. 35 U.S.C. § 32; 37 C.F.R. § 10.130(b).

34. 37 C.F.R. § 10.130(b).

35. *See* 50 Fed. Reg. 5158, 5158 (Feb. 6, 1985) (PTO response to comments concerning scope of the PTO Code).

36. *See generally Anderson v. Eppstein*, 59 U.S.P.Q.2d 1280 (Bd. Pat. App. & Inter. May 11, 2001) ("While the PTO has no specific rules which govern disqualification petitions, generally the provisions of the PTO Code, aided by decisions of federal courts, govern.").

37. *Id.* ("the provisions of the PTO Code, aided by decisions of federal courts"). In a trademark case, the Board recently wrote that "there is nothing improper in considering relevant case law of other jurisdictions with the understanding that different wording in those standards of professional responsibility may compel a different result." *Finger Furniture Co. v. Finger Interests No. 1, Ltd.*, 71 U.S.P.Q.2d 1287, 1290 (TTAB 2004) (trademark decision). *See Am. Sigma, Inc. v. QED Environmental Sys., Inc.*, 1989 Commr. Pat. LEXIS 18 (July 31, 1989) (applying PTO Code but also looking to cases applying other rules). Interestingly the *Finger* decision relied on cases from federal courts that held that federal district courts cannot allow themselves to be bound to follow state disciplinary rules in deciding the propriety of ethical issues arising in federal court. *See id.* (citing *In re Dresser Indus., Inc.*, 972 F.2d 540, 543 (5th Cir. 1992)). The reliance on such cases is dangerously misplaced. Putting to the side the question of whether *Dresser* is correct, the reason for the *Dresser* court's decision has to do with obtaining uniformity across the federal system: If every federal court had to follow the state rules in which the district court sits, then there would be balkanization of legal ethics among the federal courts. Uniformity among federal courts is served by *Dresser*. In contrast, if the PTO begins to follow the conflicting rules that apply in the states, then there will be balkanization of standards within the confines of the PTO: For example, what one practitioner

are often based on disciplinary rules that are worded differently from the PTO Code, making it difficult to know when those rules, or decisions interpreting them, can be relied on in practice before the office.

Returning again to the question of whether a practitioner could appear in an interference proceeding adverse to a current client, the Board has specifically rejected a per se or "strict liability" rule of disqualification.[38] Thus, choice of law matters: Even within the USPTO, it might be that the OED will apply the traditional per se approach and discipline, although other USPTO branches will apply a different standard to the question of current client conflicts of interest.

The issue of identifying the controlling standard is only the first step. Even if the PTO Code applies, a practitioner must determine whether he or she can rely on the PTO Code or must instead follow state law if state law is more restrictive. Again, suppose the Board denies a motion to disqualify filed against a practitioner who is adverse to a current client. Can the aggrieved client, nonetheless, seek to enjoin the lawyer, or sue him or her, based on violation of state standards?[39] That issue is explored in the following section.

C. Preemption by the Patent and Trademark Office Code of Professional Conduct

The PTO Code applies to *ex parte* and *inter partes* USPTO practice, and a practitioner can be disciplined for violating it. Many patent lawyer-practitioners are also licensed by a state. Must they consult state law while engaged in activities before the USPTO and governed by the PTO Code?

The answer is unclear. By regulation, the PTO Code preempts state law only "to the extent necessary for the Patent and Trademark Office to accomplish its Federal objectives."[40] Unless preempted, state law continues to govern the conduct of practitioners even with respect to conduct occurring during

---

could disclose to satisfy the duty of candor, another could not. The reason why the *Dresser* court held as it did has nothing to do with whether the PTO should base disqualification on anything other than the PTO, and in fact, that court's rationale compels the opposite approach in matters before the PTO.

38. *Univ. of New Mexico v. Fordham Univ.*, No. 104,761, 2002 WL 529661, at *3 (Bd. Pat. App. & Interf. Apr. 2, 2002).

39. Normally, of course, clients use motions to disqualify to enforce conflicts of interest rules. However, clients may also do so through suits for injunction. *E.g., Morrison Knudsen Corp. v. Hancock, Rothert & Bunshoft, LLP,* 81 Cal. Rptr. 2d 425 (Cal. App. 1999) (granting injunction). At least one court has questioned whether an injunction or other proceeding may be used to prevent a practitioner from appearing before the PTO. *Englishtown Sportswear, Ltd. v. Tuttle,* 547 F. Supp. 700, 216 U.S.P.Q. 486 (S.D.N.Y. 1982).

40. PTO Definitions, 37 C.F.R. § 10.1 (2005).

patent prosecution.[41] As a result, to know which rules apply, a practitioner must often engage in a "preemption" analysis to determine whether it is necessary for the USPTO to achieve its federal objectives and thus preempt state law. If it is necessary, then the PTO Code applies and excludes contrary state law.[42] If it is not necessary, then a practitioner may be disciplined by a state in accordance with its rules, even for conduct that is proper under the PTO Code that occurs during patent prosecution.

It is rare to find decisions specifically addressing this issue. In one opinion, however, a lawyer inquired of a state bar association whether he could withhold a reference from the USPTO even though he believed it was material because the client had ordered him not to disclose it. The bar association advised the lawyer to follow the USPTO's rules and approach, noting that the state could discipline him only if he violated the USPTO's approach.[43]

The preemption analysis might affect both choice of law in ethical matters and the determination of the standard of care in malpractice cases, at least in those states where the ethical rules inform or underlie the standard of care.[44] The PTO Code has been interpreted to permit conduct that could violate state law duties to a client. As seen earlier, the USPTO in the *University of New Mexico* case permitted practitioners to be adverse to current clients in interference proceedings, even though being adverse to a current client generally violates both the Model Rules and Model Code. If the USPTO's interpretation does not preempt state law, then a lawyer could be disciplined or sued for conduct permitted by federal law.[45] If the PTO Code does not preempt, then a lawyer may not rely on the PTO Code in deciding whether a representation

---

41. *Kroll v. Finnerty*, 242 F.3d 1359, (Fed. Cir. 2001).
42. *See Buechel v. Bain*, 713 N.Y.S.2d 332 (N.Y. 2000) (reasoning that PTO Code precluded enforcement of directly contrary state law but did not preclude enforcement of more restrictive state law); David Hricik, *Aerial Boundaries: The Duty of Candor as a Limitation on the Duty of Patent Practitioners to Advocate for Maximum Patent Coverage*, 44 S. Tex. L. Rev. 205, 213–15 (2002) (describing how PTO Code only preempts state law to the extent it interferes with the PTO's federal objectives). Others likewise recognize that conflicts of interest during prosecution must be analyzed under the PTO Code. *E.g.*, Lisa B. Kole, *Conflicts of Interest in Technology Law*, 616 PLI/Pat 513, 521 (2000) ("If a patent practitioner represents a client in patent prosecution, and then is asked to represent a new client in prosecution of related subject matter, there is no per se conflict of interest for the practitioner, even if the established and potential clients are economic competitors. However, the attorney should review the situation in terms of the PTO Code.").
43. Phil. B. Ass'n. Prof. Guidance Comm. Op. No. 96-12 (Dec. 1996); *see* N.Y. City L. Ass'n. Comm. Prof. Eth. Op. 668 (May 15, 1989) (noting that the "New York Code . . . may still apply to the conduct of patent lawyers practicing in this state.").
44. *See, e.g., In re Kirsh*, 973 F.2d 1454, 1461 (9th Cir. 1992) ("while the rules can be evidence of a breach of fiduciary duty, they do not, standing alone, prove the breach.")
45. A further question is whether the OED's interpretation of the rule would inform the standard of care, or whether the decision of the Board in denying the disqualification motion would do so. Even where preemption is found, the choice of law issue persists.

before the USPTO is appropriate. The fact that the PTO Code permits conduct would, if there was no preemption, be practically irrelevant. Consequently, even where a lawyer concludes that the PTO Code permits the conduct, he or she might want to determine whether state law imposes a more stringent standard, and follow it.[46]

For these reasons, practitioners must engage in a preemption analysis after identifying the applicable USPTO standard. They might, for practical reasons, choose to follow the more stringent of the potentially applicable standards.[47] As next shown, the question of choice of law is murky when federal court litigation is involved, but for reasons other than preemption.

D. Federal Circuit Choice of Law

This section furthers the discussion on the choice of law rules that apply during patent litigation in federal court. This issue is secondary to patent

---

46. This is not always the solution, however. For example, a lawyer must withdraw when he or she is faced with a conflict of interest. But, if a lawyer relies on the "more stringent" state law standard in determining whether a conflict exists, and seeks to withdraw even though withdrawal is not required under the PTO Code, that act could be argued to breach a fiduciary duty to the client whom the lawyer stops representing. Following "the more stringent standard" may not always be the simple solution it appears to be.

An interesting question is whether state law could be applied to the question of whether representation of two clients during patent prosecution is unethical. It is clear that, as noted above, the PTO will apply the PTO Code to determine whether a conflict exists in *inter partes* proceedings. The PTO has stated that during *inter partes* proceedings, state codes are "not applicable in the PTO." *Anderson v. Eppstein*, 2001 Pat. App. LEXIS 1 (Bd. App. & Inter. 2001). In our view, state law should not apply to the question of whether a lawyer can properly represent a client in such a proceeding, since otherwise the PTO would be required to apply state standards to disqualification proceedings in the PTO. The need for uniformity is clear.

Suppose, however, that a lawyer prosecutes an application for one client which, ostensibly, interferes with another but for whatever reason no interference is declared in the PTO. Should the question of whether a conflict exists turn on state law? We believe not, since that would make the question of whether a lawyer can ethically represent clients in patent prosecution turn, not on ethics, but on the happenstance of whether an interference proceeding is declared. It would be incongruous for state rules not to apply during *inter partes* interference PTO proceedings but yet apply to the question of whether a conflict of interest exists between patent clients where, by happenstance, an interference is not declared.

47. What obviously needs to occur is for the PTO to have clearer rules on when its rules apply to the exclusion of state law. The PTO may be making an attempt to do so in its proposed new disciplinary rules. *See, e.g.*, Proposed PTO Rule 11.805(b)(1) (stating that the PTO's rules apply to conduct "in connection with practice before the Office").

prosecution, but we will see connections to litigation in certain chapters of the book, and so discuss the issue somewhat fully here.

Patent cases must be appealed to the Federal Circuit,[48] but Federal Circuit law does not apply to all issues in patent cases. Regional circuit law applies to "procedural" issues, but Federal Circuit law applies to "patent" issues.[49] More specifically, the Federal Circuit applies regional circuit law to procedural matters "that are not unique to patent issues,"[50] but it applies its own law to procedural matters that "are related to patent issues."[51]

The division between issues "unique to patent law" and those which are not can be critical. In its latest pronouncements, the Federal Circuit stated that a procedural issue is subject to Federal Circuit law if it (1) "pertain[s] to" the substance of a patent right; (2) "bear[s] an essential relationship to matters committed to [the Federal Circuit's] exclusive control by statute"; or (3) "clearly implicate[s] the jurisprudential responsibilities of [the Federal Circuit] in a field within its exclusive jurisdiction."[52]

The Federal Circuit has so far held that ethical issues are not unique to patent law and has instead looked to the proper regional circuit.[53] Accordingly, a lawyer litigating a case in Texas must consult the approach of the Fifth Circuit, whereas a litigator in federal court in New York consults the law of the Second Circuit, and so on. Although a complete canvas of the varying approaches of federal courts to the issue of choice of law can form the basis of its own chapter, a brief description of two circuits illustrates the range.

The Fifth Circuit has held that even federal district courts that specifically adopt state disciplinary rules cannot be bound by them; instead, federal law governs "whether and how" the rules are applied.[54] In adopting this approach, the Fifth Circuit, for example, rejected the reasoning of the district court in *Red Eagle Resources Corp. v. Baker Hughes*,[55] that "[a]doption of a local rule specifying a particular code of professional responsibility provides clear

---

48. 28 U.S.C. § 1295(a)(1) (2005); *see Holmes Group, Inc. v. Vornado Air Circulation Sys., Inc.*, 535 U.S. 826, 62 U.S.P.Q.2d 1801 (2002).
49. *See Midwest Indus., Inc. v. Karavan Trailers, Inc.*, 175 F.3d 1356, 1360, 50 U.S.P.Q.2d 1672 (Fed. Cir. 1999).
50. *Panduit Corp. v. All States Plastic Mfg. Co.*, 744 F.2d 1564, 1574–75, 223 U.S.P.Q. 465 (Fed. Cir. 1984).
51. *Id.* at 1575 n.14.
52. *Bose Corp. v. JBL, Inc.*, 274 F.3d 1354, 1360, 61 U.S.P.Q.2d 1216 (Fed. Cir. 2001).
53. *Sun Studs, Inc. v. Applied Theory Assocs., Inc.*, 772 F.2d 1557, 1566, 227 U.S.P.Q. 81(Fed. Cir. 1985).
54. *In re American Airlines, Inc.*, 972 F.2d 605, 610 (5th Cir. 1992); *see also Resolution Trust Corp. v. Bright*, 6 F.3d 336, 341 (5th Cir. 1993). Even though the Model Code has been "superseded" by the Model Rules in federal court, in several circuits and many district courts the Model Code is still viable and relevant. *See, e.g., In re Dresser Indus.*, 972 F.2d 540, 544 (5th Cir. 1992).
55. No. H-91-0627, 1992 WL 170614, at *3 (S.D. Tex. Mar. 4, 1992).

guidance to counsel practicing before the Court." Instead, the Fifth Circuit held that the "district court clearly erred in holding that its local rules, and thus the Texas rules, which [the court] adopted, are the 'sole' authority governing a motion to disqualify."[56] The Fifth Circuit held that even the Model Code is merely "useful . . . but . . . not controlling."[57]

The Ninth Circuit's position stands in stark contrast. The Ninth Circuit reasoned that because "[a]dvance notice is essential to the rule of law [and] since it is desirable that an attorney or client be aware of what actions will not be countenanced," if the federal district court adopted the California rules in its local rules, they would apply to ethical issues arising in federal court.[58] Other circuits and district courts have reached different conclusions as to whether the district court's selection of the forum's rules controls.[59]

Federal court choice of law is a complex matter. Because courts often disagree on ethical obligations, and do so even when interpreting identically worded disciplinary rules, lawyers must be sure to consult the approach taken by the regional circuit to determine whether and to what extent state law plays a role in determining ethical issues that arise during patent litigation.

E. Conclusion on Choice of Law

The propriety of particular conduct can often hinge on the determination of which rules apply. In addition, courts often rely on applicable ethical rules in determining the standard of care.[60] For that reason, lawyers must consider

---

56. *In re Dresser*, 972 F.2d at 543.

57. *Id.* at 543–44.

58. *Paul E. Iancono Structural Eng'r, Inc. v. Humphrey*, 722 F.2d 435, 438–39 (9th Cir. 1983) (stating that application of Model Code was also proper in certain instances). *See also County of Los Angeles v. Forsyth*, 223 F.3d 990, 995 (9th Cir. 2000) (holding "we apply state law in determining matters of disqualification").

59. *See* McMorrow, *supra* note 1.

60. Some courts hold that applicable ethical rules are admissible as evidence of the standard of care under some circumstances, *see, e.g., Two Thirty Nine Joint Venture v. Joe*, 60 S.W.3d 896 (Tex. Ct. App. 2001), *rev'd on other grounds*, 145 S.W.3d 150 (Tex. 2004), whereas others hold they are inadmissible, *see, e.g., Hizey v. Carpenter*, 830 P.2d 646 (Wash. 1992). *See generally* Stephen E. Kalish, *How to Encourage Lawyers to Be Ethical: Do Not Use the Ethics Codes as a Basis for Regular Law Decisions*, 13 GEO. J. LEGAL ETHICS 649 (2000); Douglas L. Christian & Michael Christian, *Twice Bitten: Violations of Ethical Rules As Evidence of Legal Malpractice*, 28 THE BRIEF 62 (1999); Gary A. Munneke & Anthony E. Davis, *The Standard of Care in Legal Malpractice: Do the Model Rules of Professional Conduct Define It?*, 22 J. LEGAL PROF. 33, 33 (1997/1998); David J. Fish, *The Use of the Illinois Rules of Professional Conduct to Establish the Standard of Care in Attorney Malpractice Litigation: An Illogical Practice*, 23 S. ILL. U.L.J. 65 (1998); note, *The Evidentiary Use of the Ethics Codes in Legal Malpractice: Erasing a Double Standard*, 109 HARV. L. REV. 1102, 1118 (1996); James I. Sullivan, *Impact of Ethical*

whether and to what extent each of the following bears on their conduct: (a) state ethics rules; (b) the PTO Code, and whether it is the OED's interpretation or that of some other USPTO entity; (c) state substantive law (fiduciary duty, agency, and so on); (d) whether the Federal Circuit or regional circuits have jurisdiction over the issue; (e) "federal" ethical standards, however formulated by the regional circuit; and (f) the appropriate circuit's law interpreting the Federal Rules of Civil Procedure. When the conduct is in connection with prosecution, then a preemption analysis might be needed as the final step.

F. Special Choice of Law Issues
Facing Patent Agents

Patent agents are discussed several times in the book because particular issues face them. One particular issue is choice of law.

Patent agents are not lawyers. Instead, they are nonlawyers who are registered to practice patent law before the USPTO.[61] To be registered, the patent agent must have certain legal, scientific, and technical qualifications and must demonstrate good moral character.[62] A lawyer who wants to practice patent law must pass the same test as that required of a nonlawyer. State bar admission is insufficient to qualify a lawyer to practice before the USPTO.[63] The result of this is that being licensed to practice law by a state is neither sufficient to appear before the USPTO, nor a condition to doing so. In addition, the USPTO requires specific educational requirements beyond a JD degree, all of which relate to a technical background.[64]

Once registered, a patent agent becomes subject to and must comply with the PTO Code. Some contend that the implication of this is that "[f]or all purposes, lawyers and non-lawyers seeking to practice patent law before the United States Patent and Trademark Office find themselves on the

---

Rules and Other Quasi-Standards on Standard of Care, 61 Def. Couns. J. 100, 101 (1994) ("Analysis of the legal malpractice standard of care frequently requires consideration of the potential impact of ethical rules."); Teresa Schafer Sullivan, &Thomas H. Blaske, *Legal Ethics and Legal Malpractice: A Beauty and a Beast in Search of Each Other*, 74 Mich. B.J. 150 (1995); Laura Callaway Hart, Carl B. Epps, III, & Steven E. Williford, *From Offense to Defense: Defending Legal Malpractice Claims*, 45 S.C. L. Rev. 771, 776 (1994).

61. *See* 37 C.F.R. § 11.6(b).
62. *See* 37 C.F.R. § 11.7(a)(2)(i)–(ii).
63. *See* 37 C.F.R. § 11.7(b)(1)(ii).
64. *See Premysler v. Lehman*, 71 F.3d 387 (Fed. Cir. 1996),

same footing."[65] This contention is a half-truth. The standards applied to patent agents and patent lawyers by the USPTO are identical.[66] However, because patent lawyers are licensed by a state, they are likely subject to additional licensing requirements—such as continuing legal education requirements—that do not apply to patent agents. Thus, in terms of their treatment by the USPTO, patent lawyers and patent agents are the same for the purpose of prosecuting a patent. The fact that only patent lawyers are licensed by, and so subject to regulation of, state lawyer disciplinary boards, does matter, however, as becomes clear below.

Both the USPTO and state and federal courts continue to face unanswered questions concerning the status of patent agents for purposes of disqualification motions. This section addresses what is known and what remains to be discovered about how the USPTO and the courts characterize patent agents. Surprisingly, the following discussion shows that consistency and clarity would be best served if patent agents were treated as lawyers for purposes of discipline in the USPTO but as nonlawyers for all other purposes.

The OED has authority to reprimand, suspend, or exclude patent agents, either generally or from a particular matter, but only if it proves that the patent agent has violated a disciplinary rule in the PTO Code.[67] Thus, a patent agent can only be disciplined by the OED for violations of the PTO Code. As a result, the PTO Code controls the question of whether the OED may bring a disciplinary proceeding against a patent agent.

The same is true with the discipline of patent lawyers: The OED can succeed in disciplining a patent lawyer also only by establishing a violation of the PTO Code. For purposes of discipline, therefore, patent agents are treated like patent lawyers. Both are subject to discipline by the OED only on violation of the PTO Code. That treatment is consistent, and correct, because by its terms, the PTO Code applies to lawyers or agents who practice before the USPTO.

---

65. *Mold-Masters Ltd. v. Husky Injection Molding Sys., Ltd.,* 01 C 1576, 2001 WL 1268587, at *2 (N.D. Ill. Nov. 15, 2001) (citing *In re* Ampicillin Antitrust Litig., 81 F.R.D. 377, 393 (D.D.C. 1978)). The statement is true only with respect to the USPTO. Patent lawyers can be disciplined by a state bar for violating state ethics rules, but patent agents may not be. *See Buechel v. Bain,* 713 N.Y.S.2d 332, 340 (App. Div. 2000). However, nonlawyers who practice patent law can be subject to state proceedings for the unauthorized practice of law, and patent agents can be subject to such proceedings if their conduct exceeds the boundaries authorized by federal law. Congress did not authorize those who have not become registered with the USPTO to practice patent law, nor authorize those who are registered with the USPTO to practice law broadly—only to practice before the USPTO.

66. *In re Amalgamated Dev. Co.,* 375 A.2d 494, 496 (D.C. 1977) ("The only difference between the two is that patent agents are not also attorneys.").

67. *See* 35 U.S.C. §§ 2(b)(2)(D), 32; 37 C.F.R. § 10.130(a).

CHAPTER

4

Client Identity, Matter Scope, Ending Matters, and Prospective Consent

A. Client Identity   25
    1. Inventors   26
       A. The Law   26
       B. What to Do   30
    2. Business Entities   31
       A. The Law   31
       B. What to Do   37

B. Representation Ending Dates in Patent Matters   37
    1. The Law   37
    2. What to Do   39

C. Scope of the Representation   39

D. Prospective Consent   40
    1. Standards Governing Prospective Consent   40

This chapter addresses common issues concerning client identity, the scope of a representative, and the point at which a representation ends. It also addresses prospective consent, an issue we will return to later and also in the Appendix.

A. Client Identity

The absence of client identity in patent prosecution can lead to difficulties, including malpractice as well as simply failing to warn those who might reasonably rely on a practitioner to protect their interests that he or she cannot do so.

Two relatively common client identity issues arise in patent practice. The first is created by the fact that the Patent Act generally requires patent applications to be filed in the name of the inventor, not the owner or assignee. Thus, where an employee invents subject matter that is subject to an obligation of assignment to the employee's corporate employer, the fact that the employee must be involved can create the potential for ambiguity. Second, even if the practitioner avoids ambiguity as to whether, or not, he or she represents only the corporate employer, ambiguity can still exist as to whether he or she represents only the corporate employer, or affiliated entities (such as parents, subsidiaries, and the like). The following section discusses these issues.[1]

1. Inventors

A. The Law

Often practitioners prosecute applications where an inventor is employed and is subject to assign of all inventions to a corporate employer. However, under U.S. Patent and Trademark Office (USPTO) regulations and the 1952 Act, a "patent must be applied for in the name of the actual inventor or inventors."[2] Corporations cannot be "inventors."[3] Hence, the patent must be prosecuted in the name of the inventor. A practitioner must obtain authority from the inventor to do so. This creates potentially awkward circumstances.

The USPTO requires that practitioners get a Declaration from the inventors at the time that an application is filed or immediately thereafter.[4] Although only a Declaration by the inventors is required for filing an application, the Declaration is frequently filed as a joint Declaration and Power of Attorney. The Power of Attorney portion is directed under 37 C.F.R. sections

---

1. See also *We're Talkin' Mardi Gras, LLC v. Davis*, 192 F. Supp. 2d 635 (E.D. La. 2002) (analyzing malpractice claim based on failure to advise corporation of need to have inventor assign his rights); *Kaempe v. Myers*, 367 F.3d 958, 71 U.S.P.Q.2d 1147 (D.C. Cir. 2004) (affirming dismissal of malpractice claim against law firm based on conversion of patent rights); *Am. Stock Exchange, LLC v. Mopex, Inc.*, 230 F. Supp. 2d 333, 52 U.S.P.Q.2d 1385 (S.D.N.Y. 2002) (analyzing claim for constructive trust over patents based on misuse of trade secrets); *Bausch & Lomb Inc. v. Alcon Labs., Inc.*, 64 F. Supp. 2d 233 (W.D.N.Y. 1999) (analyzing claim on indefiniteness and counterclaims of misappropriation of trade secrets, unfair competition, and constructive trust).
2. 37 C.F.R. § 1.41(a); *see* 35 U.S.C. § 111 ("application for patent shall be made, or authorized to be made, by the inventor"); *Comtech, Inc. v. Reuter*, 1986 WL 6829 (E.D.N.Y. Mar. 18, 1986) (explaining need for inventor to sign; denying motion to disqualify).
3. *Beech Aircraft Corp. v. EDO Corp.*, 990 F.2d 1237, 1247 (Fed. Cir. 1993).
4. There are of course times when the inventor refuses to sign or cannot be found. In these circumstances, the requirements under 37 C.F.R. § 1.47 are followed.

1.31 and 1.32. The Declaration is generally obtained from the inventor (as is the Power of Attorney), unless the inventor is dead, insane, a minor, or legally incapacitated. At that point, the executor or legal representative makes the Declaration and grants Power of Attorney when it is a joint document.

For general communications with the USPTO, such as for responding to office actions, one does not require Power of Attorney. Instead, a registered agent or attorney can file the response while acting in a representative capacity under 37 C.F.R. section 1.34. This power is applicable to responses to the Office filed during the course of prosecution. It also eases the rush to obtain Power of Attorney when moving files between corporations and between firms. However, action in a representative authority does exclude certain actions, such as written assertions.[5] Thus, it is advisable to obtain a Power of Attorney in an application in an expedient fashion.

Companies generally require assignments by employee-inventors of the invention to the corporation. After that point, inventors generally have nothing further to do with the application. It is wise to remind inventors at times that you do not represent them, but rather the company or entity. Future revocations and new powers of attorney needed because of the corporate purchase of patent portfolios and transfer of portfolios between law firms will be obtained from the corporation and not the inventor. Revocations and withdrawal of power are performed pursuant to 37 C.F.R. section 1.36.

Given the issues that typically arise during representation (e.g., dead inventors, insane inventors, child inventors, missing inventors, and angry inventors), it may be more advisable to obtain the Declaration from the inventor or legal custodian and an assignment to the entity than a combined Declaration and Power of Attorney. Then, a separate Power of Attorney can be obtained from the entity. Separating the documents also will make communication from the USPTO to the practitioner less prone to error in continuation and divisionals in applications transferred to a different law firm or sold. Frequently such applications result in USPTO communications going to the address listed on joint Declarations and Power of Attorney, which may no longer be correct.

Given the general approach, however, of obtaining the Combined Declaration and Power of Attorney from the inventor, it is perhaps understandable why some inventors operate under the false belief that they, too, were also clients of the practitioner retained by the corporate employer. After all, the employee-inventor will likely have met with or communicated with the practitioner, and will have perhaps signed a document styled "power of attorney." It is also understandable why these facts can give rise to strategic behavior, such as where in a dispute between inventor and assignee, the inventor's attorney either seeks to disqualify the assignee's counsel or attempts

---

5. *See* 37 C.F.R. § 1.34(b).

to assert a malpractice claim against the assignee's lawyer, claiming that assignee's counsel also represented the inventor.

As a general rule, courts are properly recognizing that actions that a practitioner takes pursuant to a power of attorney granted by an inventor subject to an absolute obligation[6] of assignment are not necessarily made during an attorney-client relationship.[7] That holding reflects several key points. First, a lawyer does not have to have a power of attorney to act as a lawyer. Likewise, powers of attorney can authorize nonlawyers to act (i.e., patent agents). Thus, a power of attorney does not create an attorney-client relationship.[8] Consistent with this, courts generally recognize "the mere existence of a power of attorney may be insufficient to establish a confidential or fiduciary relationship."[9]

In a case involving an absolute obligation of assignment, the Federal Circuit held that the execution by an employee of a power of attorney for the benefit of his employer did not create an express or implied attorney-client relationship: "In the present case there was not even a 'technical' attorney-client relationship between Chernoff and Hunter because of the prior agreement that all rights in the invention belonged to Sun Studs."[10]

Thus, where the corporate employer previously had the inventor-employee assign all inventions to the corporation, generally the assignee, not the employee, is deemed to be the only client.[11] Several courts in both

---

6. "If doubts exist as to the extent of the inventor's obligation to assign the invention, the practitioner may need to advise the inventor to seek separate counsel to resolve this question even before work begins on the patent application." Tarek N. Fahmi, *Who's Your Client? Issues Involved in Representing Inventors and Their Assigneees in Patent Matters*, 824 PLI/Pat 737, 746 (Mar. 2005). *See Dunbar v. Baylor College of Med.*, 984 S.W.2d 338 (Tex. Ct. App. 1998) (suit against lawyers and others for not disclosing that she was obligated to assign inventions to corporate employer).

7. *Nebraska v. Flores*, 622 N.W.2d 632 (Neb. 2001) (recognizing that attorney's actions taken pursuant to a power of attorney were not done in an attorney-client relationship).

8. *See* Restatement (Second) Agency § 14H (1974) ("One who holds a power created in the form of an agency authority, but given for the benefit of the power holder or of a third person, is not an agent of the one creating the power."). *See also id.* § 387 cmt. a.

9. *Transamerica Ins. Fin. Corp. v. Pennmed Consultants, Inc.*, 1996 WL 605131, *5 (Oct. 18, 1996). *See In re State Street Assocs., L.P.*, B.R. 2005 WL 887151 (Bankr. N.D.N.Y. Mar. 23, 2005) ("A POA does not necessarily create an attorney-client relationship, however").

10. *Sun Studs, Inc. v. Applied Theory Assocs., Inc.*, 772 F.2d 1557, 1568 (Fed. Cir. 1985) (emphasis added).

11. *Synergy Tech & Design Inc. v. Terry*, 2007 U.S. Dist. LEXIS 34463 (N.D. Cal. May 2, 2007) ("The listing of Mr. Terry as the individual inventor was made necessary by the rules governing the filing of patents and does not alter the parties' previous discussions and the memorialization of those discussion in the law firm's engagement letter with its corporate client."); *Ultimax Cement Mfg. Corp. v. CTS Cement Mfg. Corp.*, 2007 US Dist. LEXIS 44096 (May 7, 2007) (denying motion to disqualify by inventor even though assignment was not executed because power of attorney was granted to benefit assignee, not inventor); *In re Ducane Gas Grills, Inc.*, 320 B.R. 312, 320–21 (Bankr. D. S.C. 2004); *University of W. Va. Bd. of Trustees v. Vanvoorhies*, 33 F. Supp. 2d 519 (N.D. W.Va. 1998); *Telectronics Proprietary, Ltd. v. Medtronic,*

the disqualification and malpractice context have held that a practitioner prosecuting a patent does not have an attorney-client relationship with the inventor.[12]

However, these general principles, absolute obligations, and basic fact patterns can give rise to fact questions and ambiguity. For example, at least one court has held in the context of a motion to disqualify that the practitioner had represented the inventor, and not just the assignee.[13] The muddy waters of real life often lead to circumstances that can present a fact question as to who the lawyer represented, particularly in jurisdictions that give weight to the subjective belief of the person claiming to have been a client.

Foremost, ambiguity or a fact question requiring trial by jury can arise if the practitioner in the course of prosecuting the application met with the inventor and casually referred to the inventor in correspondence or billing records as a "client." This type of evidence—common in malpractice cases—has special importance in those jurisdictions that take into account the subjective belief of the person who claims to have been a client.[14] In one case, the court found the practitioner had represented inventors in prosecuting patents, reasoning:

> In this case, appellee expressly appointed Brooks and Kushman to advance its position in the Patent and Trademark Office. To further that effort, appellee

---

Inc., 836 F.2d 1332, 1337 (Fed. Cir. 1988); *Sun Studs, Inc. v. Applied Theory Assocs., Inc.*, 772 F.2d 1557, 1568 (Fed. Cir. 1985); *Kersey v. Dennison Mfg. Co.*, 1992 WL 71390, *3 (D. Mass. 1992). *See generally Comtech, Inc. v. Reuter*, 1986 WL 6829 (E.D.N.Y. Mar. 18, 1986) (holding that inventor could not have disclosed confidences to lawyer representing his employer). *See also Shannon v. Gordon*, 670 N.Y.S.2d 887 (N.Y. Sup. Ct. 1998) (affirming dismissal of suit brought by inventor against attorney who had allegedly forged assignment because there was no attorney-client relationship between inventor and attorney). *See generally* Gregory E. Upchurch, *Intellectual Property Litigation Guide: Patents and Trade Secrets*, § 12:8 ("the mere fact that a person executes a power of attorney does not ipso facto create an attorney-client relationship."); Lisa B. Kole, *Ethics in Technology Protection*, 573 PLI/Pat 71 (Oct. 1999); Tarek N. Fahmi, *Who's Your Client? Issues Involved in Representing Inventors and their Assignees in Patent Matters*, 824 PLI/Pat 737 (2005).

12. *E.g., Emory Univ. v. Nova Biogenetics, Inc.*, 2006 WL 2708635 (N.D. Ga. Sept. 20, 2006) ("a firm prosecuting a patent application on behalf of a company does not form an attorney-client relationship with any individual inventor required to assign his rights to the company"); *Univ. of W. Va. Bd. of Trustees v. Vanvoorhies*, 33 F. Supp. 2d 519 (N.D. W. Va. 1998) (same); *Shannon v. Gordon*, 670 N.Y.S.2d 887 (N.Y. App. Div. 1998) (affirming dismissal of complaint brought by inventor against assignee's attorney for malpractice).

13. *Henry Filters, Inc. v. Peabody Barnes, Inc.*, 611 N.E.2d 873, 876 (Ct. App. Ohio 1992) (holding in disqualification context that an attorney-client relationship existed between attorneys and inventor because among other things he had supplied attorneys with confidential information and paid half of the fees).

14. Even where a party needs to establish objective evidence of an agreement by the lawyer to represent the person as a client, evidence such as this may defeat a lawyer's motion for summary judgment.

supplied Brooks and Kushman with confidential information. Furthermore, appellee agreed to pay one half of the attorney fees. Finally, Brooks and Kushman were aware that one half of the fees would be indirectly paid by appellee and that appellee would directly benefit from the successful prosecution of the patent application. From these circumstances, the trial court could properly infer that appellee reasonably believed that Brooks and Kushman owed duties to appellee to the same extent that the firm owed duties to appellant and that the confidential information supplied to Brooks and Kushman would not subsequently be used to degrade its interests. Therefore, the factual finding that Brooks and Kushman had an attorney-client relationship with appellee is supported by substantial evidence and will not be disturbed.[15]

In addition to these fact patterns, under some state's laws, a person generally need not establish that he or she was represented, but instead show only that the lawyer knew or should have known that the person thought he or she was represented or, arguably, that the lawyer was negligent in not recognizing the person's misapprehension and correcting it.[16] Jurisdictions relying on subjective beliefs are particularly troublesome for attorneys who prosecute patents because they will most frequently interact with inventors, who might not understand their role in patent prosecution as representing only the assignee's interests.

B. What to Do

As a consequence, care needs to be taken to ensure that engagement letters specify not only who is the client, but who is not the client. Perhaps more importantly, persons who the practitioner interacts with, but does not represent, must know the identity of the client, and know that they are not clients. Providing the inventor with a letter stating that the practitioner represents the assignee might not be sufficient in all circumstances. Instead, in some circumstances, a letter that expressly negates any representation of the inventor can be in order.[17] Another possibility is to have the inventor assign the

---

15. *Henry Filters, Inc. v. Peabody Barnes, Inc.*, 611 N.E.2d 873, 877–78 (Ct. App. Ohio 1992).
16. *See Parker v. Carnahan*, 772 S.W.2d 151, 157 (Tex. App.—Texarkana 1989, writ denied) (lawyer has duty to warn person he does not represent him "where the circumstances lead the party to believe that the attorney is representing him").
17. On a somewhat distinct note, a lawyer whose firm is litigating a patent that has been prosecuted by one of its lawyers should consider the potential impact on its liability of asserting privilege over any communication with the inventor. If the firm takes the position that it had represented both inventor and assignee, this may result in the firm's inability to represent either or both in any dispute that arises between them concerning, or substantially related to, the prosecution of the patent. The solution is to avoid ambiguity and to make clear in any assertion of privilege that it is being asserted over communications with the inventor solely under the control group or other appropriate test.

invention to the corporate employer, and any power of attorney should be obtained from the corporation, not the inventor. In addition, the practitioner can provide a letter to the inventor explaining that the client is only the corporate employer, and not the inventor. Finally, if a power of attorney is obtained directly from the inventor, it can clearly disclaim any attorney-client relationship. Following one or more of these suggestions will reduce risk and protect the client, the lawyer, and the inventor.

2. Business Entities

A. The Law

It is clear that a lawyer, who represents an entity, does represent the entity.[18] Put the other way, a lawyer-client relationship between a lawyer and a corporate client is only between the lawyer and the entity. This is the so called "entity approach," which assumes that the "entity" has its own fictional, separate existence apart from the constituents who make decisions on the entity's behalf. The entity approach has been applied to numerous business entity forms, including partnerships, corporations, associations, joint ventures, limited partnerships, and virtually every other form of entity.[19] But the statement that a lawyer who represents an entity represents *the* entity does not answer the question of whether the lawyer can be disqualified from being adverse to entities related to the entity-client, such as its subsidiaries, affiliates, or parent corporations.

First, in most jurisdictions, the fact that a lawyer represents an entity does not *ipso facto* mean the lawyer represents affiliated entities. The clear majority rule is that the mere fact that a lawyer represents an entity does not ipso facto mean that he or she represents any of the entity's constituents.[20]

---

18. Am. B. Ass'n Model R. 1.13(a) ("A lawyer employed or retained by an organization represent the organization acting through its duly authorized constituents.")

19. *See, e.g., Carlson v. Fredrikson & Byron, P.A.*, 475 N.W.2d 882, 890 (Minn. Ct. App. 1991) (representation of business does not amount to representation of business' owner); *McCarthy v. John T. Henderson Inc.*, 587 A.2d 280, 283 (N.J. Super. Ct. App. Div. 1991) (lawyer who represented close corporation could sue another close corporation with same officers and directors since representation of corporation was not representation of individuals); *Security Bank v. Klicker*, 418 N.W.2d 27, 31 (Ct. App. Wis. 1987) ("a limited partnership has been held to be an entity 'similar' to a corporation for purposes of determining attorney-client relationships.")

20. *Marshall v. Quinn-L Equities, Inc.*, 704 F. Supp. 1384, 1395 (N.D. Tex. 1988) (if lawyers "represented the limited partnerships . . . this does not magically transform them into counsel" for the limited partners); *Meyerland Cmty. Improvement Ass'n v. Temple*, 700 S.W.2d 263, 267–68 (Tex. App.—Houston [1st Dist.] 1985, writ ref'd n.r.e.) (no attorney-client relationship between association's lawyers and members of association); *Fortson v. Winstead,*

But the majority of courts, although rejecting a "one big client" approach, also reject an "only the 'real' client counts" approach. As a result, practitioners who are unclear about client identity, when undertaking to represent a corporation or other entity, run the risk that a court will later deem them to have represented more than just the entity that signed the engagement letter. For example, if a lawyer represents Company A in prosecuting an application, and his or her firm is asked to represent another client against Company A's parent corporation, the firm may be disqualified because by representing Company A, the lawyer will be deemed to represent Company A's parents, affiliates, or other entities.

Unfortunately, there is no uniform approach among the jurisdictions, and often there are different approaches reflected within a jurisdiction, a client identity in this context. Some authority holds that lawyers always represent affiliated entities; others hold that they never do; and, perhaps a majority, apply a vague, multifactored balancing test. A 1995 American Bar Association (ABA) opinion[21] illustrates the scope of disagreement on the proper way to address "corporate family" conflicts, and the disagreements expressed in that opinion persists in the law today. In that ABA opinion, a majority concluded that representation of one entity does not automatically disqualify the lawyer from being adverse to related entities. Two members of the Committee vigorously dissented, which is unusual in an ABA opinion. They took the bright-line position that this would always be a conflict that required consent. A third member also dissented, and espoused a third approach.

McGuire, Secrest & Minick, 961 F.2d 469, 472–74 (4th Cir. 1992) (no duty owed by counsel for partnership to limited partners). *See also Hopper v. Frank*, 16 F.3d 92, 95–96 (5th Cir. 1994) (lawyer hired by individual partners to assist in sale of limited partnership assets had attorney-client relationship only with partnership, and so individuals who retained lawyer could not sue for malpractice) (Mississippi law); *Quintel Corp. v. Citibank*, 589 F. Supp. 1235 (S.D.N.Y. 1984) (lawyer for general partner has no fiduciary duty to limited partners); *Rice v. Strunk*, 670 N.E.2d 1280, 1289 (Ind. 1996) (lawyer for partnership has no attorney-client relationship with anyone except the managing general partner); *Hackett v. Village Court Assocs.*, 602 F. Supp. 856, 858 (E.D. Wis. 1985) (limited partners could not bring a malpractice claim against partnership's lawyers); *Rose v. Summers, Compton, Wells & Hamburg P.C.*, 887 S.W.2d 683 (Mo. Ct. App. 1994) (lawyer for limited partnership owes no duty to individual partners on which they may sue for malpractice); *Morin v. Trupin*, 711 F. Supp. 97, 103–04 (S.D.N.Y. 1989) (lawyer for partnership cannot be sued by its limited partners); Am. Bar Ass'n Comm. On Ethics and Prof. Resp., Formal Op. 91-361 (1991) (lawyer for partnership represents entity, rather than individual partners); Md. St. B. Ass'n, Inc., Comm. on Ethics, Op. 95-54 (1995) (lawyer of limited partnership may continue representing limited partnership even where general partner is removed and contests removal because lawyer represents partnership, not general partner); Va. St. B. Standing Comm. on Legal Ethics, Op. 1610 (1994) (lawyer representing joint venture of three entities may ethically sue one of those entities on behalf of another client).

21. A.B.A. in Op. 95-390 (1995).

The newer version of the ABA Model Rules in a comment adopts a middle ground, highly indeterminate, weighing test that rejects both the "all" and "nothing" approach to corporate family conflicts:

> A lawyer who represents a corporation or other organization does not, by virtue of that representation, necessarily represent any constituent or affiliated organization, such as a parent or subsidiary. Thus, the lawyer for an organization is not barred from accepting representation adverse to an affiliate in an unrelated matter, unless the circumstances are such that the affiliate should also be considered a client of the lawyer, there is an understanding between the lawyer and the organizational client that the lawyer will avoid representation adverse to the client's affiliates, or the lawyer's obligations to either the organizational client or the new client are likely to limit materially the lawyer's representation of the other client.[22]

---

22. *Id.* A related issue arose in *Strausbourger Pearson Tulcin Wolff, Inc. v. Wiz Tech., Inc.* 82 Cal. Rptr. 2d 326 (Cal. App. 1999), the one of a series of cases involving the question of whether a law firm that receives confidential information from a corporation while acting on behalf of a third party can be disqualified from being adverse to that corporation. Only a very few courts have addressed this issue, and their approaches have not been uniform.

In *Strasbourger*, the Stroock firm represented Strasbourger, an investment banking firm, in its capacity as underwriter for Wiz's public offering. Among other things, Stroock prepared the registration statement, the prospectus and other filings, and did due diligence on Wiz. To perform these and other tasks, Stroocks' lawyers repeatedly met with Wiz personnel, who disclosed information to Stroock as requested. Wiz, as part of the underwriting agreement, agreed to pay Stroock's fee. Stroock performed blue sky work for Wiz as part of the arrangement. A short time later, Wiz retained Coopers & Lybrand as auditors. Stroock was also Coopers' counsel. Wiz disclosed certain information to Coopers concerning an Securities and Exchange Commission (SEC) investigation. Eventually, Coopers resigned as Wiz's auditors.

Strasbourger thereafter sued Wiz for breaching the underwriting agreement. Strasbourger alleged that Wiz was selling its shares on its own, among other things. In the suit, Strasbourger was represented by Stroock. Wiz then moved to disqualify Stroock. The district court granted the motion to disqualify, finding both that Stroock had represented Wiz and that it should be disqualified for having received Wiz's confidential information.

Strasbourger appealed. On appeal, the California appellate court reversed. The court concluded that Stroock had not represented Wiz because of the precise language of the underwriting agreement at issue. In reaching its conclusion, it distinguished two other decisions that have addressed this or similar fact patterns, stating:

> Any inference [that Stroock represented Wiz] to the contrary is rebutted by the habit and custom of parties in stock underwriting transactions. The company traditionally pays for the blue sky work done by the underwriter's counsel. A savvy company involved in a stock offering would not consider the underwriter's counsel to be its attorney simply because it performed blue sky work for the transaction.

Wiz asserts that *International Tele-Marine v. Malone & Associates*, (D. Colo. 1994) 845 F. Supp. 1427 compels a contrary conclusion. The case involved a stock offering with an underwriting agreement under which the underwriter's counsel was to perform functions similar to those Stroock performed, and the company was to pay the underwriter's counsel for its blue sky work. The company and the underwriter's

Thus, the ABA in the comment simply refers to "circumstances" that indicate the affiliate "should be considered a client," or there is an "understanding," or the adverse matter will materially limit the lawyer's ability to be

---

counsel entered into another agreement, however. That agreement was consistent with the underwriting agreement in some respects but also referred to "withdrawal as *counsel for the company.*" The court found that language could be construed as creating an attorney-client relationship and denied summary judgment. Nothing in *International Tele-Marine* mandates a finding the evidence here was sufficient to establish an attorney-client relationship, particularly in the absence of any express representation by Stroock. Indeed, the *International Tele-Marine* court noted the mere performance of blue sky work in an offering does not create an attorney-client relationship between the underwriter's counsel and the issuing company.

Wiz also relies heavily on *Jack Eckerd Corp. v. Dart Group Corp.* (D. Del. 1985) 621 F. Supp. 725. In *Eckerd*, Dart wanted to obtain shares in another company, but wanted to avoid the restrictions inherent in being labeled an "investment company" under the Investment Company Act of 1940. It hired First Boston Corporation, an investment banking firm, to advise it. First Boston obtained the services of Fried, Frank, Harris, Shriver & Jacobson (Fried, Frank) in connection with the work. Fried, Frank received permission from Dart's regular outside counsel to confer with Dart. One of Fried, Frank's attorneys obtained information from Dart and prepared a complex memorandum discussing the issue. By agreement with First Boston, Dart paid Fried Frank's fee. When jack Eckerd Corporation sued Dart later on a substantially related matter, Dart sough to have Fried, Frank disqualified as Eckerd's counsel. The district court granted the motion, finding there had been at least an implied attorney-client relationship between Fried, Frank and Dart.

Although the fact situations of *Eckerd* and this case are similar, the distinctions mandate a different result. No agreement, like the one here, designated Fried, Frank as First Boston's counsel. To the contrary, First Boston was required to obtain Dart's approval of the counsel First Boston obtained for the work. Indeed, the district court in *Eckerd* found First Boston acted as Dart's agent in obtaining Fried, Frank. And, unlike the blue sky work here, which inured to Strasbourger's benefit, the memorandum Fried, Frank prepared affected only Dart's interests. 82 Cal. Rptr.2d at 330 (citations and brackets omitted).

The court then rejected Wiz's other evidence of an attorney-client relationship—including the fact that Stroock had "advised" Wiz of certain legal needs and had made various decisions on its behalf (82 Cal. Rptr. 2d at 331). Finally, the court rejected the argument that Stroock should be disqualified by reason of Wiz's disclosure of confidential information to Coopers, as Coopers had then passed that information along to Stroock in its capacity as Coopers' counsel. After noting that "Wiz's argument on this point is not entirely clear" (82 Cal. Rptr. 2d at 332), the court then rejected Wiz's reliance on a case that held that disqualification was proper where a nonlawyer had received information while employed as a paralegal. Wiz argued that "the disqualified firm never had an attorney-client relationship with the opposing party and argue[d] for the same result" (82 Cal. Rptr. 2d at 333). The court held that because the information came from Stroock's client, Coopers, it could not serve as the basis for a motion to disqualify (82 Cal. Rptr. 2d at 334).

adverse to the affiliated entity. This has led to at least three separate "tests" for loyalty under these circumstances:[23]

1. Is the affiliate de facto a current client of the law firm?
   1.1 Does the current corporate client have an objectively reasonable belief that its affiliate has de facto become a current client of the law firm, either because of the law firm's relationship and dealings with the affiliate during the representation, or because of significant overlaps in personnel and infrastructure between the corporate client and its affiliate?;
      1.1.1. Do the current corporate client and its affiliate share the same directors, officers, management, or other personnel?;
      1.1.2. Do the current corporate client and its affiliate share the same offices?;
      1.1.3. Do the current corporate client and its affiliate share the same legal department (or report to the same general counsel)?;
      1.1.4. Do the current corporate client and its affiliate share a substantial number of corporate services?; and
      1.1.5. Is there substantial integration in infrastructure between the current corporate client and its affiliate, such as shared computer networks, e-mail, intranet, interoffice mail, health benefit plans, letterhead and business cards, etc.?
2. Is there a significant risk that the law firm's representation of either the current corporate client or the adverse client in the adverse representation will be materially limited by the law firm's responsibilities to the other client?
3. During its representation of the corporate client, did the law firm learn confidences and secrets from either the client or its affiliate that would be so material to the adverse representation as to preclude the law firm from proceeding?[24]

Although the New York City Bar Association's opinion is typical, courts and bar associations that apply these various alternative tests do not do so uniformly.[25]

Although uniformity is sorely lacking in this area, uniformly the authorities recognize that one important factor in determining whether a separate legal entity should nonetheless be treated as part of the "real" client is whether the same in-house lawyer may be or already is involved in both the matter

---

23. *Available at* http://www.nycbar.org/Publications/reports/print_report.php?rid=671&search term=Corporate-family%20conflicts;%20duty%200f%2010yalty;%20duty%20to%20preserve %20confidences%20and%20secrets.

24. *Id.*

25. *See, e.g.,* Ill. St. B. Ass'n Advisory Op. 95-15 (May 17, 1996); N.Y. County Lawyers' Ass'n Comm. on Prof. Eth. 684 (June 1991); Cal. St. B. Standing Comm. on Prof. Resp. Op. 1989-113 (1989).

on which the firm is representing the client and the matter in which the firm will be adverse to the related entity. Another factor that often is identified as important is whether the lawyer in representing the corporate client might have obtained information about the entity to which the firm is adverse.[26]

Finally, even if the engagement letter specifies that the "real" client is the practitioner's only client, nothing precludes a practitioner who is representing an entity from also—intentionally or otherwise—forming an express or implied attorney-client relationship with one or more of the entity's constituents. The Fifth Circuit's approach in *Hopper v. Frank* exemplifies the approach to whether a lawyer who represents an entity also has an attorney client relationship with its constituents. In that case, the court reasoned that, by itself representing a partnership did not constitute representation of a constituent representation of one of its partners. Instead, the court must look to "such factors as whether the lawyer affirmatively assumed a duty of representation to the individual partner, whether the partner was separately represented by other counsel when the partnership was created or in connection with its affairs, whether the lawyer had represented an individual partner before undertaking to represent the partnership, and whether there was evidence of reliance by the individual partner on the lawyer as his or her separate counsel, or of the partner's expectation of personal representation."[27]

Of course, in real practice the facts and circumstances in *Hopper v. Frank* can and often do occur. Failing to clarify up front who is and is not the client thus permits entity-constituents to argue, in hindsight, that they "had been" a client. For example, a lawyer representing a corporation might on a daily basis be in contact with individuals; those individuals (who are oblivious to what the ethical rule may say) can become confused about who the lawyer represents, particularly where the individual is a principal in the corporation or other entity being represented.

---

26. *Faughn v. Perez*, 145 Cal. App. 4th 592 (Cal. App. 2006) (noting split in California law on the approach to this issue); *Discotrade Ltd. v. Wyeth-Ayerst Int'l. Inc.*, 200 F. Supp. 2d 355 (S.D.N.Y. 2002) (weighing); *Colorpix Systems of America v. Broan Mfg. Co.*, 131 F. Supp. 2d 1499 (D. Conn. 2001) (in applying the weighing, approach, the court disqualified the firm, emphasizing that the same in-house lawyer represented both the client-entity and the adverse entity); *Gen-Cor, LLC v. Buckeye Corrugated, Inc.*, 111 F. Supp. 2d 1049 (S.D. Ind. 2000) *Baxter Diagnostics, Inc. v. AVL Scientific Corp.*, 798 F. Supp. 612 (C.D. Cal. 1992) (weighing in patent litigation); Md. State Bar Op. 87-19 (weighing); Mass. Bar Op. 3 (1992) (weighing); Pa. Op. 2001–03 (2001) (allowing firm that represents one subsidiary to be adverse to another).
27. *Hopper*, 16 F.3d at 95–96 (quoting A.B.A. Op. 91-361 (1991) [internal quotation marks omitted]).

B. What to Do

Practitioners who do not use an engagement letter "choose" the default that will apply in the context of entity representations risks letting a court later decide it for them or, more likely, of possibly having to decline a new matter because of the liability to clear conflicts. It does not take "magic language," just thoughtful language to reduce these problems. Language such as "by representing the entity that has retained us, we do not represent any of its shareholders, officers, directors, or entities which it or they owns or controls" will go a long way toward reducing uncertainty concerning client identity.[28] Consider this as another possible term in any engagement letter with a business entity:

> If you are signing the accompanying letter on behalf of a business entity, including a corporation, partnership, limited partnership, or similar entity, it is important that you be aware that our client is only the entity. We do not, by representing the entity, have an attorney-client relationship with you, or the entity's other individual executives, directors, partners, managing agents, shareholders, or other constituents, agents, or employees. Likewise, we do not represent any person or entity that owns or controls the entity, such as a parent corporation or general partner. We also do not represent entities owned by our client, such as its affiliates or subsidiaries. Where we represent an entity as a client, our professional responsibilities are to that entity alone.
>
> We will gladly explore with you whether we can ethically also represent a person or entity associated or related to our client. However, we will do so only by way of a separate written agreement.

B. Representation Ending Dates in Patent Matters

1. The Law

If representation of a client has ended, then the person or entity is a "former client." A lawyer is generally free to be adverse to a former client unless the representation against the former client is "substantially related" to the lawyer's prior representation.[29]

---

28. *Cf. Avocent Redmond Corp. v. Rose Elec.*, 2007 U.S. Dist. Lexis 39736 (W.D. Wash. May 30, 2007) (holding that firm that agreed to represent "Avocent . . . and its affiliates" had an attorney-client relationship with every Avocent affiliate).

29. *See* Model Rule 1.9. This is obviously a simplification. *See* Chapter 6, concerning former client conflicts, *infra*.

Various issues can create uncertainty as to ending dates, and so when a client has become a "former client." It is significant to note that movants in disqualification proceedings have successfully argued that they were "current clients," even though the firm was not representing them in a particular matter at the moment the disqualification motion was filed, and had not done so for months, and sometimes years. The movant argued that it had an ongoing relationship, and the fact that a matter was not active at the moment the disqualification motion was filed does not control. Doubts as to whether a client is "current" or not are, seemingly, resolved against the firm.[30]

Accordingly, to the extent that the correspondence or activities show when the representation ended, the lawyer is more likely to have more freedom to be adverse to the person. The engagement letter provision in the following section is one option; a better one is to include with the final fee statement a simple notice to the client that the representation has ended, and that the firm would of course be willing to represent the party in some other matter should the need arise—and a subsequent engagement letter be executed.

In addition, firms that send patentees reminders about maintenance fees and the like might want to reconsider the practice,[31] or clearly explain to the "client" that such reminders are not done as part of an ongoing attorney-client relationship.[32] Likewise, firms should consider whether to require attorneys

---

30. *Int'l Bus. Mach. Corp. v. Levin*, 579 F.2d 271, 281 (7th Cir. 1978); G.D. *Searle & Co. v. Nutrapharm, Inc.*, 1999 WL 249725 (S.D.N.Y. Apr. 28, 1999) (analyzing whether client was current or former client in trademark dispute); *Oxford Sys., Inc. v. Cellpro, Inc.*, 45 F. Supp. 2d 1055 (W.D. Wash. 1999) (sending newsletters and similar communications can be indicia of current attorney-client relationship); *Kabi Pharmacia AB v. Alcon Surgical Inc.*, 25 U.S.P.Q.2d 1030 (D. Del. 1992) (party disqualified firm as a "current client" even though it had not been given any advice for many months); *Manoir-Electroalloys Corp. v. Amalloy Corp.*, 711 F. Supp. 188, 193–94 (D.N.J. 1989) (firm disqualified four years after sending last letter to "current" client). *But see Strojirenstvi v. Seisakusho*, 2 U.S.P.Q.2d 1222 (Comm'r Pat. & Trademarks Aug. 29, 1986) (reasoning that not all deadlines must pass before a party can be deemed to become a former client).

31. Firms who agree to pay maintenance fees create myriad problems for themselves, including calendaring the obligation and tracking the patentee down years later when the fee is due. Firms that permit lapse have been sued for damages. *E.g., New Tek Mfg. Inc. v. Beehner*, 702 N.W.2d 336 (Neb. 2005) (remanding for trial on whether infringement would have occurred after lapse). As a consequence, there has been a firm trend to unload these burdens onto third-party annuity payment companies and thereby the high risk associated with unintentional abandonment.

32. *See Oregon* Op. 2005-146 (2005) (reasoning that the recipients of maintenance fee reminders "in the absence of . . . a clear statement [that no attorney-client relationship exists] may reasonably believe that there is a continuing relationship"). The PTO in its recent notice and comment took the same position. *See* Notice of Proposed Rulemaking Changes to Representation of Others before the United States Patent and Trademark Office, 68 Fed. Reg. 69442, 69467 (Dec. 12, 2003). However, in *Strojirenstvi v. Seisakusho*, 2 U.S.P.Q.2d 1222 (Comm'r Pat. & Trademarks Aug. 29, 1986), the commissioner stated that a client was a former client even though the firm was "paying maintenance fees" because calendaring was merely a "ministerial" service.

to formally terminate every relationship with the transmittal of the final fee statement.[33]

2. What to Do

Consider this language in an engagement letter:

> *End of Representation.* Unless we are retained by you to file continuation applications, our representation of you will end when we deliver any issued patent to you, or you agree with us that further prosecution is unnecessary even though no patent has issued.
>
> *Patent Maintenance Fee Reminders.* If a patent is granted to you as a result of our prosecution, you must periodically pay maintenance fees or the patent will lapse, perhaps rendering it worthless. Generally, fees will be due after 3½, 7½, and 11½ years after the date of issuance. We will send to your last known address maintenance fee reminders as a service, even though our attorney-client relationship has ended, if you request us in writing to do so when we forward the patent to you. If you do not ask us to do so, we strongly suggest that you either hire a commercial service to do this for you, or place reminders of maintenance fees in more than one calendaring system.

C. Scope of the Representation

The more carefully defined the representation is, the less likely a client will contend that a lawyer's obligations continue into the future, or that the lawyer is obligated (under a flat or contingent fee arrangement) to do something the lawyer had not intended to agree to. Consider this language:

> You have engaged us only to represent you in the Matter, and to provide services only as reasonably necessary to represent your interests in the Matter. Any changes to the scope of the representation must be confirmed in writing.

In *CardioGrip Corp. v. Mueller & Smith, LP,* 2008 U.S. Dist. LEXIS 2627 (S.D. Ohio Jan. 14, 2008), the court also intimated that sending reminders of maintenance fee due dates did not create an attorney-client relationship, basing its holding on undisputed testimony of the practitioner that reminders were sent as a courtesy and in the hopes of obtaining fees for being retained to pay the maintenance fees.

The Court of Appeals of Michigan has also held that the "ministerial task of sending a reminder letter" did not continue a prior attorney-client relationship. *Wright v. Rinaldo,* 2008 Mich. App. LEXIS 1411 (July 10, 2008).

33. *See Kabi Pharmacia,* 25 U.S.P.Q.2d 1030 (in treating party a current client, court noted that firm could not "isolate any point in time at which [the party] became a "former client").

We are lawyers, not experts in marketing, product design, or consumer preferences or demand. You have asked us to determine whether to file, and if so what sort of applications to file, to obtain patent protection on the subject matter identified in the accompanying letter. As you know, after an application is filed, it will be examined and could be the subject of one or more office actions. It is impossible to predict whether it will be allowed without substantial prosecution, which means expense and delay.

D. Prospective Consent

In addition to using engagement letters to clearly define the scope of a representation (as ending when the patent issues, and not when the obligation to pay maintenance fees ends, for example), and client identity (in the case of corporations and inventors), they can be used, to a more limited extent, to obtain consent in advance to certain conflicts.

1. Standards Governing Prospective Consent

One way to reduce the number of conflicts is to obtain "advance consent" to certain common forms of adverse representations. Many, but not all, conflicts of interest are consentable if the client provides informed consent after full disclosure by the attorney of the benefits and risks of the representation. Under the Patent and Trademark Office Code of Professional Conduct (PTO Code)[34] and many state rules modeled after Model Rule 1.7(b), unless the representation is prohibited by law or involves a claim by one client against another in the same lawsuit, a conflict may be waived so long as (1) the lawyer reasonably believes he or she can competently and diligently represent both clients (i.e., will be able to exercise independent professional judgment on behalf of each client), and (2) each client gives informed consent.

It is important to recognize that if a reasonable lawyer would not believe that competent and diligent representation could be given, then the lawyer may not seek consent, and any consent given is invalid. A comment to the Model Rules, for example, explains:

Ordinarily, clients may consent to representation notwithstanding a conflict. However, as indicated in paragraph (b), some conflicts are nonconsentable,

---

34. Section 10.66(c) provides that, if there is a conflict, "a practitioner may represent multiple clients if it is obvious that the practitioner can adequately represent the interest of each and if each consents to the representation after full disclosure of the possible effect of such representation on the exercise of the practitioner's independent professional judgment on behalf of each."

meaning that the lawyer involved cannot properly ask for such agreement or provide representation on the basis of the client's consent. When the lawyer is representing more than one client, the question of consentability must be resolved as to each client.

Consentability is typically determined by considering whether the interests of the clients will be adequately protected if the clients are permitted to give their informed consent to representation burdened by a conflict of interest. Thus, under paragraph (b)(1), representation is prohibited if in the circumstances the lawyer cannot reasonably conclude that the lawyer will be able to provide competent and diligent representation. See Rule 1.1 (competence) and Rule 1.3 (diligence).[35]

Where consent is sought *before* the conflict exists, it is obviously more difficult for a client to obtain sufficient information for consent to be informed. As a result, a comment to the rule states:

> The effectiveness of such waivers is generally determined by the extent to which the client reasonably understands the material risks that the waiver entails. The more comprehensive the explanation of the types of future representations that might arise and the actual and reasonably foreseeable adverse consequences of those representations, the greater the likelihood that the client will have the requisite understanding. Thus, if the client agrees to consent to a particular type of conflict with which the client is already familiar, then the consent ordinarily will be effective with regard to that type of conflict. If the consent is general and open-ended, then the consent ordinarily will be ineffective, because it is not reasonably likely that the client will have understood the material risks involved. On the other hand, if the client is an experienced user of the legal services involved and is reasonably informed regarding the risk that a conflict may arise, such consent is more likely to be effective, particularly if, e.g., the client is independently represented by other counsel in giving consent and the consent is limited to future conflicts unrelated to the subject of the representation. In any case, advance consent cannot be effective if the circumstances that materialize in the future are such as would make the conflict nonconsentable under paragraph (b).[36]

Courts and bar associations agree that prospective consent is more difficult to obtain, but disagree on the particulars.[37] The ABA opinion on the subject[38] took the position that prospective conflicts are more likely to be effective when the client is independently represented by other counsel in

---

35. Model Rule 1.7, cmt. 14–15.

36. *Id.* cmt. 22.

37. *See Fisons Corp. v. Atochem N. Am., Inc.*, 1990 WL 180551 (S.D.N.Y. 1990); *Indianapolis Podiatry, P.C. v. Efroymson*, 720 N.E.2d 376 (Ind. App. 1999); *Visa U.S.A., Inc. v. First Data Corp.*, 241 F. Supp. 2d 1100 (N.D. Cal. 2003).

38. A.B.A. Formal Op. 05-436 (May 11, 2005).

giving the consent, and the consent is limited to matters which are unrelated to the lawyer's representation of the client. The ABA concluded that the "Ethics 2000" version of the Model Rules—not yet adopted in many states— permits prospective consents in broader circumstances than either the Model Rules or the Model Code.[39]

The Trademark Trial and Appeal Board (TTAB) recently analyzed full disclosure in a trademark case and so provided some insight into how the USPTO can approach the issue of prospective consent. That decision reasoned:

> In addition, if both clients have consented, courts and ethical regulations have permitted a law firm to represent multiple clients with adverse interests. Opposer argues that Akin Gump obtained applicant's consent pursuant to the Terms of Engagement Letter. The relevant paragraph is set out below:
>
> > During the term of this engagement, we will not knowingly accept representation of another client to pursue interests that are directly adverse to your interests unless and until we have made full disclosure to you of all the relevant facts, circumstances and implications of our undertaking the two representations and you have consented to our representation of the other client. You agree, however, that you will be reasonable in evaluating such circumstances and that you will give your consent if we can confirm to you in good faith that the following criteria are met: (i) there is no substantial relationship between any matter in which we are representing or have represented you and the matter for the other client; (ii) our representation of the other client will not compromise any confidential information we have received from you; (iii) our effective representation of you and the discharge of our professional responsibilities to you will not be prejudiced by our representation of the other client; and (iv) the other client has also consented in writing based on our full disclosure of the relevant facts, circumstances and implications of our undertaking the two representations.
>
> Courts have found that a party can consent to its attorney's adverse representation of another client.
>
> > To satisfy the requirement of full disclosure by a lawyer before undertaking to represent two conflicting interests, it is not sufficient that both parties be informed of the fact that the lawyer is undertaking to represent both of them, but he must explain to them the nature of the conflict of interest in such detail so that they can understand the reasons why it may be desirable for each to have independent counsel, with undivided loyalty to the interests of each of them.

---

39. *Id.*

United Sewerage Agency, 646 F.2d at 1345–46, *quoting, In re Boivin,* 533 P.2d 971, 974 (Or. 1975).

Opposer argues that "Akin Gump notified Applicant that the legal representation provided to Applicant and Opposer were not substantially related." Opposition at 18. Opposer refers to two paragraphs to support its argument concerning its notification of applicant. The first paragraph from Mr. Fladung reports that "I notified [applicant] that Akin Gump believed the matters handled by Akin Gump for [applicant] were not substantially related or are non-related to the matters handled by Akin Gump for [opposer]." Fladung declaration, 8. Mr. Raffkind declares (7) that the "matters handled by Akin Gump for [applicant] are not substantially related or are non-related to the matters handled by Akin Gump for [opposer]." Despite these general statements in the declarations that the matters were not substantially related or non-related, it is far from clear what information was presented to applicant in order for it to make an informed consent. In an email dated August 27, 2003, applicant wrote to Eliot Raffkind as follows:

> Regarding your representation of Finger Furniture, who is suing us (Finger Interests) on a trademark issue, what is the status of the conflict of interest this raises as set forth in our engagement letter.
>
> We have discussed this on . . . two previous occasions, and I have left recent phone messages with you regarding this issue. The last response that I received form you on this issue was probably back in late June when you mentioned that you were checking with the ethics department. What response have you received from that department?

The response applicant received from Mr. Raffkind that same day simply reported:

> Sorry I have not gotten back to you. I have spoken to our ethics folks on several occasions (including yesterday most recently), but at this point have not gotten guidance for me to get back to you. I have stressed the need to do so quickly as possible and will let you know as soon as I hear from them.

Mr. Fladung's letter of August 29, 2003, does not set out how Akin Gump had complied with its requirements under its Terms of Engagement letter or that it fully disclosed "the relevant facts, circumstances and implications of our undertaking the two representations" in order that applicant could make an informed consent. Naked assurances that the matters are "not substantially related or are non-related" do not amount to "full disclosure . . . of all the facts, circumstances and implications of our undertaking the two representations."

> It is not clear how opposer maintains that it obtained applicant's consent pursuant to the terms of this agreement. There is no indication in Mr. Fladung's letter of August 29, 2003, or Eliot Raffkind's email of August 27, 2003, that Akin Gump believed that applicant had already consented to the representation of adverse clients under the Terms of Engagement letter. It is not tenable

for a law firm to sue its client and then rely on the firm's response to the petition to disqualify as a means of advising its client that the client had consented to the representation of an adverse client. Therefore, based on the record in this case, Akin Gump had not demonstrated that Akin Gump had complied with the Terms of Engagement letter and that applicant has consented or is bound to consent to the adverse representation. *See Manoir-Electroalloys,* 711 F. Supp. at 195 ("I need not reach the issue as to whether Iacono could have consented to the concurrent representation . . . because [the law firm] has not met its burden of proving full disclosure was made and Iacono's consent was obtained").[40]

The *Finger* decision by the TTAB, along with the other authority, illustrate the difficulties facing practitioners who seek prospective consent: The client must receive full disclosure of the relevant facts, but those facts are not known at the time consent is obtained. To the extent, however, that the practitioner can identify the likely adverse client (by name or by industry), the type of adverse representation (e.g., responding to an office action applying a patent owned by that client), and any other facts likely to be pertinent to the future adverse matter. However, even with lengthy and highly predictive disclosure, the degree to which prospective consent is enforceable remains a matter about which the courts disagree, and about which there is scant USPTO authority.

---

40. *Finger Furniture Co. v. Finger Interests No. 1, Ltd.,* 71 U.S.P.Q.2d 1287, 1290 (TTAB 2004) (trademark decision).

CHAPTER

5

Loyalty and Current Client Conflicts of Interest

A. The Patent and Trademark Office Code of Professional
   Conduct and Analogous State Law   47

B. The Meaning of "Adversity" and "Differing Interests"   48

C. The Meaning of "Material Limitations"   51

D. Adversity and Material Limitations Created by the
   Property Right   52
   1. Problems Created by Priority   52
      A. Narrowing Claims to Disfavor One Client
         Over Another   52
      B. Office Action Responses and Rule 131 Antedating   54

E. The Conflict Created by the Right to Exclude   59

F. Information: Liability and Conflict   60

G. Additional Possible Prosecution Conflicts   61

H. What to Do   62
   1. Prosecution Problems   62
   2. Corporate Affiliate Intellectual Property   63
   3. Lateral Hires   63

I. Conclusion   64

Practitioners are required to withdraw when a representation of a client is unethical.[1] In the next few chapters, we examine when conflicts of interest

---

1. The withdrawal provision of the PTO Code provides:

   (a) A practitioner shall not withdraw from employment in a proceeding before the Office without permission from the Office (*see* §§ 1.36 and 2.19 of this subchapter). In

arise that can require withdrawal. These include: conflicts between the practitioner's interests and his or her client's; conflicts among the practitioner's

---

any event, a practitioner shall not withdraw from employment until the practitioner
has taken reasonable steps to avoid foreseeable prejudice to the rights of the client,
including giving due notice to his or her client, allowing time for employment of
another practitioner, delivering to the client all papers and property to which the client
is entitled, and complying with applicable laws and rules. A practitioner who withdraws from employment shall refund promptly any part of a fee paid in advance that
has not been earned.

(b) Mandatory withdrawal. A practitioner representing a client before the Office shall
withdraw from employment if:

(1) The practitioner knows or it is obvious that the client is bringing a legal action,
commencing a proceeding before the Office, conducting a defense, or asserting a
position in litigation or any proceeding pending before the Office, or is otherwise
having steps taken for the client, merely for the purpose of harassing or injuring
any person;

(2) The practitioner knows or it is obvious that the practitioner's continued
employment will result in violation of a Disciplinary Rule;

(3) The practitioner's mental or physical condition renders it unreasonably
difficult for the practitioner to carry out the employment effectively; or

(4) The practitioner is discharged by the client.

(c) Permissive withdrawal. If paragraph (b) of this section is not applicable, a practitioner may not request permission to withdraw in matters pending before the Office
unless such request or such withdrawal is because:

(1) The petitioner's client:

(i) Insists upon presenting a claim or defense that is not warranted under
existing law and cannot be supported by a good faith argument for an extension, modification, or reversal of existing law;

(ii) Personally seeks to pursue an illegal course of conduct;

(iii) Insists that the practitioner pursue a course of conduct that is illegal or
that is prohibited under a Disciplinary Rule;

(iv) By other conduct renders it unreasonably difficult for the practitioner to
carry out the employment effectively;

(v) Insists, in a matter not pending before a tribunal, that the practitioner
engage in conduct that is contrary to the judgment and advice of the practitioner but not prohibited under the Disciplinary Rule; or

(vi) Has failed to pay one or more bills rendered by the practitioner for an
unreasonable period of time or has failed to honor an agreement to pay a
retainer in advance of the performance of legal services.

(2) The practitioner's continued employment is likely to result in a violation of a
Disciplinary Rule;

(3) The practitioner's inability to work with co-counsel indicates that the best
interests of the client likely will be served by withdrawal;

(4) The practitioner's mental or physical condition renders it difficult for the
practitioner to carry out the employment effectively;

(5) The practitioner's client knowingly and freely assents to termination of the
employment; or

(6) The practitioner believes in good faith, in a proceeding pending before the
Office, that the Office will find the existence of other good cause for withdrawal.

current clients; and conflicts between a current client and a former client of the practitioner.

This chapter analyzes conflicts of interest that can arise during patent prosecution between different current clients of the practitioner, as well as between current clients and the practitioner's own interests. Subsequent chapters will analyze additional conflicts, and others are discussed in Appendix 1.

A. The Patent and Trademark Office Code of Professional Conduct and Analogous State Law

Several provisions of the Patent and Trademark Office Code of Professional Conduct (PTO Code) relate to concurrent client conflicts of interest.[2] However, foremost, is section 10.62(a), which provides:

> Except with the consent of a client after full disclosure, a practitioner shall not accept employment if the exercise of the practitioner's professional judgment on behalf of the client will be or reasonably may be affected by the practitioner's own financial, business, property, or personal interests.[3]

"Differing interest" is defined to "include every interest that may adversely affect either the judgment or the loyalty of a practitioner to a client, whether it is a conflicting, inconsistent, diverse, or other interest."[4] As with the Model

---

2. In addition, section 10.66 of the PTO Code provides:

> (a) A practitioner shall decline proffered employment if the exercise of the practitioner's independent professional judgment in behalf of a client will be or is likely to be adversely affected by the acceptance of the proffered employment, or if it would be likely to involve the practitioner in representing differing interests, except to the extent permitted under paragraph (c) of this section.
> (b) A practitioner shall not continue in multiple employment if the exercise of the practitioner's independent professional judgment in behalf of a client will be or is likely to be adversely affected by the practitioner's representation of another client, or if it would be likely to involve the practitioner in representing differing interests, except to the extent permitted under paragraph (c) of this section.
> (c) In the situations covered by paragraphs (a) and (b) of this section, a practitioner may represent multiple clients if it is obvious that the practitioner can adequately represent the interest of each and if each consents to the representation after full disclosure of the possible effect of such representation on the exercise of the practitioner's independent professional judgment on behalf of each.
> (d) If a practitioner is required to decline employment or to withdraw from employment under a Disciplinary Rule, no partner, or associate, or any other practitioner affiliated with the practitioner or the practitioner's firm, may accept or continue such employment unless otherwise ordered by the Director or Commissioner.

3. 37 C.F.R. § 10.62(a). *See* Appendix 1.
4. 37 C.F.R. § 10.1(f).

Rules, generally if one practitioner in a firm is disqualified, all are.[5] Also as with the Model Rules, consent may be obtained from the affected clients under some circumstances.[6]

Similarly, Model Rule 1.7, which has been adopted in many states, contains two prohibitions concerning conflicts of interest between two current clients: (a) a lawyer may not represent one client "directly adverse to another client"; and (b) he or she may not "represent a client if the representation of that client may be materially limited by the lawyer's responsibilities to another client."[7] Under the principle of imputed disqualification, if one lawyer may not undertake a representation, no lawyer in the firm can.[8] Both rules permit clients to consent, under some circumstances, after full disclosure.

B. The Meaning of "Adversity" and "Differing Interests"

For the large part, both "adversity" and "differing interest" cover the same terrain. Although it may be that in some unusual circumstances conduct might be "adverse" but not involve "differing interests," we will not delve into those issues here but will instead assume that if conduct is "adverse" it involves "differing interests" and, conversely, if conduct does not involve "differing interests," it is not "adverse."

Many circumstances would involve an adverse representation. Obviously, for example, a practitioner would be adverse to a current client and would be representing differing interests if he or she files a suit against a current client or appears in an interference proceeding against a current client. On the other end of the spectrum, it is equally obvious that simply representing a client in obtaining a patent does not mean that the practitioner is adverse to any other

---

5. *Id.* § 10.66(d) ("If a practitioner is required to decline employment or to withdraw from employment under a Disciplinary Rule, no partner, or associate, or any other practitioner affiliated with the practitioner or the practitioner's firm, may accept or continue such employment unless otherwise ordered by the Director or Commissioner.")

6. *Id.* § 10.66(c).

7. Model Rule 1.7 provides:

   (a) A lawyer shall not represent a client if the representation of that client will be directly adverse to another existing client, unless:
       (1) [T]he lawyer reasonably believes the representation will not adversely affect the relationship with the other client; and
       (2) [E]ach client consents after consultation.

8. Model Rule 1.10(a).

client—even though, if the practitioner is successful, the patentee will be better able to compete economically with the practitioner's other clients.

Beyond that, there is very little patent-specific authority on when "differing interests" or "adversity" can arise. There is one USPTO decision examining the meaning of "adversity," and only a few courts have applied state ethics rules, similar to the Model Rules, to patent prosecution conflicts. Thus, analogies must largely control, and they are imperfect. First, we will discuss what direct authority there is.

The USPTO has held that representing both parties to an interference proceeding constitutes an adverse representation.[9] Although the Board did not disqualify the practitioner in that proceeding from representing one party to the interference against the other, it did so because, although the practitioner was representing differing interests, the Board found that prudential and practical concerns necessitated that it deny the motion. The Board's decision appeared to turn on whether there was a subject matter overlap between the work being done for the client, and the work being done against it:

> Balance is a particularly critical consideration in this case. UNM has conceded (a) that there is no substantial relationship between the subject matter of the P&E's work on UNM's patent application and the subject matter of this interference and (b) that it has not presented facts to support a sharing of confidences with P&E sufficient to warrant disqualification under the former-client standard. The question thus framed is whether a current-client conflict is a strict liability offense . . . Rejection of a per se rule is sound policy because such a rule would permit wasteful ancillary litigation for purely tactical reasons.[10]

Thus, there is no "per se" rule that an adverse representation requires disqualification. However, the Board also made clear that although disqualification was not warranted, discipline might be.[11] Presumably, the Board's comments that it would adopt something other than a per se rule for purposes of disqualification means that a per se rule does apply to discipline. Thus, finding when "adversity" arises in patent prosecution remains critical, but elusive.

There is very little authority applying to patent practice, the concept of "adversity" from the Model Rules or other state-based regulation. The courts applying the Model Rules have, contrary to the approach of the Board noted above, typically disqualified lawyers for being directly adverse to a current

---

9. *Univ. of New Mexico v. Fordham,* No. 104,761, 2002 WL 529661, at *3 (Bd. Pat. App. & Interf. Apr. 2, 2002).

10. *Id.*

11. *Id.* ("To the extent that P&E may have harmed UNM in a way unrelated to this interference, UNM can seek redress through the Office of Enrollment and Discipline or a relevant State bar").

client, with few exceptions. In appropriate cases, courts hold that disqualification is not proper where, for example, disqualification will work a substantial hardship on one client, and the matter on which the law firm is representing the client is wholly unrelated to the matter adverse to that client. That is, courts have interpreted Model Rule 1.7(a) to mean what it says: A lawyer may never be adverse to a current client, unless the client consents, waives any objection, or the lawyer demonstrates that there are exceptional circumstances that would serve either a professional or societal interests that would outweigh the public's perception of impropriety.[12]

Again, and under either set of rules, if one lawyer in a firm is disqualified, all are.[13] Thus, if one lawyer in a firm could not engage in a representation, no lawyer in a firm may do so. Disqualification is imputed and firm-wide.

There is no direct authority, yet, on when prosecuting similar patents or patents to potentially competing products for different clients constitutes adversity. The closest analog we could find relates to the question of economic competition. There are numerous authorities stating the proposition that mere economic adversity between clients does not create a conflict of interest, but which nonetheless find adversity under specific facts.[14] One District of Columbia case, *Curtis v. Radio Representatives, Inc.,*[15] provides an extended judicial discussion of this concept in a somewhat analogous environment. In that case, lawyers who had represented a client in obtaining radio broadcast licenses brought a claim for fees. The client's counterclaim alleged that the firm had represented conflicting interests by representing competitors in obtaining licenses. In addressing the motion, the court rejected the rule that merely representing economic competitors was sufficient to constitute a conflict of interest. Instead, the court focused on whether the lawyer was involved in representing differing interests. In the radio licensing context, the court concluded that the lawyer could be representing conflicting

12. *In re Dresser*, 972 F.2d 540, 545 (5th Cir. 1992).
13. Model Rule 1.10(a)("While lawyers are associated in a firm, none of them shall knowingly represent a client when any one of them practicing alone would be prohibited from doing so by Rule" 1.7").
14. *E.g.,* A.B.A. Formal Op. 05-435 (Dec. 8, 2004) (concluding that a lawyer who represents as a client an insurance company named party in litigation could represent another client in a suit against a defendant who is insured by a policy issued by the insurance company client); *Texarkana College Bowl, Inc. v. Phillips*, 408 S.W.2d 537, 540 (Tex. Civ. App.—Texarkana 1966, no writ) (rejecting as evidence that corporate directors were not acting in best interest of corporation because their lawyers represented a competing bowling alley that "[l]egal counsel may, within very narrow limits, represent clients having adverse economic interests."); *Gursky & Ederer, LLP v. GMT Corp.,* 2004 WL 2793174 (N.Y. Sup. Ct. Oct. 5, 2004) (concluding that client stated claim upon which relief could be granted where it alleged that lawyers assisted former employee of current client establish competing business).
15. 696 F. Supp. 729 (D. D.C. 1988).

interests if there was objectionable electrical interference between stations the firm was seeking for two clients.[16]

Although by itself prosecuting closely related applications is not a conflict, conflicts of interest in patent prosecution can arise because a firm prosecutes applications for different clients that are in the same, or nearly the same, area of technology. The issue is one less of line drawing then of risk identification and risk management.

There are obvious steps and positions a firm could adopt to lessen its exposure. A firm will not face conflicts arising out of patent prosecution if it represents only one prosecution client. That, obviously, is unrealistic for most firms and, just as clearly, most clients and the patent system generally.

Moving past that point, a firm could choose to represent more than one prosecution client, but not to represent any two clients in analogous art fields.[17] If a firm does so, then it should not face any of the possible conflicts discussed in this chapter, at least absent unusual circumstances (which we will explore). Again, however, this approach is likely an unrealistic business model for most firms, and represents an enormous cost to clients, and inefficiencies to the patent system because it will result in less disclosure of pertinent art. Further, this approach denies clients efficiency and imposes unnecessary costs on lawyers, clients, and the patent system.

Once a firm is past that point—once it decides to take on clients in analogous art fields—then the risk increases that a conflict of interest will arise. There are several ways this can occur. The following section explores specific issues, after first discussing the concept of "material limitations" on a representation.

C. The Meaning of "Material Limitations"

The notion of when a lawyer's obligations to one client will materially limit his or her ability to represent another client is less clearly stated than the principle that an adverse representation is improper. The limitation must not only be "material"; it must be "significantly" likely to arise. Finally, this limitation

---

16. 696 F. Supp. at 736.
17. One commentator noted that prosecuting patents in "analogous arts" can create a conflict of interest. Paul Vapnek, *Ethics and Professional Responsibility Issues*, 835 PCI/Pat. 7, 17 (June 2005). He correctly noted that "drawing boundaries in accordance with the definition of analogous art may be the only way to assure that one client's patent or patent application is sufficiently remote that it could not legitimately be cited against another client's application." *Id.* Drawing the boundaries that broadly would no doubt eliminate any conflict, but it would also unduly restrict the ability of different clients to hire the same lawyer, or under some circumstances, firm, with expertise in a narrow area of technology.

must arise out of "the lawyer's responsibilities to another client, a former client or a third person or by a personal interest of the lawyer." The concern, stated simply, is that because of the lawyer's obligations to someone else, he or she will "pull punches" in representing a client, even if one client is not adverse to another client.

To apply the principle, one must compare how (1) a lawyer reasonably would represent a client without any other relationship between the lawyer and another person, with (2) a lawyer with the relationship. If there is a significant risk that the lawyer with the relationship or clients will provide the client with materially less zeal or dedication than the reasonable lawyer would without the relationship, and that diminution in zeal or dedication is caused by the relationship, then a material limitation exists.[18]

As noted below, there are malpractice cases based on this principle that have been filed against patent practitioners. They provide examples of conduct to watch for.

D. Adversity and Material Limitations Created by the Property Right

1. Problems Created by Priority

A. Narrowing Claims to Disfavor One Client Over Another

In the broadest sense, a practitioner who obtains a patent for one client thereby reduces to all other clients the property available to those clients. What one client patents, no other can. Thus, merely obtaining a patent for one client is in that sense adverse to every other client. Yet, the mere patenting of subject matter for one client creates no conflict of interest with all other clients, even though by definition the lawyer has helped to take property away from them. The concept of adversity plainly cannot be stretched that far.

On the other end of the spectrum, it is certain that a lawyer could not represent two clients with interfering subject matter in an interference proceeding. This is no different than representing two clients with competing claims to title to the same property, or indeed, a plaintiff and defendant to the typical lawsuit. What one wins, the other loses.

Risks can arise without actual pending claims to the same subject matter, however. Foremost, one client may contend that the practitioner's duty of

---

18. *See Berkeley Ltd. Partnership v. Arnold, White & Durkee.* 118 F. Supp. 2d 668 (D. Md. 2000) (firm breached fiduciary duty when it represented patentee-client without telling it that it represented a party who should have been sued for infringement).

loyalty to another client constituted an impermissible limitation on the practitioner's ability to represent it. In a nutshell, the client will contend that, by reason of his or her obligations to the other client, the practitioner "pulled punches" in the USPTO, and got the client less than it deserved.

In *Sentinel Prods. Corp v. Platt*,[19] a law firm prosecuted patents for two clients, Sentinel and Knaus. The evidence showed that the firm had filed applications for Sentinel, and then two weeks later filed applications for Knaus.[20] There was evidence that the firm changed the disclosure provided to it by Sentinel, but no evidence that changes had been made to avoid Knaus' application.[21] However, the firm's attorneys testified that they thought the applications "overlapped" and lacked a "patentable difference."[22] Knaus' application was issued first, and Sentinel's claims were then rejected in light of Knaus.[23] Sentinel narrowed its claims to avoid Knaus, and eventually Sentinel was issued patents with narrower claims.[24]

Not only was there evidence that the claims of one client, Sentinel, had been narrowed to avoid reading on the claims of the other client, Knaus, Sentinel's applications were rejected in light of the other client's patents, which the firm had obtained for it. Despite this evidence, the court granted the attorneys' motion for summary judgment, holding that—although "the defendants may have had a conflict of interest when they simultaneously represented Knaus and Sentinel—there was no evidence that the plaintiff had been damaged as a result of this alleged breach of fiduciary duty," and further stating that:

> At best, the evidence shows that Sentinel's applications were delayed and narrowed because of Knaus' patents. What is not shown by any of the evidence offered is that if Sentinel had been represented by a different, conflict-free attorney, it would not have experienced the same delays and narrowing. That is to say, Sentinel has not offered evidence to prove that the [the lawyers] intentionally or inadvertently pulled their punches in prosecuting Sentinel's interest. Instead, it appears that any potential or actual conflict of interest was not the cause of Sentinel's difficulties. Though the Knaus patents themselves may have limited Sentinel's ability to achieve broad patents, there is no evidence offered that if Sentinel had had different representation, its patent applications would have fared any better. The client will not need to show that the patents interfered; it will contend that they *should have interfered* but the practitioner "pulled her punches" in order to obtain coverage for the favored client.[25]

---

19. 64 U.S.P.Q.2d 1536 (D. Mass. 2002).
20. *Id.* at 1538.
21. *Id.*
22. *Id.*
23. *Id.* at 1537.
24. *Id.* at 1538.
25. *Id.* at 1539.

This case illustrates that the client will not need to show that the patents interfered; it can contend that they should have interfered but the practitioner "pulled her punches" to obtain coverage for the favored client.

Suppose instead, for example, that one client's patent is cited against a pending client's application, and a reasonable lawyer would invoke an interference. However, because he or she represents the client who owns the cited patent, the lawyer does not invoke an interference but, instead, amends the claim to avoid the issued patent.[26] That would be an instance—much like in *Sentinel Prods. v. Platt,* where a material limitation exists. (Of course, as that court held, it may not necessarily cause damage.) Consequently, lawyers who represent clients in closely related fields can be accused of narrowing the scope of disclosure in a client's application or of not including claims or certain coverage to leave the subject matter available to other clients, either to patent or to operate in.

B. Office Action Responses and Rule 131 Antedating

We located no authority addressing whether a practitioner acts adversely to a client when he or she responds to an office action that applies a patent owned by another client. This happens frequently, and most firms do not necessarily know whether a patent applied by an examiner in a rejection is owned by a current client, or not. Only when the practitioner is aware of ownership does a conflict check perhaps need to be performed, and even then only in some circumstances.

There are obvious problems, and yet few bright lines. It is impossible to catalog all the possibilities or to predict precisely how a court would respond to the various fact patterns, but some circumstances that ought to at least give practitioners pause include these:

- Arguing in response to an office action for one client that a patent obtained by the firm for another client is narrower than the examiner portrays it to be
- During prosecution, having the examiner cite "killer" prior art, and discovering that it is owned by another client and will be infringed if the prosecution client practices its invention

---

26. It is worthwhile to note that interferences have become increasingly difficult to invoke. Thus, although interfering subject matter may exist between a patent and an application, if the dates are sufficiently diverse, then amending the claims may be the only practical objective left to the practitioner and the client, regardless of representation. The complicating factor may be the practitioner, who must also provide argumentation in addition to the amendments to distinguish over the issued patent, and in doing so construe or otherwise limit the meaning of claims in that patent.

- During prosecution for one client, the examiner cites a reference that is material to another client's application, meaning that it must be submitted by information disclosure statement (IDS) in that case, resulting in the other client receiving narrower claims
- Antedating a patent obtained by the firm for another client
- Arguing that the reference does not inherently teach that which it is asserted to teach
- Arguing that a patent obtained by the firm for another client lacks enablement or written description to support the interpretation proffered by the examiner

We located no cases addressing whether these are, or are not, adverse representations. Clearly, however, lawyers who face these circumstances ought to at least consider the possibility that they might be deemed to constitute an adverse representation, or that the lawyer will be accused of "pulling punches" for one client because of obligations owed to the other. These issues are particularly troublesome because the "conflict" might be caused by a clear examiner error—the examiner incorrectly interpreted the prior art patent to disclose ABC when it only mentioned A and B, for example. The rest of this section attempts to further probe this important but difficult-to-define limitation.

On one end of the spectrum, a firm should refrain from responding to an office action to the extent it rejects one client's claims in light of a patent that the firm previously obtained for another client. Without regard to whether such action is adverse, or not, the firm can be viewed as interpreting or even challenging work product that it obtained for a former client.[27] The practical issues that could arise need to be considered: A statement made by a practitioner to the USPTO about a client's assets—a patent—may be used against the client in other fora. The lesson from a different context are worth noting. In one recent case, a lawyer filed a pleading relating to his client's divorce where he characterized the client's patent as "worthless"—a statement that later was used against the patentee in subsequent infringement and reissue proceedings.[28]

On the other end of the spectrum, we do not believe that a firm acts adversely when it responds to an office action that rejects a claim without first determining whether the applied patent is owned by a current client. Although the average application might cite less than twenty references, some areas such as the chemical and biotechnological arts might cite hundreds of references for issues relating to anticipation, obviousness, as well as written description and enablement. Accordingly, the burden of determining current

---

27. *See* Chapter 6, *infra,* discussing former client conflicts.
28. *Fawer, Brian, Hardy & Zatzkis v. Howes,* 639 So. 2d 329 (Ct. App. La. 1994).

ownership (or licensing interest) of those patents and applications cited as art by the practitioner or by the USPTO could be extremely burdensome from both a fiscal and time standpoint. Additionally, through mergers and acquisitions of companies and law firms and the sales of patent portfolios, tracking ownership over time, not just at the time it was reviewed, would add another burden to the overall conflicts determination. Thus, determining whether a conflict exists with prior art patents just is not standard screening practice used by law firms.

Likewise, it is not unheard of for examiners to apply a reference in an office action that clearly—indeed, almost indisputably—does not disclose what the examiner says it does. We do not believe that a practitioner is barred from responding to a rejection that applies a reference owned by a current client of the firm where no reasonable practitioner would read the reference as does the examiner. A mistake by an examiner does not create a conflict of interest, in other words.

Similarly, we do not believe that it is adverse for a practitioner to respond to an office action by antedating the cited reference. Although it can have economic impact, this is not adverse because antedating the patent or published application reference does nothing to impact the scope of the other client's patent, and indeed cannot do so.[29] Similarly, even if the application in which the antedating occurs issues, if there is claimed interfering subject matter, then an interference can and should occur. In that sense, we see antedating a reference owned by another client of the firm as no different from simply obtaining a patent for one client: There is "harm" only in the sense that a patent will issue, but that is not sufficient to constitute adversity, for otherwise every patent prosecution would be "adverse" to every other client.

In the middle of these examples lie other more difficult issues, and they are made more difficult because of the quality of patent examination, but even some of these, we believe, can be addressed with clarity. As noted above, the simple fact that a patent reference applied by an examiner to reject a claim does not preclude the practitioner from responding to the office action. It is not rare for examiners to cite a reference as disclosing subject matter that the reference cannot reasonably be read to disclose. In our view, it is not adverse for a practitioner to traverse an examiner's argument in an office action to the extent that a reasonable practitioner would conclude that the cited patent or patent publication reference does not in fact disclose what the examiner asserts. Thus, for example, if an examiner appears to have misread a reference as disclosing four components, when in fact it literally only discloses three, it is not adverse for the lawyer to respond and make that point.

---

29. A reference can be antedated without corroboration, for example. Likewise, antedating has no effect on the antedated reference.

But where a reasonable practitioner would conclude that the examiner's position has merit, then a practitioner who only represented the applicant should respond to the office action with zeal, and yet a practitioner who also represents the owner of the applied reference might feel constrained by his or her obligations to its owner not to respond with full zeal. Thus, it can be that the lawyer's obligation to the patent owner would materially limit his or her obligations to the applicant. Obviously, this is a fact-specific issue, and one that must be addressed on a case-by-case basis. The risk of being accused of "pulling punches" is real, however.

We do not believe that responding to an office action that applies a patent or published application to reject the claim of another client is adverse to the patent owner, however, at least absent other specific facts that raise the practical impact to a greater level than simply responding to an examiner's interpretation of a patent. We reach that conclusion by analogy to cases involving claim interpretation and patent litigation. That analogy is not perfect, but we believe it is compelling.

In two recent cases, district courts reached different conclusions on whether there was "adversity" for a law firm to represent a patent owner against a non-client accused of infringement where in parallel, pending litigation, a separate firm was representing the patent owner against the first firm's client. In the first case, *Enzo Biochem, Inc. v. Applera Corp.*,[30] the court found no adversity; a month later, the second court in *Rembrandt Technologies, LP v. Comcast Corp.*,[31] did. In doing so, the Rembrandt court described the first case and explained why a different result should lie in the second:

> A Connecticut District Court recently addressed a similar issue. *Enzo Biochem, Inc. v. Applera Corp.*, 2007 WL 30338 (D. Conn. Jan. 5, 2007). In *Enzo*, the Hunton firm represented a client in a patent case against one defendant. The same plaintiff, represented by the Greenberg firm, sued a different defendant. Some of the same patents were asserted in both cases. A client of the Hunton firm, GE, later acquired the defendant being sued in the second case. The Hunton lawyers representing the plaintiff in the first case aided, to a certain extent, the Greenberg lawyers representing the plaintiff in the second case. GE contended that the Hunton firm's concurrent representation of Enzo in the first case and the GE subsidiary sued by Enzo in the second case amounted to an impermissible conflict of interest. GE intervened in the first case and moved to disqualify the Hunton firm. The court evaluated the evidence and concluded that GE had not demonstrated a sufficient showing of direct adversity. The court stated that "while the construction of [the plaintiff's] patents applicable to the infringement claims brought against two separate accused infringers . . . implicates pretrial *Markman* overlap, *the trials of how those constructions apply to the*

---

30. 468 F. Supp. 2d 359 (D. Conn. 2007).

31. 2007 WL 470631 (E.D. Tex. Feb. 8, 2007).

respective accused products or conduct are wholly separate." *Enzo*, 2007 WL 30338 at *7 (emphasis added). As a result, the court refused to disqualify the Hunton firm from representing the plaintiff in the first case. The court agrees with Enzo that the mere possibility of overlapping Markman proceedings is insufficient to show direct adversity, particularly when the trials of how the constructions apply to accused products or conduct varies from defendant to defendant.

Here, in contrast to *Enzo*, F & R is not simply advocating claim construction positions that might, at some later date, adversely impact Time Warner. F & R advocates that the Comcast defendants infringe the patents because the defendants comply with industry standards. In particular, F & R advocates in this case that Comcast infringes because it adheres to the ATSC standard for United States Patent No. 5,43,627 ("the 627 patent") and DOCSIS for United States Patent Nos. 5,852,631, 4,937,819, and 5,719,858 ("the 631, 819, and 858 patents"). The practical significance of Rembrandt's infringement theory is to indict for patent infringement all major cable companies who follow the industry standards. A finding of infringement and an injunction issued by this court against a cable company for compliance with industry standards would have a significant practical effect on Time Warner.

There are additional distinctions between this case and the *Enzo* decision that lead the court to find the requisite direct adversity. Rembrandt filed its cases in the same district. Its case against Time Warner is pending before the same judge at roughly the same time as this case, but this case was filed first. Although it is true that the claim construction rulings in this case would not be binding on Time Warner, there is a likelihood that the positions taken by F & R in this case could, as a practical matter, prejudice Time Warner in subsequent proceedings. As a result, on these facts, this court reaches a different conclusion from the one in Enzo. F & R's representation of Rembrandt in this case is directly adverse to Time Warner.[32]

Boiled down, the lawyers in *Rembrandt* were adverse because of the practical impact of the involvement of the firm. In *Rembrandt*, the case against the client was pending at the same time and before the same judge as the case against the non-client, and so the likelihood that the firm's representation adverse to the non-client would have a practical impact on the client were clear: In representing the patentee against the non-client, the lawyer would argue for claim interpretations, for example, that would no doubt be followed by that same judge when he was deciding those questions in the case against the lawyer's client. That same problem did not exist in *Enzo*. And, further, in *Rembrandt*, the patentee made the remarkable argument that the claims covered a standard. Thus, infringement by the non-client meant infringement by the client. The practical impact on the client of the lawyer's representation of

---

32. *Id.*

the patentee against the non-client was clear, although there was probably no legal impact whatsoever.

Where a firm is simply responding to an office action by one examiner concerning the scope of a patent reference owned by another client, the practical impact appears minimal: Just as in *Rembrandt*, the statements in the office action response obviously are not admissions or statements against interest because the practitioner is making the statements in the course of representing the patent's owner. There is no legal impact on the patentee. Likewise, the practical impact typically will be minimal as well: Statements made by a practitioner to one examiner about the scope of an issued patent will, at least typically, have little or no practical impact on the scope of the claims of the issued patent. The practical impact is that such statements are not readily capable of being found to have a practical impact—it would the proverbial needle in a haystack search, with the hope that the needle in fact even existed.

Thus, as a general principle, a firm does not act adversely to a current client when it responds to an office action that applies a patent owned by that current client. The practice does, however, create obvious business issues: A client may not appreciate the firm filing with the federal government statements about the scope of property owned by the client. Further, in some cases, it might be so clear that any statement made by the practitioner will be used by third parties in later infringement suits to attack the issued patent that adversity could arise, raising the practical concerns that led the *Rembrandt* court to find adversity. However, those situations will be the exception, not the norm.

E. The Conflict Created by the Right to Exclude

A limitation or perhaps adversity could also arise where, for example, a practitioner prosecuting an application for one client could draft claims that cover another client's products or processes. This probably happens every day in patent practice, although most likely it happens unintentionally. Again, however, there is a spectrum of conduct with only a few bright lines.

On one end of the spectrum, the firm might be representing the potential infringer in that subject matter, and the applicant might request the lawyer to intentionally draft claims to cover the firm's own client's product, and the firm possesses the "infringing" client's relevant confidential information and uses it to draft the claim. Such conduct would be adverse.

On the other end of the spectrum, it may often be the case that a lawyer drafts claims for one client that will coincidentally happen to cover products, in full or in part, of another client. In our view, "adversity" cannot be stretched that far. Were the law otherwise, a firm would have to engage in an infringement analysis of all of its clients' products to determine whether it could draft a patent application for a client. Adversity cannot be stretched that far.

In between, there is enough doubt to exercise caution, as drafting a claim to cover another client's product has already been the basis of breach of fiduciary duty claims.[33] We believe that the question of adversity will be viewed as a case-specific matter, not as a bright-line rule.

Even if there is no adversity, however, a lawyer who is drafting a claim that he knows may cover a product or process made by another client should be concerned about the possibility that the applicant will later contend that the practitioner "pulled his punches" while prosecuting the claim: that is, that he deliberately did not draft the claims to cover his own client's products.

F. Information: Liability and Conflict

As noted in Chapter 8, the Federal Circuit has held that a lawyer may have an obligation to disclose in one case confidential information of another client. If that is correct, then a lawyer could face a conflict of interest if the confidential information of one client is material to another client's application. Suppose, for example, one company discloses a trade secret to a lawyer. Later, that lawyer realizes that the confidences are material to another client's application. If the lawyer must disclose the information, this would create a conflict between the duty of confidentiality to one client and the duty of candor to the USPTO. Conversely, if the lawyer keeps the information confidential, any issued patent might be subject to attack for the lawyer's failure to disclose.

Information can also create liability. Foremost, of course, are trade secret misuse claims—arguments that a practitioner used the confidential information of one client to favor another client, either by expanding the scope of their patent or otherwise favoring it.[34]

---

33. *See generally GD Searle & Co. v. Pennie & Edmonds, LLP,* 2004 WL 3270190 (N.Y. Sup. Ct. Jan. 14, 2004) (discussing but not deciding whether drafting claims to cover another client's product constituted a breach of duty); *Universal Mfg. Co. v. Gardner, Carton & Douglas,* 207 F. Supp. 2d 830 (N.D. Ill. 2002) (allegation that firm breached its duty to client by not warning it of impending infringement suit).

34. *See, e.g., Hutchins v. Fish & Richardson, PC,* Civ. A. No. 05-30062-MAP (Filed Mar. 4, 2005) (complaint alleging, among other things, trade secret misuse); *Am. Silver LLC v. Gen'l Resonance LLC,* 2007 WL 4828352 (D. Md. Dec. 21, 2007) (complaint filed by applicant against lawyer and its other client alleging firm had conflict of interest and used trade secrets of applicant to benefit itself and its other client by, among other things, naming himself as an inventor).

G. Additional Possible Prosecution Conflicts

Conflicts can come from many directions and at different times, not just at the time of the initial intake. There are the conflicts that arise during and out of prosecution directly. There are also the business conflicts that arise from running a law firm or from a client's own business.

Other prosecution conflicts not already discussed include arguments regarding a patent reference to (1) erode credibility regarding written description of genus by asserting lack of working examples of any species and thus lack of description for the genus; (2) assert that a reference is not enabled for what it teaches either as a stand-alone enablement rejection or to prove that the reference cannot be anticipatory; or (3) assert that the reference cannot inherently result with certainty in the end product as argued by the USPTO. Most of the arguments tend to arise under 35 U.S.C. sections 102, 103, and 112, first paragraph.

In addition, as discussed elsewhere, calendaring or maintenance fees has been construed to mean that a lawyer represents the client concerning patent. Thus, even simple payment of a U.S. maintenance fee can pose a conflict with other work, as the patent is considered to be fully part of the firm.

Business conflicts include, for example, those regarding (1) the sale of transfer of patents to another entity, wherein perhaps the practitioner said something adverse to the patent when it was owned by an entity other than the client, and it is now owned by the client or its subsidiary; and (2) mining for new claims not originally conceived of in a new direction that now tracks the claims of another client.

Firm-related conflicts can arise with the acquisition of lateral attorneys and agents and their business. Generally, a search must be performed for all of the proposed clients and their known subsidiaries and affiliates to determine if a conflict of interest exists. Direct adversity wherein the firm already is adverse to a potential new client is easy to ascertain through various databases (e.g., docketing, marketing, or accounting databases). However, subject matter searches using keywords should also be performed to identify if there is overlapping subject matter that could block the work. Such searches are only as good as the key words entered to search the database as well as the key words and/or title used to describe the invention in the database. Frequently, invention titles fail to adequately describe the invention such that a high number of false-positive hits can be generated (e.g., "laser" or "machining tool").

Additional conflicts can arise through the sale of corporate business units, as well as through bankruptcies and mergers. For example, the economic downturn that occurred at the end of 2008 resulted in many banking and investment institutions merging, which in turn created difficulty generally in determining the status of "when" the client changed its entity from the standpoint of determining adversity. A Dun & Bradstreet analysis to ascertain business relationships simply was not easily performed for the purpose of identifying the nature of the "new client" post merger.

H. What to Do

1. Prosecution Problems

The key component is to make sure key words in conflicts databases are practically accurate and precise for the description of the claims and perhaps also the specification. The keywords should be included for all applications and patents, even those which are just calendared for annuities or maintenance fees. Even if your firm did not prosecute the case, calendaring maintenance fees give the impression—and, under some authority, the legal conclusion—that your firm has power for the case, and the subject matter of that case could now block working on related subject matter for a different client. Ideally, given the malpractice risks posed by maintenance fees and annuities, their payment should not be an action performed by a law firm, but rather by the patent owner.

Regarding search terms, practitioners should strive to be consistent. Terms should be used consistently in the claims, as well as in the specification. Terminology consistency can be monitored using programs such as LexisNexis Patent Optimizer, which can process lists of words used and words that are ill defined. When the application is complete, a review of the title might be in order to determine whether it captures the nature of the invention. Frequently only the invention title gets placed in a docketing database and searched, thus an accurate title can have downstream consequences in determining scope. The same guidelines apply for preparation of the abstract of the invention.

The major issues of any search are those relating to the words used given the number of synonyms known for those words. Frequently, synonyms exist for any term, and the synonyms should be searched as well to ascertain overlapping subject matter at the firm. As those synonyms might only be known to the practitioner, the practitioner should provide them when possible for performing the conflicts analysis. In biotechnology, many genes have multiple synonyms and names received as they were identified by multiple parties. In chemistry, there are different naming criteria that again can lead to problems in identifying whether there is overlapping subject matter. Thus provision of synonyms and accurate word lists to the databases searcher is needed to feel certain that there is no subject matter overlap for a new incoming application.

Finally, when dealing with overcoming rejections under sections 102, 103, and section 112, first paragraph, although there is no industry standard to run every office action through conflicts, if the patent or published application applied by an examiner against the client's claims belongs to another client, and you know it, tread carefully. If the practitioner merely has to prove the reference was inappropriately applied or mischaracterized, then it is unlikely the practitioner will undermine or compromise the value of the other client's patent. However, if the practitioner must present an argument that would potentially question the issued claims in the other client's patent, this should be avoided. Although a potential needle-in-a-haystack issue, and one that even reasonable care often cannot preclude or identify always, it nevertheless should be avoided.

2. Corporate Affiliate Intellectual Property

Some firms institute an affiliate/subsidiary exclusion, such that if no immediate work is being done for the subsidiary or affiliate of the client, then the firm may act adversely to a client's subsidiary's interest. Such a "waiver" or limitation on the scope of the representation may also apply to patents and published applications that belong to the affiliate or subsidiary of a current client. However, law firms differ in their handling of conflicts for client affiliates and subsidiaries, and the approach under state law varies, as discussed earlier in this chapter. Some law firms, as a result, maintain a bright-line rule that no firm lawyer may be adverse to any current client's affiliate or subsidiary with few exceptions. If responding to an office action applying a patent owned by a current client is "adverse," then, presumably, so too would be responding to an office action where the patent is owned by an affiliate or subsidiary of the client.

3. Lateral Hires

In the case of lateral attorney and agent hires, there are several issues that can arise. For associates and patent agents, it is knowledge of cases in which they work that can provide issues of materiality or even adversity. Adversity only arises for associates in the instance of having staffed a litigation and having represented a party adverse to the new firm's client. This can be handled by creating an ethical wall for that new hire on entry.

The same issues arise for lateral partners. However, partners usually also bring work with them to their new firm. Searches should be done for the subject matter and for the clients prior to the partner joining the firm. On joining the firm, it should be determined if there is an inability to easily transfer the docket information (e.g., from PATTSY (Patent and Trademark Tracking System) to Computer Packages, Inc. (CPi)). If this situation arises, the hiring firm should pay to have the second software installed and have two systems running until the data is known to have been accurately placed in the hiring firm's main docketing system. This can also be done for corporations purchasing portfolios and merging portfolios if the work was performed in-house. The cost of the software is minor compared to the malpractice costs associated with a missed annuity or maintenance fee or a missed response to an office action.

I. Conclusion

In conclusion, prospective client consent might be a means to reduce or avoid many misunderstandings, although obviously not all. One option is to advise clients at the outset of a prosecution representation that the firm prosecutes patents in related fields for different clients, and to request that client to agree that if information disclosed by it is or becomes material to another client's application, the client will agree to allow the firm to disclose it unless the information is its proprietary information. Many clients might agree to that approach because it might merely memorialize what they anticipate the law, expectations, or best practices to already be.

In the end, the practitioner must take reasonable steps throughout the course of prosecution to spot conflicts. Simple intake of an application into the firm and clearance of conflicts does not terminate the potential for conflicts.

CHAPTER

6

Former Client Conflicts

A. The Three Principal Prohibitions   65
   1. The Substantial Relationship Test   66
   2. Disqualification for Possession of Confidences   69
   3. Challenging or Interpreting Work Product   70
B. Examples of Former Client Conflicts   71

As shown in Chapter 5, although a practitioner represents a client in prosecuting an application—and, perhaps, for some time thereafter—the practitioner owes the client loyalty, competency, and confidentiality. The same cannot be said with respect to former clients because the core duty owed to former clients is largely one of confidentiality, although the duty of loyalty still persists in modified, narrower forms.

A. The Three Principal Prohibitions

The most common conflict that arises when a lawyer seeks to be adverse to a former client comes from the prohibition against becoming adverse to a former client in a matter which is "substantially related" to a prior representation of that former client. Most courts hold that lawyers may not be adverse to former clients where there is a substantial relationship between the work the lawyer did for the former client and the work the lawyer proposes to do against it. The precise details of that test vary widely, however, both between state and federal courts as well as among federal courts.

Another common, although less prevalent, basis for disqualification is proof that the lawyer involved actually obtained confidential information in the prior representation that is relevant to the adverse representation. As becomes clearer below, the substantial relationship test generally serves as a surrogate for proof that a lawyer obtained confidential information in the initial representation; no proof that the lawyer actually obtained confidences is required. In contrast, to disqualify a lawyer for actually possessing relevant confidences, the movant must generally show that the lawyer in fact did obtain such information. Again, the precise details of this basis for disqualification vary greatly between jurisdictions.

Although each of these three can be the source of disqualification and discipline, as a general matter proof that a lawyer is adverse to a former client in a substantially related matter should not support a malpractice claim, in our view. This is because disqualification is granted in matters that are substantially related to prevent harm to a client; a malpractice claim arises only with harm. Thus, allowing a malpractice claim based solely on an adverse substantially related representation is not appropriate.

1. The Substantial Relationship Test

Courts do not hesitate to find a "substantial relationship" and to disqualify firms where one lawyer in the firm had prosecuted the patent-in-suit if the client, or former client, is the same party for whom the lawyer prosecuted the patent, and sometimes if it is an assignee.[1] When identicality is missing, the answer becomes more fact-intensive. In *Biax Corp. v. Fujitsu Computer Systems Corp.*,[2] for example, Biax filed an infringement suit against Fujitsu

---

1. *E.g., Sun Studs, Inc. v. Applied Theory Assocs., Inc.*, 772 F.2d 1557, 1567 (Fed. Cir. 1985) (no "court would hold that it is within the bounds of propriety to permit a law firm to assist a client in obtaining a patent which was equitably owned by another and then to lead the attack against the patent's validity once it is transferred to its rightful owner."); *Telectronics Proprietary, Ltd. v. Medtronic, Inc.*, 836 F.2d 1332 (Fed. Cir. 1988) (under facts presented, attorney could attack patent he had prosecuted for assignor of patent because there was no attorney-client relationship between assignee and attorney); *Schloetter v. Railoc of Indiana, Inc.*, 546 F.2d 706, 710 (7th Cir. 1976) (dicta); *Monon Corp. v. Wabash Nat'l Corp.*, 764 F. Supp. 1320 (N.D. Ind. 1991); *Hilleby v. FMC Corp.*, 25 U.S.P.Q.2d 1413 (N.D. Cal. 1992) (in-house counsel prosecuted patent, then went to law firm; law firm disqualified from representing infringer); *Koehring Co. v. Manitowoc Co.*, 418 F. Supp. 1133 (E.D. Wis. 1976); *Strojirenstvi v. Toyoda*, 1986 Commr. Pat. LEXIS 14 (Comm'r. Pat. Aug. 29, 1986). *But cf. New York Institute of Tech. v. Biosound, Inc.*, 658 F. Supp. 759, 762 (S.D.N.Y. 1987) (no appearance of impropriety where attorney had represented licensee in suit defending licensor's patent, and had helped prosecute the patents on behalf of licensee); *Levin v. Ripple Twist Mills, Inc.*, 416 F. Supp. 876, 884–85 (E.D. Pa. 1976) (denying motion to disqualify, but noting that in "most circumstances an attorney may not represent the alleged infringer over the objection of his former client, the patentee"); *Flo-Con Sys., Inc. v. Servsteel, inc.*, 759 F. Supp. 456 (N.D. Ind. 1990) (firm disqualified from representing patentee where it had represented defendant in an infringement suit, withdrew, and later another of its clients purchased the patentee).
2. 2007 U.S. Dist. LEXIS 35770 (E.D. Tex. May 16, 2007).

and Sun Microsystems, claiming they infringed its patent on server architecture. Sun moved to disqualify Biax's law firm because it had previously represented Sun. However, the firm had only provided an opinion to Sun as to whether a third party was infringing an unrelated Sun patent, but a patent that did relate to an invention concerning server architecture. The district court denied the motion finding no substantial relationship or risk of violating confidences.

As *Biax* indicates, it is a fact-intensive and specific inquiry to determine precisely when two patents are "substantially related." One court has held that the fact that two patents are in the same technology "field" did not mean they were substantially related to each other.[3] In general, if two patents have been assigned to the same art group, then a finding of substantial relationship is more likely. If one patent interferes with another, then the two would appear even more likely to be substantially related.

That was the holding of a recent case decided by the Board of Patent Appeals and Interferences that might provide some insight into how the U.S. Patent and Trademark Office (USPTO) will view conflicts. In *Anderson v. Eppstein*,[4] Anderson filed a motion to disqualify the Pillsbury, Madison firm from representing Eppstein in an interference proceeding. The alleged conflict presented was narrow because of the particular facts involved; the Board's approach to the question of whether there was a conflict under the "substantial relationship" test, however, might apply in many other cases. As a result, the decision is worth analyzing in detail.

Anderson had been employed by the National Institutes of Health (NIH). He was the named inventor on the '567 application. A law firm, Cushman, Darby & Cushman, had been retained by NIH to prosecute that application. Scott, a Cushman partner, signed the agreement between Cushman and NIH. Kokulis, another Cushman partner, signed an order directing that Cushman lawyers prosecute the '567 application. That order also certified that there was no conflict with Cushman going forward in prosecuting the application. Kokulis and several other Cushman partners were named in the Power of Attorney in the '567 application.[5]

Kokulis, Scott, and several other Cushman lawyers worked on the case. Cushman then merged with the Pillsbury Madison firm. At both Cushman and at Pillsbury, NIH files apparently were not readily accessible to all lawyers, Instead, access was limited to those who were actively involved in prosecuting the applications.

---

3. *Moyroud v. Itek Corp.*, 528 F. Supp. 707, 708 (S.D. Fla. 1981).
4. 59 U.S.P.Q.2d 1280 (Bd. Pat. App. & Interf. May 11, 2001).
5. It is notable that most firms list all registered attorneys and agents affiliated with a customer number regardless of whether they may work on a particular application.

The '567 application was the first of a series of continuing applications that led to another Anderson patent, which was the subject of the interference proceeding. Kokulis was then retained by Eppstein to represent him against Anderson in the interference proceeding. Kokulis essentially stated that he accepted the representation without recognizing that he had signed the order directing that the '567 be prosecuted, nor that he had been involved in its prosecution.

Anderson then moved to disqualify Kokulis and Pillsbury because Kokulis had been involved in prosecuting the '567, which was a parent to the patent in the interference proceeding. The Board denied the motion. With respect to the substantial relationship issue, the Board noted that there were different views of what constituted a substantial relationship. The Board adopted a "narrow[]" interpretation, and held that "Anderson must demonstrate that (1) the subject matter of the '567 application is identical or essentially the same as the subject matter in the Anderson patent involved in" the interference.[6]

Applying this test without explaining whether it was applying New York cases because the lawyers were from there, or because those cases applied under the Patent and Trademark Code of Professional Conduct (PTO Code), the Board found there was no "substantial relationship," because there was no evidence "that the '567 application describes or essentially describes the interfering subject matter."[7] The Board recognized that the interfering patent was a continuation-in-part (CIP) of the '567, with a different specification and different claims. It also repeatedly noted that the '567 was not relied on for priority in the interference proceeding.[8]

Again, the precise scope of the substantial relationship test varies greatly from jurisdiction to jurisdiction. For instance, some jurisdictions state that possession of *public* information can be used to establish a "substantial relationship" if it was acquired during an attorney-client relationship. Some jurisdictions have exceptions, the effect of which is that information that was acquired in confidence cannot be used to show a "substantial relationship" if the information has since become generally known. These and other issues have not yet been resolved by the USPTO.[9]

---

6. *Id.*, citing *N.Y. Marine & Gen'l Ins. Co. v. Tradeline and Deepak Fertilizers and Petrochemicals Corp.*, 186 F.R.D. 317 (S.D.N.Y. 1999).

7. *Id.*

8. *Id. See also, Strojirenstvi v. Toyoda*, 1986 Commr. Pat. LEXIS 14 (Comm'r. Pat. Aug. 29, 1986) (applying substantial relationship test and denying disqualification). *See generally* Eric G. Marcks et al., *Ethical Issues in Patent Prosecution*, PLI No. G0-0130 (Dec. 2002) (discussing substantial relationship test).

9. *See* Virginia Legal Eth. Op. 1456 (analyzing substantial relationship test).

2. Disqualification for Possession of Confidences

The *Anderson* case provides a somewhat typical example of how the courts treat disqualification motions based on possession of confidences.[10] After finding that the movant had failed to establish a "substantial relationship" between the two matters, the Board went on to reason:

> Anderson arguably could prevail if it could successfully demonstrated [sic] that Kokulis [the attorney] actually received confidential information. Anderson says Kokulis received confidential information, relying on the fact that (1) Kokulis was listed on the Power of Attorney in '567 and (2) Kokulis signed off on the task order for preparing and prosecuting '567. Anderson concludes that, for Kokulis to sign his name to the task order certifying that there was no conflict between the interest of the Government and other clients of the firm, Kokulis had to be intimately involved with the subject matter of '567.
>
> We agree with Eppstein that listing all partners in a law firm as having power of attorney is customary and does not properly convey the idea that all of the listed attorneys are actually involved in the preparation and prosecution of an application. . . .
>
> Kokulis testifies that he did not receive any information regarding '567. Kokulis further testifies, along with supporting evidence, that he had no involvement in the preparation of prosecution of '567. Kokulis still further testifies that he believes that he signed the specific task order in the absence of Scott. Both Kokulis and Doescher testify that Scott, not Kokulis, was the project director for all NIH projects. Further, there is no indication that Kokulis, upon signing the task order, had to be intimately involved with the subject matter of '567 to signify that there was no conflict of interest. The record convincingly establishes that the Cushman attorneys that actually worked on the '567 application are no longer affiliated with the Pillsbury law firm . . . .
>
> We find that the declaration testimony of Kokulis . . . is highly credible. In this respect, we credit the declaration testimony of Eppstein's witnesses . . . over the declaration testimony of Anderson's witness . . . whenever there is a conflict . . .
>
> Where one lawyer at a firm possesses client confidences gained in the course of a prior representation, it can be presumed that the confidences were shared with other attorneys within the lawyer's firm. However, the presumption is rebuttable. Based on the record before us, Eppstein has sufficiently rebutted any presumption that confidences were shared by Scott with Kokulis or any attorney now at Pillsbury.[11]

---

10. *See also Halcon Int'l, Inc. v. Werbow*, 228 U.S.P.Q. (BNA) 611, 613 (Comm'r Pat. 1985) (disqualifying lawyer in interference proceeding where lawyer may have obtained information in prior representation that could be used against former client)
11. *Id.*

Again, the precise scope of this test varies greatly from jurisdiction to jurisdiction. For instance, some jurisdictions state that possession of *public* information can be "confidential" information if it was acquired during an attorney client relationship. Some have exceptions that state that even information that was acquired in confidence can be used adversely if it has become generally known. These and other issues have not yet been resolved by the USPTO.[12]

In addition, the courts and bar associations disagree on whether the presumption that each lawyer in a firm acquired confidential information known to one lawyer is rebuttable in disqualification contexts (it ought not apply outside that context). In the USPTO, it appears that this is rebuttable, at least with respect to former clients, which might suggest that firms should establish "walls" between prosecuting attorneys to allow for greater rebuttability of the presumption of shared confidences. ABA Model Rules of Professional Responsibility (Model Rules) 1.6 and 1.9(b)(2) preclude revealing "confidential information" of former clients.[13] The precise scope of this test varies greatly from jurisdiction to jurisdiction. For instance, some jurisdictions state that possession of *public* information can be "confidential" information if it was acquired during an attorney client relationship.[14] Some have exceptions that state that even information that was acquired in confidence can be used adversely if it has become generally known.

3. Challenging or Interpreting Work Product

Some state rules expressly prohibit lawyers from challenging the validity of work that they previously performed for a client, whereas other states do so by judicial decision.[15] Even where a lawyer is adverse to a former client in a matter that is not substantially related to a prior representation, and one that does not involve the potential misuse of client information, this rule could bar an adverse representation.[16]

Other courts, such as the Supreme Court of New Hampshire, also have taken a seemingly broader prohibition, precluding lawyers from not just challenging work product created for former clients, but also from interpreting it.[17]

---

12. *See* Virginia Legal Eth. Op. 1456 (analyzing substantial relationship test).
13. *See* R.I. Rule 1.6 cmt. 7 (duties of confidentiality continue after representation ends).
14. *See In re Hoar Constr. Co.*, 2008 WL 2262087 (Tex. App.–Houston [14th Dist.] 2008, no pet. h.).
15. *E.g.,* Tex. Disc. R. Prof. Conduct 1.09.
16. *In re Basco*, 221 S.W.3d 637 (Tex. 2007).
17. *See Sullivan County Regional Refuse Disposal Dist. v. Town of Acworth*, 686 A.2d 755, 758 (N.H. 1996) ("even in the absence of any confidences, an attorney owes a duty of loyalty to a former client that prevents that attorney from attacking, or interpreting, the work she

In prosecution, this could arise when practitioners respond to an office action that applies a patent that the practitioners or their firm drafted for another client. It could be that the client owning the patent would argue the firm is challenging or interpreting the practitioner's own work product, depending on the form of the office action.[18] As noted in Chapter 5 this is more likely to be an issue in the current client context.

B. Examples of Former Client Conflicts

As noted in Chapter 5, various forms of conflicts can arise during prosecution. A patent owned by a former client could, for example, be applied by an examiner in an office action to reject a claim of a current client's application. Because the owner of the applied patent is a former client, however, even if responding were "adverse" (a matter we deal with in Chapter 5), the practitioner would not be disqualified from responding to the office action solely on that basis. Instead, the practitioner could respond so long as, in addition to being adverse, responding also means that the lawyer is in position to misuse confidential information, to challenge or interpret prior work product, or puts the lawyer in an adverse matter that is substantially related to the prior representation of the client who owns the applied patent.

Obviously, the most likely scenario for any one of these issues to arise is if the patent applied by the examiner was obtained by the firm for the former client. In such circumstances, the firm should tread carefully. The immediate concern is whether doing so places the firm in violation of the protections of former clients. In the longer term, too, however, there are issues. For example, if the firm states that the patent does not disclose certain subject matter, and the new application claims it, if the firm had been in position to disclose and claim that subject matter, the firm might have created evidence that could be used against it later.

---

performed, or supervised, for the former client"). Interestingly, this is analogous to prior patent examiners not being able to work with patents that they actively handled as an examiner.

18. *See Strojirenstvi v. Toyoda,* 1986 Commr. Pat. LEXIS 14 (Comm'r. Pat. Aug. 29, 1986) ("A long series of decisions have clearly established that an attorney who represented a client during the prosecution of a patent application will not be permitted to represent a party attacking the validity of the resulting patent.").

CHAPTER
7

Competency in Patent Prosecution

A. Introduction   74

B. Selecting the Proper Form of Protection   75
    1. Patent, Trade Secret, Copyright, Trademark,
        or a Combination   75

C. Which Type of Patent or Other Form of Protection to Use?   77

D. Which Type of Claim: Process, Product, or Product-by-Process?   78

E. Which Form(s) of Claim?   79

F. Definiteness   80

G. Drafting Claims as Broadly as Practicable   81

H. Drafting Claims to Avoid Unnecessary Amendment   83

I. Appealing Improper Rejections   84

J. Being Clear and Precise in Claims and Specification   85

K. Drafting Specifications That Comply with the Patent Act   87
    1. Best Mode   87
    2. Written Description   88
    3. Enabling Disclosure   89

L. Including All, but Only, True Inventors   90
    1. The Basic Requirement   90
    2. Special Issues Concerning Joint Inventors   92
        A. Who Is a Joint Inventor?   92
        B. What Does Joint Inventorship Convey by Way
            of a Property Right?   94
        C. What to Do   94
        D. Problems Lawyers Face When Representing
            Joint Inventors   97
        E. Conclusion   98

M. Responding to Office Actions   98

N. Meeting Deadlines and Prosecuting Diligently   99

O. Handing-Off or Giving Notice of the Maintenance
    Fee Obligation   100

P. Using Continuation-in-Part Applications to Obtain
    Earlier Filing Dates When Proper   101

A. Introduction

One core ethical duty is competency,[1] with the other two being confidentiality and loyalty. The next several chapters explore each of these duties in detail.

Patent practice, perhaps more than any other, challenges the abilities of even skilled professionals. Deadlines must be met; claims must be drafted carefully; specifications must be drafted to comply with, at times, esoteric and complex doctrines that are quite divorced from the practical question of what is the invention. Patent practitioners face both obligations that require meeting bright-line deadlines, and others that require complying with indeterminate legal principles here in the United States. This chapter addresses those issues of competency. The chapter does not address issues of competency in the preparation of specifications that meet requirements in foreign jurisdictions. However, practitioners should be versed not only with U.S. filing practices and prosecution procedures but also the evolving changes to Patent Cooperation Treaty (PCT) practice.

There are many circumstances that make patent practice challenging. By definition, many patents disclose cutting-edge technology. Thus, practitioners must have an understanding, often, of complex or at least evolving technologies. Related to that, often inventions must be described in terms that are adequate to fully capture the invention because of the inherent limitations of language itself. In addition, patent law has evolved, rapidly and sometimes sporadically, particularly since the formation of the Federal Circuit in 1982. Claim formats, for example, that once were very useful to practitioners, now should be avoided, and vice versa. No doubt, that might change again. So, too, the U. S. Patent and Trademark Office (USPTO) has with increasing frequency changed governing regulations or the provisions of the Manual of Patent Examining Procedure (MPEP).[2] In sum, not only must

---

1. *See Voight v. Kraft*, 342 F. Supp. 821 (D. Idaho 1972) (suit by client against lawyers who allegedly advised it to pursue patent on unpatentable invention).
2. In 2004 alone, title 37 of the Code of Federal Regulations was amended at least three times.

patent practitioners be up to date on technology, they must be up to date on the law, and in patent practice, both represent accelerating, moving targets.

The closely related issue of complying with the duty of candor is discussed in Chapter 8. Apart from violations of the duty of candor, firms have been sued for failing to disclose facts to the USPTO that would have reduced or eliminated invalidity arguments later presented by accused infringers.[3]

B. Selecting the Proper Form of Protection

1. Patent, Trade Secret, Copyright, Trademark, or a Combination

A threshold question is whether patent protection, as opposed to some other form of intellectual property protection, is the best choice. Obviously, whether patent protection is superior to any other available form of protection is a fact- and law-intensive issue.

A significant limitation on the ability of a patent agent, not supervised by a lawyer, to advise about these alternative forms of protection is important to note. The limitation also impacts patent attorneys because registration to practice does not permit attorneys to practice law in a state in which they are not licensed beyond the authority granted by the office. Under new regulations, patent agents, as well as patent attorneys, may advise an applicant to consider the advisability of relying on alternative forms of protection that may be available under state law.[4] However, the regulation means only what it says: Patent agents may advise the client to consider whether other forms of protection may be available, but not go further, and patent attorneys cannot provide about the law of a state in which they are practicing unless they are registered there:

> Patent agents should consider the advisability of relying on the alternative forms of protection available under statute law. Inasmuch as the state laws are public, agents should refer clients to the statutes and suggest that the client consult with an attorney of the client's choice in the state whether the statute has been adopted about the alternative forms of protection available under statute law. The same would obtain for a registered patent attorney who is not

---

3. *Air Measurement Tech., Inc. v. Hamilton,* 2005 WL 425411 (W.D. Tex. Feb. 22, 2005). *See also Beasley v. Avery Dennison Corp.,* 2005 WL 1719222 (W.D. Tex. July 22, 2005) (discussing general allegations of prosecution incompetence). *See also Jackson Jordan, Inc. v. Leydig, Voit & Mayer,* 633 N.E.2d 627 (Ill. 1994) (lawyers failed to discuss pertinent prior art in providing opinion of counsel to client).

4. 37 C.F.R. § 11.15(b)(1)(i) (effective Sept. 15, 2008).

licensed in the state where the attorney is practicing unless the state where
the attorney is practicing has authorized the attorney to provide legal services.
For example, if the attorney is "corporate counsel" or "in-house counsel" and
is licensed to practice law in another state, the attorney may provide legal
advice about the state's statutes to the attorney's corporate employer if the
state where the attorney is practicing has authorized the attorney to provide
legal services for the attorney's employer in the state where the attorney is
practicing.[5]

Trade secret protection varies by state, but often it only protects against
"misappropriation" and not independent creation or reverse engineering. As
a consequence, trade secret protection often may be a poor choice; conversely,
patents today expire 20 years after the filing of the first nonprovisional application, and the patent disclosure must explain how a person of ordinary skill
in the art can make the invention.

Each form of protection has its benefits, and limitations, to put it simply.
A practitioner should consider whether patent protection in fact is the best
means to protect the intellectual property at issue. It might be, for example,
that the client would be best served by analyzing trade secret protection,
determining whether safeguards are in place, and keeping the subject matter
protected in the form of a trade secret.

There might be some inventions that should be covered by multiple forms
of intellectual property protection.[6] For example, if the invention involves
bioinformatics, protection in the form of a patent application (to cover the
software and output), copyright protection of the software, and a trademark
for the name of the software to be marketed all must be considered. If it is
a combination of software and hardware, then there might be a need for
design patent protection. All might be necessary, or only one.

Another example that can be faced by a practitioner is protection of a new
plant species. This raises the issue of whether to protect the plant through
a regular nonprovisional application, a plant patent, or through the Union
for the Protection of New Varieties of Plants (UPOV), or a combination of
these.

One industry tendency is that many larger firms are going to specialty
practices that allow the practitioner to more readily keep on top of changes
in both the law and technology. However, without the training as a generalist

---

5. *See* 73 Fed. Reg. 4650 (Aug. 14, 2008).
6. Interestingly, even the simple act of filing a patent application may cause people to consider,
   of all things, copyrighting the application. Although it is industry practice, and arguably the
   best form of flattery, to cannibalize or plagiarize another's specification to produce a model
   specification, some corporate entities have been going to a standard of copyrighting their
   applications to prevent competitors from copying their inventions. The practice also provides
   two grounds of pursuing a competitor in the event that they should copy the patent: copyright
   and patent.

in intellectual property (IP), practitioners can miss issue spotting for multi-disciplinary IP issues, such as the overlap between the Food and Drug Administration (FDA) and patents. As illustrated above, a practitioner must have a general understanding of the issues and the nature of the business to develop strategies that best protect the intellectual property.

C. Which Type of Patent or Other Form of Protection to Use?

If patent protection is available, then the next issue competent counsel must address is what form of protection: design patents, utility patents, or plant patents—each is available under certain circumstances, and each has its benefits and limitations. There are also provisional patent applications and PCT patent applications, which again offer additional routes and strategies when developing a patent portfolio. Again, which type of patent and which filing strategy is most appropriate will vary depending on the facts and circumstances of each case.

As briefly discussed above, the patent application for an invention can be combined with other forms of intellectual property protection to cover other aspects of the invention, such as a trade name, a design, or for software, the copyright to that software. In the instance of plants, in some circumstances, a utility application, plant patent application, and protection under UPOV all can be sought. These applications offer different scopes of coverage for different terms. A plant patent application and utility application on a plant cannot be filed in all circumstances. For example, plant patents cannot be filed on tuber type plants (e.g., potatoes and Jerusalem artichokes). Thus, familiarity with IP protection options is necessary to best assess the various protective strategies for a client and their intellectual property.

From a competency standpoint, plant patents illustrate another issue, that is, technical competencies. Although electrical engineers and mechanical engineers can frequently prosecute patents in each other's area, many biotechnology practitioners would not feel comfortable prosecuting applications directed to semiconductors or software. However, even within biotechnology, there can be areas wherein one biotechnology background is not the same as another. Plant technology, as opposed to prokaryotic or nonplant eukaryotic technology, is exemplary of this issue. Although one can learn the material, it is oftentimes better if the practitioner preparing and prosecuting the plant application is a plant biologist because of the great degree of difference between plants at a cellular and molecular level from other nonplant eukaryotes and most prokaryotes.

The choice of one form of intellectual property over another or a combination of protections again will be fact intensive. For example, the design of a particular medicinal tablet design with logo, if nonfunctional, could be covered in a design patent. If the tablet design, however, has a specific function (e.g., time release), then a design patent may no longer be an option. A design may also be protected in the form of a trademark or trade dress for the item. A competent practitioner must be familiar with the limitations and benefits of each type of patent and intellectual property protection.

Thus, the choice on which type of intellectual property protection or combination can vary. The practitioner will have to have enough experience, either as reviewing attorney, or as preparer, to make the fact determinations necessary to best protect all aspects of the inventive idea.

D. Which Type of Claim: Process, Product, or Product-by-Process?

Once the proper form of patent protection is chosen, different types of claim format are available. There are various forms of protection available to inventions, including product claims, process claims, or product-by-process claims. Each of these forms has its benefits, and some, or all, might be available to a practitioner to protect different aspects of the same basic invention. Many factors affect which type of claim is proper.

The choice of the claim(s) selected are based on the novelty or nonobviousness of the inventive subject matter. For example, for a known compound, it might not be possible to claim the compound. However, it might be possible to protect the invention by using a claim for new methods of manufacturing the compound or new methods of using the compound. A competent practitioner, as a result, must consider whether certain claim formats are unavailable, or offer less protection than other available choices.

As this shows, the choice of claim type can hinge on, or at least be influenced by, the invention itself. Some inventions, for example, might only be capable of being claimed as a product-by-process because the precise nature of the composition or compound cannot otherwise be accurately defined. For example, stem cells today are better claimed as a product-by-process claim, as the full understanding of the subject matter defies ready description as a product. The product exists by the steps of manufacture, hence a product-by-process claim method, wherein the steps of manufacture define the product. Typically, the steps of manufacture do not define the product. Subject matter, such as cell lines, can also be more narrowly claimed through a reference to a biological deposit. Other areas wherein product-by-process claims have been used to describe the inventive subject matter include antibiotics (in the 1940s to 1970s), and polymers. Generally, however, at least under current law to the extent practicable, a practitioner should avoid using product-by-process claims when product claim coverage is available.

Because this type of issue relates to the technical capabilities and therefore competencies of the practitioner, finding someone who is competent to the field of the invention can be relevant for best protecting the subject matter. Thus, a mechanical engineer or electrical engineer might be no more competent in discerning the best ways to claim a stem cell and obviate the existing art, than a practitioner with a doctoral or master's degree in molecular biology necessarily would be working on subject matter relating to microchip design or laser design. One must have experience, either practical or by education, that would allow the skilled artisan to distinguish the prior art issues and determine the best claims for fully covering the invention. Simply having a registration number from the USPTO does not award competency in every scientific field.

E. Which Form(s) of Claim?

In addition to the differing protections afforded to product, product-by-process, and process claims discussed above, certain types of claim formats have been recognized over the years as having specific limitations.

For example, Markush style claims offer the practitioner an ability to list certain types of alternatives. They can be set forth for example as "a compound selected from the group consisting of A, B and C," or "a compound of A, B, or C." These both get interpreted in a similar manner. However, the former recitation is the true Markush style as set forth in *Ex parte Markush*, 1925 Dec. Comm'r Pat. 126, 128 (1924).

The USPTO is proposing new rule language which could make such "alternative claims" ever more problematic, as each alternative would be considered as an obvious variant over the other unless the applicant could evince otherwise.[7] In the event that this rule change occurs, this could cause applicants to reconsider the usage of Markush style claims, instead wanting to claim each member of a Markush group as a separate dependent claim.

Conversely, Jepson format claims—which typically begin with a preamble that includes the transition, "the improvement comprising"—are beneficial for some inventions, but the use of Jepson format indicates that everything preceding the transition is prior art to the improvement described after the transitional phrase.[8]

Finally, means-plus-function type claims are defined by and limited to the structure disclosed in the specification plus any equivalents of that structure.

---

7. *See* "Examination of Patent Applications That Include Claims Containing Alternative Language, Notice of proposed rule making," 72 Fed. Reg. 44992 (Aug. 10, 2007).
8. *See Catalina Marketing Int'l, Inc. v. Coolsavings.com, Inc.*, 289 F.3d 801 (Fed. Cir. 2002).

If the specification does not disclose structure to perform the function, then the claim can be invalid for indefiniteness under 35 U.S.C. section 112.[9] Although means-plus-function claims are useful for certain types of inventions, the format obviates protection that may be available through other claim formats, and so should be used only deliberately.[10]

Multiple factors affect whether any of these claim formats should be used and, if so, which one. Again, the type of invention might indicate which type of claim format should be used. A competent practitioner should consider the benefits, and limitations, attendant to each type of format before filing claims.

F. Definiteness

To be definite, each claim must "particularly point[] out and distinctly claim[] the subject matter the applicant regards as his invention.[11] The definiteness requirement "focuses on whether those skilled in the art would understand the scope of the claim when the claim is read in light of the rest of the specification."[12] Its purpose is to ensure that claims are "sufficiently precise to permit a potential competitor to determine whether or not he is infringing."[13]

To avoid an indefiniteness problem, a practitioner should provide definitions necessary to adequately define the invention, while not providing mixed or conflicting definitions. Computer programs such as LexisNexis Patent Optimizer are becoming available to assess word usage in an application, to avoid confusing terms or lack of redundancy. Redundancy and not artistic license is a patent practitioner's mantra. By providing clear metes and bounds to any claim and yet still providing sufficient breadth, one provides reasonable coverage to the client. Mixed definitions can cause the patent to be invalid, and definitions that are too narrow overly limit the invention.

---

9. *Aristocrat Tech. Australia Pty Ltd. v. Int'l Game Tech.*, 2008 WL 819764 (Mar. 28, 2008).
10. Deliberate use of "means for" language is one thing, but functional language may also inadvertently limit the claims without using the means-plus-function format. *E.g., K-2 Corp. v. Salomon S.A.*, 191 F.3d 1356, 1363 (Fed. Cir. 1999) (analyzing functional language as an additional limitation to an apparatus claim for an in-line skate). Thus, if the claim uses functional language but recites insufficient structure, § 112, ¶ 6 may apply despite the lack of "means for" language. *See, e.g., Personalized Media Commc'ns, LLC v. Int'l Trade Comm'n*, 161 F.3d 696, 703–04 (Fed. Cir. 1998) (discussing cases).
11. 35 U.S.C. § 112(2).
12. *Union Pac.*, 236 F.3d at 692.
13. *Morton Int'l Inc. v. Cardinal Chem. Co.*, 5 F.3d 1464, 1470 (Fed Cir. 1993).

G. Drafting Claims as Broadly as Practicable

As a general principle, and absent contrary instruction from a client, a practitioner should seek for a client the broadest valid claims available.[14] The problem with that simple statement is that many practical and legal concerns can call for a competent practitioner to avoid seeking claims that the applicant arguably is entitled to. For example, a practitioner might conclude that an applicant is entitled to certain coverage, but seeking all that coverage could result in a rejection. Avoiding delay in overcoming the rejection could be more important than obtaining the broadest coverage theoretically available. Likewise, a practitioner who drafts to the absolute limit believed to be allowable at the time, might reach a conclusion different than the examiner and might find it necessary to amend claims, creating an estoppel (discussed below). That said, with decreasing allowance rates, claim amendments are expected, and depending on the type of technology, might even require multiple rounds of amendments before an accord of patentability is met between the applicant and the examiner.

Having said that, certain broad goals should be kept in mind.

First, some claims should cover the preferred embodiment as well as any other specific embodiment of the invention. As noted below, some claims should be broader than the specific embodiment, but in the event those claims are rejected or are later held invalid, the narrower claims may issue without amendment.

Second, the claims should also cover any known or obvious possible variations that could compete or replace the patented invention. This could even include inferior variations that might still pose an easy end-run around the instant invention. To meet that objective, a practitioner should be sure to ask the inventor whether specific limitations disclosed by the inventor are in fact necessary. For example, the inventor might have visualized the invention as requiring a metal screw at a certain point, although in fact any sort of fastener would work, metal or wood, screw or nail, for example. The claims should cover, to the extent permitted by the prior art, competing products as well as possible alternatives to the "core" of the invention.

The practitioner and the client should also keep in mind the practical need at the time to get claims allowed versus the opportunity cost of delay because of appeal and further argumentation preventing any claims from maturing to allowance. The 20-20 hindsight of what "woulda" or "coulda" been achieved,

---

14. See generally *Collard & Roe, P.C. v. Vlacancich,* 2004 WL 2453219 (N.Y. Sup. Ct. App. Term Oct. 29, 2004) (dismissing because of speculative damages claim that patent specification had been drafted too narrowly); *Warren v. Eckert Seamans Cherin & Mellott,* 2000 WL 1060652 (Pa. Com. Pl. Apr. 25, 2000) (alleged failure to "obtain a patent of appropriate breadth and scope").

like obviousness, should be set from the perspective of what was feasible to obtain from the USPTO at the time, what the company was fiscally interested in pursuing, and the like. Not all clients can afford pursuing a case to the Federal Circuit, let alone arguing every case to that extent.

Third, each claim should be drafted as expansively as possible yet still avoid the known prior art. It is not always possible, of course, to know precisely where an examiner will determine the prior art ends, and novelty begins, but to the extent possible claims should be drafted to avoid the prior art, so as to avoid unnecessary rejections. However, the practitioner should draft the claims to the extent possible to seek and obtain the broadest possible coverage.

Fourth, omit reference to any element or limitation that is not strictly necessary to achieve the goal of the invention. If the gizmo needs to be attached to the widget, that is all that should be said; the claim should not include limitation that the gizmo needs to be attached with a screw, for example, let alone a metal screw, unless it is essential to the invention.

In sum, determining the maximum allowable coverage is not a matter of math or measurement, but instead depends on judgment, and reasonable minds—such as those of an examiner—might disagree with the practitioner's read of the scope of the prior art, and for that reason the scope of the claims must be weighed against various issues. This section discusses the duty of competency as it applies to claim scope.

Having said that, we emphasize that drafting claims is perhaps the most difficult task patent practitioners face—and the most important. We also emphasize that often the practice that was accepted or the norm when the application was first written, let alone at the onset of prosecution sometimes more than 44 months later, also may be disfavored at the time the patent is litigated, making the issue all the more troublesome.[15]

One requirement is that the claimed subject matter be novel and nonobvious.[16] As becomes clear below, it is important to avoid drafting claims

---

15. Applications may be filed as a provisional application and then as an International PCT application. The international PCT application will enter national stage here in the United States thirty months from the original filing date of the provisional application. It is another 14 months before the PTO is required to pick up the application without adding to patent term because of PTO delay under 35 U.S.C. § 154. Therefore, it may take 44 months or more after the filing of the initial provisional application before prosecution begins. The PTO has issued rule changes generally annually since the late 1990s, with an increasing pace in recent years. Thus, much can occur in the practice field in a period of three years or more. These changes should be considered when trying to review practitioner competency.

16. *See, e.g., Sakraida v. Ag Pro, Inc.*, 425 U.S. 273 (1976) (novel method of cleaning dairy barn floor was nonetheless obvious); *Dann v. Johnston*, 425 U.S. 219 (1976) (novel method of processing checks nonetheless invalid as obvious); *Anderson's-Black Rock, Inc. v. Pavement Salvage Co.*, 396 U.S. 305 (1969) (novel product to fuse pavement nonetheless obvious and so invalid); *Graham v. John Deere Co.*, 383 U.S. 1 (1966) (novel plow design nonetheless

that clearly would cover the prior art because that will result in a rejection that will result in the need to amend the claims, and that will create an estoppel.[17] To draft claims that reach near, but not beyond, the maximum allowed by the prior art and consistent with the scope of the invention, a practitioner should find multiple ways of covering the subject matter, and this may occur in one application or over several applications. This can be exemplified well with pharmaceutical patent applications. The first patent oftentimes is directed to a genus of compounds and perhaps then to a few species known at the time. Future applications may then be directed to other chemical species, formulations (e.g., tablet, capsule, micronized for increased bioavailability, or formulated for suspended release or combination treatment), and methods of treatment using the various compositions. Additional efforts to expand protection may include new patent applications that focus on polymorphs or racemates of the compound claimed in the original genus application. All of these patents would serve to increase the coverage of an invention. Process claims directed to methods of making the compounds may also be claimed along the way. Thus, strategy for writing the initial application, as well as subsequent applications in view of the patent laws, must be considered when trying to provide the most extensive patent coverage of the IP white space of interest for a particular client.

H. Drafting Claims to Avoid Unnecessary Amendment

As explained above, if a claim is rejected for reasons related to patentability, and if the claim is amended to overcome the rejection then, generally, the applicant will be estopped to claim that the subject matter surrendered to overcome the rejection is an "equivalent." Obviously, a first step in this

---

invalid for nonobviousness); *cf. U.S. v. Adams*, 383 U.S. 39 (1966) (patent on battery not obvious where claimed combination operated in a wholly unexpected way). *See also KSR Int'l Co. v. Teleflex Inc.*, 127 S. Ct. 1727 (2007) (novel pedal design invalid under § 103).

17. It is fascinating to note that Japanese patent applications that are filed as national stage applications will do just that; they will describe the closest prior art known at the time because that is a requirement in Japan. Despite doing this, in a paper by Paul Janicke that did an analysis of patent litigations, Japanese companies did not have their patents invalidated despite the alleged concern of this estoppel or even inequitable conduct concerns over potentially mischaracterizing a reference. Perhaps the fear of estoppel is greater than the reality. Additionally, distinguishing one's invention over the prior art may place a proper stage for the subject matter of the invention in a clearer context more ready for allowance.

process is determining what the scope of the prior art will allow—at least to the extent that it can be said to be determinable with much predictability.[18]

Prosecution history estoppel—also known as "file wrapper estoppel"—has been the subject of recent Supreme Court and Federal Circuit case law and can arise from amendment of claims. In *Festo Corp. v. Shoketsu Kinzoko Kogyo Kabushiki Co., Ltd.,*[19] the Supreme Court placed on the patentee the burden of showing that an amendment to a claim during prosecution does not surrender a particular equivalent in question. The patentee can rebut the presumption only by showing that the equivalent was not foreseeable at the time of the amendment, that the rationale for the amendment was no more than tangentially related to the equivalent, or for "some other reason" that the patentee could not reasonably have been expected to have described the "insubstantial substitute in question."[20] Roughly a year later, the Federal Circuit held that prosecution history estoppel not only applied to the application in which the amendment occurred, but also barred its assertion as to claim language in a grandchild application of a patent in which similar language had been amended.[21] Thus, amendments in a parent application can impact applications much later in a patent family chain, *if* the arguments are not overcome in some manner during the prosecution of one of the progeny.

As a result, and also because a rejection will result in delay of issuance of a patent, to the extent practicable, practitioners generally should seek to avoid submitting claims that will result in an amendment to the claim in order to obtain issuance.

I. Appealing Improper Rejections

Because an amendment can lead to an estoppel, it can be necessary for practitioners to more frequently appeal rejections. Some immediate responses to *Festo* were to list all possible claim variants and when amending claims, cancel all existing claims and rewrite the claims so that there was no clear road mapping of claim evolution. This lead to some applications being filed with more than 1000 claims. With increasing claim fees for more than three independent claims and more than twenty claims total, this should become

---

18. *See generally Carabotta v. Mitchell,* 2002 Ohio 8 (2002) (suit claimed lawyer failed to find prior art that hindered client's ability to obtain patent). David Hricik, *Aerial Boundaries: The Duty of Candor as a Limitation on the Duty of Patent Practitioners to Advocate for Maximum Patent Coverage,* 44 So. Tex. L. Rev. 205, 227 (2002) (discussing duty to maximize claim coverage).

19. *Festo Corp. v. Shoketsu Kinzoku Kogyo Kabushiki Co., Ltd.,* 535 U.S. 722, 740–41 (2002).

20. *Id.*

21. *Biovail v. Andryx Pharms.,* 239 F.3d 1376 (Fed. Cir. 2001).

less of a problem. The issue will be further impacted with the new significant claim fees instituted under the London Agreement, which will impact European claim strategy, and perhaps claim strategy overall.[22] However, few applications are in fact being filed today with more than 1000 claims. Thus, although issues of estoppel as set forth under *Festo* continue, practical considerations of costs of going forward will have to govern. Although it is easy for the litigator to say that simply no amendments should be introduced to the application's claims, realistically, this might not be an option.

J. Being Clear and Precise in Claims and Specification

It is beyond the scope of this book to provide a complete tome on how to draft patent claims. There are several good articles in print, as well as good books.[23] What we provide in this section, however, is a review of the basic competency issues that claim drafting presents.

"Comprising" versus "consisting" versus "consisting essentially of." Each of these transitional phrases when used in a patent claim has distinct meaning, with comprising being the broadest.[24] Malpractice claims have been filed based on the incorrect choice—one that unnecessarily obtains narrower coverage to which the applicant otherwise would have been entitled.[25] A practitioner should use the broadest transition that the prior art and the invention permit.

Practitioners should also consider providing definitions of "consisting essentially of" if there are multiple components involved, only some of which are the active components.

---

22. With claim limitations and even higher fees in Europe, the number of claims reasonably being submitted must be contemplated in advance of filing. Additionally, some foreign jurisdictions only permit one independent claim, thus the first claim should be the broadest that can be used to tie the other claims together, if possible, so as to avoid divisional applications abroad.

23. *See* Stephen Durant et al., *Preparing and Prosecuting a Patent that Holds Up in Litigation,* PLI No. 11589 (2007); Lock See Yu-Jahnes, *Selected Topics in Advanced Patent Prosecution,* PLI No. 11375 (July 2007); Stephen J. Lee et al., *Claim Drafting, Amendments and Patent Prosecution for Chemical Inventions,* PLI No. 11375 (July 2007); Rochelle K. Seide et al., *Drafting Claims for Biotechnology Inventions,* PLI No. 11375 (July 2007); Robert C. Faber, *The Winning Mechanical Claim,* PLI No. 11375 (July 2007).

24. *See Vehicle Techs. Corp. v. Titan Wheel Int'l,* 212 F.3d 1377, 1382 (Fed. Cir. 2000) ("The phrase 'consisting of' is a term of art in patent law signifying restriction and exclusion, while, in contrast, the term 'comprising' indicates an open-ended construction.")

25. *Immunocept, LLC v. Fulbright & Jaworski, LLP,* 504 F.3d 1281 (Fed. Cir. 2007).

Avoid Using the Word "Means" in Claims. As noted above, use of the word "means" in a claim can create ambiguity as to whether a "means-plus-function" type claim is intended. Means-plus-function claims create unique interpretive issues and impose dramatic limitations on scope and should be avoided unless a means-plus-function claim is, in fact, desired.

Be Consistent. It is important to avoid synonyms and to be utterly consistent in the use of terminology. If a particular aspect of the invention is referred to as a "module" in the specification, it should always be referred to by that term, and that term should be used in the claim (if necessary), and not some other synonym. Variety might be the spice of life and literature, but it's the bane of patents.[26]

Consistency of language may be important and can pose a tangential conflict if not uniformly applied. Consistency can be used against a practitioner if arguments, such as between families of cases, are inconsistent. It is not unheard of to argue the use of inconsistent language between an application for one client and an application for another client. Although not a direct conflict between clients, the inconsistency in arguments and language could be used by a skilled litigator to undermine the validity of patent.

Define New Terms. Patent applicants are of course free to be their own lexicographers, but applicants must define any new terms clearly and should not have differing term definitions within the same application.[27]

Avoid Absolute, Unprovable Claim Limitations. Although clarity and absolutes are usually helpful in claim language, limitations that require proof that something is "not present in" the claimed invention can prove impossible to prove in litigation.[28]

Avoid Unnecessary Verbiage in the Preamble. Although the general rule is that language in a claim's preamble does not limit the scope of the claim, if the preamble does not merely recite the context for the invention, then omit it. Often, short preambles are better than longer preambles, and so are those that merely recite the class of invention—"a product," "a process," or "a composition of matter." Alternatively, if the preamble is important, the applicant

---

26. As previously noted, programs are available to analyze word usage in a draft specification to assess indefiniteness as well as to remove improper synonyms and single word usage during the preparation of applications. Although the software is still being perfected, it can be useful.

27. *Sinorgchem Co., Shandong v. Int'l Trade Comm'n.*, 511 F.3d 1132 (Fed. Cir. 2007) ("Our opinions have repeatedly encouraged claim drafters who choose to act as their own lexicographers to clearly define terms used in the claims in the specification."); *CCS Fitness, Inc. v. Brunswick Corp.*, 288 F.3d 1359, 1366 (Fed. Cir. 2002) ("[A] claim term will not receive its ordinary meaning if the patentee acted as his own lexicographer and clearly set forth a definition of the disputed claim term in . . . the specification"); *Vitronics Corp. v. Conceptronic, Inc.*, 90 F.3d 1576, 1582 (Fed. Cir. 1996) ("The specification acts as a dictionary when it expressly defines terms used in the claims or when it defines terms by implication.").

28. *Morphosys AG v. CAT,* 158 F. Supp. 2d 84 (D. D.C. 2001).

should consider reciting the text of the preamble again in the body of the claim.

K. Drafting Specifications That Comply with the Patent Act

To be valid, a claim must comply with various provisions of the Patent Act. This section surveys the principal forms of invalidity and explains the issues that must be understood for a practitioner to draft valid claims.

1. Best Mode

The best mode requirement is contained in the first paragraph of section 112, which requires that the specification "set forth the best mode contemplated by the inventor of carrying out his invention." A failure to disclose the best mode occurs only when "the inventor both knew of and concealed a better mode of carrying out the claimed invention than was set forth in the specification."[29] Best mode differs from enablement (discussed below): "failure to enable an invention will produce invalidity whether or not the omission was deliberate, whereas invalidity for omission of a better mode than was revealed requires knowledge of and concealment of that better mode."[30]

To draft specifications that comply with the best mode requirement, a practitioner must, of course, ensure that if the inventor in fact knew of a best mode, and that the best mode known at the time is disclosed in the specification. Later improvements to how the invention is practiced are not covered. Only the best mode at the time the application was filed needs to be disclosed in the specification.

Although the facts of each case vary, a practitioner should determine what the best mode of making and using the subject matter is at the time of drafting the application. The best mode can be disclosed as any one of the actual working examples provided in the specification or as an exemplary example of making and using the claimed invention. The best mode does not have to be specifically pointed out and only must be the best mode known at the time of filing the application.

---

29. *Young Dental Mfg. Co. v. Q3 Special Prods, Inc.*, 112 F.3d 1137, 1144 (Fed. Cir. 1997).
30. *Cardiac Pacemakers, Inc. v. St. Jude Med., Inc.*, 381 F.3d 1371, 1378 (Fed. Cir. 2004).

2. Written Description

The written description requirement is satisfied only if the specification demonstrates that "the applicant was in possession of the claimed invention, including all of the elements and limitations" at the time the application was filed.[31] Its purpose is fundamental: "to ensure that the scope of the right to exclude, as set forth in the claims, does not overreach the scope of the inventor's contribution to the field of art as described in the specification."[32] Put another way, its purpose is "to prevent an applicant from later asserting that he invented that which he did not; the applicant . . . is therefore required to recount his invention in such detail that his future claims [of what the patent covers] can be determined to be encompassed within his original creation [i.e., the specification]."[33] The specification must convey "with reasonable clarity to those skilled in the art that the inventor was in possession of" the later-claimed invention.[34] It is not enough that the later-claimed invention would have been obvious to those skilled in the art; it must be reasonably conveyed in the specification.[35]

To draft specifications that comply with the written description requirement, a practitioner should provide the level of detail necessary to place the public in possession of the limits of the subject matter, but does not have to provide a blueprint of every aspect of the invention, when certain aspects were known in the art. This can vary depending on the nature of the invention, for example, a plant pot versus a genus of compounds that bind to a ligand. The level of detail to place someone in possession depends on nature of the invention, with certain inventions requiring increased amounts of description or examples to be found to have sufficient description. Over time, the degree of description required for an invention can decrease as more understanding and details of the technology become publicly available. Unfortunately, there is no perfect algorithm to provide the practitioner with clear guidance on when a specification possesses sufficient written description and when it does not, especially when the USPTO changes its internal guidelines on interpreting such statutes.[36]

---

31. *Univ. of Rochester v. G.D. Searle & Co.*, 358 F.3d 916, 926 (Fed. Cir. 2004).
32. *Reiffin v. Microsoft Corp.*, 214 F.3d 1342, 1345–46 (Fed. Cir. 2000).
33. *Vas-Cath Inc. v. Mahurkar*, 935 F.2d 1555, 1563 (Fed. Cir. 1991).
34. *Purdue Pharma LP v. Faulding Inc.*, 20 F.3d 1320, 1323 (Fed. Cir. 2000).
35. *Lockwood v. Am. Airlines, Inc.*, 107 F.3d 1565, 1571–72 (Fed. Cir. 1997); *see also TurboCare*, 264 F.3d at 1119 (to be inherently disclosed the "missing descriptive matter must necessarily be present" in the original specification).
36. Written Description Guidelines were published in 1999. A new set of Written Description Training Materials were released in April 2008 further refining examples of what had and what lacks sufficient written description. Written Description Training Materials can be obtained *at* http://www.uspto.gov/web/menu/written.pdf. The Guidelines for Written

3. Enabling Disclosure

It is a fundamental requirement that "the specification must enable a person of ordinary skill in the art to make and use the invention."[37] This arises from the requirement in section 112 that the specification set forth "the manner and process of making and using [the invention] in such full, clear, concise, and exact terms as to enable a person skilled in the art to which [the invention] pertains . . . to make and use the same."[38] Enablement serves a critical public function—to ensure that "the public knowledge is enriched by the patent specification to a degree at least commensurate with the scope of the claims." The enablement requirement helps ensure that claims cover no more than the invention the person fully disclosed how to make and use the claimed invention.[39]

The question is whether one skilled in the art could "make and use the full scope of the invention without undue experimentation."[40] Considerations established in *In re Wands*[41]—not surprisingly called the *"Wands* Factors"—bearing on enablement include: "(1) the quantity of experimentation necessary, (2) the amount of direction or guidance presented, (3) the presence or absence of working examples, (4) the nature of the invention, (5) the state of the prior art, (6) the relative skill of those in the art, (7) the predictability or unpredictability of the art, and (8) the breadth of the claims."

Providing an enabling disclosure can be a fact intensive effort. Although the facts of each case vary, a practitioner should make sure all the materials and details on procedure are provided for the purpose of teaching how to make. Frequently, details are omitted in working examples or in the general discussion such that the skilled artisan would not have all the materials necessary to make and/or use the invention. This raises the issue of competency and whether the practitioner is familiar enough with the art the invention falls into to determine whether sufficient disclosure is provided to be enabling.

---

    description issued as Guidelines for Examination of Patent Applications Under the 35 U.S.C. 112, ¶ 1, "Written Description" Requirement and published in 66 Fed. Reg. 1099 (Jan. 5, 2001).

37. *Union Pac. Resources Co. v. Chesapeake Energy Corp.*, 236 F.3d 684, 690 (Fed. Cir. 2001).
38. *Nat'l Recovery Techs., Inc. v. Magnetic Separation Sys., Inc.*, 166 F.3d 1190, 1195–96 (Fed. Cir. 1999).
39. Absent an enabling disclosure in a reference, the reference cannot be held to anticipate a claim. For example, where a process for making the compound is not developed until after the date of invention, the mere naming of a compound in a reference, without more, cannot constitute a description of the compound. *In re Hoeksema*, 399 F.2d 269, 158 U.S.P.Q. 596 (CCPA 1968).
40. *Warner-Lambert Co. v. Teva Pharm. USA, Inc.*, 418 F.3d 1326, 1337 (Fed. Cir. 2005).
41. *In re Wands*, 858 F.2d 731, 737 (Fed. Cir. 1988).

Turning to the *Wands* factors, how closely a practitioner tries to meet each factor depends on the nature of the invention and the state of the prior art. On the continuum of unpredictability and developments in the field, the more undeveloped and unpredictable, the more detail the practitioner should provide. The more the applicant provides in the form of description and examples to demonstrate how to make and use the invention, the more the practitioner will also meet requirements of written description at the same time, even though these are legally distinct requirements.

The necessity for detailed information will relax over time as a field develops and matures. Thus, in an undeveloped field with a great deal of unpredictability, there will be a need to provide detailed descriptions of the materials and methods for performing the examples and carrying out the various claimed embodiments. If there is variation in embodiments or a genus is claimed, for example, then examples of the variation or representative species should be provided. Again, no algorithm exists on the proper number of representative examples for any one application especially given examiner subjectivity. However, if the data is available, it should generally be submitted. This is the "more is better" approach to specification drafting.[42]

One cautionary note from the perspective of enablement relates to providing prophetic examples. Clearly set forth that the example is prophetic and not real. Use preferably future tense, or if necessary present tense. Do not use past tense in presenting prophetic examples. To state that an experiment "was performed" when the example is only prophetic (has not been performed) has been used to find patents unenforceable.[43] If used, it serves to misrepresent the nature of the example, and such events have caused patents to be held unenforceable for inequitable conduct.[44]

L. Including All, but Only, True Inventors

1. The Basic Requirement

It "is the responsibility of applicants and their attorneys to ensure that the inventors named in a patent application are the only true inventors."[45]

---

42. With the introduction of page fees for specifications in excess of 100 pages, the more is better approach is somewhat limiting depending on the amount of funds the applicant is willing to pay.

43. *See, e.g., Novo Nordisk Pharmaceuticals Inc. v. Bio-Technology General Corp.*, 424 F.3d 1347 (Fed. Reg. 2005) for presentation and assertions made in application relating to a prophetic example.

44. *See id.*

45. *Bd. of Ed. ex rel. Florida v. Am. Bioscience, Inc.*, 333 F.3d 1330 (Fed. Cir. 2003).

Not only do practitioners have an affirmative substantive legal duty to ensure that only inventors are named, but federal law precludes naming as "inventors" persons who did not contribute to the subject matter of an invention, and knowingly doing so may: (1) render the patent unenforceable under 35 U.S.C. section 282; (2) violate the duty of candor imposed by 37 C.F.R. section 1.56; (3) violate the Patent and Trademark Office Code of Professional Conduct (PTO Code), which proscribes violations of section 1.56; and (4) constitute malpractice.[46]

Under the Patent Act, every inventor, but only inventors, must be named on an application. The failure to include every inventor can result in patent invalidity as can the inclusion of a person who is not an inventor. If there is intentional deception of the USPTO, the patent can be held unenforceable.[47] The USPTO has stated that the duty of candor must be satisfied even over the objections of a client, and even if the client "fires" the lawyer under state law.[48]

As a result, a practitioner must determine either alone, or with the assistance of the corporate attorney responsible for the case, the role of each of the "inventors" has relative to the "novel" limitations. There has to be a real contribution to the inventive subject matter. Once a final set of claims is obtained, it may be useful to associate at least one claim (or limitation) with each of the inventors. In patent savvy environments, the issue of inventor determination may be more routine and tied to an invention disclosure that has at least one of the inventors attesting to the attributions. However, in corporate start-ups and university settings, inventorship determination can be more difficult because of the lack of procedural guidance for determination. In non-savvy settings, patent inventorship can frequently be considered the same as paper authorship. It is not. If the person did the work under the direction of or at the behest of another, the person is not an inventor. Thus, many laboratory personnel, interns, graduate students, or advisors might not advance to the level necessary to be an inventor. Alternatively, the department chair may not be the inventor, when the idea arose from a post-doctoral fellow in the laboratory. Thus, it can be necessary for the practitioner to explain to those

---

46. *See generally Frank's Casing Crew & Rental Tools, Inc. v. PMR Technologies, Ltd.,* 292 F.3d 1363 (Fed. Cir. 2002).

47. *See* David Hricik et al., *Save a Little Room for Me: The Necessity of Naming as Inventors Practitioners Who Conceive of Claimed Subject Matter,* 55 MERCER L. REV. 635 (2004). If an attorney conceives of subject matter, special care needs to be exercised. *See id.; see also Virginia St. B. v. Lynt,* Chancery No. CH04001593 (suspending lawyer for conduct relating to naming himself as inventor on CIP application); Harry I. Moatz, *Some Observations About Two Topics: The Duty of Disclosure and a Practitioner's Asserted Inventorship* (Dec. 5, 2005) (discussing assertion of inventorship by practitioner).

48. 50 Fed. Reg. 5158–01, 5165 (Feb. 6, 1985).

involved the differences between authorship and inventorship. Such conversations can require delicate explanations to avoid a political quagmire.

Although the in-house attorneys frequently determine issues relating to inventorship based on invention disclosures,[49] outside counsel are called in to handle more murky issues, including determining ownership when inventors belong to different corporate or university entities. Such an analysis frequently requires determination of the facts by talking to the various parties and reviewing documentation. The analysis should involve talking with the putative inventors, as well as reviewing relevant documents.

If there is more than one inventor, and if each has an obligation of assignment to the same entity, then generally naming each person as an inventor, even when one may not have contributed to every claim, is proper. However, if inventors do not have the same obligation of assignment, then it can be important for the practitioner to consider filing separate applications, including in each one the subject matter conceived of only by those inventors who have a common assignee.

Inventorship must be revisited again at the time of a restriction requirement or when a divisional application is to be filed. The separation of the claims into inventive groups may split up the originally listed inventors. As a practice note, it can be beneficial to have a listing of inventors with some of the claims, especially the independent claims, to simplify prosecution of divisional applications later. Prosecution is usually started 14 to 46 months after the nonprovisional application is filed. During this time, inventors can leave the company or university, retire, become incapacitated, or die. Having this information in advance can assist with dealing with inventorship issues later.

2. Special Issues Concerning Joint Inventors

A. Who Is a Joint Inventor?

Determining whether a person is a joint inventor is highly fact specific and there is "no bright-line standard" that suffices in every case."[50] However, "one does not become an inventor either by suggesting a desired end or result, with no suggestion of means, or by merely following the instructions of the person(s) who conceive the solution."[51]

---

49. *See also* Or. St. B. Ass'n Formal Op. No. 1994-136 (Jan. 1994) (analyzing whether in-house counsel who refused to intentionally name incorrect inventors could disclose those facts in subsequent wrongful termination suit).

50. *Fina Oil & Chemical Co. v. Ewen*, 123 F.3d 1466, 1473 (Fed. Cir. 1997).

51. *Id.*

The fundamental policy behind joint inventorship issues underlies the Constitutional provision for securing patent rights to the originator of an invention, rather than simply to the first applicant. This policy underlies two general requirements for recognition of inventorship: First, only an "actual" inventor or originator of an invention is entitled to a patent, whereas a person who appropriates or derives the invention from another is not so entitled. Second, only the "first" actual inventor is entitled to a patent. Still today, our patent system operates under the concept of first in time, first in right.

Ownership of something invented by another is insufficient to make one an inventor. Ownership can be seen as a special category of lawful appropriation, rather than actual inventorship. An owner of an invention, for example, an employer to whom an employee assigns all patent rights, is not a joint inventor by the mere fact of his or her appropriation or ownership. Although an employer-assignee might claim to have some form of natural right in the fruits of an innovation when his or her financing was necessary to support the inventor's creative work, he or she has no legal entitlements of inventorship.

Standards of naming inventors as determined by companies, universities, and others may not be the proper way of determining inventorship under federal law. It may be that, for example, a person is entitled to receive a bonus as an "inventor" even though he or she cannot properly be named as such on the patent.

Inventorship cannot be based on whether someone performed an experiment at the behest of another and was listed as an author of a related journal article. Inventorship cannot be based on position in a company or a university. For example, a university department chair cannot be named as an inventor merely because he or she is the department chair, unless he or she contributed to a claimed invention. In the past, attempts may have been considered to list individuals as inventors to avoid prior art from prior inventions that had different inventive entities. This issue has been overcome somewhat with the advent of 35 U.S.C. section 103(c) and 37 C.F.R. section 1.321.

An even starker conflict of interests occurs when inventors employed by different companies collaborate on a joint research project.[52] Each inventor has an incentive to be recognized for his or her contribution. Each employer, however, has an incentive to name only its own employees to obtain full ownership through assignment. Here again, the true inventors must be determined according to their contribution to the claimed invention and without regard to any assignment or other contractual obligations that might affect ownership of the patent rights. In this situation, as in the one discussed above,

---

52. *See also In re Goldstein*, 16 U.S.P.Q.2d 1963 (Comm'r. Pat. 1988) (discussing inability of attorney to prosecute in name of assignee where each inventor had not assigned interest to same corporation).

under the first requirement for inventorship, only the "actual" originators are entitled to a patent.

B. What Does Joint Inventorship Convey by Way of a Property Right?

Patents may be jointly owned. Each co-owner holds an undivided interest in the whole patent. Thus, each co-owner can practice or license the patented invention without accounting to any other co-owner as to his or her activities.[53]

The relationship among joint investors is, as a result, similar to tenants in common in real property holdings. Thus, the practical component for all is that there should be assignment of the patent rights to a common entity. If there is more than one inventor, the risk that a joint inventor may be a maverick and license someone else or do something with his or her rights, diminishes the overall rights to the invention. Thus, the practitioner should always counsel joint inventors to commonly assign their rights to a corporate entity, which reduces this risk. Alternatively, the joint inventors can assign their rights to one inventor in exchange for remuneration thereby leaving only one person with ownership of the invention.

Not only does joint inventor ownership of invention pose problems for licensing and venture deals relating to the invention, joint ownership also poses a fertile ground for conflict of interest to the patent attorney or agent representing the joint inventors. The questions that should come to mind when preparing an engagement letter are (1) who do you represent; and (2) what happens to the representation should problems arise between the joint inventors?

C. What to Do

When asked to represent joint inventors, the practitioner should always first consider whether to even undertake the representation. Perhaps turning down the work is the better answer. Joint inventors present an extremely

---

53. *See* 35 U.S.C. § 262 ("In the absence of any agreement to the contrary, each of the joint owners of a patent may make, use, offer to sell, or sell the patented invention within the United States, or import the patented invention into the United States, without the consent of and without accounting to the other owners."); *Schering Corp. v. Roussel-UCLAF SA*, 104 F.3d 341, 344 (Fed. Cir. 1997) (affirming summary judgment that co-owner's grant of a license to an accused infringer provided a complete defense to infringement claims brought by other co-owner and ruling that even though terms of co-ownership agreement addressed third-party infringement claims and provided each co-owner with a unilateral right to sue and a duty for each co-owner to provide "reasonable assistance" to the other in the event of a third-party infringement suit those clauses did not nullify the co-owner's right to license its interest at will) (citation omitted).

complicated situation for any practitioner, whether seasoned or a first-year associate.

If the practitioner decides to represent the joint inventors, the practitioner and the joint inventors should be prepared for potential scenarios. A checklist of questions is a valuable tool for the practitioner when considering whether representing joint inventors is worthwhile.

1. Who owns the invention?
2. Who do you represent?
3. Was the invention assigned to an individual or entity?
4. What rights does the assignee have to the invention?
5. Are the inventors employed at the same company?
6. Does the company have rights under shop right laws or employment agreements?
7. Does the assignee have full or partial ownership?
8. Are there any corporate collaborators?
9. Who has standing to bring a suit?

Because of the nature of the answers to these questions, the practitioner needs to be careful. The answers could serve as grounds for disqualification, and depending on the number and size of the parties involved, and the law firm's size, all can play to a conflict of interest during the information acquisition and client-attorney courtship period.

Disputes can arise after joint representation is undertaken. Suppose later the inventors hate each other and want to pursue separate paths. Does the engagement letter provide clear means of terminating the relationship or means of dealing with the problem? For example, 37 C.F.R. section 10.66 provides:

(a) A practitioner shall decline proffered employment if the exercise of the practitioner's independent professional judgment in behalf of a client will be or is likely to be adversely affected by the acceptance of the proffered employment, or if it would be likely to involve the practitioner in representing differing interests, except to the extent permitted under paragraph (c) of this section.

(b) A practitioner shall not continue multiple employment if the exercise of the practitioner's independent professional judgment in behalf of a client will be or is likely to be adversely affected by the practitioner's representation of another client, or if it would be likely to involve the practitioner in representing differing interests, except to the extent permitted under paragraph (c) of this section.

(c) In the situations covered by paragraphs (a) and (b) of this section a practitioner may represent multiple clients if it is obvious that the practitioner can adequately represent the interest of each and if each consents to the representation after full disclosure of the possible effect of such representation on the exercise of the practitioner's independent professional judgment on behalf of each.

(d) If a practitioner is required to decline employment or to withdraw from employment under a Disciplinary Rule, no partner, or associate, or any other practitioner affiliated with the practitioner or the practitioner's firm, may accept or continue such employment unless otherwise ordered by the Director or Commissioner.[54]

In a scenario that is less strident, what happens if one joint inventor no longer wants to, or cannot, pay the practitioner? Does the engagement letter address issues relating to remuneration with respect to the joint representation? If receiving money from third parties who are not the joint inventors, then there may be a concern of influence by others, which is governed by Rule 10.68 and was recently discussed in the *Bender v. Dudas* case.[55] Once there are issues between joint inventors, there develops a problem whether the practitioner can continue to represent the client zealously or not.[56]

Once wedded to a client, divorce can prove difficult—and the degree of living in sin that will allow disengagement later is impossible to gauge with certainty. Conflicts of interest generally may be waived or consented to.[57] Joint representation needs to be laid out at the outset as a complex representation with potential outcomes set forth clearly to the joint inventors. They must consent to the representation, and to the practitioner's means of extricating him or herself should the amicable joint inventors become adverse to each other. The joint inventors must understand that the historical knowledge that is shared, should the practitioner withdraw representation will be lost to them absent new engagement letters and appropriate waivers. "Waiver refers to the voluntary or intentional relinquishment of a known right" and "emphasizes the mental attitude of the actor."[58] So, in any event, a practitioner should err on the side of overeducating joint inventors on future possibilities and what they might relinquish.

For example, suppose joint inventors want a practitioner to prepare an application for them. In their minds, they are joint inventors. But, the practitioner must ask whether, as a legal matter, each is an inventor? If not, then who is the client? Although our book does not exhaustively analyze how to determine what constitutes inventorship, one does not become a joint inventor by merely suggesting a desired end or result, with no suggestion of means

---

54. 37 C.F.R. § 10.66.
55. *Bender v. Dudas*, 490 F.3d 1361 (Fed. Cir. 2007).
56. *See* 37 C.F.R. 10.84.
57. *Black v. Missouri*, 492 F. Supp. 848 (W.D. Mo. 1980).
58. *Id.* at 866.

of achieving the result.[59] To be considered a joint inventor, one must contribute to the conception of the solution that constitutes the claimed invention.

The practical suggestion is to discuss quickly what inventorship means with the individuals and educate them. Then put in the engagement letter a clause stating that the representation will include the joint inventors as determined by that analysis. Should the people initially identified in the letter change, it can be worthwhile to execute a new engagement letter at that time with those individuals.

D. Problems Lawyers Face When Representing Joint Inventors

General principles of agency law indicate that a power of attorney does not ipso facto create an attorney-client relationship. For example, one who grants a power of attorney for the benefit of a third person does not create an attorney-client relationship between the grantor and the attorney.

The relationship between the inventor and the assignee's patent counsel, who is appointed to prosecute the patent application, must be considered in conjunction with the patent laws governing the acquisition and assignment of rights to inventions. When the client is the corporation, the practitioner should always get an assignment from the inventor to the corporation to make clear ownership issues. Additionally, if there is any question, the inventor should be made to understand quickly that the practitioner represents the corporation and not the inventor's interests, should those interests be adverse to the client's. Such scenarios frequently arise in inventorship disputes or if the inventor is planning to leave the company or has left the company. There is a desire by the inventor to confide in the attorney. They should be cautioned that the practitioner represents the university, corporation, or other entity and not them, and if they have legal questions they will have to procure their own legal counsel.

Inventors hired or employed by a company who develop an invention in the course of their work, which they agreed to assign to the company are generally by contract required to execute whatever papers are necessary for the company's patent counsel to prosecute a patent application on behalf of the company. Thus, it is routine for an inventor to execute an application appointing the attorney who prepared the application at the direction of the party to whom the application must be assigned and on whose behalf it will be prosecuted. The choice of attorneys, like the filing, is a decision by the assignee, not the inventor. And, both sides must realize that they have to make it work, even if the inventor believes that another attorney should be handling the job.

---

59. *Brown v. Regents of the University of California*, 866 F. Supp. 439, 440 (N.D. Cal. 1994).

E. Conclusion

Representation of joint inventors should be made with care. The first suggestion is to request the inventors assign their rights to a company, and the practitioner represents the company. However, this is frequently not an option. Then a preliminary investigation should be made to determine whether the individuals truly are inventors. Finally, if all sides agree to the joint representation, the practitioner must clearly set out an engagement letter.

M. Responding to Office Actions

An examiner can issue an office action for all sorts of reasons. Frequently, the first office action is in the form of a restriction requirement. Assessing the restriction requirement for correctness in following USPTO guidelines, especially with the high number of new examiners, is important. The restriction requirement is equivalent to the start of a chess match and just as initial moves can control game outcome, the restriction can map out the ultimate family. Determination of propriety of the restriction requirement, its errors, and detailing the errors is important. Petitions to the restriction requirement can be necessary depending on whether the restriction is made final. Although petitions are frequently not used, given the downstream impact on the number of filings necessary to claim all aspects of the invention, making sure the restriction is proper is important. Incorrect groupings of claims, claims in more than one group, claims missing from consideration in the restriction, lack of burden to substantiate the restricted groups, and so forth, if handled improperly, will set a muddied and possibly expensive path for the application and its progeny if not corrected or ameliorated.

Likewise, when receiving an office action, determination of the propriety of the rejection and objections must be made early on. Additionally, making sure all aspects of the office action are in order for response must also be made. If the office action is so defective as to not be capable of reply, then seeking a new office action and resetting the time for response can be in order. Not doing so can result in the practitioner having to put unnecessary arguments in the record.

A system of quality control handling should be implemented for all office actions, checking acknowledgments on information disclosure statements and other application formalities. Determining USPTO errors or clarifying USPTO ambiguities early in prosecution frequently will maintain proper prosecution direction. By doing so, the practitioner not only detects USPTO errors but remains on as direct a prosecutorial pathway as is available, without deviating because of unperceived USPTO errors or misconstrued USPTO meanings.

As noted in chapter 5 on loyalty and current client conflicts of interest, in addition to requiring competency, under some circumstances office action responses can create conflicts of interest.

N. Meeting Deadlines and Prosecuting Diligently

There are two issues that relate to deadlines: A deadline must be met, but even meeting all deadlines can still result in harm to a client through prosecution laches.

Many deadlines in patent practice can be extended by the payment of a relatively small fee. Others, however, are absolute. It is important that practitioners use a docketing system that tracks these deadlines accurately. In addition, practitioners should consider redundant systems—one on computer, the other on paper, for example—in case of a failure of one system.

Although deadlines can be extended, extensions should be obtained at the client's direction, or out of necessity, but not as a result of practitioner delay or convenience.[60] Extensions of time will reduce any patent term adjustment received as a result of USPTO delay under 35 U.S.C. section 154. Although term accrual at the end of a patent's term might not be valuable for a microchip, it can be extremely valuable to a pharmaceutical composition patent. Accordingly, unless otherwise necessary, such delays should be avoided to award the maximum amount of term possible to the patent.[61]

---

60. In this regard, if the need to pay for the extension is caused by the practitioner, not the client, the practitioner may ethically pay the fee and not seek reimbursement from the client. N.Y. County Lawyers' Ass'n Comm. on Prof. Eth. Op. No. 668 (May 15, 1989). Under some circumstances, of course, it may be improper for the practitioner to seek reimbursement. *See id.*

61. Malpractice claims based on missing various deadlines are perhaps the most common form of malpractice suit brought arising out of patent prosecution. *See, e.g., Delta Process Equip., Inc. v. New England Ins. Co.,* 560 So.2d 923 (La. App. 1990) (failure to file before 102(b) barred application); *Keller v. Clark Eqip. Co.,* 715 F.2d 1280 (8th Cir. 1983) (same); *Minatronics Corp. v. Buchanan Ingersoll PC,* 1996 WL 76508 (Pa. Comm. Pl. Feb. 7, 1996) (failure to file application and concealment of same); *Fotodyne, Inc. v. Barry,* 1989 WL 142846 (Wis. App. Sept. 26, 1989) (missed PCT deadline); *Igen, Inc. v. White,* 672 N.Y.S.2d 867 (N.Y. Sup. Ct. App. Div. 1998) (failure to timely file in EPO); *Inkine Pharma. Co. v. Coleman,* 759 N.Y.S.2d 62 (N.Y. Sup. Ct. App. Div. 2003 (failure to timely file in Asia); *Boehm v. Wheeler,* 223 N.W.2d 536 (Wis. 1975) (102(b) deadline missed by practitioner); *People v. Williams,* 915 P.2d 669 (Colo. 1996) (discipline involving allegations of gross neglect in abandoning application); *Kairos Scientific Inc. v. Fish & Richardson, P.C.,* 2006 Cal. App. Unpub. LEXIS 667 (2006) (mostly upholding award of $30 million in case where firm admitted missing PCT deadline). *See also People v. Herring,* 2001 WL 1161242 (Colo. O.P.D.J. 2001) (suspending lawyer who abandoned application and did not notify client of event); *Chopra v.*

Systems designed to meet deadlines should be put in practice that all paralegals, secretaries, and attorneys know and follow. The systems for docketing and maintaining dockets should be redundant, in at least one order, to minimize the impact of human error or machine failure. Communication of systems and process should not be siloed among a small group but should be universal across the practice. This includes preparation and use of forms and processes. When errors are identified, the firm should determine how the error arose, and the processes and procedures should be modified as necessary to avoid recurrence of the problem.

It is worthwhile to consider having a clear organizational structure tied to defined (and communicated) processes and procedures and responsibilities assigned to individuals, along with management oversight and responsibility. This practice is not far different from the models used for good manufacturing practices (GMPs) in the drug industry. Like that industry, the practice is to minimize risk. The issue of communicating these aspects regularly to all professionals and nonprofessionals is especially important in large firms, where turnover of staff and attorneys can be high.

But even meeting every deadline as written does not insulate a client from harm. The USPTO may subject an application to forfeiture; and even if a patent issues, it may under some circumstances be subject to the equitable defense of "prosecution laches."[62] Although subject to few bright lines, if the examiner gives notice that forfeiture is a consequence of failing to substantively advance prosecution, and an application has been pending for several years, forfeiture may be proper. Thus, merely rote compliance with USPTO deadlines is insufficient to protect a client, but such accusations are rare.

O. Handing-Off or Giving Notice of the Maintenance Fee Obligation

When a patent is issued, it is accompanied by a statement of the number of months until a maintenance fee is due. Malpractice actions have been based on the failure of a firm to send maintenance fee reminders,[63] or for actually

---

Townsend, Townsend and Crew, LLP, 2008 WL 413944 (D. Colo. Feb. 13, 2008) (abandonment).

62. In *Symbol Tech., Inc. v. Lemelson Med.*, 277 F.3d 1361, 1368 (Fed. Cir. 2002), the Federal Circuit held prosecution laches was an equitable defense to infringement, and in *In re Bogese*, 303 F.3d 1362 (Fed. Cir. 2002), it held the PTO had even greater power to sanction undue delay during prosecution by denying issuance to an application. *See generally* Lisa A. Dolak, *The Ethics of Delaying Prosecution*, 53 Am. U. L. Rev. 739 (2004).

63. *Accuweb, Inc. v. Foley & Lardner,* 2007 WL 259829 (Wis. App. 2007).

failing to pay maintenance fees where, ostensibly, the firm had agreed to do so.[64]

A best practices action would be to obtain instructions in writing at the time of reporting to the assignee the notice of allowance. This should cover payment of all the maintenance fees. This may be better than at the time of grant, when the assignee may no longer have the urgency to respond to the practitioner's correspondence. Instructions from the client on handling the maintenance fees should be obtained and updated in the firm's docketing system.

Another final practice note is that the practitioner should always recheck whether entities have gone from small to large for each maintenance fee, either through licensing or through growth. Payment of a maintenance fee at the level of small, when it should have been large, can be a ground for holding a patent unenforceable if anyone can prove knowing knowledge of large entity status and payment at low entity rates.[65]

In conclusion, remaining competent for the practice is never ending, given constant court decisions, changes to the statutes, changes by the USPTO, and new science. It is not an end goal that once achieved never has to be revisited.

P. Using Continuation-in-Part Applications to Obtain Earlier Filing Dates When Proper

A nonprovisional patent application can claim an invention disclosed but not claimed in an earlier, still-pending nonprovisional application if the later application shares at least one common inventor with the earlier-filed co-pending application. A continuation application adds no new matter to the earlier-filed application, but a continuation-in-part, or CIP, does add some new matter. More specifically, a CIP is "an application filed during the lifetime of an earlier nonprovisional application by the same applicant, repeating some substantial portion or all of the earlier nonprovisional application and adding matter not disclosed in the said earlier nonprovisional application."[66]

Thus, any time a practitioner is asked by a client with a co-pending application to file a new application, the practitioner should examine whether the

---

64. *New Tek Mfg. Inc. v. Beehner,* 702 N.W.2d 336 (Neb. 2005) (remanding for trial on whether infringement would have occurred after lapse).

65. *See* Chapter 8, on Inequitable Conduct, *infra.*

66. Manual of Patent Examining Procedure (MPEP) 201.08, citing *In re Klein,* 5 U.S.P.Q. 259 (Comm'r. Pat. 1930). *See Ex Parte Wiener,* 125 U.S.P.Q. 594 (Comm'r Pat. 1958) (an application that does not carry forward any part of the earlier disclosure is not a CIP).

claims are already supported in a then-pending application of that same client, or whether at least some of the claims are supported, and new matter could be added to the pending application.[67] The result can be claims that, in whole or in part, are entitled to an earlier filing date than would be those filed in an original application. Today, CIP practice is generally avoided because of patent term loss that CIPs would be subject to given a term of 20 years from original films.

---

67. *But see IMT, Inc. v. Haynes & Boone, LLP,* 1999 WL 58838 (N.D. Tex. Feb. 1, 1999) (client alleged in a malpractice suit that the filing of a CIP rather than an original application made it easier to attack the resulting patent); *Adamasu v. Gifford, Krass, Groh, Sprinkle, Anderson & Citkowski, PC,* 409 F. Supp. 2d 788 (E.D. Mich. 2005) (malpractice suit alleging that lawyer had erred in reviving an earlier-filed application that, because of amendments to GATT, resulted in shorter patent term than otherwise would have been available).

CHAPTER
8

The Duty of Candor and Inequitable Conduct

A. Background 105
   1. Preemption of State Law 105
   2. First Principles of Inequitable Conduct 111
   3. Materiality Is Not Limited to the Circumstances
      Specified in Rule 1.56 112

B. Knowledge of the Information Is Not Necessarily Required:
   The Duty to Investigate May Exist, but Imputation
   Should Not Apply 116

C. Knowledge That the Information Is Material Is Not
   Necessarily Required 123

D. Intent to Deceive May Be Inferred 125
   1. *Whose* Knowledge Counts? 127
   2. *When* Must Information Be Disclosed? 128

E. Recurrent Fact Patterns Constituting Inequitable
   Conduct 129
   1. Nondisclosure of Prior Art 129
   2. Submitted but Buried Material Information 131
   3. Submitted but Mischaracterized References 133
   4. Misleading Translations of Foreign-Language Prior
      Art References 135
      A. Withholding Full or Partial Translations the Applicant
         Possesses 135
      B. Submitting a Partial Translation That Omits the Most
         Material Aspects of the Reference 136
      C. Characterizing the Whole Reference on a Partial
         Translation 138
   5. Withholding Information That Contradicts Statements
      to the U.S. Patent and Trademark Office 139
   6. Test Data 139

7. Relationships between Declarants and Applicants   143

8. Section 112 Requirements   144

    A. Enablement   144

    B. Best Mode   146

9. Prior Sales   146

10. Co-Pending Applications   148

    A. Of Same Client of Same Lawyer   148

    B. Of Different Clients of Same Lawyer   149

    C. Of Different Clients of Other Firm Lawyers   149

11. Rejection of Substantially Similar Claims by
    Another Examiner   150

12. *McKesson* Disclosure Statements   151

13. Existence of and Information Gleaned from
    Ongoing Litigation   153

14. Misrepresentations of Information Relating to
    Inventorship   155

15. Misclaiming Priority of Disclosure   157

16. Maintenance Fees, Small Entity Status,
    and Inequitable Conduct   158

17. Petitions to Reinstate   159

18. Petitions to Make Special   160

19. Reexamination   160

A patent is granted in exchange for disclosing a new, useful, and nonobvious invention.[1] To ensure that patents are not granted patents on inventions that are not new or that are merely obvious variants on those that the public already has the right to use, and that the disclosure is sufficient to permit those skilled in the art to make and use the invention and to practice its preferred embodiments,[2] every person substantively involved in the prosecution of an application has a duty to disclose to the U.S. Patent and Trademark Office (USPTO) information material to the patentability of the claimed invention.[3]

---

1. *See* 35 U.S.C. §§ 101, 102, 103 (2000).
2. *See* 35 U.S.C. § 112 (2000).
3. 37 C.F.R. § 1.56 (1999). *See generally Refac Int'l., Ltd. v. Lotus Dev. Corp.,* 81 F.3d 1576, 1581, 38 U.S.P.Q.2d (BNA) 1665, 1668–69 (Fed. Cir. 1996) (discussing the elements of the inequitable conduct defense).

A practitioner's[4] substantive involvement in prosecution creates duties independent of the inventor.[5] Specifically, the intentional failure of a prosecuting attorney to disclose material information can result in the patent being held unenforceable in a later suit for infringement of that patent, even if the applicant was unaware of that information or of its importance to whether the invention was patentable.[6] The duty of candor is nondelegable.[7]

In light of this broad duty, it is tempting to state that there is no such thing as too much disclosure, but practical realities, including the time pressure on attorneys, the need for efficient and economic prosecution, and the risk of being accused of burying the most material information, demonstrate that is not true. Instead, while prosecuting an application, a practitioner must exercise skill and judgment in determining whether, and if so, how, to disclose information to the USPTO in a way that complies with the duty of candor and balances the needs of the USPTO and the client.

This chapter addresses the recent and fundamental shifts in the breadth of inequitable conduct doctrine and surveys conduct that has recently resulted in findings of inequitable conduct or at least found to evidence bad faith and provides some practical guidance.[8]

A. Background

1. Preemption of State Law

At least two commentators believe that state law can apply even to fundamental conduct at the core of patent prosecution.[9] Specifically, these

---

4. Although this chapter often refers to "attorneys," for the most part the issues discussed here apply equally to nonattorney registered patent agents.
5. See *Brasseler, U.S.A. I, L.P. v. Stryker Sales Corp.*, 267 F.3d 1370, 1381–86, 60 U.S.P.Q.2d (BNA) 1482, 1488–92 (Fed. Cir. 2001) (Separately analyzing conduct of attorney and inventors).
6. *FMC Corp. v. Manitowoc Co.*, 835 F.2d 1411, 1415 n.8, 5 U.S.P.Q.2d (BNA) 1112, 1115 n.8 (Fed. Cir. 1987) (stating that knowledge and actions of an applicant's representative are chargeable to applicant for purposes of determining enforceability of the patent); *Brasseler*, 267 F.3d at 1381–85, 60 U.S.P.Q.2d at 1488–91 (holding attorneys' conduct was sufficient to find unenforceability).
7. See generally *Levenger Co. v. Feldman*, 516 F. Supp. 2d 1272 (S.D. Fla. 2007).
8. A finding of inequitable conduct buries not just the patent, but the lawyers who prosecuted it. Clients whose patents have been held unenforceable have sued their lawyers for breach of fiduciary duty and malpractice—often years after prosecution ended. For example, in *Lex Tex Ltd., Inc. v. Skillman*, 579 A.2d 244, 16 U.S.P.Q.2d (BNA) 1137 (D.C. App. 1990), the patents were issued in 1963, but were not held unenforceable by the Federal Circuit until 1985. The result was the reversal of a $9 million judgment in favor of the patentee against an infringer. Lex Tex, the patentee, then sued the lawyers for having failed to disclose the pertinent prior art to the PTO twenty years before.
9. See Daniel Ovanezian & Suk Lee, *Ethical Conflicts for the Patent Practitioner*, 29 NEW MATTER 1, 13 (2004) (concluding that it is at best unclear whether a state could discipline a lawyer for

commentators have concluded that state confidentiality rules apply during prosecution and are not preempted. One consequence of this conclusion is that a lawyer who is told by a client, "don't disclose this material information to the USPTO"[10] may not ethically do so.[11] Does the Patent and Trademark Office Code of Professional Conduct's (PTO Code) requirement that a lawyer disclose certain information to the USPTO[12] preempt state law that requires that it be kept confidential?

That question raises a crucial example of when the PTO Code requires what state law may prohibit. If the PTO Code preempts state law, then a lawyer could not be sued for disclosing information that state law requires be held in confidence. For example, suppose that under state law, a client's termination of a lawyer's authority to act (i.e., the client says "don't disclose the information and, by the way, you're fired") terminates the lawyer's authority to act on behalf of the client. Must the lawyer still disclose the art? If he or she does so, can he or she be disciplined, or sued, for violating conflicting obligations under state law?

The USPTO has clearly and unequivocally stated that a lawyer has no choice but to disclose information when required by the PTO Code, and without regard to what state law may require. Specifically, in responding to comments when it was originally adopting the PTO Code, the USPTO acknowledged that—whatever the responsibilities of a practitioner under state law to maintain the confidentiality of a client's information—if that information was material to patentability, then it had to be disclosed.[13]

---

complying with Rule 1.56); Rose & Jessup, *supra* note 3 (concluding that state ethics rules applied to whether a lawyer may disclose material information during prosecution of an application).

10. Under 37 C.F.R. § 1.56 (2005), every person substantively involved in the prosecution of an application has a duty to disclose to the examiner all information which is material to the patentability of a claim. *See generally* Lisa Dolak, *The Inequitable Conduct Doctrine: Lessons from Recent Cases*, 84 J. PAT. & TRADEMARK OFF. SOC'Y 719 (2002) (examining recent inequitable conduct cases).

11. *Id.*

12. 37 C.F.R. § 1.56 requires disclosure of all information "material" to the patentability of a claim. *See generally* Lynn C. Tyler, *Kingsdown Fifteen Years Later: What Does It Take to Prove Inequitable Conduct?*, 13 FED. CIR. B.J. 267 (2004) (describing nature of the duty of disclosure which attorneys owe to the PTO).

13. Specifically, the PTO, when adopting the PTO Code, responded to comments and observed that the duty of candor could conflict with state law confidentiality law by requiring lawyers to disclose information to the PTO over their clients' objections and even after being terminated by the client by emphasizing that the duty of candor required disclosure—even over the client's objections. 50 Fed. Reg. 5158-01, 5165 (Feb. 6, 1985). Consistent with those statements, the PTO Code repeatedly requires disclosure of information to comply with the duty of candor and makes *no exception* based on the source of that information: Section 10.85(a)(3) of the PTO Code prohibits him from failing to disclose information he is required by law to disclose; section 1.56 requires him to disclose material information;

The USPTO made its position clear: Federal law[14] requires disclosure, and that obligation overrides both state law and a client's specific instruction not to do so, and even termination of the representation. Therefore, the express language of the PTO Code,[15] as well as the USPTO's comments when it adopted that language, requires disclosure.[16]

The state's law could prohibit disclosure of information that the USPTO requires be disclosed, either because state law provides that the client's statement terminates authority of the practitioner to act, or that state law requires the information be maintained in confidence absent a state law exception. The critical question thus becomes one of preemption. Some commentators say state law applies during prosecution, and so a lawyer cannot disclose information when required by the PTO Code but prohibited by state rules. For several reasons, the better view is that state law does not apply, and that any effort by a state to apply its law to the question of compliance with the duty of candor in a manner that is inconsistent with the PTO Code should fail.

First, applying state law—particularly state rules governing confidentiality—would clearly interfere with the federal objectives of the USPTO.[17] Specifically, if state law is applied, then in most states virtually

---

section 10.23(c)(1) prohibits him from committing or causing to be committed inequitable conduct; and, section 10.40(b)(2) requires him to withdraw if the "continued employment will result in violation of a Disciplinary Rule." There is no doubt—none—that an attorney cannot withhold even "confidential" material information of the same client whose application is being prosecuted. *See* Phila. Bar Ass'n. Prof. Guidance Comm., Op 96-12 (1996) (holding that state rules do not apply, and advising that "the Inquirer ascertain his obligations under the PTO's rules and act accordingly"). However, a few commentators have stated that the PTO Code "does not include an exception for disclosures required under Rule 56." Rose & Jessup, *supra*, at 319.

14. The PTO Code is a form of federal regulation. As such, it is treated for preemption purposes for the most part just as is a federal statute. *See* David Hricik et al., *Save a Little Room for Me: The Necessity of Naming As Inventors Practitioners Who Conceive of Claimed Subject Matter*, 55 Mercer L. Rev. 635, 662 (2004) (discussing preemptive impact of federal regulations).

15. *See* Bradley William Baumeister, *Critique of the New Rule 1.99: Third-Party Information Disclosure Procedure for Published Pre-Grant Applications*, 83 J. Pat. Off. Soc'y 381, 403 (2001) (explaining various provisions of the PTO Code and federal law requiring disclosure of material information); *supra* (discussing 37 C.F.R. § 10.85(a)(3) (2005)).

16. 50 Fed. Reg. 5158-01, 5165.

17. The phrase "federal objectives" was adopted from the Supreme Court's decision in *Sperry v. Florida ex rel. Florida Bar*, 373 U.S. 379, 402 (1963), which held that a state could not impose additional licensing requirements on a person who was authorized by the PTO to prosecute patents. The *Sperry* Court held those licensing requirements were preempted because they imposed "upon the performance of activity sanctioned by federal license additional conditions not contemplated by Congress." 373 U.S. at 385. Additional light on the meaning of the preemption provision is shed by the PTO's actions in adopting the PTO Code. In response to a comment stating that the term "federal objectives" was vague, the PTO stated that "[t]hat the federal objectives of the PTO center around" numerous *inter partes* proceedings including

all information related to a representation could not be disclosed to the USPTO absent client consent.[18] The duty of candor would almost completely be eliminated if state law governing confidentiality were applied.

Second, the USPTO, in adopting the current PTO Code, repeatedly rejected the suggestion that state law would apply during prosecution. The USPTO, in response to comments, repeatedly emphasized that the PTO Code "shall not be construed to preempt the authority of any State to maintain control over the practice of law within its borders"—except as necessary for the USPTO to achieve its federal objectives.[19] The USPTO also emphasized that "the rules of the various State bars do not govern proceedings before the USPTO."[20] The USPTO emphasized its view of supremacy because "the decisions made by the USPTO in patent and trademark cases"—unlike other matters—"affect the public interest."[21] The USPTO believed that the "standards for federal conduct and the evidence used to prove or defend against allegations of misconduct involving federal matters should be uniform throughout the United States."[22] Thus, application of state laws to matters at the heart of patent prosecution—at the core of the federal objectives of the USPTO—should be preempted if application of those laws would frustrate the USPTO's achievement of those objectives.

Applying state rules or law to patent prosecution would frustrate those objections. Specifically, using state rules would mean that whether a patent is unenforceable under section 282 of the Patent Act[23] would turn on state law—not federal patent law. States lack authority to define when a patent should be enforced;[24] allowing them to define when material information can be withheld would not only accomplish the same impermissible purpose,

---

"engag[ing] in examination of applications for patents [and] reexamination of issued patents." 50 Fed. Reg. at 5161.

18. *See* MODEL RULES 1.6, 4.4(b) (requiring that any information relating to the representation of a client be kept in confidence, with limited permissive exceptions and few mandatory ones). *See generally* Susan R. Martyn, *In Defense of Client-Lawyer Confidentiality . . . and Its Exceptions . . .* , 81 NEB. L. REV. 1320 (concisely reviewing the scope of the duty of confidentiality and its exceptions under the Model Rules).

19. 49 Fed. Reg. 33790–01 (proposed Aug. 24 1984) (to be codified at 37 C.F.R. pts. 1, 2, and 10); *id.* at 33792 ("only conduct which is relevant to the practice of patent, trademark or other law before the PTO is what the PTO seeks to regulate."); *see also* 49 Fed. Reg. 33790–01, 33795 (proposed Aug. 24 1984) (to be codified at 37 C.F.R. pts. 1, 2, and 10) (explaining that the PTO was not adopting certain other standards and so they did not apply).

20. 49 Fed. Reg. at 33796.

21. 49 Fed. Reg. 10012-01, 10017 (proposed Mar. 16, 1984) (to be codified at 37 C.F.R. pts. 1, 2, and 10).

22. 49 Fed. Reg. at 33801.

23. 35 U.S.C. § 282 (2005).

24. *Cf. Dow Chem. Co. v. Exxon Corp.*, 139 F.3d 1470, 1473–74 (Fed. Cir. 1998) (state courts are not preempted from allowing proof of enforcement of a patent obtained through inequitable conduct as an element in a state tort claim).

it would allow states to define when patents are *enforceable* despite the withholding of information that federal regulations and federal case law requires to be disclosed to the USPTO.[25] This obviously is not correct.[26]

Third, the express terms of the duty in section 1.56 of the PTO Code do not end on termination of a lawyer's representation by a client.[27] Instead, as shown above, it continues until the USPTO allows for withdrawal.[28] Application of state law to this question would result in patents being held enforceable—or not—depending on whether *state law* authorized the patent practitioner to act. The enforceability of a patent would, consequently, turn on state law.

The disagreement on "what" appears to be a fairly straightforward application of the preemption issue should give practitioners pause in relying solely on the PTO Code. Even if conduct is held to be subject only to the PTO Code, the costs of litigating the issue could be substantial. In addition, the preemption provision implicitly recognizes that not every aspect of conduct governed by the PTO Code will be governed only by the PTO Code: Preeemption occurs only when necessary for the USPTO to achieve its federal objectives. Thus, even where a lawyer concludes that the USPTO standard permits the conduct, the lawyer may want to determine whether state law imposes a more stringent standard, and follow it.[29]

---

25. Currently, the PTO regulations in 37 C.F.R. § 1.56 impose a narrower duty of disclosure to avoid discipline than federal substantive law to avoid unenforceability. *See* David Hricik, *Where the Bodies Are: Current Exemplars of Inequitable Conduct and How to Avoid Them,* 12 Tex. Intell. Prop. L.J. 287, 291–94 (2004) (concluding that the PTO's regulations cannot affect whether a patent is enforceable).

26. The fact that state law claims can be brought against a patentee who committed inequitable conduct in obtaining a patent is not to the contrary. *E.g., Dow Chem. Co.,* 139 F.3d at 1473–74. Nor is the fact that state courts may at times have jurisdiction to adjudicate such claims. *E.g.,* Consol. Kinetics Corp. v. Marshall, Neil & Pauley, Inc., 521 P.2d 1209, 1212 (Wash. Ct. App. 1974). In both circumstances, the court deciding the state law claim would still "be required to make its inequitable conduct determination in accordance with federal law." *Dow Chem. Co.,* 139 F.3d at 1476 n.4. Preemption bars allowing a state law claim to proceed without anything other than a showing of "inequitable conduct," as determined by federal law. *See id.* at 1477 (discussing *Abbott Labs. v. Brennan,* 952 F.2d 1346, 1357 (Fed. Cir. 1991)).

27. Clients have, however, attempted to prevent disclosure by revoking the attorney's power of attorney. *See generally Semiconductor Energy Lab. Co. v. Samsung Elec. Co.,* 4 F. Supp. 2d 477, 488 (E.D. Va. 1998) (noting without addressing the issue that the client had revoked attorney's power of representation after attorney stated his intent to disclose information to the PTO).

28. 37 C.F.R. § 1.56 (2005).

29. This is not always the solution, however. For example, a lawyer must withdraw when he or she is faced with a conflict of interest. But, if a lawyer relies on the "more stringent" state law standard in determining whether a conflict exists and seeks to withdraw even though withdrawal is not required under the PTO Code, that act could be argued to breach a fiduciary

For these reasons, state law has some, albeit limited, applicability during patent prosecution, and lawyers must engage in a preemption analysis after identifying the applicable USPTO standard. They may, for practical reasons, choose to follow the more stringent of the potentially applicable standards.[30] But identifying the more stringent standard with respect to whether a conflict of interest exists or the duty of candor prevails over state confidentiality laws turns on perspective: Is it measured from the perspective of the client whose loyalty obligation the lawyer protects by withdrawing by following the more stringent definition of loyalty, or is it measured from the perspective of the client who is "dropped" when it was not required by the "less stringent rule?" The dropped client could contend the lawyer has adopted the less stringent definition of loyalty by withdrawing when he or she was not ethically required to do so. Similarly, is "more stringent" measured from the perspective of the client whose confidentiality obligation the lawyer protects by not disclosing information under the more stringent state law rules, or from the point of view of the USPTO, which is denied access to material information? Following the "more stringent rule approach" is not as simple as it seems. Lawyers who abjure that approach and instead conduct a preemption analysis could still be sued and be left to litigate the question of whether their preemption analysis was correct.[31]

---

duty to the client who the lawyer stops representing. Following "the more stringent standard" may not always be the simple solution it appears to be.

30. An interesting question is whether state law could be applied to the question of whether representation of two clients during patent prosecution is unethical. It is clear that, as noted above, the PTO will apply the PTO Code to determine whether a conflict exists in *inter partes* proceedings. The PTO has stated that during *inter partes* proceedings, state codes are "not applicable in the PTO." *Anderson v. Eppstein*, 2001 Pat. App. LEXIS 1 (Bd. App. & Interf. 2001). In our view, state law should not apply to the question of whether a lawyer can properly represent a client in such a proceeding, because otherwise the PTO would be required to apply state standards to disqualification proceedings in the PTO. The need for uniformity is clear.

   Suppose, however, that a lawyer prosecutes an application for one client that, ostensibly, interferes with another but for whatever reason no interference is declared in the PTO. Should the question of whether a conflict exists turn on state law? We believe not, as that would make the question of whether a lawyer can ethically represent clients in patent prosecution turn, not on ethics, but on the happenstance of whether an interference proceeding is declared. It would be incongruous for state rules not to apply during *inter partes* interference PTO proceedings but yet apply to the question of whether a conflict of interest exists between patent clients where, by happenstance, an interference is not declared.

31. What obviously needs to occur is for the PTO to have clearer rules on when its rules apply to the exclusion of state law. The PTO may be making an attempt to do so in its proposed new disciplinary rules. *See, e.g.,* Proposed PTO Rule 11.805(b)(1) (stating that the PTO's rules apply to conduct "in connection with practice before the Office").

2. First Principles of Inequitable Conduct

Every person substantively involved in patent prosecution owes a duty of good faith to the examiner.[32] That duty is often called "the duty of candor." A breach of the duty has several consequences. A breach of the duty of candor constitutes a violation of applicable ethical rules.[33] More pertinent here, a breach of the duty of candor serves as a foundation for inequitable conduct, which is an equitable defense to patent infringement.[34] Both consequences can, of course, lead to a malpractice claim against the practitioner.

Although often referred to as "fraud on the Patent Office," in fact "inequitable conduct" is not fraud.[35] Among other things, reliance is not an element.[36] Instead, the elements of the defense of inequitable conduct are settled.[37] It requires proof by clear and convincing evidence of (1) either an affirmative misrepresentation, or an omission of (2) material information (3) coupled with intent to deceive.[38] If both materiality and intent are established, the

---

32. 37 C.F.R. § 1.56.

33. *E.g.*, 37 C.F.R. § 10.23(c)(10) (2003). Despite continuing to be a violation of governing federal regulations, in the late 1980s the PTO announced that it would no longer investigate whether applicants had attempted to deceive it. The office stated that it was doing so in light of the fact that the Federal Circuit—apparently in *Kingsdown Medical Consultants, Ltd. v. Hollister, Inc.*, 863 F.2d 867, 9 U.S.P.Q.2d (BNA) 1384 (Fed. Cir. 1988)—had imposed "a high level of proof of intent to mislead." PTO Notice Regarding Implementation of 37 C.F.R. § 1.56, 1095 Off. Gaz. Pat. & Trademark Office 16 (Sept. 8, 1988). *See generally* Donald S. Chisum, 4 Chisum on Patents § 11.03[4][b][iv] (1996); soon after making this announcement, the PTO formalized its decision to discontinue investigating allegations of inequitable conduct, except in the most egregious and clear cases, such as when a court has made a final decision that inequitable conduct has occurred. Dept. of Commerce, Notice of Proposed Rulemaking, Duty of Disclosure, 56 Fed. Reg. 37321, 37323 (Aug. 6, 1991).

34. 35 U.S.C. § 282(1) (2003); *Critikon Inc. v. Becton Dickinson Vascular Access Inc.*, 120 F.3d 1253, 1255, 43 U.S.P.Q.2d (BNA) 1666, 1668 (Fed. Cir. 1997); *J. P. Stevens & Co. v. Lex Tex Ltd.*, 747 F.2d 1553, 1560–61, 223 U.S.P.Q. (BNA) 1089, 1092–94 (Fed. Cir. 1984) (holding that inequitable conduct "fits best" within § 282(1) as a ground for unenforceability).

35. *See* David Hricik, *Wrong About Everything: The Application by the District Courts of Rule 9(b) to Inequitable Conduct*, 86 Marq. L. Rev. 895, 912–16 (2003) (discussing Federal Circuit decisions holding that inequitable conduct is not "fraud").

36. *See id.*

37. *But compare Brasseler, U.S.A. I, L.P. v. Stryker Sales Corp.*, 267 F.3d 1370, 1381 60 U.S.P.Q.2d (BNA) 1482, 1488 (Fed. Cir. 2001) (reasoning that *Kingsdown* requires a finding of intent to deceive) *with* Charles M. McMahon, *Intent to Commit Fraud on the U.S.P.T.O.: Is Mere Negligence Once Again Inequitable?* 27 Am. Intell. Prop. L. Ass'n. Q. J. 49 (1999) (questioning whether negligence is still relevant).

38. *See* Lisa A. Dolak, *As If You Didn't Have Enough to Worry About: Current Ethics Issues for Intellectual Property Practitioners*, 82 J. Pat. & Trademark Off. Soc'y 235, 237–38 (Apr. 2000).

judge must decide, through "equitable balancing," whether the conduct was so culpable that the patent should be held unenforceable.[39]

If the judge concludes the patent is unenforceable, the effect is not on a claim-by-claim basis, as it is with validity, but instead means that the affected patent is unenforceable in its entirety. Even if the inequitable conduct only pertained to one claim of a patent (most have more than one),[40] every claim in the patent is unenforceable.[41] Indeed, it is possible that inequitable conduct during the prosecution of one application can cause patents that issue on different, but related, applications to be held unenforceable.[42]

The following section analyzes the elements of inequitable conduct to expose how recent case law has once again expanded the doctrine.

3. Materiality Is Not Limited to the Circumstances Specified in Rule 1.56

The standard for determining whether information was "material" has changed over the years.[43] Prior to 1992, Rule 1.56 required applicants to submit information if there was "a substantial likelihood that a reasonable examiner

---

39. *Id.* at 238. Although a district court can submit the ultimate question of equitable balancing to the jury, *Hebert v. Lisle Corp.,* 99 F.3d 1109, 1114, 40 U.S.P.Q.2d (BNA) 1611, 1614 (Fed. Cir. 1996), whether the judge can allow the jury to make a binding determination of equitable balancing appears to be an open question. *Juicy Whip, Inc. v. Orange Bang, Inc.,* 292 F.3d 728, 746 n.3, 63 U.S.P.Q.2d (BNA) 1251, 1263 n.3 (Fed. Cir. 2002) ("In light of our disposition on the inequitable conduct issue, we do not reach Juicy Whip's contention that the district court erred by making the jury finding binding upon the parties."). In contrast, if the jury decides a factual question that is intertwined with inequitable conduct—such as, for example, the fact that a prior art reference anticipates a claim—that fact finding would be binding in determining the materiality of the anticipatory reference, and so the jury's determination must come first and controls. *See Cabinet Vision v. Cabnetware,* 129 F.3d 595, 600–01, 44 U.S.P.Q.2d (BNA) 1683, 1686–67 (Fed. Cir. 1997) (Seventh Amendment precludes holding jury's findings on question of fact common to legal and equitable issues as merely advisory).

40. *See* David Hricik, Aerial *Boundaries: The Duty of Candor as a Limitation on the Duty of Patent Practitioners to Advocate for Maximum Patent Coverage,* 44 So. Tex. L. Rev. 205, 227 (2002).

41. *Kingsdown,* 863 F.2d at 877, 9 U.S.P.Q.2d at 1392.

42. *E.g., Consolidated Aluminum Corp. v. Foseco Int'l Ltd.,* 910 F.2d 804, 809, 15 U.S.P.Q.2d (BNA) 1481, 1487 (Fed. Cir. 1990); *see also Monsanto Co. v. Bayer Bioscience N.V.,* 514 F.3d 1229, 85 U.S.P.Q.2d 1582 (Fed. Cir. 2008).

43. *See Dayco Prods., Inc. v. Total Containment, Inc.,* 329 F.3d 1358, 1364, 66 U.S.P.Q.2d (BNA) 1801, 1806 (Fed. Cir. 2003) (describing some of the varying standards applied by both the USPTO and the courts).

would have considered th[e] information important in deciding whether to issue as a patent."[44]

Responding to criticism concerning lack of certainty as to this standard of materiality, the USPTO amended the rule in 1992. As amended, Rule 1.56 requires "[e]ach individual associated with the filing and prosecution of a patent application . . . to disclose to the Office all information known to that individual to be material to patentability as defined in this section."[45] The significant change is "as defined in this section." Rule 1.56 goes on to provide that information is "material" only if it is not cumulative and:

(1) It establishes, by itself or in combination with other information, a prima facie case of unpatentability of a claim; or
(2) It refutes, or is inconsistent with, a position the applicant takes in:
  (i) Opposing an argument of unpatentability relied on by the Office, or
  (ii) Asserting an argument of patentability. A prima facie case of unpatent-ability is established when the information compels a conclusion that a claim is unpatentable under the preponderance of evidence, burden-of-proof standard, giving each term in the claim its broadest reasonable construction consistent with the specification, and before any consideration is given to evidence which may be submitted in an attempt to establish a contrary conclu-sion of patentability.[46]

Many saw the USPTO's restriction of the definition of "materiality" as a contraction of the inequitable conduct doctrine. For a time, the Federal Circuit postponed deciding whether information that is not "material" under amended Rule 1.56 can nonetheless be "material" for purposes of determin-ing inequitable conduct.[47]

However, the Federal Circuit has indicated that the narrow standard of materiality in Rule 1.56 does not control in determining whether information is material for purposes of finding a patent unenforceable. Instead, it has rea-soned that information covered by Rule 1.56 is presumptively material; but simply because it is not covered by Rule 1.56 does not preclude it from being

---

44. *Molins PLC v. Textron, Inc.,* 48 F.3d 1172, 1179 n.8, 33 U.S.P.Q.2d (BNA) 1823, 1827 n.8 (Fed. Cir. 1995).
45. 37 C.F.R. § 1.56(a). The USPTO clearly views this duty to disclose material information as part of a broader duty of candor, because the amended rule states that the duty of candor "includes" this duty to disclose material information.
46. 37 C.F.R. § 1.56(b).
47. *Dayco Prods., Inc. v. Total Containment, Inc.,* 329 F.3d 1358, 1363–64, 66 U.S.P.Q.2d (BNA) 1801, 1805–06 (Fed. Cir. 2003) (recognizing that whether the amended rule applies in ineq-uitable conduct matters is an open question). *See generally Dolak, supra* note 12, 82 J. PAT. & TRADEMARK OFF. SOC'Y at 239–40 (discussing the question of whether "old" Rule 56 standards of materiality continues to be applicable); *see also* Margaret A. Boulware & Tamsen Valoir, *Inequitable Conduct,* 619 PLI/PAT 1245, 1249 (Oct. 2000).

material under the "reasonable examiner" standard that controls in determining unenforceability of a patent.[48]

We believe the Federal Circuit's decision is correct, at least with respect to unenforceability (but not discipline). For the reasons that follow, although the Office of Enrollment and Discipline (OED) could not *discipline* a practitioner for conduct that constitutes inequitable conduct, but which does not violate Rule 1.56,[49] the Federal Circuit's conclusion that a patent can be *unenforceable* even if the information that is withheld is outside the scope of Rule 1.56 is correct.

First, there is the matter of *supremacy*. The defense of unenforceability is expressly authorized by statute.[50] The USPTO cannot by federal regulation affect the substance of the statutory defense of unenforceability.[51] Second, when in 1992 the USPTO adopted the narrower standard, it expressly disclaimed any intent to modify the standard that applies to inequitable conduct. Specifically, in promulgating its 1992 version of Rule 1.56, the USPTO stated that its amended rule did "not define fraud or inequitable conduct which have elements both of materiality and intent."[52] Although cryptic, this comment suggests that the USPTO recognized that it lacked power to affect inequitable conduct, and clearly that it did not intend to do so.[53]

For these reasons, compliance with the narrower definition of materiality in amended Rule 1.56 does not put the practitioner (or applicant) in a safe harbor with respect to unenforceability. That is, even if amended, Rule 1.56 does not require disclosure of a particular piece of information, and so the practitioner cannot be disciplined; the failure to disclose that information nonetheless can still constitute inequitable conduct and render the patent unenforceable.

---

48. *Monsanto Co. v. Bayer Bioscience N.V.*, 514 F.3d 1229, 1237 & n.10 (Fed. Cir. 2008).

49. Obviously, the OED's ability to discipline requires proof of violation of a provision of the PTO Code. Thus, engaging in conduct that results in unenforceability, as such, does not violate the PTO Code.

50. 35 U.S.C. § 282(1) (2000) (stating that unenforceability "shall be" a defense to infringement).

51. For similar reasons, those who contend that information that is material can, nonetheless be withheld from the USPTO if it is "confidential" in terms of the USPTO's code of ethics—let alone state law—are incorrect. *See* Simone Rose & Debra Jessup, *Whose Rules Rule? Resolving Ethical Conflicts During the Simultaneous Representation of Clients in Patent Prosecution*, 12 FED. CIR. B.J. 571 (2003) (contending that if information is confidential under state law, it cannot be disclosed to the USPTO).

52. 57 Fed. Reg. 2021, 2024 (Jan. 17, 1992). *See id.* at 2025. (explaining that "there is a duty of candor and good faith which is broader than the duty to disclose material information").

53. *Cf. Dayco Prods.*, 329 F.3d at 1364, 66 U.S.P.Q.2d at 1805 ("the extent, if any, to which the Patent Office rulemaking was intended to provide guidance to the courts concerning the duty of disclosure in the context of inequitable conduct determinations is not clear").

The proposed Information Disclosure Statement Rules that issued July 10, 2006, threaten to augment this dichotomy further still by placing a limit on the number of references that can be submitted absent a statement distinguishing the reference over the claimed invention.[54] Although these remain proposed rules, there is an expectation that final rules might yet be instituted sometime in 2009.

As a consequence, using Rule 1.56 as a checklist—and assuming that if the information is not covered by it that the information cannot be "material"—is unwise. Accordingly, information that is material to patentability, whether covered by the list of information deemed to be material in amended Rule 1.56 or not, should be disclosed.[55] The consequence of applying the broader standard is that practitioners prosecuting patents must refer to the law of inequitable conduct and not to Rule 1.56 to determine materiality. That result arguably allows the inequitable conduct tail to wave the duty of candor dog because only a tiny fraction of issued patents are actually litigated.[56] Nonetheless, it is correct because only Congress, not the courts or the USPTO, has the authority to narrow the scope of "unenforceability."

Finally—no matter which definition applies—the concept of materiality is broader than, and so requires disclosure of, more than just "patent-defeating" information. Applicants are required to disclose information to the USPTO even though the information would not, by itself, require rejection of a claim.[57]

---

54. Changes to Information Disclosure Statement Requirements and Other Related Matters, 71 Fed. Reg. 38808.
55. *See also Trinity Indus., Inc. v. Road Sys., Inc.*, 235 F. Supp. 2d 536 (E.D. Tex. 2002) (holding that even the failure to disclose statutorily mandated information may not be "material").
56. R. Polk Wagner, *Reconsidering Estoppel: Patent Administration and the Failure of Festo*, 151 U. PA. L. REV. 159, 191 (2002) (concluding only .03% of patents are litigated).
57. *Norton v. Curtiss*, 433 F.2d 779, 795, 167 U.S.P.Q. 532, 545 (C.C.P.A. 1970). The court recognized that requiring disclosure only of facts that would in and of themselves require rejection of the pending claims, or invalidate them after issuance, was too narrow:

> Findings of materiality should not be limited only to those situations where there can be no dispute that the true facts, or the complete facts, if they had been known, would most likely have prevented the allowance of the particular claims at issue or alternatively, would provide a basis for holding those claims invalid. In such cases, the claims at issue would probably be invalid, in any event, because of the *existence* of those facts, *in and of themselves.* Whether the claims would also be unenforceable because a fraud was committed in misrepresenting the facts to the Patent Office would really be of secondary importance. *Id.*

Consequently, the *Norton* court held that information could be "material" even if it would not have, from an objective perspective, directly affected patentability of the claims at issue. *Id.* Instead, the court held that the subjective views of the examiner and applicant must be considered, and that if the court determines that "the claims would *not* have been allowed

B. Knowledge of the Information Is Not Necessarily Required: The Duty to Investigate May Exist, but Imputation Should Not Apply

Negligence principles may apply in determining whether a person involved in prosecution, who did not actually know of material information, nonetheless should be treated as if he or she did. Normally, it is black letter law that only information "known" by a person involved in prosecution must be disclosed.[58] For good reason, the notion that practitioners or their clients can be charged with knowledge that they "should have known" has been, with one exception, rejected by the Federal Circuit.[59]

In a remarkable case where the attorney was told to file the application within three days because of an approaching 102(b) critical date, the Federal Circuit held that a duty to investigate exists, and that an attorney can be charged with knowledge of facts he or she does not know for purposes of inequitable conduct. The court began its discussion with a passage that rejects the idea of imputed knowledge:

> [A] duty to investigate does not arise where there is no notice of the existence of material information. The mere possibility that material information may exist

---

but for the misrepresentation, then the facts were material regardless of their effect on the objective question of patentability." *Id.*

The broader standard of looking at whether a reasonable examiner would have considered the information material—as opposed to whether, in light of the information the claims are patentable from an objective view point—serves several purposes. The *Norton* court emphasized that it served to give "real meaning" to the "relationship of confidence and trust between applicants and the Patent Office." *Id.* In addition, it reduces search costs, which is particularly important because, as government employees, examiners have a limited amount of time to spend on each application. Requiring applicants to submit only information that they know would result in denial of their claims would thus require examiners to spend more time on each application.

It bears noting that later developments have made the *Norton* court's statement that an applicant's withholding of art that invalidates a claim only of secondary importance incorrect. As shown more fully below, inequitable conduct with respect to one claim renders the entire patent—all other claims, not just the one claim—unenforceable and could lead to unenforceability of related applications. In contrast, invalidity is generally determined on a claim-by-claim basis. *See Connell v. Sears, Roebuck Co.*, 722 F.2d. 1542, 1552, 220 U.S.P.Q. (BNA) 193, 201 (Fed. Cir. 1983) (holding that the validity of each claim must be determined separately). As a result of these differing consequences, an applicant who establishes that a claim is invalid invalidates only that claim; whereas an accused infringer who proves that a patentee intentionally withheld prior art that would have invalidated a claim, renders the entire patent and perhaps other patents—wholly unenforceable.

58. *See* 34 C.F.R. § 1.56.
59. Cases holding that "should have known" of the existence of the information is not the standard are legion. *E.g., Nordberg, Inc. v. Telsmith, Inc.*, 82 F.3d 394, 397, 38 U.S.P.Q.2d 1593, 1595–96 (Fed. Cir. 1996) (failure to disclose can only be shown if the applicant knew of the information).

will not suffice to give rise to a duty to inquire; sufficient information must be presented to the attorney to suggest the existence of specific information the materiality of which may be ascertained with reasonable inquiry. Indeed, a finding of deceptive intent may not be based solely on gross negligence, including instances in which the patent attorney is completely unaware of the existence of specific information later discovered and found to be material.[60]

However, the court then held that such a duty to investigate does arise, and it noted that it could do so under two circumstances. First, relying on *Black's Law Dictionary*, the court stated:

> There is no need for an attorney to pursue a fishing expedition to obtain information. Counsel can reasonably rely on information provided by the client, unless, as here, there is reason to question the accuracy or completeness of the information or to doubt the adequacy of the client's own investigation into material facts. Thus, no duty to inquire arises unless counsel is on notice of the likelihood that specific, relevant, material information exists and should be disclosed. Here, Price and Brody were aware that sales of the invention had been made approximately one year before the filing of the application and, in light of the questionable information given to them by "someone at Brasseler," they had a duty to investigate.
>
> Implied notice of a fact is defined in Black's Law Dictionary, as "[n]otice that is inferred from facts that a person had a means of knowing and that is thus imputed to that person; actual notice of facts or circumstances that, if properly followed up, would have led to a knowledge of the particular fact in question." Thus, notice of a possibly material event—a sale, public use, publication, issuance of a patent, occurring on or about one year before the application is filed—arises when information of which the attorney is aware suggests the existence of specific information that may be material.[61]

In addition to "implied notice," the court invoked the willful blindness doctrine, and stating that "one should not be able to cultivate ignorance,

---

60. 267 F.3d at 1383 (citations omitted).
61. 267 F.3d at 1384 (citations omitted). The court went on to discuss and harmonize earlier decisions:

> In *Hennessy*, we warned that "one should not be able to cultivate ignorance, or disregard numerous warnings that material information or prior art may exist, merely to avoid actual knowledge of that information or prior art." Where one does, deceptive intent may be inferred. Once an attorney, or an applicant, has notice that information exists that appears material and questionable, that person cannot ignore that notice in an effort to avoid his or her duty to disclose. Similarly, in *Paragon Podiatry Laboratory, Inc. v. KLM Laboratories, Inc.*, 984 F.2d 1182, 25 U.S.P.Q.2d (BNA) 1561 (Fed. Cir. 1993), we explained that absent credible evidence of good faith, evidence of a knowing failure to disclose sales that "bear all the earmarks of commercialization reasonably supports an inference that the inventor's attorney intended to mislead the PTO.

Id.

or disregard numerous warnings that material information or prior art may exist, merely to avoid actual knowledge of that information or prior art."[62]

Thus, under at least these two circumstances, practitioners are imputed with knowledge of facts that they knew should have existed. Whether they "should have" known them is inherently a negligence concept.[63]

Although controlling, the *Brasseler* panel clearly misapprehended the case law it relied on in reaching its conclusion. Foremost, the cases that the court relied on for finding that facts known to a client were "chargeable" to the patent attorney have nothing to do with that proposition of law. What those cases hold is that inequitable conduct by a practitioner is chargeable to a client; that is simply another way of saying that the duty of the practitioner to comply with the duty of candor is independent of the client's, and vice versa. It says nothing about the propriety of imputing knowledge for determining inequitable conduct. In our view, doing so is incorrect.

Although some inventors are more patent savvy than others, materiality of information (e.g., information that raises issues of written description, enablement, obviousness, and novelty) can be fact based or law based, and thus require a patent practitioner to provide guidance through the perceived materiality maze. Imputation of knowledge from practitioners or personnel to the practitioner prosecuting a case should not apply to determine inequitable conduct. Clearly, a person substantively involved in prosecuting a patent application who has "actual knowledge" of facts material to that application and who fails to disclose that information to the USPTO will result in the patent being held unenforceable. It is also clear, on the opposite end of the spectrum, that a person has no duty to investigate the prior art for material information, that is, proof of actual knowledge is required, rather than proof that the person could have or should have known the information. Thus, merely because one attorney in a firm knows a fact material to the prosecution of a patent application currently being prosecuted by another attorney in that firm is of no consequence to the enforceability of the resulting patent, even if the first attorney's knowledge makes it unethical for the firm to prosecute the application.

Unfortunately, principles of imputed knowledge have been applied to find inequitable conduct. Under this approach, knowledge of each attorney in a firm will be imputed to every other attorney in the firm, and a patent may be held unenforceable when the firm, but not the individual attorney who prosecuted the patent application, knew undisclosed material information.

---

62. *Id.* (citation and quotation omitted).
63. The key to properly reacting to a "red flag" indicating that specific material information exists is to ensure that those who are prosecuting applications understand that they cannot turn a blind eye to them. Repeated warnings cannot be ignored.

Cases have held that imputation is proper,[64] and commentators have likewise concluded that imputation is appropriate.[65]

For example, in *W.R. Grace & Co. v. Western U.S. Industries, Inc.,*[66] the Ninth Circuit affirmed the district court's finding that a patent is unenforceable, as a matter of law because of knowledge imputed among corporate employees. In *W.R. Grace,* Grace sought to overcome a rejection during prosecution of the patent at issue by submitting an affidavit showing that its design for car wheels had achieved commercial success. In the affidavit, the president of the relevant division, Mr. Merritt, swore that only minor advertising had been done for the particular design. Therefore, Grace argued, the commercial success of the design was caused by its merits, not advertising. The argument succeeded, and the patent was issued to Grace.

When Grace brought suit for patent infringement, the defendants responded that the affidavit was false because Grace had significantly advertised the design. Therefore, the defendants asserted that Grace's patent was unenforceable. The district court agreed, and the Ninth Circuit affirmed on appeal:

> Merritt admits he erred in the affidavit, but insists it was only because he personally misunderstood his subordinates' reports about the advertising. Grace thus argues that there was a jury question presented on scienter. It is important to remember, however, that the plaintiff and patent holder here is not Merritt, but a corporation, Grace. Under well established agency doctrines a corporate principal is considered to know what its agents discover concerning those matters in which the agents have the power to bind the principal. And even when an agent has no reason to know the falsity of the representations he or she makes, the principal is liable if it knows the falsity and has reason to know the agent would make the statement. Under these rules, Grace clearly must answer for intentional or reckless misrepresentation as a matter of law. The evidence was undisputed that some agent of Grace had to know about the corporation's

---

64. *See, e.g., Insultherm, Inc. v. Tank Insulation Int'l, Inc.,* 64 F.3d 671, 36 U.S.P.Q.2d (BNA) 1271 (Fed. Cir. 1995) (stating that inequitable conduct may be proven by "knowledge chargeable to the patentee," and examining whether the district court properly "imputed knowledge" to the inventor of facts that the inventor claimed ignorance of); *W.R. Grace & Co. v. Western U.S. Indus., Inc.,* 608 F.2d 1214, 1218–19, 203 U.S.P.Q. (BNA) 721, 725 (9th Cir. 1979) (relying on agency principles to find inequitable conduct because "some agent of " the corporation had to know that the statement in question was false); *Transitron Elec. Corp. v. Hughes Aircraft Co.,* 487 F. Supp. 885, 902, 205 U.S.P.Q. (BNA) 799, 813 (D. Mass. 1980) (imputing knowledge among corporate actors but finding no fraud).

65. *See* Restatement (Third) of Law Governing Lawyers § 40 reporters' note c & cmt. c (Proposed Final Draft No. 1 Mar. 29, 1996). The Restatement confuses the concept of imposing the consequences of an attorney's knowledge and acts on the client with imputing the attorney's knowledge to the client. *See id. (citing Argus Chem. Corp. v. Fibre Glass-Evercoat Co. Inc.,* 759 F.2d 10, 225 U.S.P.Q. (BNA) 1100 (Fed. Cir. 1985)).

66. 608 F.2d 1214, 203 U.S.P.Q. (BNA) 721 (9th Cir. 1979)

advertising for the wheels; thus, Grace must be said to have known it. And even if we assume that Merritt himself harbored no doubts about the truth of his affidavit . . . on this record the corporation, which knew the truth and had ample reason to know of Merritt's actions and statements, must be said as a matter of law to have known that the statements were false.[67]

Despite the holding of *W.R. Grace*, imputing knowledge to find inequitable conduct is inappropriate, which other courts have recognized.[68] Information known by one attorney in a firm should not be imputed to the client of another attorney in the same firm.[69] Further, as discussed below, the USPTO rules demonstrate that imputation is not appropriate to determine compliance with Rule 1.56, which strongly indicates that inequitable conduct should not be based on imputed knowledge.

Rule 1.56 provides that "[e]ach individual associated with the filing and prosecution of a patent application has a duty of candor and good faith in dealing with the [USPTO], which includes a duty to disclose to the [USPTO] all information known to that individual to be material to patentability as defined in this section." Significantly, Rule 1.56 defines "individuals associated with the filing or prosecution of a patent application" as:

(1) Each inventor named in the application;
(2) Each attorney or agent who prepares or prosecutes the application; and
(3) Every other person who is substantively involved in the preparation or prosecution of the application and who is associated with the inventor, with the assignee or with anyone to whom there is an obligation to assign the application.[70]

As with the Code of Federal Regulations (CFR), the Manual of Patent Examining Procedure (MPEP) does not extend the duty of disclosure to those

67. *Id.* at 1218.
68. *See, e.g., Litton Sys., Inc. v. Honeywell, Inc.*, No. CV.90–93 MRP, 1995 WL 366468 (C.D. Cal. Jan. 6, 1995) (finding intent to deceive because someone "at Litton knew about the article"), *rev'd*, 87 F.3d 1559, 1571 39 U.S.P.Q.2d (BNA) 1321, 1328 (Fed. Cir. 1996) ("relative to the issue of culpable intent, the record does not disclose that anyone involved in the prosecution at Litton knew of" the article) (emphasis added); *Haworth, Inc. v. Steelcase, Inc.*, 685 F. Supp. 1422, 1449–50, 8 U.S.P.Q.2d (BNA) 1001, 1022–23 (W.D. Mich. 1988) (refusing to impute knowledge among corporate employees and stating that inventors "had no duty to search their employees' files to discover information regarding prior art"); *Wycoff v. Motorola, Inc.*, 502 F. Supp. 77, 93, 209 U.S.P.Q. (BNA) 115, 129 (N.D. Ill. 1980) (stating in dictum that "only actual knowledge of an attorney or agent can be imputable to the client or principal")
69. Restatement (Second) of Agency § 275 cmt. b (1957) (where knowledge, as opposed to a reason to know, "is the important element in the transaction and the agent who has the knowledge is not one acting for the principal in the transaction, the principal is not affected by the fact that the agent has the knowledge").
70. 37 C.F.R. § 1.56.

who merely belong to an organization that employs: (1) the inventor, (2) the prosecuting attorney, or (3) every person substantively involved in prosecuting the patent. Instead, the MPEP emphasizes that the

> [W]ord "with" appears before "the assignee"and "anyone to whom there is an obligation to assign" to make clear that the duty applies only to individuals, not to organizations. For instance, the duty of disclosure would not apply to a corporation or institution as such. However, it would apply to individuals within the corporation or institution who were substantively involved in the preparation or prosecution of the application, and actions by such individuals may affect the rights of the corporation or institution.[71]

However, the fact that the *Brasseler* decision is unsupported does not matter much for patent practitioners left in its wake. The case is a clear expansion of inequitable conduct doctrine, although subsequent decisions by the Federal Circuit have narrowed the circumstances in which the "duty to investigate" becomes triggered.[72]

Nonetheless, the "duty to investigate" and the "willful blindness" doctrines persist. What this means for practitioners is a need for vigilance, especially in expansive application families, with international prosecution and multiple law firms and lawyers involved on some cases. For example, when dealing with an overseas originating source of applications, frequently cases can be split up between U.S. firms and foreign firms. Thus, an ability to readily report to the different firms may be hampered or even prevented. A paragraph in a reporting letter sent to the foreign associate handling the case should state something as follows:

> In the event that there are related applications pending, please provide us with any references cited in those related applications. Likewise, please report all references cited by us and the PTO to the patent office in those respective applications.

We should note that when the USPTO provides references listed on a PTO-892 form (the analogous form to a practitioners PTO-1449 form), a recommendation is to send to the foreign associate handling related cases something along the lines of the following:

> Please note that the PTO has cited references in its Office Action and on a PTO-892 form. We recommend that the Office Action and its references may need to be reported to all jurisdictions having reporting requirements, such as

---

71. Manual of Patent Examining Procedure (MPEP) § 2001.01
72. *E.g., Flex-Rest, LLC v. Steelcase, Inc.,* 455 F.3d 1351, 1361–64 (Fed. Cir. 2006) (affirming district court's conclusion that facts did not warrant imposing a duty to investigate).

> Australia, Canada, and Israel. Additionally, if there is either a related U.S. application or a U.S. application with related subject matter that our firm is not handling, we recommend submitting copies of the art and this Office Action in those cases as well.

Although the U.S. practitioner is not likely to be registered in a foreign jurisdiction, the ultimate client may have corresponding applications pending in those jurisdictions. Addition of this statement is just one further reminder to all handling the portfolio of the issue of cross reporting.

Another aspect that can be relevant is the duty to investigate related applications. It is generally easier to keep track of cases when application families are prepared and prosecuted from beginning to end by a single practitioner. However, depending on the number of applications, there is frequently more than one law firm or lawyer involved in the prosecution of cases. When a single lawyer or firm is involved, the family trees are easily retained in memory or drawn out using software; it becomes more dodgy when dealing with more people and firms. This can be further complicated for practitioners handling applications of foreign origin. The ties of related applications may be less clear or unknown, especially when arriving from multiple foreign law firms. Hence, we recommend using something such as the paragraph above when the USPTO cites art.

With use of keywords and titles in the docketing database, it can be easier to determine related applications that a single attorney has, but other attorneys in the same firm are handling. When organizing docket numbering schemas, it is useful to have families tied together, noting divisional and continuation status in the docket number. If the docket number is completely unrelated to family status but only relates to the client (e.g., #####–###, wherein the last three digits are consecutively numbered for each new case from that client but not necessarily related to the case before or after it), it makes having the docketing software tying the application relationships together that much more important. However, if the relationship of the cases is not provided or maintained, then there is an increased risk that willful blindness could be asserted against the practitioners in a malpractice case, albeit incorrectly.

Advisably, once a relationship has been ascertained, having a drawing or listing of the related cases, or an information disclosure statement (IDS) checklist of related cases for reporting purposes in each of the identified cases can be useful to have in the file. That will serve as a visual reminder, instead of the duty to investigate and search on the docket software, where again the search is only as good as the key terms entered. Although the family tree drawing or IDS checklist are useful ideas, for malpractice purposes, it should be noted that these ideas do not appear to be an industry practice.

Finally, with regard to imputation, the concept should not apply across a firm. It is nonsensical. For example, in large general practice firms, the likelihood that an environmental lawyer would be aware of references between related applications for reporting purposes would be nil. Likewise, even within a patent department, the idea that an electrical patent attorney would know of references to cross report between related applications for a biotechnology patent attorney would likewise be nil. Geographical siloing between multiple offices in a firm can also result in one practitioner in city X not knowing what the other is doing in city Y. Siloing can also occur within a patent department between agents handling compound claims and an other gene therapy claims. For example, a junior attorney only handling antibody cases, would be unaware of small chemical compound cases and the relationship of its prior art to the antibody application.

In conclusion, although systems should be put in place especially when handling applications in known internationally filed portfolios, there are no industry-wide practices commonly used by all either for docket numbering, key words, and docket programs, intake searching, family portfolio tree representation, and the like. The question should remain of whether there was a willful disregard of all practices that represents gross negligence and not of imputation, willful blindness, or a duty to investigate. The latter perhaps representing a slippery slope of where that duty starts and stops.

C. Knowledge That the Information Is Material Is Not Necessarily Required

According to the Federal Circuit, negligence concepts come into play in determining whether a person substantively involved in prosecution knew of the materiality of the information. Whereas generally there must be proof that the person in fact knew that the information existed,[73] negligence principles, including whether the person "should have known" of the materiality of the information, are applied, and recently have been applied with greater frequency. As a district court recently explained, "to succeed on their failure to disclose allegation, defendants must show that the plaintiff had *knowledge* of the existence of prior art but need show only that the plaintiff *should have known* of that prior art's materiality."[74] The issue of whether a person "should

---

73. *Bruno Indep. Living Aids, Inc. v. Acorn Mobility Serv.*, Ltd., 277 F. Supp. 2d 965, 69 U.S.P.Q.2d 1229 (W.D. Wis. 2003) (discussing *Brasseler U.S.A. I.L.P. v. Stryker Sales Corp.*, 267 F.3d 1370, 1380, 60 U.S.P.Q.2d 1482 (Fed. Cir. 2001); *Nordberg v. Telsmith, Inc.*, 82 F.3d 394, 397, 38 U.S.P.Q.2d 1593 (Fed. Cir. 1996); and *Dayco Prods., Inc. v. Total Containment, Inc.*, 329 F.3d 1358, 1362, 66 U.S.P.Q.2d 1801 (Fed. Cir. 2003).

74. *Bruno Indep. Living Aids*, 277 F. Supp. 2d at 968–69. *See GFI, Inc.*, 265 F.3d at 1273–74.

have known" of the materiality of information obviously turns on negligence principles.

The Federal Circuit applied an even more unusual gloss on this issue when it applied what amounts to an almost strict liability standard in determining whether inventors committed inequitable conduct for failing to disclose an on-sale bar.[75] The court held that "knowledge of the law is chargeable to the inventor."[76] Thus, the clients were charged with knowing what constituted a "sale" under patent law, and that there was no exception for transfers between unrelated companies under a "joint development" exception.[77] The court held that the inventors could not "reasonably believe[]" otherwise.[78]

Thus, the standard for determining whether an inventor "should have known" of the materiality of information apparently is based upon a reasonable inventor standard to the extent that inventors are ostensibly charged with knowledge of the law. This, again, is an expansion of inequitable conduct law, allowing findings of inequitable conduct where a person knowledgeable in patent law knows of materiality, but the person subjectively involved in prosecution does not.

For practitioners, this means educating the inventors and corporations on the benefits of invention reports and providing the closest prior art known. Having invention reports in writing with an area wherein prior art can be listed should then be provided to the practitioner handling the case. That way those references can be later submitted in an IDS as well as helping the practitioner draft claims to the invention with a better understanding of the art. The inventors frequently have the best idea regarding what is known versus not known. However, some garage inventors may have no idea. With regard to the on-sale bar, this is an element that most inventors have no idea about. Although not as much of an issue in the pharmaceutical industry, this can be

---

75. *Brasseler, U.S.A. I, L.P. v. Stryker Sales Corp.,* 267 F.3d 1370, 1385, 60 U.S.P.Q.2d (BNA) 1482, 1491 (Fed. Cir. 2001).

76. *Id.,* quoting *Molins PLC v. Textron, Inc.,* 48 F.3d 1172, 1178, 33 U.S.P.Q.2d (BNA) 1823, 1826 (Fed. Cir. 1995) and *FMC Corp. v. Manitowac Co.,* 835 F.2d at 1415 n.8, 5 U.S.P.Q.2d at 1115 n.8 (Fed. Cir. 1987). Neither *Molins* nor *FMC* support the proposition that knowledge of the law is chargeable to applicants to determine whether an applicant knew of the materiality of the information. Instead, what each holds is that if a person substantively involved in prosecution of an application commits inequitable conduct, that person's misconduct is chargeable to the applicant, and thus the applicant's patent is unenforceable. *See Molins,* 48 F.3d at 1178, 33 U.S.P.Q.2d at 1826, *FMC Corp.,* 835 F.2d at 1415 n.8, 5 U.S.P.Q.2d at 1115 n.8. The *Brasseler* court's imputation of information from one person to another is, I believe, unprecedented in inequitable conduct law. *See* David Hricik, *The Risks and Responsibilities of Attorneys and Firms Prosecuting Patents for Different Clients in Related Technologies,* 8 TEX. INTELL. PROP. L.J. 331, 348–49 (2000) (concluding that imputation of knowledge for purposes of determining inequitable conduct is incorrect as a matter of law).

77. *Brasseler,* 267 F.3d at 1385, 60 U.S.P.Q.2d at 1492.

78. *Id.*

vexing with mechanical devices, where sales can more easily occur prior to the filing of a patent application. The question as to whether an invention has been sold and date of sale should be inquired about.

With regard to foreign-origin applications, actual access to the inventors becomes more difficult. Thus, reporting letters should always state clearly that material information known by anyone with familiarity to the case including foreign practitioners, inventors, and so on, should be provided and submitted to the USPTO.

Access to inventors, education of inventors, and persistence on these issues are the common features to be remembered by the practitioners.

D. Intent to Deceive May Be Inferred

Many believe that intent to deceive is the fundamental modern requirement of inequitable conduct, and indeed the Federal Circuit held en banc in *Kingsdown Med. Consultants, Ltd. v. Holister, Inc.,*[79] that inequitable conduct occurs only if there is proof of an intent to deceive the USPTO. The court stated:

> Some of our opinions have suggested that a finding of gross negligence compels a finding of intent to deceive. Others have indicated that gross negligence alone does not mandate a finding of intent to deceive.
>
> "Gross negligence" has been used as a label for various patterns of conduct. It is definable, however, only in terms of a particular act or acts viewed in light of all the circumstances. We adopt the view that a finding that particular conduct amounts to "gross negligence" does not of itself justify an inference of intent to deceive; the involved conduct, viewed in light of all the evidence, including evidence of good faith, must indicate sufficient culpability to require a finding of intent to deceive.[80]

Despite the clarity of these words, negligence concepts still enter into the determination of whether there has been proof of an intent to deceive. These nuances are important to practitioners.

First, because there will seldom be direct evidence of intent to deceive, courts examine the materiality of the information. The greater the materiality,

---

79. 863 F.2d 867, 9 U.S.P.Q.2d (BNA) 1384 (Fed. Cir. 1988). *See* Lynn C. Tyler, *Kingsdown Fifteen Years Later: What Does It Take To Prove Inequitable Conduct*, 13 Fed. Cir. B.J. 267 (2004).
80. *Id.* at 876, 9 U.S.P.Q.2d at 1392 (citations omitted).

the more likely it is that there will be a finding of intent to deceive.[81] Put simply, people do not bother to misrepresent information that would not affect patentability. Thus, if a highly material reference is withheld, a finding of intent to deceive is permissible. Negligence still matters. Even so, and despite the permissible use of inferences based on the materiality of the information, "intent to deceive can not be inferred *solely* from the fact that information was not disclosed; there must be a factual basis for a finding of deceptive intent."[82]

Second, in determining "intent to deceive, a court must weigh all the evidence, including evidence of good faith."[83] Often courts when faced with a misrepresentation or omission of material information will look to the applicant to come forward with a credible, good faith explanation that allows the court to find that the omission or misrepresentation was a mistake, not an intentional act.[84]

Thus, some factors perhaps relevant to the issue to be considered when making a determination of action constituting inequitable conduct include:

- Was more than one attorney handling the applications?
- Was more than one law firm handling related applications?
- If more than one law firm was handling the related applications, how was the client making sure that information could get cross reported?
- What procedures were in place to make sure the inventor provided information?
- What procedures were in place to make sure cross reporting of references could occur between applications?
- What kind of docket numbering system is used and were relationships between applications tracked with computer-generated reminders to report in related cases when a PTO-1449 or PTO-892 form appeared?
- Does the firm's or company's docketing system track all related applications?
- Is the docketing system electronically tied in to Patent Application Information Retrieval (PAIR) at the USPTO?

---

81. *Bristol-Myers Squibb Co. v. Rhone-Poulenc Rorer, Inc.*, 326 F.3d 1226, 1234, 66 U.S.P.Q.2d (BNA) 1481 (Fed. Cir. 2003) ("when balanced against high materiality, the showing of intent can be proportionally less"); *Abbott Labs. v. Torpharm, Inc.*, 300 F.3d 1367, 1380, 63 U.S.P.Q.2d (BNA) 1929, 1937 (Fed. Cir. 2002).
82. *Catalina Lighting, Inc. v. Lamps Plus, Inc.*, 295 F.3d 1277, 1289, 63 U.S.P.Q.2d (BNA) 1545 (Fed. Cir. 2002).
83. *GFI, Inc. v. Franklin Corp.*, 265 F.3d 1268, 1274 (Fed. Cir. 2001).
84. *Nilssen v. Osram Sylvania, Inc.*, 504 F.3d 1223, 1235 (Fed. Cir. 2007); *Ferring B.V. v. Aventis Pharm., Inc.*, 437 F.3d 1181, 1193 (Fed. Cir. 2006).

The more of the steps taken, the less likely gross negligence, let alone intent, can be adduced. However, it is unlikely that all the steps will be taken by any firm or company.

This section has shown that negligence concepts are still highly relevant to inequitable conduct, even though there must be a finding of intent to deceive. Because accused infringers usually prove intent by circumstantial evidence, this will cause them to scour the file wrapper for any misstatement, mischaracterization, or omission. Any steps that the practitioner can take to avoid creating evidence that can lead to an inference of deceptive intent are obviously steps well taken.[85] Evidence of good faith can be considered to negate the inference of deceptive intent.[86]

1. *Whose* Knowledge Counts?

Rule 1.56 is quite broad. Inarguably, each named inventor and each prosecuting practitioner is covered by Rule 1.56.[87] But, it is not so limited: *All* persons substantively involved in the merits of prosecuting an application, excluding clerical workers and the like, have a duty of disclosure.

Persons other than the named inventor and the prosecuting practitioner may not know that they are under an obligation of disclosure. Accordingly, the MPEP recommends that the practitioner ensure "that all of the individuals who are subject to the duty of disclosure . . . are informed of and fulfill their duty."[88] One way to do this is to distribute to each person who is

---

85. When faced with a particularly troublesome question, perhaps a prosecuting attorney should imagine him or herself on the stand three or four years later, with a jury or federal judge, listening intently to the lawyer's defense under cross-examination of his or her actions. A lawyer prosecuting an application, who faces a tough issue is then, and only then, in a position to affect the future. Many options open during the prosecution, such as amending the claims or apprising the examiner of new information, will not be available after issuance. As noted below, disclosure in close cases is often the answer, but too much disclosure can create its own problems. Patent prosecution takes care.

86. *See Dolak, supra* note 12, 82 J. Pat. Off. Soc'y at 242.

87. *See id.; see, e.g., Brasseler*, 267 F.3d at 1385-86. In pertinent part, Rule 1.56 provides:

   (c) Individuals associated with the filing or prosecution of a patent application within the meaning of this section are:

   (1) Each inventor named in the application;

   (2) Each attorney or agent who prepares or prosecutes the application; and

   (3) Every other person who is substantively involved in the preparation or prosecution of the application and who is associated with the inventor, with the assignee or with anyone to whom there is an obligation to assign the application.

   (d) Individuals other than the attorney, agent or inventor may comply with this section by disclosing information to the attorney, agent, or inventor.

88. Manual of Patent Examining Procedure (MPEP) § 2004(17).

substantively involved in prosecution a form or letter describing the sorts of materials and information that must be disclosed to the USPTO and explaining the consequences of failing to do so, as well as the benefits of disclosing even marginally material information. A copy of a prototype of such form is in Appendix 2.

2. *When* Must Information Be Disclosed?

Undue delay in submitting material information can result in increased risk to the applicant. The USPTO has regulations proscribing when information must be disclosed, and preferably no later than three months of filing the application or before substantive examination (i.e., first action on the merits); if filed after this period, either a fee must be paid or an averment made that the discovery of the reference is to a foreign search report less than three months old.[89] Ninety days (i.e., 3 months) can, at critical junctures of prosecution, be "too long." In this regard, the MPEP states:

> Submit information promptly. An applicant, attorney, or agent who is aware of prior art or other information and its significance should submit same early in prosecution, e.g., before the first action by the examiner, and not wait until after allowance. Potentially material information discovered late in the prosecution should be immediately submitted. That the issue fee has been paid is no reason or excuse for failing to submit information.[90]

As one commentator put it, the "earlier the disclosure of a known piece of information relative to the examination the better."[91] Obviously, if material information is disclosed to the USPTO only *after* the examiner has allowed a patent to issue, or otherwise adopted the position of the applicant, it is more likely that an accused infringer will later argue that the examiner had been sandbagged.[92] Today, if substantive art is discovered after final rejection or

---

89. 37 C.F.R. § 1.97.
90. MPEP § 2004(12), *citing Elmwood Liquid Prods., Inc. v. Singleton Packing Corp.*, 328 F. Supp. 974, 170 U.S.P.Q. (BNA) 398 (M.D. Fla. 1971).
91. Margaret A. Boulware & Tamsen Valoir, *Inequitable Conduct*, 619 PLI/PAT 1245, 1252 (Oct. 2000). *See, e.g., Golden Valley Microwave Foods Inc. v. Weaver Popcorn Co., Inc.*, 837 F. Supp. 1444, 1476, 24 U.S.P.Q.2d (BNA) 1801, 1809 (N.D. Ind. 1992) (in a case finding inequitable conduct, court noted that the applicant had cited art only after claims had been allowed).
92. Examiners have financial incentives that arguably make it less likely for them to reopen examination after receiving information once they have decided to allow an application. *See* David Hricik, *Aerial Boundaries: The Duty of Candor as a Limitation On the Duty of Patent Practitioners to Advocate for Maximum Claim Coverage* 44 So. Tex. L. Rev. 205, 228–29 (2002) (discussing financial incentives of examiners).

after notice of allowance, many will seek entry of the reference and its acknowledgement by requesting continued examination (RCE). Although this comes at a cost, it does insure acknowledgement of the reference, and when necessary, further amendment to the claims. The RCE also provides an easy count to the examiner to reopen the case.

To avoid such accusations and to speed examination, disclosure should be prompt. Justifying undue delay can be difficult, and so can increase risk to the applicant.

E. Recurrent Fact Patterns Constituting Inequitable Conduct

The following section describes various fact patterns and forms of conduct that have been repeatedly found to constitute inequitable conduct. In each subsection, we also provide some possible best practices on how to avoid these problems, although obviously they are simply suggestions not guidelines or requirements. At the end, we provide some broader guidance and thoughts.

1. Nondisclosure of Prior Art

The failure of the practitioner to disclose known material prior art to the examiner constitutes the most fertile ground for inequitable conduct claims. Typically, the battleground then becomes whether the withheld prior art was more material than prior art that was disclosed, or whether instead it was merely cumulative or even more remote than art that was disclosed and considered by the examiner. If the undisclosed reference was more material than the disclosed art, then a finding of materiality is likely; the sole remaining issue will be whether the practitioner withheld it with an intent to deceive.

Practitioners have difficult decisions to make during prosecution that require judgment and care. They must analyze whether they are aware of prior art that is material to patentability of each claim. The MPEP provides some useful insights into making this determination:

> It is desirable for an attorney or agent to carefully evaluate and explain to the applicant and others involved the scope of the claims, particularly the broadest claims. Ask specific questions about possible prior art which might be material in reference to the broadest claim or claims. There is some tendency to mistakenly evaluate prior art in the light of the gist of what is regarded as the invention or narrower interpretations of the claims, rather than measuring the art against

the broadest claim with all of its reasonable interpretations. It is desirable to pick out the broadest claim or claims and measure the materiality of prior art against a reasonably broad interpretation of these claims.

It may be useful to evaluate the materiality of prior art or other information from the viewpoint of whether it is the closest prior art or other information. This will tend to put the prior art or other information in better perspective. However [amended Rule 1.56] may still require submission of prior art or other information which is not as close as that of record.[93]

Even assuming the information is material, the USPTO advises not to disclose material information cumulative of that already submitted.[94] Generally, if the reference discloses a more complete combination of the claimed elements than the art that has been submitted, or if it discloses an element that has become a focal point of prosecution and which is not disclosed in the submitted art, the reference is likely not merely cumulative.[95]

Practitioners, who decide that information is cumulative and withhold it on that basis, run the obvious risk of being second-guessed later. By not submitting a piece of prior art of which the applicant or attorney is aware, the practitioner permits an accused infringer to later argue that the withheld reference was not cumulative. This perhaps explains why the MPEP currently encourages submission of information, even of questionable relevance and even if arguably cumulative:

> When in doubt, it is desirable and safest to submit information. Even though the attorney, agent, or applicant doesn't consider it necessarily material, someone else may see it differently and embarrassing questions can be avoided. . . . In short, the question of relevancy in close cases, should be left to the examiner and not the applicant.[96]

Further, as a practical matter, practitioners have the incentive to submit references. A patent that is issued after the examiner has considered a prior art reference is more readily defended against charges of invalidity.

---

93. MPEP § 2001(5) & (6).
94. *Baxter Int'l. Inc. v. McGaw, Inc.,* 149 F.3d 1321, 1328, 47 U.S.P.Q.2d 1225, 1229 (Fed. Cir. 1998).
95. *See id.* at 1329, 47 U.S.P.Q.2d at 1230. (finding withheld reference was not cumulative where the submitted prior art, as a whole, had disclosed all of the elements of the claimed invention, but only the withheld reference disclosed all of the elements in a single reference); *Semiconductor Energy Lab. Co. v. Samsung Elec. Co., Ltd.,* 204 F.3d 1368, 1374, 54 U.S.P.Q.2d (BNA) 1001 (Fed. Cir. 2000) (holding that withheld reference was not cumulative as it "contained a more complete combination of the elements claimed in the'636 patent than anything else before the PTO").
96. MPEP § 2004(10) (internal quotation marks and citations omitted).

Interestingly, despite the USPTO's recent views as espoused in the MPEP, the USPTO issued proposed rules that would dramatically curtail the number of references submitted without supportive statements, and the timing of the submissions. For example, even the use of an RCE to submit new art would be prohibited under these proposed rules.[97]

Today, when confronted with issue with the possible redundant reference, the practitioner errs on the side of over inclusion. Even with foreign search reports, which are generally based on different rules and searching principles, Applicants will try to submit the art relating to the general area, in addition to the art destroying novelty and inventive step as well as the search report itself. If the new rules are put in place, to avoid having to make statement regarding the reference, applicants will limit the number of references submitted, try and avoid putting a whole reference that is over the page number limit, and try to find ways to avoid having to translate references from foreign languages. This will add a significant amount of time in the judgment and balancing of what gets introduced and what does not. Also as mentioned above, this set of IDS rules will really have the inequitable conduct tail wagging the duty of candor dog. However, it should be noted that complying with the MPEP's suggestion to submit all references, however, has its own problems, as next shown.

2. Submitted but Buried Material Information

" 'Burying' is the submission of a highly material reference in a long list of less relevant references in the hopes that the examiner will not notice the material reference."[98] Accused infringers can portray the submission of long lists of supposedly cumulative prior art as a deliberate effort by the prosecuting attorney to bury the critical prior art reference.[99]

The balance struck by the MPEP is helpful to consider. Despite encouraging submission of references in close cases, the MPEP specifically discourages submitting a long list of references. In addition, it requires that if a long list is submitted, that the most significant reference(s) be highlighted for the examiner:

> It is desirable to avoid the submission of long lists of documents if it can be avoided. Eliminate clearly irrelevant and marginally pertinent cumulative information. If a long list is submitted, highlight those documents which have

---

97. Changes to Information Disclosure Statement Requirements and Other Related Matters 71 Fed. Reg. 38808 (2006).
98. Boulware & Valoir, 619 PLI/PAT at 1251.
99. *Molins PLC v. Textron, Inc.,* 48 F.3d 1172, 1183, 33 U.S.P.Q.2d (BNA) 1823, 1831 (Fed. Cir. 1995).

been specifically brought to applicant's attention and/or are known to be of most significance.[100]

As with the MPEP, the courts consider the realities of patent practice in analyzing claims of burying references.[101] Despite the practical realities and the fact that burying by itself is highly unlikely to constitute inequitable conduct, the Federal Circuit has held that burying is probative of "bad faith."[102] Consequently, an accused infringer will obviously attack the practice of listing a reference of more importance among those of lesser importance without calling its significance to the examiner's attention. Whether a court will ultimately find this behavior to constitute inequitable conduct depends on the materiality of the reference, evidence of intent, and other facts. Clearly, however, burying a reference by itself is probably insufficient to constitute inequitable conduct, but burying it and mischaracterizing it in some way makes a finding of inequitable conduct far more likely.[103]

Every practitioner, particularly those prosecuting in crowded arts, must balance the need for disclosure against the need to avoid burying references. If practitioners do not disclose references, they will later be argued to be more material than those that were disclosed. If they disclose them in one long list, the accused infringer will contend that they buried the wheat with the chaff. The practice of submitting hundreds of references to make sure no one could contend that a reference was withheld has been addressed head on by the USPTO, which in 2007 released proposed rule changes to IDSs. The rule changes effectively would limit the number of references that could be submitted without characterization and would require that the submitter have read each reference to make the characterization.

---

100. MPEP § 2004(13). *See Sunrise Med. HHG, Inc. v. AirSep Corp.*, 95 F. Supp. 2d 348, 460 & n.767 (W.D. Pa. 2000).
101. *Molins*, 48 F.3d at 1184, 33 U.S.P.Q.2d at 1832.
102. *Id.*
103. For courts finding inequitable conduct based upon burying, see *Golden Valley Microwave Foods Inc. v. Weaver Popcorn Co., Inc.*, 837 F. Supp. 1444, 1477, 24 U.S.P.Q.2d 1801 (N.D. Ind. 1992) (finding inequitable conduct where attorney listed reference but discussed less relevant aspects of it); *Penn Yan Boats, Inc., v. Sea Lark Boats, Inc.*, 359 F. Supp. 948, 175 U.S.P.Q. (BNA) 260 (S.D. Fla. 1972) (finding inequitable conduct where 13 references were listed in letter stating that they had been found in prefiling search, but in fact 13th reference was a patent that had issued afterward). For courts finding no inequitable conduct, see *Molins*, 48 F.3d at 1184 (finding that attorneys' mere submission of long list of references soon after they were discovered did not evidence intent to deceive); *Sunrise Med. HHG*, 95 F. Supp. 2d at 460–61 (finding no inequitable conduct based on lack of materiality of buried reference); *Boehringer Ingelheim Yetmedica, Inc. v. Schering-Plough Corp.*, 68 F. Supp. 2d 508 (D.N.J. 1999) (finding accused infringer unlikely to prevail on claim of "burying references" because of lack of evidence of intent to mislead); *C&F Packing Co., Inc. v. IBP, Inc.*, 916 F. Supp 735, 750 (N.D. Ill. 1995) ("An examination of the IDS at issue . . . does not support a finding that the applicants buried" the prior art).

An option that was available to the practitioner in addition to submitting everything, was at one time done while preparing the "background of the invention." This can also be done in an IDS itself. However, these practices have increasingly fallen out of favor, as being subject to increasing scrutiny for mischaracterization and thus charges of inequitable conduct. Obviously, there is a significant degree of judgment and balancing that this requires. As a general principle however, most applications have less than fifty references submitted and many less than twenty references submitted. References are submitted in several ways: (1) with a foreign search report that can list whether the reference destroys novelty or inventive step; (2) part of a patentability report; (3) closest prior art listed in the background of the invention, which is required in countries such as Japan; (4) as cited in a parent application; or (5) newly identified. The number of applications wherein the references that are "newly identified" and amounting to more than 50 or more are few indeed. Additionally, much of the art cited may be in fact a result of the crowded nature of the field. Thus, how the reference is submitted (e.g., in which lumped group) can be significant in determining whether the practitioner was trying to hide the reference. In truth, the practitioner may receive all the references, be told that they are all relevant, and after a survey of publication dates and titles, decide to submit all of them out of caution.

However, one option is to submit the reference along with a concise explanation as to its significance or lack thereof. This can be beneficial when submitting an IDS listing more than 100 references, where in truth that reference can become lost in the list. As next shown, use of this option must be done with care.

3. Submitted but Mischaracterized References

A practitioner who characterizes a reference must do so fully, accurately, and fairly. The examiner's attention should not be directed to the less material portions of the reference. As the MPEP explains:

> Care should be taken to see that prior art or other information cited in a specification or in an information disclosure statement is properly described and that the information is not incorrectly or incompletely characterized. It is particularly important for an attorney or agent to review, before filing, an application which was prepared by someone else, e.g., a foreign application.[104]

---

104. MPEP § 2001(7).

Even assuming an inaccurate characterization is made, inequitable conduct will not likely be found because the art was submitted, and the USPTO is presumed to have examined it and allowed the claims over the art. Because the art was in fact disclosed and the examiner had it to examine during prosecution, establishing materiality or intent is difficult.[105] For that reason, courts continue to reject arguments based on mischaracterization where the reference was disclosed to, described, and considered by the examiner.[106]

However, once again, mischaracterization of a reference will be relied on as evidence of "bad faith."[107] It will be part of the circumstantial evidence built up by counsel for the accused infringer to establish an inference, and evidence, of an intent to deceive the USPTO. Thus, although mischaracterization has rarely resulted in inequitable conduct by itself, any description should be done with care.

Obviously, there is a significant degree of judgment and balancing that this requires. Ironically, the bogeyman of inequitable conduct has become so great, that many practitioners now avoid preparing a background of the invention section in an application listing the closest art because of fears that they may mischaracterize a reference. This is now extending to the fear that references may be mischaracterized in summaries submitted with an IDS.

As a general principle however, if you decide to characterize the reference, block quote it from the abstract of the patent or the abstract of the journal article. If you are concerned that the abstract may not accurately describe the reference (and oftentimes they do not because they may be poor translations), then look at the last paragraph of the introduction section of a journal article, which might sum up the hypothesis and conclusion of the experimental question asked. If you block quote it, there is less of a fear that you mischaracterized it. The only problem may be that the quote does not accurately describe the reference *as a whole.*

In the end, if we ridded ourselves of the inequitable conduct bogeyman, perhaps we would have greater freedom in being more candid in our presentation of information to the USPTO.

---

105. *See Nisus Corp. v. Perma-Chink Sys., Inc.,* 497 F.3d 1316 (Fed. Cir. 2007) (attorney argument was not inequitable conduct because it was an "attempt[] to distinguish the claims from the prior art, not gross mischaracterizations or unreasonable interpretations" of the prior art).

106. *Id. See also Gambro Lundia AB v. Baxter Healthcare Corp.,* 110 F.3d 1573, 1581–82, 42 U.S.P.Q.2d (BNA) 1378 (Fed. Cir. 1997) (reversing finding of inequitable conduct based on alleged mischaracterizations of prior art).

107. *See Gambro,* 110 F.3d 1573, 1581–82, 42 U.S.P.Q.2d (BNA) 1378, 1386 (Fed. Cir. 1997) (reversing finding of inequitable conduct based on alleged mischaracterizations of prior art); *Golden Valley Microwave Foods, Inc. v. Weaver Popcorn,* 837 F. Supp. 1444, 1474, 24 U.S.P.Q.2d (BNA) 1801 (N.D. Ind. 1992) (concluding that mischaracterizations evidenced an intent to deceive).

4. Misleading Translations of Foreign-Language Prior Art References

Because of the increasing importance of protecting intellectual property internationally, it is becoming increasingly common for practitioners to learn of a translation, or at least a partial translation, of a pertinent foreign reference and to submit the full or partial translation, along with the complete reference in the foreign language, during prosecution. This practice is consistent with PTO regulations that require submission of complete or partial translations in the possession of the applicant:

> (i) A concise explanation of the relevance, as it is presently understood by the individual designated in § 1.56(c) most knowledgeable about the content of the information, of each patent, publication, or other information listed that is not in the English language. The concise explanation may be either separate from applicant's specification or incorporated therein.
>
> (ii) A copy of the translation if a written English-language translation of a non–English-language document, or portion thereof, is within the possession, custody, or control of, or is readily available to any individual designated in § 1.56(c).[108]

Section 1.98(3) thus creates two distinct obligations.

First, if someone substantively involved in prosecution understands the language that a foreign reference is written in, that person has an obligation to explain his or her understanding of its relevance to patentability.[109] The fact that the lawyer does not speak the language does not excuse this obligation, because the duties of client and lawyer are independent.

The second obligation is to submit English translations of foreign references that the applicant possesses. Despite the clarity of this obligation, inequitable conduct has arisen in connection with translations. Three varieties exist.

A. Withholding Full or Partial Translations the Applicant Possesses

Applicants currently do not have an obligation to obtain translations of foreign language references.[110] However, when they have obtained one, failing to submit it can violate section 1.98(3). If the other elements of

---

108. 37 C.F.R. § 1.98(3); *see also* MPEP § 609(A)(3) (providing additional guidance to applicants).

109. 37 C.F.R. § 1.98(3)(i).

110. In the event that the proposed IDS rules issued in 2006 are instituted, then *all* foreign language references would be required to have a complete translation submitted to the PTO. *See* proposed changes to rule 1.98, 71 Fed. Reg. 38822.

inequitable conduct are present, failing to submit a translation can result in unenforceability.[111] Courts will not excuse the failure of the applicant to submit a translation, even though the USPTO has some authority to obtain translations, unless perhaps the applicant has given to the examiner a reason to obtain a complete translation.[112] In *Atofina v. Great Lakes Chem. Corp.,* the Federal Circuit held that the infringement defendant failed to prove by clear and convincing evidence that applicants for the patent had acted with an intent to deceive the USPTO by failing to disclose a full English translation of a Japanese publication. In this case, the patent holder had a full English language translation, which they had failed to provide to the USPTO. Yet, the Court found no intent to deceive the USPTO, and thus the patent was not found invalid for failure to submit the full translation.[113]

B. Submitting a Partial Translation That Omits the Most Material Aspects of the Reference

The submission of a partial translation, along with a concise explanation and the full reference—literal compliance with section 1.98(3)—does not insulate the applicant from a charge or finding of inequitable conduct. For example, intentionally submitting a partial translation and concise explanation concerning aspects of the reference that are *known* to be less significant to patentability than the portions not translated can constitute inequitable conduct. The Federal Circuit emphasized the fact that compliance with section 1.98(c) and the MPEP provisions relating to it,[114] do not put the applicant in a safe harbor.[115] This is because an applicant may know that the untranslated portions of the reference are more material to patentability

---

111. *See Poly-America, Inc. v. GSE Lining Technology, Inc.,* 1998 WL 355477 at *4 (N.D. Tex. 1998) (allegation that applicant intentionally withheld material translations stated a defense of inequitable conduct).

112. *See Semiconductor Energy Lab. Co. v. Samsung Elec. Co., Ltd.,* 204 F.3d 1368, 1377, 54 U.S.P.Q.2d 1001, 1007–08 (Fed. Cir. 2000) ("Though the examiner is presumed to have done his job correctly, there is no support in the law for a presumption that the examiner will understand foreign languages such as Japanese or will request a costly complete translation of every submitted foreign language document, particularly in the absence of any reason to do so.") (affirming finding of inequitable conduct). *See also Atofina v. Great Lakes Chem. Corp.,* 441 F.3d 991 (Fed. Cir. 2006) (reversing finding of intent to deceive where applicant did not submit full translation which it possessed because of lack of proof of intent to deceive).

113. *Atofina v. Great Lakes Chemical Corp.,* 78 U.S.P.Q.2d 1417, 1425–1427 (Fed. Cir. 2006). It is notable that Judge Dyk dissented in the opinion, arguing that Atofina had misrepresented the information contained in Japanese Patent JP 51–82206 to the court, and recommended reconsideration of the inequitable conduct determination. *Id.* at 1427–1428.

114. MPEP § 609.

115. *Semiconductor Energy Lab. Co. v. Samsung Elec. Co., Ltd.,* 204 F.3d 1368, 1376, 54 U.S.P.Q.2d 1001, 1007–08 (Fed. Cir. 2000) ("Though Rule 98 requires that the applicant provide any

than the translated portion. An applicant who knowingly fails to translate the most material portions of a foreign language reference has neither complied with those rules nor insulated the patent from a finding of inequitable conduct.

The Federal Circuit analyzed a similar issue in *Semiconductor Energy Lab. Co. v. Samsung Elec. Co., Ltd.*,[116] where the applicant had submitted the full foreign language reference, along with a summary and concise statement, both of which indicated that the reference was not particularly pertinent. The court rejected the argument that the examiner's ability to obtain a full translation obviated the charge of inequitable conduct, reasoning:

> We perceive no clear error in the district court's conclusion that SEL effectively failed to disclose the Canon reference to the PTO by providing a one-page partial translation of the entire 29-page application. By submitting the entire reference to the PTO along with a one-page, partial translation focusing on less material portions and a concise statement directed to these less material portions, SEL left the examiner with the impression that the examiner did not need to conduct any further translation or investigation. Thus, SEL deliberately deceived the examiner into thinking that the Canon reference was less relevant than it really was, and constructively withheld the reference from the PTO. SEL's submission hardly satisfies the duty of candor required of every applicant before the PTO.
>
> SEL's contention that the examiner must have both read and fully understood the entire untranslated Canon reference based on his having read the misleadingly incomplete one-page translation and concise statement is absurd. Though the examiner is presumed to have done his job correctly, there is no support in the law for a presumption that the examiner will understand foreign languages such as Japanese or will request a costly complete translation of every submitted foreign language document, particularly in the absence of any reason to do so. . . .
>
> SEL's contention that the PTO should not require applicants to translate all foreign references into English misses the critical point. The duty at issue in this case is the duty of candor, not a duty of translation. The duty of candor does not require that the applicant translate every foreign reference, but only that the applicant refrain from submitting partial translations that it knows will misdirect the examiner's attention from the reference's teaching. Here, the desirability of the examiner securing a full translation was masked by the affirmatively misleading concise statement and one-page translation.[117]

---

existing translation of a foreign reference, Rule 98 provides neither a safe harbor nor a shield against allegations of inequitable conduct").

116. 204 F.3d 1368, 1376, 54 U.S.P.Q.2d (BNA) 1001 (Fed. Cir. 2000).

117. 204 F.3d at 1377–78 (affirming finding of inequitable conduct).

The facts of *Samsung* appear unusual, but one can imagine practitioners being accused of inequitable conduct under more innocent circumstances. For example, an attorney prosecuting a U.S. case with foreign counterparts might submit a partial translation obtained in a foreign case without analyzing whether the portions material to the U.S. case were translated. Care needs to be given in determining whether the translation discusses the portions that are material to the U.S. case. This may or may not be aided by characterizations set forth by foreign patent office of a reference relative to invention patentability. In any event, it is generally advisable to request the client to provide at least a machine translation of the entire reference, even if the quality of the machine translation is poor. In the end, characterizations of a reference often mean careful adherence to literalisms.

C. Characterizing the Whole Reference on a Partial Translation

A practitioner who submits a partial translation needs to be quite literal. A charge of inequitable conduct can arise if the practitioner characterizes the entire reference based on the portion. For example, if the attorney overcomes a rejection by arguing that there is no teaching in the foreign reference of the critical feature or element, then the attorney has made a representation as to the scope and teaching of the entire foreign reference, not just the translated portion. At least two courts have addressed inequitable conduct charges in the context of partial translations and statements respecting the entire reference, with the outcome largely turning on whether the accused infringer was able to gather sufficient circumstantial evidence to establish intent to deceive.[118] The intent to deceive may be increased with the increasing ability to perform machine translations of foreign documents. Although these translations are not perfect, they may augment the partial value of the partial translation.

Obviously, there is a significant degree of judgment and balancing that this requires. Clearly, practitioners should not assume that partial translations contain the portion most pertinent to the U.S. case, for example. No representation as to what the "reference" teaches as a whole can or should be made—only to what the translation states. Again, being literal and precise is important. In addition, when providing the reference in the PTO-1449 form, it is best to indicate that this is a partial translation and of what.

---

118. *See, e.g., Key Pharmaceuticals v. Hercon Labs. Corp.,* 161 F.3d 709, 712–13, 48 U.S.P.Q.2d (BNA) 1911 (Fed. Cir. 1998) (affirming finding of no inequitable conduct based on applicant's submission only of abstract of Japanese patent, but stating that "while the finding of no materiality is problematic" the finding of an absence of intent to deceive provided a basis for affirming the trial court); *LNP Engineering Plastics, Inc. v. Miller Waste Mills, Inc.,* 2000 WL 33341185 (D. Del. 2000) (finding that submission only of partial translation was not material because complete translation was cumulative).

That way it is clear on the record that the entirety of the reference has not been considered by the USPTO.

5. Withholding Information That Contradicts Statements to the U.S. Patent and Trademark Office

Withholding information that contradicts a position asserted in support of patentability has been found to constitute inequitable conduct, when done with an intent to deceive. This can take the form of submitting only test data that supports the applicant's position, as discussed in the next subsection.

It can include, however, simply withholding internal notes that contradict the arguments being made in prosecution.[119] So long as that information is something a reasonable examiner would consider important in allowing an application to issue, it is "material." However, not every internal document must be submitted, just those that in the particular case constitute information a reasonable examiner would want to consider—a highly fact-intensive inquiry.[120]

6. Test Data

Test data can become relevant to patentability in various ways. Among other things, tests can be used to show criticality, unexpected results, an additive effect, synergism, and other tangible benefits of a claimed invention over the prior art. Thus, for example, to overcome a rejection based on obviousness, an applicant may file a Rule 132 affidavit with evidence, often in the form of test data.[121] Likewise, to antedate a reference, an applicant can file a Rule 131 affidavit and submit test data.[122]

Because of its materiality and the fact that the USPTO has no ability to verify or challenge the data, accused infringers often focus on test data as a basis for finding inequitable conduct. Their effort is made easier because an affidavit submitted specifically to overcome a rejection is likely to be deemed

---

119. *Monsanto Co. v. Bayer Bioscience N.V.*, 514 F.3d 1229 (Fed. Cir. 2008).
120. *Id.* at 1240.
121. 37 C.F.R. § 1.32. *See generally* MPEP, *supra* note 52, § 716.02 (allegations of unexpected results); *Monsanto Co. v. Bayer Bioscience, N.V.*, 264 F. Supp. 2d 852, 855 (E.D. Mo. Dec. 27, 2002); Alan H. MacPherson et al., *Ethics in Patent Practice (A Brief Visit to Several Areas of Concern)*, 574 PLI/PAT 657, 700–02 (1999).
122. 37 C.F.R. § 1.31. *See, e.g., In re Zletz*, 893 F.2d 319, 13 U.S.P.Q.2d (BNA) 1320 (Fed. Cir. 1989).

material for that reason alone.[123] As a result, submission of test data has been a focal point of inequitable conduct claims.

Portraying that a test had been conducted, when in fact it had not, has been the subject of recent successful inequitable conduct claims. The test must actually have been run, unless it is described in the present tense or future tense as a prophetic example.[124] Implying that an experiment "was run" when it was not is a misrepresentation:

> Care should be taken to see that inaccurate . . . experiments are not introduced into the specification, either inadvertently or intentionally. For example, stating that an experiment "was run" or "was conducted" is a misrepresentation of the facts. No results should be represented as actual results unless they have actually been achieved. Paper examples should not be described using the past tense.[125]

Representation of whether the example is prophetic or real is important and has been used to find inequitable conduct. In *Novo Nordisk Pharmaceuticals Inc. v. Bio-Technology Gen. Corp.*, the Federal Circuit found that Claim 1 was invalid because Novo Nordisk failed to disclose that Example 1, which it relied on in asserting enablement (human growth hormone), was prophetic. Additionally, Novo Nordisk had never successfully produced the ripe hGH according to the methodology taught by Example 1. Novo attempted to mitigate the issue by asserting that the inventors purportedly had failed to

---

123. *See eSpeed, Inc. v. Brokertec USA, LLC,* 480 F.3d 1129, 1138 (Fed. Cir. 2007) ("An inference of intent may arise where material false statements are proffered in a declaration or other sworn statement submitted to the PTO."); *Refac Int'l, Ltd. v. Lotus Dev. Corp.,* 81 F.3d 1576, 1583–84, 38 U.S.P.Q.2d (BNA) 1665, 1671 (Fed. Cir. 1993) ("Affidavits are inherently material, even if only cumulative. The affirmative act of submitting an affidavit must be construed as being intended to be relied upon."); *Ferring B.V. v. Barr Labs., Inc.,* 437 F.3d 1181, 1190 (Fed. Cir. 2006) (failure to disclose bias in affidavit found material); *Digital Control Inc. v. Charles Mach. Works,* 437 F.3d 1309, 1317 (Fed. Cir. 2006) ("submission of a false affidavit may be determined to be 'inherently material.'"); *Rohm & Haas Co. v. Crystal Chem. Co.,* 722 F.2d 1556, 1571, 220 U.S.P.Q. (BNA) 289, 300 (Fed. Cir. 1983) ("there is no room to argue that submission of false affidavits is not material"); *Procter & Gamble Co. v. Kimberly-Clark Corp.,* 740 F. Supp. 1177, 1199 (D.S.C. 1989) ("the court cannot imagine a more material representation than a declaration submitted specifically to overcome a prior art rejection").

124. MPEP § 608.01(p).

125. MPEP § 2004(8). *See Hoffmann-La Roche, Inc. v. Promega Corp.,* 323 F.3d 1354, 1363, 66 U.S.P.Q.2d 1385, 1391–92 (Fed. Cir. 2003) (upholding finding that statement in specification that experiments "were run" was a false material misrepresentation when no test had been run, because the example was "written in the past tense" and inventors understood that "at least in a scientific publication, the use of the past tense means that an experiment was actually performed" and could not explain "why a different principle would apply in a patent application."); *Use Techno Corp. v. Kenkco USA, Inc.,* 515 F. Supp. 2d 1086 (N.D. Cal. 2007) (specification described clinical tests but in fact tests, but not clinical tests, had been run).

disclose to Novo's counsel the truth behind Example 1. However, knowledge and actions of an applicant's representatives are chargeable to the applicant, whether they are by the inventor-employee or by patent counsel.[126] Thus, although prophetic examples can be useful in providing an enabling disclosure, they should be clearly set forth by using future verb tense, or at least present verb tense. Additionally, in the event that data contrary to the teachings of the prophetic example is ultimately realized, this data may also have to be disclosed to the USPTO.

In another context, running experiments, but submitting only those that support patentability, has proven fruitful grounds for inequitable conduct defenses.[127] It is easy for judges to understand the impact on patentability of submitting only favorable data and withholding adverse results.[128] Yet in the real world, experiments are often "failures" for practical reasons—a gauge fails, power fluctuates, or for some other reason the experiment is invalid. It is important for lawyers who withhold test data that "fails" to document (not for the USPTO, but for the later infringement suit) that the reasons for the "failure" were experimental or equipment flaws.[129] It is also important that the client understand that cherry-picking data is not permitted. Yet, failure to provide negative data to the USPTO is not per se evidence of inequitable conduct.[130] Thus, review of relevant data and whether it should or

---

126. *Novo Nordisk Pharmaceuticals Inc. v. Bio-Technology Gen. Corp.*, 76 U.S.P.Q.2d 1811, 1818–1823 (Fed. Cir. 2005).

127. *Avco Corp. v. PPG Indus., Inc.*, 867 F. Supp. 84, 34 U.S.P.Q.2d (BNA) 1026 (D. Mass. 1994) ("An affidavit offering comparison test data . . . constitutes a representation to the Patent Office that the showing is a fair and accurate demonstration of the closest prior art of which the applicant is aware").

128. *See Monsanto Co. v. Bayer Bioscience, N.V.*, 264 F. Supp. 2d 852, 862 (E.D. Mo. 2002) (on summary judgment, finding inequitable conduct where applicant omitted unfavorable results to avoid narrowing claims), *rev'd*, 2004 WL 612877 (Fed. Cir. 2004) *Sigma-tau Industrie Farmaceutiche Riunite, S.p.A. v. Lonza, Ltd.*, 62 F. Supp. 2d 70 (D.D.C. 1999) (denying patentee's motion for summary judgment that inequitable conduct had not occurred); *Golden Valley*, 837 F. Supp. at 1475 (finding inequitable conduct where test data reported to examiner contradicted test data reported to different examiner). *But see Upjohn Co. v. Mova Pharmaceutical Corp.*, 225 F.3d 1306, 56 U.S.P.Q.2d (BNA) 1286 (Fed. Cir. 2000) (affirming finding of no intent to deceive based on failure to submit tests conducted in different ingredient range).

129. *See Cargill, Inc. v. Canbra Foods, Ltd.*, 476 F.3d 1359 (Fed. Cir. 2007).

130. The Federal Circuit in *Eli Lilly & Co. v. Zenith Goldline Pharmaceuticals Inc.*, 81, U.S.P.Q.2d 1369, 1332–1333 (Fed. Cir. 2006), held that the patentee's failure to mention during prosecution of a patent for the compound olanzapine idiosyncratic blood toxicity problems detected in a dog study did not constitute inequitable conduct. In this case, the patentee was able to discount the problems of the dog study, such that the data did not contradict is patentability arguments or rise to an intent to deceive. The court noted that "[g]ross negligence alone is insufficient to justify an inference of intent to deceive the PTO." *Id.*, citing to Kingsdown Med. Consultants, Ltd. v. Hollister, Inc., 863 F.2d 867, 876 (Fed. Cir. 1988) and *FMC Corp. v. Manitowoc Co.*, 835 F.2d 1411, 1415 n.9 (Fed. Cir. 1987). The court goes on

should not be provided to the USPTO is recommended. The advice, however, has been to err on the side of submitting such information to the USPTO.

In addition to looking for nonexistent tests and cherry-picking, accused infringers will examine the prosecution history and supporting laboratory notebooks for variations of any kind. Among them: (a) variations in test conditions; (b) variations in ingredients or materials; (c) any failure to follow the closest prior art, or the closest example in the closest prior art; (d) any inconsistent test methods (e.g., testing the prior art in one fashion but the claimed invention in another, where there is no principled reason for testing differently); and (e) any failure to advise the USPTO of the known impact of variations or changes in test conditions or ingredients.

There are often practical issues that applicants face that make charges of wrongdoing based on variations of these kinds easy to make. For example, the prior art can require the use of an ingredient or machine that is no longer available. To reduce the likelihood of finding inequitable conduct, any substitution or change to the prior art should be highlighted for the USPTO. For example, if the prior art calls for the use of a machine that is no longer readily available, the practitioner should explain why the applicant used a different machine. Likewise, applicants may be faced with a prior art disclosure that the examiner contends renders the claimed invention obvious, but which has no clear direction as to which of a myriad of listed ingredients should be combined. Recognizing these practical issues, the MPEP advises:

> Care should be taken to see that inaccurate . . . experiments are not introduced into the specification, either inadvertently or intentionally. . . . Also, misrepresentations can occur when experiments which were run or conducted are inaccurately reported in the specification, e.g., an experiment is changed by leaving out one or more ingredients.[131]

Because of the heightened materiality of test data and the practical difficulties that testing creates, practitioners need to exercise particular care in disclosing test conditions and methodologies, and consider whether to disclose "bad" tests—those with results that undermine the assertions being made—and explaining to the examiner why the test is inapposite or was scientifically unsound.[132] An accused infringer cannot argue that the examiner did not

---

to point out that "[i]n a case involving an omission of material reference to the PTO, the record must contain clear and convincing evidence that the applicant made a deliberate decision to withhold a known material reference." *Id.*

131. MPEP § 2004(8).

132. *See Cargill, Inc. v. Canbra Foods, Ltd.*, 476 F.3d 1359 (Fed. Cir. 2007) (where applicant withheld test data allegedly for good reason, court emphasized that in "close cases" there should be "disclosure" rather than the applicant unilaterally "making and relying on their own determinations of materiality.") (quotations and citations omitted).

even though the court held that the patent was enabled.[143] Thus, the failure to disclose information material to enablement can constitute inequitable conduct even when the patent is fully enabled.[144]

Enablement can take various forms. In one recent case, for example, the inventors had filed an application claiming a process and apparatus to make integrated circuits. During prosecution and through commercial use of the claimed invention, they learned that it did not work—the wafers were contaminated and "filthy." In light of their knowledge, they apparently filed either a divisional or separate application on an improved invention. That application and the resulting '761 patent covered an improvement on the original application.

Even though the applicants realized that the invention disclosed in the original application did not work, they continued prosecution of that application. During its prosecution, the inventors filed declarations describing the supposed benefits of their invention, including the fact that it reduced contaminants. This, of course, was contradicted by their experience in commercially using the system. Eventually, two patents issued from this application, one on the process and one on the apparatus.

The patentee first sued YieldUP for infringing the improved '761 patent. After settling with YieldUP, the patentee then sued again, but this time for infringing the two patents that had issued from the original application. YieldUP argued that the failure by the applicants to disclose the fact that during commercial use of the invention the inventors had learned that it did not produce clean wafers constituted inequitable conduct because the failure of the invention to operate was material to the enablement requirement. The district court agreed, holding the patents unenforceable.

Obviously, attorneys should pay particular attention to enablement when inventors are perfecting the invention while the attorney is prosecuting continuing applications. In addition, the initial form provided to persons skilled in the art should mention that the duty to disclose goes beyond requiring disclosure of prior art: Section 112 is material to patentability.

As a result, if the data presented in the specification does not meet the limitations of the claims, the practitioner should question the actual scope of the claims, and whether they realistically portray the invention. If not, then the scope should be scaled back to what is realistic.

---

143. 326 F.3d at 1238–39. *See generally* William F. Lang, *Lawyer May Avoid Inequitable Conduct by Disclosing Patent Material,* 5 LAWYERS J. 3 (May 16, 2003) (discussing *Bristol-Myers*).

144. *CFMT, Inc. v. YieldUP Int'l Corp.*, 144 F. Supp. 2d 305 (D. Del. 2001), *rev'd on other grounds*, 349 F.3d 1333 (Fed. Cir. 2003).

B. Best Mode

Intentionally failing to disclose the best mode of carrying out an invention results in a finding of invalidity of a claim.[145] It can also result in unenforceability of the entire patent if the failure to disclose the best mode for even just one claim is done with an intent to deceive.[146]

Although it will be rare for accused infringers to need to establish inequitable conduct because a best mode violation invalidates the patent, the MPEP advises to "ask questions of the inventor about the disclosure of the best mode."[147] Practitioners must ensure that the best mode is disclosed by the inventor and included in the specification.

This can be done by simply asking what is the best way of doing the invention and is it exemplified in the examples. The practitioner does not need to state what is the best way of making or using the invention in the specification, the best mode merely must be presented and present somewhere in the specification. Usually when asking all the questions to push the scope of each variable of the claimed invention, the practitioner will become aware of what the best variable combination is.

9. Prior Sales

Omitting prior sales is obviously material in light of section 102(b).[148] In addition, a commercial embodiment can constitute prior art that is pertinent to nonobviousness, and so material to patentability.[149] "The concealment of sales information can be particularly egregious because, unlike the applicant's failure to disclose, for example, a material patent reference, the examiner has no way of securing the information on his own."[150] For these reasons, the MPEP advises that it "may be desirable to submit information about prior

---

145. *Glaxo Inc. v. Novopharm Ltd.*, 52 F.3d 1043, 1049–50 (Fed. Cir. 1995).
146. *See Consolidated Alum. Corp. v. Foseco Int'l, Ltd.*, 910 F.2d 804, 807–08, 15 U.S.P.Q.2d 1481, 1483–84 (Fed. Cir. 1990) (affirming finding of inequitable conduct based on omission of best mode, and also the inclusion of fictitious best mode); *Imperial Chem. Indus., PLC v. Barr Labs.*, 795 F. Supp. 619, 22 U.S.P.Q.2d 1906 (S.D.N.Y. 1992), *vacated*, 991 F.2d 811 (Fed. Cir. 1993).
147. MPEP § 2004(3). *See generally MacPherson*, 574 PLI/PAT at 691–96 (explaining why inequitable conduct based on best mode violations will be rare). *See also Li Second Family Ltd. Partnership v. Toshiba Corp.*, 231 F.3d 1373, 1381, 56 U.S.P.Q.2d (BNA) 1681 (Fed. Cir. 2000) (affirming finding of inequitable conduct in case involving misrepresentation of facts involving priority).
148. *See Allen Eng'g Corp. v. Bartell Indus., Inc.*, 299 F.3d 1336, 1351, 63 U.S.P.Q.2d 1769, 1777 (Fed. Cir. 2002).
149. *Dippin' Dots, Inc v. Mosey*, 476 F.3d 1337 (Fed. Cir. 2007).
150. *Paragon Podiatry Lab., Inc. v. KLM Labs. Inc.*, 984 F.2d 1182, 1193 (Fed. Cir. 1993).

uses and sales even if it appears that they may have been experimental, not involve the specifically claimed invention, or not encompass a completed invention."[151]

The Federal Circuit affirmed summary judgment of inequitable conduct for failing to disclose prior sales in a remarkable decision, *Brasseler U.S.A. I, L.P. v. Stryker Sales Corp.*[152] There, the attorney who prepared the application had been told to file it quickly, because the applicant was running into the one-year bar. In fact, the application was barred before it was filed. In affirming not only the decision of the district court that the claims were barred by section 102(b) but also that the patent was unenforceable, the Federal Circuit affirmed, holding that an attorney who was told to file the application in three days should have further inquired into precisely when the sale had taken place.[153]

Finally, in evaluating or investigating prior sales or offers to sell, the attorney should consider the impact of *Pfaff* on the need for disclosure. *Pfaff* creates a standard for what constitutes a "sale," and hence, what constitutes material information, that may not comport with an inventor's or business' understanding.[154] According to *Brasseler*, clients are charged with lawyers' knowledge of patent law.

As a result, practitioners should discuss with the client what sale activities relating to the claimed invention have occurred. Sometimes this will require a series of questions that try to determine whether the invention was for sale, or whether prior prototypes were placed for sale or not.

In the event that the practitioner determines there has been a violation of the 102(b) on sale bar, then the practitioner should advise the client to expressly abandon the application. This should obviate most issues of inequitable conduct, although there may still be an issue of provisional rights, if the application was published prior to the intentional abandonment.

---

151. MPEP § 2004(11). *See In re Dippin' Dots Patent Litig.*, 249 F. Supp. 2d 1346, 1364–65 (N.D. Ga. 2003) (precritical date activities "should have been disclosed even if it is eventually determined that [they] were experimental").

152. 267 F.3d 1370, 60 U.S.P.Q.2d (BNA) 1482 (Fed. Cir. 2001). *See* Dave A. Ghatt & Michael A. Graham, *Brasseler IV Case Comment: Is the Court Imposing New Duties on Patent Counsel?*, 84 J. Pat. Off. Soc'y 641 (Aug. 2002).

153. *Id.* at 1384–85, 60 U.S.P.Q.2d at 1489–90.

154. 267 F.3d at 1385 ("The court correctly concluded that the inventors knew that the sale was material. First, knowledge of the law is chargeable to the inventor."). *See Allen Eng'g*, 299 F.3d at 1352, 63 U.S.P.Q.2d at 1778–79 (explaining *Pfaff*). Practitioners should also take into account the fact that courts are applying *Pfaff* retroactively, even though the decision arguably changed the definition of what constitutes a "sale" under § 102. *See, e.g., Novadigm, Inc. v. Marimba, Inc.*, 2000 WL 228356 (N.D. Cal. 2000); *Brasseler U.S.A., I, L.P. v. Stryker Sales Corp.*, 93 F. Supp. 2d 1255 (S.D. Ga. 1999) (finding offer to sell material under either *Pfaff* or "totality of the circumstances" test).

10. Co-Pending Applications

It is common, acceptable, and socially desirable for practitioners to prosecute applications for the same, or different, clients in closely related technologies. However, such practices create risk to practitioners and patentees arising from the fact that applications may be material to each other. In that regard, the MPEP admonishes:

> Do not rely on the examiner of a particular application to be aware of other applications belonging to the same applicant or assignee. It is desirable to call such applications to the attention of the examiner even if there is only a question that they might be "material to patentability" of the application the examiner is considering. It is desirable to be particularly careful that prior art or other information in one application is cited to the examiner in other applications which it would be material. Do not assume that an examiner will necessarily remember, when examining a particular application, other applications which the examiner is examining, or has examined.[155]

As shown below, inequitable conduct allegations have been based not only upon the failure to disclose co-pending applications of the same clients, but also on the co-pending applications of different clients, and also of different clients of different lawyers in the same firm. Significantly, the issue presented in these cases is not limited to the question of disclosure of co-pending applications. Rarely will one client's application be material to another client's, because applications are not, generally, "prior art" and not likely to otherwise be material to patentability of each other. However, the fundamental issue of whether a lawyer has a duty to disclose information that is confidential to one client in prosecuting the application of another client is a growing concern.

A. Of Same Client of Same Lawyer

MPEP sections 2004 and 2001.06(b) specifically address the need for attorneys to point examiners to co-pending applications of the same client. Where a co-pending but unrelated application is material to patentability, the intentional failure of an attorney to disclose the application can constitute inequitable conduct, if done with an intent to deceive.[156] In *Dayco Prods., Inc. v. Total Containment, Inc.,*[157] the district court held that inequitable conduct occurred when a lawyer failed to disclose a co-pending application that could have formed the basis of a double patenting rejection. The Federal Circuit affirmed the finding of materiality, but held that the fact that the applicant disclosed

---

155. MPEP § 2004(9).
156. *Golden Valley,* 837 F. Supp. at 1474.
157. 329 F.3d 1358, 1365–66, 66 U.S.P.Q.2d 1801 (Fed. Cir. 2003).

the co-pendency to one of the two examiners involved was evidence of good faith, and thus negated a finding of intent to deceive.[158]

B. Of Different Clients of Same Lawyer

Much has been written about the Federal Circuit's decision in *Molins*, where a divided panel addressed the question of whether a lawyer must disclose the application of one client during prosecution of a different client's application where the failure to do so would violate the duty of candor.[159]

A lawyer who knows that one client's application is material to an application of a different client has some serious issues to address. Generally, the lawyer must consider whether he or she has the ethical freedom to disclose confidential information of one client during representation of another. He or she may need the consent of the client to do so, and he or she may need to withdraw if consent is not forthcoming.

C. Of Different Clients of Other Firm Lawyers

The Federal Circuit has only once analyzed whether it is inequitable conduct for two lawyers in the same firm to knowingly—a key word—prosecute applications that are material to each other for different clients. In *Akron Polymer Container Corp. v. Exxel Container, Inc.*,[160] the court held that because the attorneys disclosed the co-pending applications, which had overlapping subject matter, to one of the examiners, although not both, this obviated the claim of inequitable conduct.[161]

There is scant law in this area. Where two lawyers in the same firm become aware that they are prosecuting applications that are material to each other, extreme care needs to be exercised. The lawyers may be unable to continue to prosecute one or both applications without disclosing the existence of the other application to the examiner, and the existence of a pending application may be a client confidence that the lawyer may not disclose without the client's informed consent. As with the solo practitioner who discovers he or she is prosecuting applications that are material to each other, the firm may have to withdraw from one or both representations.

---

158. *Id.* at 1366, 66 U.S.P.Q.2d at 1807.
159. *See, e.g.,* David Hricik, *The Risks and Responsibilities of Attorneys and Firms Prosecuting Patents for Different Clients in Related Technologies,* 8 Tex. Intel. Prop. L.J. 1 (2000).
160. 148 F.3d 1380, 47 U.S.P.Q.2d (BNA) 1533 (Fed. Cir. 1998).
161. *Id.* at 1384. The court reached the same result in *Dayco Prods., Inc. v. Total Containment, Inc.,* 329 F.3d 1358, 1366, 66 U.S.P.Q.2d (BNA) 1801 (Fed. Cir. 2003) ("Here, members of the family of applications that issued as the patents-in-suit were disclosed to the examiner assigned to the co-pending application," a fact which "'points away from an intent to deceive.'") (quoting *Akron Polymer,* 148 F.3d at 1384).

Finally, some commentators have suggested that principles of imputed knowledge might apply in determining whether a lawyer in a firm must disclose information concerning other applications being prosecuted by other attorneys in the same firm.[162] The better view is that imputed knowledge does not apply for purposes of determining inequitable conduct. If a lawyer does not have actual knowledge of a material, co-pending application, there is no duty to disclose it. Some disagree. Individual firms need to analyze how to address this issue.

11. Rejection of Substantially Similar Claims by Another Examiner

Merely disclosing to an examiner the pendency of a related application may not be enough. The Federal Circuit has held that applicants have a duty to inform examiners of the rejection of substantially similar claims by other examiners.[163] The court recognized that "examiners are not bound to follow other examiners' interpretations," but nonetheless held that "knowledge of a potentially different interpretation is clearly information that an examiner could consider important when examining an application."[164]

The court gave two policy reasons for its holding. First, it posited that if applicants were not required to disclose prior rejections of substantially similar claims by other examiners, then "applicants may surreptitiously file repeated or multiple applications in an attempt to find a 'friendly' examiner."[165] Likewise, it emphasized that patent applications "are often very complicated, and different examiners with different technical backgrounds and levels of understanding and experience may often differ when interpreting such documents."[166]

The practical implication of this rule could be quite onerous. Although practitioners no doubt by now know of their responsibility to disclose substantively related applications to an examiner, disclosure of pendency is

---

162. *See, e.g.,* MacPherson, 574 PLI/PAT at 665.
163. *Dayco Prods., Inc. v. Total Containment, Inc.,* 329 F.3d 1358, 1367–68, 66 U.S.P.Q.2d (BNA) 1358 (Fed. Cir. 2003). The only other court to have so held is *Golden Valley Microwave Foods, Inc. v. Weaver Popcorn Co.,* 837 F. Supp. 1444, 1474 (N.D. Ind. 1992) ("it was important for [an examiner] to know that another knowledgeable Patent Examiner had carefully examined and rejected all claims of [another] application, including claims that were directly related to claims in the [present] application, on the grounds that the claims were obvious in light of prior art patents").
164. *Dayco,* 329 F.3d at 1368. The court also stated in *dicta* that such rejections were "material" in terms of the post-1992 version of Rule 1.56.
165. *Id.* at 1367 (quoting A.B.A. Section of Intell. Prop. L. *Annual Report 1993–1994* (1994)) (brackets omitted).
166. *Id.* at 1368.

not enough. Applicants must now examine office actions in related applications to see if the examiner has rejected "substantially similar" claims. The examiner's attention must be directed to the rejection in a prior office action of "substantially similar" claims. Arguably, the related office action can be listed in an IDS.

12. *McKesson* Disclosure Statements

More recently, with the Federal Circuit's decision in *McKesson*[167] several issues have arisen or been amplified. Certainly, it carries the potential of increasing inequitable conduct motions in patent litigation. Essentially, the court appears to require that all office actions and references in substantively similar but unrelated applications as well as related applications should be brought to the attention of the examiner. *McKesson* arrives at the crossroads of proposed new information disclosure rules that could limit the number of references capable of citation without statements regarding their relevance to twenty or fewer as proposed.[168] The decision also has led to increased tension between prosecutors and examiners, as examiners argue that these additional disclosures should not be submitted because some references have post-filing publication dates and are not prior art. That particular argument is without merit because postdated references can be provided and are cited all the time in an effort to show that claims were enabled when filed.

McKesson appears to be part of a recent trend by the Federal Circuit to apply the inequitable conduct doctrine and create a more expansive view of materiality and intent.

As a result of this complex duty, practitioners must be more rigorous on which applications to cross cite, as well as the office actions and contents of those office actions and other USPTO communications. Although divisional applications are viewed as being independent and distinct, and therefore nonobvious, frequently divisionals may lose their divisional status during the course of prosecution. At that point, they may become more vulnerable to issues of materiality, raising the spectre of whether these as well should have all materials from the parent applications cited in them, and vice versa.

After *McKesson*, the practitioner must be careful to consider citing all the references from a parent application if the application is a continuation or continuation-in-part. There is less of a concern if the application is a divisional application. Also, a warning of an obviousness-type double-patenting

---

167. *McKesson Information Solutions, Inc. v. Bridge Med., Inc.,* 487 F.3d 897 (Fed. Cir. 2007).
168. *See* Changes to Information Disclosure Statement Requirements and other Related Matters, 71 Fed. Reg. 38808 (July 10, 2006).

rejection should immediately caution the practitioner to cross reference all references between the two applications.

If the application is not before the same examiner, the practitioner might also now want to consider whether to provide copies of the office actions from the related cases. This said, examiners have the requirement to identify claims for purposes of interference prior to allowance of the application as well as raise double-patenting rejections. Searches for obviousness double patenting as well as interferences by the USPTO should potentially identify references, office actions, and arguments by the USPTO, thereby negating the need to inundate the office. Notably, most firms have not created procedures to cross cite office actions between related applications, unless perhaps there are references cited by the USPTO in a PTO-892 form. The PTO-892 form triggers the need to determine the necessity of cross reporting between applications, especially related applications not in the same family. *McKesson* practitioners appear to be not only listing Office Actions, but also Notices of Allowance, Restriction Requirements, and other USPTO communications. Certainly, if the applications are before different examiners, as in *McKesson*, the applicant should make sure that the references and today even the office actions are cross reported.[169] Nevertheless, if the applications are before the same examiner, there may be less of a need to cross report. However, we recommend erring on the side of caution by trying to make sure all the references are cited nevertheless.

However, the difficulty arises given how many practitioners handle the prosecution of applications present in a single portfolio to allowance. The different practitioners may not have the benefit of knowing in detail the issues that have come about during the prosecution of the parent or related-applications. Reviewing prosecution of the instant application is time consuming. Keeping up with the prosecution history of the instant case, versus those of the other applications in the portfolio is rarely performed because of the increasing costs of prosecution and the time constraints of cost effectively seeking allowance in the application. Thus, tracking the portfolio family members will be more important to make sure that cross reporting is being performed consistently.

In today's prosecution world, wherein for foreign origin cases coming through multiple routes, the family may be split out, making it impossible for the U.S. practitioner to knowingly supply details on related cases. Additionally, given firm turnover, differences in docketing wherein there is no numbering relationship between families, and people moving from firm to firm cause loss of historical and relationship information on patent portfolios, all become more compounded in their implications in view of the decision in *McKesson*.

---

169. *McKesson*, 487 F.3d at 904, 82 U.S.P.Q.2d 1873–75.

Judge Newman in her dissent in the *McKesson* decision captures the loss of balance well. *McKesson* placed greater emphasis on materiality than on the intent to deceive, let alone a weighing of the equities. A practitioner with an active practice can have several hundred to a few thousand applications to review or work with. *McKesson* will exacerbate litigation-driven distortion of the complex procedures of patent prosecution. *McKesson* has taken the clear and convincing evidence of deceptive intent necessary for finding inequitable conduct, and reduced it to a mere mistake with any degree of intent or even lack of intent.[170] So, although judges disparage motions for inequitable conduct, *McKesson* opened the flood gates a bit further.

13. Existence of and Information Gleaned from Ongoing Litigation

The fact that there is ongoing litigation concerning the subject matter of a patent application likely is itself material information.[171] "It is important because it signals to the examiner that other material information relevant to patentability may become available through the litigation proceedings."[172]

In addition, the litigation may lead to discovery of information that is material.[173] Consequently, the MPEP advises:

> Where the subject matter for which a patent is being sought is or has been involved in litigation, the existence of such litigation and any other material information arising there from must be brought to the attention of the Patent and Trademark Office. Examples of such material information include evidence of possible prior public use or sales, questions of inventorship, prior art, allegations of "fraud," "inequitable conduct," and "violation of duty of disclosure." Another example of such material information is any assertion that is made during litigation which is contradictory to assertions made to the examiner. Such information might arise during litigation in, for example, pleadings, admissions, discovery including interrogatories, depositions, and other documents and testimony.[174]

---

170. *McKesson*, at 487 F.3d at 904; 82 U.S.P.Q.2d at 1886.
171. *Nilssen v. Osram Sylvania, Inc.*, 504 F.3d 1223, 1234 (Fed. Cir. 2007).
172. *Id.*
173. *See also Nisus Corp. v. Perma-Chink Sys., Inc.*, 497 F.3d 1316, 1348–49 (Fed. Cir. 2007) (discussing timeliness of such disclosures).
174. MPEP § 2001.06, *citing Environ Prods., Inc. v. Total Containment, Inc.*, 43 U.S.P.Q.2d (BNA) 1288, 1291 (E.D. Pa. 1997). *See also* 37 C.F.R. 1.565 (requiring disclosure of litigation during reexamination proceedings); MPEP § 1442.04 (disclosure during reissue proceedings).

Myriad circumstances can make litigation or the information disclosed during litigation material to a pending application. For example, if the litigation involves a parent application, the litigation or the information from it could be relevant to continued prosecution of continuation applications.[175] Litigation could turn up evidence of prior sales, public uses, or other information that was not apparent earlier in prosecution.[176] In one recent case, the Federal Circuit affirmed summary judgment of unenforceability where the practitioner knew of but failed to disclose in a reexamination proceeding court opinions construing the claim language.[177]

The practical problem is that practitioners prosecuting an application might not be involved in litigation over an issued patent that is related to a still-pending application. Their client or the named inventors, however, might become aware of facts because of their involvement in litigation that must be disclosed to the USPTO. Thus, it is important that inventors and others substantively involved in prosecution understand that ongoing litigation can result in the need to disclose information during prosecution of related applications, such as a continuation-in-part, for example.

Accordingly, practitioners should create reference lists from both the pending applications and issued patents in the portfolio related to the patent under litigation and determine if any references have been missed. If new references are identified, then an analysis should be performed to determine whether a reissue or reexamination is required for a related issued patent. For the patent application, the references should be submitted. If a related application is after final, then a request for continued examination (RCE) should be filed. If the application is at allowance or even if the issue fee is paid, then the practitioner should review the reference and determine the level of materiality. If necessary, file the RCE and withdraw the allowance, or request withdrawal from issue to reopen prosecution and get the references considered. Alternatively, submit the references in the record to have them present but unacknowledged.

On a cautionary note, practitioners should also cite references that have been identified during the course of a foreign opposition or trial for invalidation of a patent in the same patent portfolio family. This frequently is identified and occurs in patent interferences, wherein there may be parallel opposition proceedings occurring in Europe or elsewhere. Life search reports from foreign patent offices, the references cited in the invalidation proceedings should also be cited as well as the papers from the invalidation

---

175. *See also Critikon Inc. v. Becton Dickinson Vascular Access Inc.*, 120 F.3d 1253, 1257, 43 U.S.P.Q.2d (BNA) 1666, 1669 (Fed. Cir. 1997) (finding inequitable conduct based in part on attorney's failure to disclose ongoing litigation during reissue proceeding).
176. *See Golden Valley,* 837 F. Supp. at 1477, 24 U.S.P.Q.2d at 1827.
177. *Marlow Indus., Inc., v. Igloo Prods. Corp.*, 2003 WL 21212626 (Fed. Cir. 2003).

proceeding itself. Frequently these arguments and application of the references could be construed as material to a related case under prosecution or that has issued in a U.S. application.

Additionally, as U.S. prosecution advances more frequently than some foreign jurisdictions, whenever a U.S. patent is reopened in a reexamination or through reissue, all foreign search reports, oppositions (or trials for invalidation), as well as related U.S. application citations and office actions should be accumulated and submitted to the extent that the claims of those related applications are similar to the case in question.

In the end, all of this translates to more time and effort on the part of the practitioner, and thus more cost to the client, and also more time and effort on the part of the examiner to consider the references.

14. Misrepresentations of Information Relating to Inventorship

"[I]nformation about inventorship is material under 37 C.F.R. § 1.56."[178] "In practice, patent examiners do not normally engage in determination of the respective contributions of the individual members of an inventive entity as part of making an *ex parte* examination; rather, it is the responsibility of the applicants and their attorneys to ensure that the inventors named in an application are the only true inventors."[179] Although under some circumstances, invalidity caused by misjoinder and nonjoinder can be corrected under 35 U.S.C. section 256,[180] leaving off an inventor, or (more rarely) naming as an inventor a person who did not contribute to claimed subject matter can result in unenforceability.[181]

At least twice, the Federal Circuit affirmed findings of inequitable conduct based on issues concerning misjoinder or nonjoinder of inventors. First, in *Frank's Casing Crew & Rental Tools, Inc. v. PMR Techs., Ltd.*,[182] the court

---

178. *Perseptive Biosystems, Inc. v. Pharmacia Biotech, Inc.*, 225 F.3d 1315, 1321 (Fed. Cir. 2000). See generally Antigone Kriss, *Misrepresentation of Inventorship and the Inequitable Conduct Defense: Perseptive Biosystems, Inc. v. Pharmacia Biotech, Inc.*, 12 FED. CIR. B.J. 285 (2002).

179. *See Bd. of Educ. v. Am. Bioscience, Inc.*, 333 F.3d 1330, 1344, 67 U.S.P.Q.2d (BNA) 1252, 1262 (Fed. Cir. 2003) (reversing finding of inequitable conduct because it concluded that each named inventor and only true inventors were named).

180. *See Fina Oil & Chem. Co. v. Ewen*, 123 F.3d 1466, 43 U.S.P.Q.2d (BNA) 1935 (Fed. Cir. 1997).

181. Leaving off an inventor is worse than naming a "non-inventor" because only those persons substantively involved in prosecuting an application have a duty to disclose material information under section 1.56. Thus, if an inventor is left off, the PTO will not receive information concerning patentability from the person most likely to know it—an actual inventor.

182. 292 F.3d 1363, 63 U.S.P.Q.2d (BNA) 1065 (Fed. Cir. 2002).

affirmed a finding of unenforceability where the two named inventors deliberately concealed a true inventor's involvement in the conception of the claimed invention and "engaged in a pattern of intentional conduct designed to deceive the attorneys and the patent office as to who the true inventors were." It is not clear that derivation occurred, however, nor that the finding of inequitable conduct was based on that. Instead, the Federal Circuit in affirming noted that the district court had focused on evidence that the named inventors had omitted the inventor as part of a "deliberate schem[e]" "to claim the patents for themselves and to omit" the omitted inventor "from participation."[183]

Second, in *PerSeptive Biosystems v. Pharmacia Biotech*,[184] the court affirmed unenforceability, not because true inventors were omitted, but because of statements made to obfuscate that there might have been a dispute about that question. In so holding, the Federal Circuit seemed to suggest that, even if inventorship *were* correct, statements intended to hide the fact that it might not be correct could be material:

> There can be no doubt that—irrespective of whether the district court was correct in holding . . . that the inventorship was incorrect—the intentional "misrepresentations, omissions and half-truths to the PTO," made as a "persistent course" of conduct, are highly material. As the court found, these falsehoods and omissions were calculated to "obfuscate the threshold issue of inventorship." As a critical requirement for obtaining a patent, inventorship is material. Examiners are required to reject applications under 35 U.S.C. § 102(f) on the basis of improper inventorship. Accordingly, the Manual of Patent Examining Procedure details the "rules" of inventorship to be used by examiners, see *id.*, and specifically notes that information about inventorship is material under 37 C.F.R. § 1.56.
>
> Furthermore, the intentional falsehoods and omissions found by the district court easily meet our oft-stated test for materiality: [I]nformation is material if there "is a 'substantial likelihood that a reasonable examiner would consider it important in deciding whether to allow the application to issue as a patent.'" As we noted above, an examiner must attend to the question of inventorship, pursuant to 35 U.S.C. § 102(f). A full and accurate disclosure of the true nature of the relationship between PerSeptive and Polymer Labs, and the contributions of Warner, Lloyd, and Rounds, would have been "important" to a reasonable examiner's consideration of the inventorship question.
>
> PerSeptive's argument that the patents' claims were narrowed during prosecution, thereby curing any possible inventorship problem, misses the point. First, whether the inventorship of the patents as issued is correct does not determine the materiality of the statements in this case, just as whether

---

183. *Id.*
184. 225 F.3d 1315, 56 U.S.P.Q.2d (BNA) 1001 (Fed. Cir. 2000).

issues relating to 1.56 are triggered and are applicable to the same extent as previously discussed. A similar standard applies for an *inter partes* reexamination as set forth in 37 C.F.R. section 1.915.

Thus, the same considerations apply here as discussed for the prosecution of an application. Additionally, as reexamination affords the applicant the ability to introduce art, a careful review of all related applications both in the United States and abroad should be made to make sure all art has been cited, and any new intervening art should now be cited.

CHAPTER
9

Maintenance Fees and Annuities

A. Maintenance Fees   164

B. Other Issues   166

The failure to pay U.S. maintenance fees and foreign annuities has led to an increasing number of malpractice claims.[1] As a result, malpractice insurers have placed greater pressure on law firms to outsource their annuity and maintenance fee payments to third parties such as Computer Patent Annuities. This chapter reviews obligations concerning maintenance fees and annuities, as well as practical business methods of addressing these issues.

---

1. *See, e.g., Svedala Indus., Inc. v. Winston & Strawn,* 1993 WL 198918 (N.D. Ill. June 10, 1993) (lapse of Australian patents).

    An additional, interesting twist arose in *CardioGrip Corp. v. Mueller & Smith, LP,* 2008 U.S. Dist. LEXIS 2627 (S.D. Ohio Jan. 14, 2008). There the lawyers obtained a patent for a client and calendared maintenance fees on their docketing system. The client later sold the patent to a third party. When the lawyers did not remind the third party of maintenance fees, it sued. The court held there was no attorney-client relationship sufficient to sustain a legal malpractice claim, granting summary judgment to the defendant lawyers. The assignee argued that the lawyers had continued to represent the patentee and, by reason of the assignment, it, too, because the firm had calendared and mailed maintenance fee reminders and had also worked to revive two patents that lapsed for failure to pay maintenance fees. The court held there was no attorney-client relationship with the assignee. Conversely, in *Mindscape, Inc. v. Media Depot, Inc.,* 973 F. Supp. 1130 (N.D. Cal. 1997), the court found an ongoing attorney-client relationship existed under somewhat similar facts because there "were unsettled matters tangential to a case." Undocumented ending dates in patent practice can, in other words, create fact-dependent ambiguities and circumstances.

A. Maintenance Fees

The U.S. Patent and Trademark Office (USPTO) has no duty to remind patent holders of maintenance fee due dates.[2] Thus, the patent holder or the agent for the patent holder has to make sure that docketing systems are in place to make certain that the maintenance fees are timely paid. Several well-known commercial docketing systems are available to set up electronic ticklers.

Late payment can be cured by paying additional fees to the USPTO, so long as the delay is no more than six months. Beyond that, it becomes more difficult to seek revival of a patent. Specifically, 35 U.S.C. section 41 provides that the patent holder can always pay the maintenance fee if it is within six months of the due date. Then, the payment is always accepted.

Once beyond the six-month window, however, it becomes more difficult to revive the patent. The patent holder and/or practitioner would have to show either unintentional or unavoidable abandonment. There are instances in which the patent holder can seek reinstatement and pay the maintenance fee if the failure occurred after six months but within thirty months of the payment due date. Under 35 U.S.C. section 41(c), within that window the patent holder can seek reinstatement by reason of unintentional abandonment. After thirty months, the request to accept the late payment and reinstate the patent must be submitted as unavoidable.

Because the Office of Enrollment and Discipline (OED) is becoming increasingly active, practitioners should limit the number of both unintentional and unavoidable abandonments sought, as OED has promised to tracking the numbers of reinstatements sought by practitioners. These should be submitted with appropriate documentation preferably with facts supporting reasonable finding of unintentional abandonment let alone unavoidable abandonment. In addition, it may be wise to protect against changed recollections and miscommunications by having a letter from the client in the file authorizing the patent to be allowed to go abandoned for failure to pay a maintenance fee.

The patent owner is considered to have notice of the duty to pay the maintenance fee because the notice function is satisfied by the communication to the patent holder's attorney.[3] Given the notice function and the increasing

---

2. Manual of Patent Examining Procedure (MPEP) § 2575 ("Under the statutes and the regulations, the Office has no duty to notify patentees when their maintenance fees are due. It is the responsibility of the patentee to ensure that the maintenance fees are paid to prevent expiration of the patent . . . The notice provided by the Office are courtesies in nature and intended to aid patentees.").

3. "[N]otice to an 'applicant' under the practice of the Patent Office is satisfied by notice to his attorney." Thus, the applicant/patentee is constructively aware of issuance of the patent and the need to pay maintenance fees. *Rosenberg v. Carr Fastener Co.*, 51 F.2d 1014, 10 U.S.P.Q. 448 (2d Cir. 1931).

malpractice claims for failure to pay maintenance fees, once a case is allowed, the attorney should clearly set forth to the client what the attorney's and client's respective duties are. In fact, the patent holder's delay in payment "caused by the mistakes or omissions of his voluntarily chosen representative does not constitute unavoidable delay within the meeting of 35 U.S.C. § 41."[4] Thus, the patent holder is bound by the acts of his or her lawyer or agent and cannot avoid the consequences incurred by his or her acts or omissions.[5]

Practically, on allowance, the attorney or agent should contact the client to agree on whether the patent maintenance fees are to be paid by the attorney, the client, or the third party. The agreement should be confirmed in writing.

If the practitioner is not responsible, then the client should be advised to change the correspondence address for the patent to the address designated by the client. We note that the fee address must be an address associated with a customer number, and smaller clients may not have a customer number. Thus, changing the correspondence address could be a problem and can require the practitioner to educate the client. Information regarding change of fee address to receive notice is discussed in the Manual of Patent Examining Procedure (MPEP) at sections 2540 and 2542 pursuant to 37 C.F.R. section 1.363.

It should be emphasized that if the practitioner is no longer responsible for maintenance fees, then power of attorney also should be changed.[6] Otherwise, the practitioner maintains the duty in the eyes of the USPTO. Additionally, if the practitioner switches firms or moves, then the practitioner must update the power of attorney for issued cases. A mere change of address filed only with the OED is insufficient to change the correspondence address for patents in which the practitioner has power of attorney.[7]

Increasingly, law firms are not handling annuities all together. Even minimal supervision of their party payers such as Computer Patent Annuities, can result in the law firm shouldering the burden for failure to pay annuities. For example, in *Campbell v. Holland & Knight L.L.P.*, Case No. 24C05007868, Circuit Court for Baltimore City—Civil System, a Johns Hopkins professor sought $20 million from Computer Patent Annuities for failure to pay a

4. *In re Patent No. 5,100,001*, Paper No. 19 (Comm'r Pat. July 27, 2006), *available at* http://www.uspto.gov/web/offices/com/sol/foia/comm/maint/5100001.pdf.
5. *Smith v. Diamond*, 209 U.S.P.Q. 1091 (D.D.C. 1981) (relying on *Link v. Wabash R.R. Co.*, 370 U.S. 626 (1962)).
6. Although this can occasionally be mitigated by the facts of the case, if avoidable, practitioners should seek to avoid. *See, e.g., Univ. of Iowa Research Found. v. Beveridge, DeGrandi, Weilacher & Young L.L.P.*, 50 U.S.P.Q.2d 1620 (S.D. Iowa 1998) wherein the law firm was alleged to be negligent for failure to pay the maintenance fee. The case was dismissed for lack of personal jurisdiction because there was no sufficient minimal contact between the Washington, D.C.–based law firm and the forum.
7. *See, e.g., In re Patent No. 4,409,763*, 7 U.S.P.Q.2d 1798 (Comm'r Pat. 1988).

Japanese annuity.[8] Although the case was dismissed with prejudice after the start of discovery, it emphasizes the need to get out of the business of handling annuities, especially in countries such as Japan. Japan is well known for the inability to revive patents for failure to pay an annuity or applications for a failure to respond, although recently there has been an indication that this may eventually change.

B. Other Issues

If the law firm is in the business of paying maintenance fees and annuities, then quality control practices should be instituted to make sure matters are handled correctly. This is particularly acute in dealing with lateral attorneys or acquisitions of patent groups and making sure that the integrity of the docketing data as to maintenance and annuity fees is accurately transferred and/or docketed so that the acquiring law firm does not automatically newly acquire a liability. For general practice firms, wherein many have gone through the vogue of gaining individuals and groups, there must be an understanding of the business needs to avoid the liability. Frequently, general practice firms lack an initial understanding of the foundation and initial costs of handling a practice that involves patent prosecution. Additionally, issues remain about merging data from disparate docketing systems and maintenance of the integrity of such data. Although costly, until the integrity of the data can be confirmed, it is frequently recommended that two docketing systems be run for 6 to 12 months to insure that the data is intact, current, and complete. Remember, the cost of the second docketing system is minimal as compared to the actual costs and public relations costs of a malpractice suit.

Another issue is one of retirement or death of a practitioner. For solo practitioners, notices should go out to the client as well as to the USPTO that the individual has retired and is no longer responsible for the case. Likewise, firms should notify clients if the attorney with power of attorney has died to collect instructions to proceed. Otherwise, the firm will keep the responsibility, even if the practitioner dies.

---

8. Daniel Ostrovsky, *Johns Hopkins Professor Seeks $20M from Computer Patent Annuities*, THE DAILY RECORD (BALTIMORE), Sept. 1, 2005, *available at* http://findarticles.com/p/articles/mi_qn4183/is_20050901/ai_n15336570.

CHAPTER

10

Combining Prosecution with Other Forms of Representation

A. Identifying the Applicable Standards   168

B. Combining Prosecution and Litigation   169
    1. The Possibility of Misuse of Discovery Materials While
        Prosecuting Applications   169
        A. Is Prosecution of Patents by Itself Sufficient to Bar
            Access to Highly Confidential Information?   170
    2. *In re Sibia*   172
    3. The Majority View   176
    4. A Suggested Analysis   180

C. A Proposed Prosecution Bar Raises Potential
    Conflicts and Liability   182

D. Issues to Consider in Crafting Protective Orders   186
    1. Liability and Disqualification of Prosecuting Litigators   190

E. Inequitable Conduct as a Conflict   191

F. Depositions of Prosecuting Litigators   192
    1. Advocate-as-Witness Disqualification   194

G. Combining Opinion and Trial Representations   197
    1. Advocate-as-Witness Disqualification   197
        A. The Courts Split on Advocate-as-Witness
            Disqualification   198
        B. What to Do   200
    2. Enhanced Risk of Waiver of Work Product   201
        A. What to Do   209

H. Conclusion   209

This chapter addresses ethical issues that face attorneys and firms that combine the prosecution of patents with other forms of representation, including opinion work and litigation. It begins by briefly discussing choice of law.

A. Identifying the Applicable Standards

The propriety of particular conduct can often hinge on the determination of which rules apply. In addition, courts often rely on applicable ethical rules in determining the standard of care.[1] For that reason, lawyers must consider whether and to what extent each of the following bears on their conduct: (a) state ethics rules; (b) the Patent and Trademark Office Code of Professional Conduct (PTO Code), and whether it is the Office of Enrollment and Discipline's (OED) interpretation or that of some other USPTO entity that has control; (c) state substantive law (fiduciary duty, agency, and so on); (d) whether the Federal Circuit or regional circuits have jurisdiction over the issue; (e) "federal" ethical standards, however formulated by the regional circuit; and (f) the appropriate circuit's law interpreting the Federal Rules of Civil Procedure. When the conduct is in connection with prosecution, then a preemption analysis may be needed as the final step.

With the choice of law issues in mind, this chapter now addresses the problems that can arise by combining other forms of representation with patent prosecution.

---

1. Some courts hold that applicable ethical rules are admissible as evidence of the standard of care under some circumstances, *see, e.g., Two Thirty Nine Joint Venture v. Joe*, 60 S.W.3d 896 (Tex. Ct. App. 2001), *rev'd on other grounds*, 145 S.W.3d 150 (Tex. 2004), whereas others hold they are inadmissible, *see, e.g., Hizey v. Carpenter*, 830 P.2d 646 (Wash. 1992). *See generally* Stephen E. Kalish, *How to Encourage Lawyers to Be Ethical: Do Not Use the Ethics Codes as a Basis for Regular Law Decisions*, 13 Geo. J. Legal Ethics 649 (2000); Douglas L. Christian & Michael Christian, *Twice Bitten: Violations of Ethical Rules As Evidence of Legal Malpractice*, 28 The Brief 62 (1999); Gary A. Munneke & Anthony E. Davis, *The Standard of Care in Legal Malpractice: Do the Model Rules of Professional Conduct Define It?*, 22 J. Legal Prof. 33, 33 (1997/1998); David J. Fish, *The Use of the Illinois Rules of Professional Conduct to Establish the Standard of Care in Attorney Malpractice Litigation: An Illogical Practice*, 23 S. Ill. U.L.J. 65 (1998); Note, *The Evidentiary Use of the Ethics Codes in Legal Malpractice: Erasing a Double Standard*, 109 Harv. L. Rev. 1102, 1118 (1996); James I. Sullivan, *Impact of Ethical Rules and Other Quasi-Standards on Standard of Care*, 61 Def. Couns. J. 100, 101 (1994) ("Analysis of the legal malpractice standard of care frequently requires consideration of the potential impact of ethical rules."); Teresa Schafer Sullivan & Thomas H. Blaske, *Legal Ethics and Legal Malpractice: A Beauty and a Beast in Search of Each Other*, 74 Mich. B.J. 150 (1995); Laura Callaway Hart et al., *From Offense to Defense: Defending Legal Malpractice Claims*, 45 S.C. L. Rev. 771, 776 (1994).

B. Combining Prosecution and Litigation

A practitioner whose firm both litigates patent infringement suits and prosecutes applications faces at least two broad categories of potential liability or allegations of unethical conduct: those that arise from having access to a third-party's proprietary information *while* prosecuting patents for a client, and those that arise from acting as a litigator in a matter concerning a patent or patents that the lawyer *previously* obtained for the client. The former category of issues arise when the same lawyer is *concurrently* retained by the same client in multiple roles; the latter when the lawyer is *successively* retained by the same client in multiple roles.

1. The Possibility of Misuse of Discovery Materials While Prosecuting Applications

An attorney who litigates can gain access to an opposing party's proprietary information through the exchange of discovery. Where litigators also prosecute patents for a client, they face the risk that the opposing party may contend that they should not be allowed to obtain information through discovery, which would permit them to misuse that information during prosecution by, for example, using that information to obtain a patent on behalf of their client. If a lawyer prosecutes applications in a highly specialized area of technology on behalf of a client and obtains proprietary information from an opposing party as a result of discovery exchanges in infringement litigation, the opposing party will seek to prevent misuse of the information by seeking a protective order that prevents the lawyer from access to that information.[2] Entry of a protective order denying access to critical information will effectively disqualify a lawyer from representing the client in infringement litigation; however, this generally leaves other lawyers in the disqualified lawyer's firm able to continue the representation.

But avoiding "disqualification" by avoiding entry of such a protective order creates potential liability for the prosecuting litigator. He or she can be accused of using the opposing party's information during prosecution and be sued for money damages. In addition, the client of a prosecuting litigator may be sued by the opposing party, who can argue that it has equitable ownership of patents obtained through misused information.

---

2. *See, e.g., Nazomi Commc'ns, Inc. v. Arm Holdings PLC*, No. C 02-02521-JF, 2002 U.S. Dist. LEXIS 21400, 2002 WL 32831822 (N.D. Cal. Oct. 11, 2002) (also seeking to prevent lawyers from negotiating licenses in the field), *vacated on other grounds*, 403 F.3d 1364, 74 U.S.P.Q.2d 1458 (Fed. Cir. 2005).

The issue of access to information by a prosecuting litigator creates important issues for both courts and counsel. The courts must be careful whether and to what extent they bar prosecuting litigators from access to discovery materials: Imposing a bar too frequently will unnecessarily drive up litigation expenses, whereas permitting unfettered access by prosecuting litigators to a competitor's most current and important product development information could result in inadvertent or even intentional misuse of the information during prosecution. Similarly, counsel must be careful in seeking access where inadvertent disclosure could occur, because a prosecuting litigator's exposure to such information could result in liability by the lawyer and his or her client for misappropriation of trade secrets. This section analyzes the cases addressing this issue and provides guidance for the courts and for practitioners when confronting the competing interests raised when a prosecuting attorney is also a litigator.[3]

A. Is Prosecution of Patents by Itself Sufficient to Bar Access to Highly Confidential Information?

Federal Rule of Civil Procedure 26(c)(1) states that a "court may, for good cause, issue an order to protect a party or person from annoyance, embarrassment, oppression, or undue burden or expense, including . . . (G) requiring that a trade secret or other confidential research, development, or commercial information not be revealed or be revealed only in a specified way."[4] Courts "routinely" recognize the fact that such information is going to be exchanged in most patent cases, and that often such information is of critical commercial importance.[5] Sensitive information is almost always relevant in a patent case.[6] And even in a patent case where the litigators do not prosecute

---

3. The need to protect confidential information from disclosure to prosecuting attorneys has been addressed even where the prosecuting attorneys are in separate firms from those litigating the case. *See, e.g., BASF Corp. v. United States,* 321 F. Supp. 2d 1373 (Ct. Int'l Trade 2004) (granting protective order requiring that an ethical screen be established between firm representing party in litigation and another firm that prosecuted patents for that party). Normally, the usual prohibition in a protective order limiting use of information disclosed during litigation to "the litigation" would seem to obviate the need for such steps, but in extreme cases practitioners should consider whether to include provisions which more firmly restrict use and disclosure of information.

4. Fed. R. Civ. P. 26(c)(1), (c)(1)(G) (2007).

5. *Commissariat a L'Energie Atomique v. Dell Computer Corp.,* No. 03-484-KAJ, 2004 U.S. Dist. LEXIS 12782, at *6 (D. Del. May 25, 2004) ("This court has routinely recognized the importance of protecting technical information, particularly in patent cases."); *see, e.g., Safe Flight Instrument Corp. v. Sundstrand Data Control Inc.,* 682 F. Supp. 20, 21–22, 7 U.S.P.Q.2d 1823, 1824 (D. Del. 1988).

6. *See* John M. Benassi & Colbern C. Stuart III, *Discovery and Privilege, in* Laurence H. Pretty, Patent Litigation § 4:12.3 (2003) ("In virtually every patent case, the parties will have trade secret, confidential or proprietary technical, business and marketing information and

patents and no in-house counsel is involved, district courts will almost without question enter a protective order that limits the use and disclosure of information exchanged during discovery. Generally, such protective orders prohibit use or disclosure of information beyond that necessary to prosecute the lawsuit.[7]

Under some circumstances, courts have recognized that it is insufficient to merely restrict use of information to the litigation itself. Foremost, courts often hold that in-house counsel who, in addition to representing his or her employer in the litigation, has responsibilities to his or her employer for product design, pricing, and similar competitive business activities should be precluded from having access to materials exchanged during discovery to the extent that the materials could be deliberately or inadvertently used in business-related activities.[8] It is settled that in-house counsel who are engaged in such "competitive decision-making" can be denied access to certain sensitive discovery.[9] But even though that proposition is settled, the scope of what constitutes competitive decision-making by in-house counsel remains unclear, at least at the margins. For example, in one recent case the head of the intellectual property (IP) department was found *not* to be engaged in competitive decision-making.[10]

Does disclosure of information to outside counsel who prosecutes patents for the opposing party create similar concerns that would justify denial of access to sensitive information? The question of whether attorneys who prosecute patents may be similarly barred has split the courts.[11] As the following

---

documents that they do not want to show to the other side, especially if the other side is a direct competitor.").

7. *See generally* Wayne F. Reinke, Comment, *Limiting the Scope of Discovery: The Use of Protective Orders and Document Retention Programs in Patent Litigation*, 2 ALB. L.J. SCI. & TECH. 175 (1992).

8. *See U.S. Steel Corp. v. United States*, 730 F.2d 1465, 1467–68 (Fed. Cir. 1984); *Infosint S.A. v. H. Lundbeck A.S.*, 2007 U.S. Dist. LEXIS 36678, 2007 WL 1467784 (S.D.N.Y. May 16, 2007) (analyzing whether in-house counsel engaged in competitive decision-making); *Affymetrix, Inc. v. Illumina, Inc.*, 2005 U.S. Dist. LEXIS 15482 (D. Del. 2005) (barring certain in-house lawyers from access); *Intel Corp. v. VIA Techs., Inc.*, 198 F.R.D. 525, 531–32 (N.D. Cal. 2000) (barring access); *News Am. v. Marquis*, No. CV 000177440S, 27 Conn. L. Rptr. 195, 2000 Conn. Super. LEXIS 1273, 2000 WL 726821, at *1 (Conn. Super. Ct. May 3, 2000) (granting access); *Volvo Penta of the Americas, Inc. v. Brunswick Corp.*, 187 F.R.D. 240, 242–44 (E.D. Va. 1999) (granting access); *In re Indep. Serv. Orgs. Antitrust Litig.*, No. CIV. A. MDL-1021, 1995 U.S. Dist. LEXIS 4698, 1995 WL 151739 (D. Kan. Mar. 9, 1995) (granting access).

9. *See generally* Louis S. Sorrell, *In-House Counsel Access to Confidential Information Produced During Discovery in Intellectual Property Litigation*, 27 J. MARSHALL L. REV. 657 (1994).

10. *Intervet, Inc. v. Merial Ltd.*, 241 F.R.D. 55 (D.D.C. 2007). *See also R.R. Donnelly & Sons Co. v. Quark, Inc.*, 2007 U.S. Dist. LEXIS 424, 2007 WL 61885 (D. Del. Jan. 4, 2007) (analyzing which house counsel were competitive decision-makers).

11. *See generally* James Pooley, *Update on Trade Secret Law*, 764 PLI/Pat 173 (2003) (discussing cases generally).

cases show, even though the Federal Circuit has specifically held that a denial of access "cannot rest on a general assumption that one group of lawyers are more likely or less likely to breach their duty under a protective order,"[12] one dominating line of cases holds that proof that a lawyer is engaged in patent prosecution is sufficient to bar access. This divide grows from whether courts should treat outside counsel as if they are involved in competitive decision-making solely by reason of their prosecution activities.[13] Those courts that conclude that the activities of patent prosecutors create sufficient risk have left prosecuting litigators with a choice: They may either have access to the information, or they may prosecute patents, but they may not do both.[14]

2. *In re Sibia*

Several courts—including the Federal Circuit (in an unpublished decision)— hold that patent prosecution by itself is not enough to justify denial of access. This section discusses this line of cases, which represents the minority view.

The origins are a district court case that resulted in an unpublished decision by the Federal Circuit. In *Sibia Neurosciences, Inc. v. Cadus Pharmaceutical Corp.*,[15] the prosecuting litigator, DeConti, had been prosecuting patents in the field of cell surface receptors and related proteins and assay methods for his client, Cadus, for two years before Sibia filed an infringement suit against Cadus. The suit involved that same technology that DeConti had described as being "kind of the everyday stuff of biotechnology assays."[16] Sibia sought a protective order to preclude DeConti from prosecuting patents in that field if he was allowed access to certain information during the suit. The lawyer stated at the hearing on entry of the protective order that he did not provide advice on inventions because they "are made . . . by inventors. We basically receive information from inventors and we make sure that that information is protected to . . . the [full] scope of the law as best we can,

---

12. *U.S. Steel*, 730 F.2d at 1468.
13. *See generally* Julia S. Ferguson et al., *Conflicts in Intellectual Property Law: A Brief Survey*, 616 PLI/Pat 539, 580–83 (2000).
14. *See, e.g., Cummins-Allison Corp. v. Glory Ltd.*, No. 02 C 7008, 2003 U.S. Dist. LEXIS 23653, at *26–27 (N.D. Ill. Jan. 2, 2004) ("[T]he party could choose not to disclose confidential information to patent prosecution counsel, in which case that counsel could continue to prosecute patent applications; or, the party could choose to reveal confidential information to patent prosecution counsel, and accept limitations on the attorney's ability to prosecute certain patent applications for a period of time.").
15. No. 96-1231-IEG (POR), 1997 U.S. Dist. LEXIS 24130 (S.D. Cal. July 15, 1997).
16. *Id.* at *12.

so our work goes into basically making sure that the invention once made is properly protected by patent."[17] He further testified that he was not generally aware of marketing information, nor was he involved in product development or pricing information, but instead simply protected, through patenting, inventions disclosed to him by the client.[18] Significantly, he also testified that he had more than fifty biotech clients, "many of which are involved in the field of cell surface proteins and receptors."[19] In this vein, he stated that he had "a lot of confidential trade secret information" from each client, and yet he kept the information compartmentalized and distinct.[20]

Based on these facts, the magistrate entered a protective order precluding anyone with access to certain information from prosecuting patents "in the area of cell surface receptors and assay methods relating to the same" until one year after any appeals in the case were resolved.[21] However, the district court modified the magistrate's order,[22] noting that DeConti had no involvement in pricing or similar business-related activities that had been found to constitute competitive decision-making.[23] Then, the court turned to the argument that a ban was justified because of "the unique role which patent attorneys play in a client's competitive patenting decisions."[24] The court rejected it because it would create a "per se rule that counsel who prosecute patents in a particular field should always be subject to disqualification by protective order from viewing confidential information produced in . . . enforcement litigation. . . . Under this rule, a patent holder . . . would be precluded as a practical matter from retaining its outside patent counsel to defend it . . . or to prosecute an enforcement action on its behalf."[25] Instead, the district court credited the testimony of the DeConti that he could "segregate this information" and held that the magistrate had "erred in finding that DeConti' involvement in the prosecution of patents for Cadus, by itself, demonstrated the existence of a risk of inadvertent disclosure."[26]

---

17. *Id.* at *10.
18. *Id.* at *10–11.
19. *Id.* at *11.
20. *Id.* at *11–12.
21. *Id.* at *3.
22. *Id.* at *21 (holding the entry of the bar was "clearly erroneous and contrary to law").
23. *Id.* at *21–22 (noting that he did not serve on the board of his client; did not share employees with it; had no involvement in pricing, design, or similar activities; and generally had "a typical outside counsel relationship").
24. *Id.* at *23.
25. *Id.* at *23–24.
26. *Id.* at *24–25. The court went on to note that the case that Sibia relied on, *Motorola, Inc. v. Interdigital Tech. Corp.*, No. 93-488-LON, 1994 U.S. Dist. LEXIS 20714 (D. Del. 1994), had itself distinguished the same situation as in *Sibia* where an attorney would have "prosecut[ed] patent applications for a long period of time." *Motorola, Inc.*, 1994 U.S. Dist. LEXIS 20714,

Sibia then sought mandamus from the Federal Circuit, which denied the petition in an unpublished decision.[27] In refusing to grant the writ, the court expressly rejected the argument that involvement in patent prosecution was, by itself, sufficient to justify a bar, stating: "denying access to Cadus' outside counsel on the ground that they also prosecute patents for Cadus is the type of generalization counseled against in *U.S. Steel* (*v. United States*, 730 F.2d 1465 [Fed. Cir. 1984]). The facts, not the category, must inform the result."[28] Thus, the Federal Circuit in *Sibia* clearly held that patent prosecution does not mean the prosecuting attorney is a competitive decision-maker nor does not by itself require denial of access to information. The court denied the petition for mandamus because, although the "magistrate judge found that Mr. DeConti was very involved in the prosecution of patents," it "did not make any findings regarding outside counsel's involvement in 'competitive decision-making,' such as involvement in pricing or product design."[29] It affirmed the district court's denial of entry of a protective order with the bar because "none of the indicia of 'competitive decision-making' was present here."[30]

Several courts have agreed with the Federal Circuit that someone who prosecutes patents will not automatically be considered a competitive decision-maker.[31] Courts following *In re Sibia* generally hold that the fact

---

at *16. The *Sibia* court concluded that "Cadus will suffer a serious and unnecessary hardship from the disqualification of . . . its patent counsel for more than a year before Sibia commenced this litigation." *Sibia Neurosciences*, 1997 U.S. Dist. LEXIS 24130, at *26.

27. *In re Sibia Neurosciences, Inc.*, 1997 U.S. App. LEXIS 31828 (Fed. Cir. Oct. 22, 1997).
28. *Id.* at *7.
29. *Id.* at *8.
30. *Id.* The court emphasized that "'the standard is not 'regular contact' with other corporate officials who make policy, or even competitive decisions, but 'advice and participation' in 'competitive decision making.'" *Id.* at *8–9 (quoting *Matsushita Elec. Indus. Co. v. United States*, 929 F.2d 1577, 1580 (Fed. Cir. 1991)).
31. *E.g., Avocent Redmond Corp. v. Rose Elec., Inc.*, 2007 WL 1549477 (W.D. Wash. May 24, 2007) (denying entry of motion for protective order); *Infosint S.A. v. H. Lundbeck A.S.*, 2007 U.S. Dist. LEXIS 36678, 2007 WL 1467784 (S.D.N.Y. May 16, 2007) (barring certain prosecuting attorney from access); *MGP Ingredients, Inc. v. Mars, Inc.*, 245 F.R.D. 497 (D. Kan. 2007) (analyzing two-tiered approach to protective orders); *Trading Techs. Int'l, Inc. v. eSpeed, Inc.*, No. 04 C 5312, 2004 U.S. Dist. LEXIS 19429, at *2, 2004 WL 2534389, at *1 (N.D. Ill. Sept. 24, 2004) (refusing to enter protective order that would deny outside litigation counsel access to certain materials because he was not involved in "pricing, marketing, product design or the like"); *MedImmune, Inc. v. Centocor, Inc.*, 271 F. Supp. 2d 762, 775 (D. Md. 2003) (refusing to enter protective order that would deny outside counsel access to confidential information even though he prosecuted patents for his client because there was no indicia he was a competitive decision-maker); *Nazomi Commc'ns, Inc. v. Arm Holdings PLC*, No. C 02–02521-JF, 2002 U.S. Dist. LEXIS 21400, 2002 WL 32831822 (N.D. Cal. Oct. 11, 2002), *vacated on other grounds*, 403 F.3d 1364, 74 U.S.P.Q.2d 1458 (Fed. Cir. 2005); *Interactive Coupon Mktg. Group, Inc. v. H.O.T.! Coupons, LLC*, No. 98 C 7408, 1999 U.S. Dist. LEXIS 9004, 1999 WL 409990 (N.D. Ill. June 7, 1999), *modified*, 1999 U.S. Dist. LEXIS

that prosecution without more is insufficient to deny access.[32] Instead, these courts look at the facts of the case—including the relationship of the practitioner with the client and her actual practice—to determine whether the practitioner is involved in product design, marketing, pricing, or other business-related decision-making in the pertinent field, and not just prosecutes patents.[33] These courts interpret the Federal Circuit's decision *In re Sibia* to mean that prosecution by itself does not constitute competitive decision-making, but that the specific facts may show that the practitioner's actual activities are sufficient to compel a finding that he or she is engaged in competitive decision-making.

For example, in *Interactive Coupon Marketing Group, Inc. v. H.O.T! Coupons, LLC*,[34] the evidence showed that the prosecuting litigator had "become intimately familiar with Coolsavings' [the plaintiff's] technology and business operations"; had "become involved with various licensing and litigation matters"; and knew "our personnel . . . reviewed our documents, and participated in several high level management meetings regarding intellectual property."[35] Furthermore, the court found that the firm was "deeply involved in representing the client . . . in the context of a fluid, developing technology."[36] Accordingly, the court held that the firm should be precluded from having access to certain discovery information *or* be barred from prosecuting applications until one year after all appeals of the case were resolved.[37]

12437, at *8, 1999 WL 618969 (N.D. Ill. Aug. 9, 1999) ("The court is not persuaded that it is appropriate to disqualify patent prosecution counsel from an active role in its client's litigation as a matter of course."); *In re Certain Magnetic Switches for Coaxial Transmission Lines & Products Containing Same*, No. 337-TA-346, 1993 ITC LEXIS 143, at *4 (Int'l Trade Comm'n Mar. 2, 1993) ("[I]t is not required that counsel cease involvement in patent prosecutions, even in areas of related subject matter, in order to gain access to confidential business information."); *Certain Amorphous Metal Alloys & Amorphous Particles, Inv.* No. 337-TA-143 (July 22, 1983) (refusing to preclude counsel from having access to information unless he agreed not to prosecute patents in related areas)

32. *See, e.g., MedImmune*, 271 F. Supp. 2d at 774 n.13 (recognizing that any other rule would be tantamount to a per se prohibition on access by prosecuting litigators).

33. *Id.* at 775.

34. No. 98 C 7408, 1999 U.S. Dist. LEXIS 9004, 1999 WL 409990 (N.D. Ill. June 7, 1999) *modified*, 1999 U.S. Dist. LEXIS 12437, 1999 WL 618969 (N.D. Ill. Aug. 9, 1999).

35. U.S. Dist. LEXIS 12437, at *4. Ironically, the party had submitted an affidavit touting the firm's close connections with the party to avoid disqualification on another basis—the advocate-as-witness rule. The affidavit was intended to, and did, show that the firm's relationship with the party was such that it would have worked a substantial hardship on the party to have it disqualified. *See id.*

36. *Id.* at *8–9.

37. *Id.* at *11. Although the facts probably warrant the holding, along the way the court stated that "competitive decisionmaking is not limited to decisionmaking about pricing and design but can extend to the extent to the manner in which patent applications are shaped and prosecuted." *Id.* at *10. The statement, viewed in the context of the facts of the case, is correct

Thus, several courts hold that, absent involvement by the prosecuting litigator in pricing, product design, or similar activities, access to sensitive discovery by prosecuting litigators should be allowed and prosecution bars denied.[38] One court appears to reject the need to bar access to any prosecuting litigator. The court in *Nazomi Communications* reasoned that it was sufficient to enter a protective order prohibiting misuse of information disclosed during litigation; otherwise, it would "presume that attorneys are unable to abide by both the terms of the protective order and the Rules of Professional Conduct."[39]

But other district courts have either entered protective orders restricting access to information or enjoined (in so many words) the person from prosecuting applications in "related" areas for a period of time.[40] The following section examines the majority view from cases at the opposite side of the divide.

3. The Majority View

Although often purporting to reject the position, several courts have held that patent prosecution by itself, without inquiry into the actual facts and circumstances of the practitioner's approach to prosecution or the scope of his representation, is sufficient to bar access. This section discusses these cases.

At the outset is the question: How can courts ignore *In re Sibia*?[41] They feel they can do so for three reasons. First, some of the courts reject reliance on

---

since the court did not hold that patent prosecution per se constitutes competitive decision-making.

38. For example, the *MedImmune* court distinguished *Interactive Coupon Mktg. Corp. v. H.O.T.! Coupons LLC* on the basis that "[i]f 'shaping' patent applications amounts to competitive decision-making, the Court has trouble imagining a patent prosecutor who would not meet that standard." *MedImmune, Inc. v. Centocor, Inc.*, 271 F. Supp. 2d 762, 774 n.13 (D. Md. 2003). *See also Presidio Components, Inc. v. Am. Technical Ceramics Corp.*, 2008 WL 608407 (S.D. Cal. Mar. 4, 2008) (applying a fact intensive analysis).

39. *Nazomi Commc'ns, Inc. v. Arm Holdings PLC*, No. C 02–02521-JF, 2002 U.S. Dist. LEXIS 21400, at *8, 2002 WL 32831822 (N.D. Cal. Oct. 11, 2002), *vacated on other grounds*, 403 F.3d 1364, 74 U.S.P.Q.2d 1458 (Fed. Cir. 2005).

40. *See, e.g., Mikohn Gaming Corp. v. Acres Gaming, Inc.*, 1998 U.S. Dist. LEXIS 22251, 50 U.S.P.Q.2d 1783 (D. Nev. 1998).

41. *Sibia* is not the only decision by the Federal Circuit relevant to this discussion. The Federal Circuit in 1997 also addressed a similar question, and as in *Sibia* issued an unpublished decision. *In re Voith Sulzer Paper Tech. of Heidenheim Germany*, No. 506, 1997 U.S. App. LEXIS 12854, 1997 WL 264842 (Fed. Cir. May 6, 1997) (refusing to grant petition for mandamus to have trial court enter an order requiring that lawyers who obtained certain documents refrain from prosecuting patents).

In re Sibia because it was an unpublished decision.[42] Technically, a court is not required to give any weight to an unpublished decision of the Federal Circuit (although that does not mean that the logic and reasoning of the opinion are wrong and should be ignored). Second, some recognize that because *In re Sibia* was a mandamus case in which the court merely refused to grant a writ of mandamus that would require the district court to enter a protective order prohibiting disclosure of information to prosecuting counsel, its impact was somewhat limited.[43] But rejecting *In re Sibia* because of its procedural posture is not appropriate. The court refused to grant mandamus relief where it was undisputed that the litigator was involved in patent prosecution. If involvement in prosecution were enough to warrant a bar, then the petition for writ of mandamus would have been granted because allowing a lawyer who was engaged in prosecution to remain in the case would have been a clear abuse of discretion, and one that resulted in harm to the petitioner. The fact that the court denied the petition also clearly indicates that *something more than prosecution* is required. Third, some courts decide the issue by applying only regional circuit law. If the issue is "unique to patent law,"[44] then the Federal Circuit's decisional law controls, and district courts are not free to apply regional circuit law to the issue. But the courts split, often without addressing whether the Federal Circuit's view is controlling.[45] However, if this is a matter of Federal Circuit law, then the Federal Circuit's views control, even if *In re Sibia* does not.

---

42. *E.g., Mikohn Gaming Corp.*, 1998 U.S. Dist. LEXIS 22251, 50 U.S.P.Q.2d at 1786 n.3 (agreeing with the plaintiff that the Federal Circuit "deemed its opinion unsuitable for publication [and that] [f]or this reason alone *Sibia* should not be considered.").

43. *E.g., id.*

> The case was before the circuit court on a petition for a writ of mandamus, in support of which Sibia had the difficult burden of making a "clear and indisputable" showing that the district court had engaged in "a clear abuse of discretion or usurpation of judicial power." Mikohn's burden here is not so onerous; it need only demonstrate "'good cause'" for its proposed protective order.

> *See generally* Kevin Casey et al., *Standards of Appellate Review in the Federal Circuit: Substance and Semantics*, 11 FED. CIR. B.J. 279 (2001) (analyzing the standards of review as applied by the Federal Circuit).

44. *See generally* Julia S. Ferguson et al., *Conflicts in Intellectual Property Law: A Brief Survey*, 616 PLI/Pat 539, 582–83 (2000) ("[I]t is an open question whether the Federal Circuit shares the restrictive views many district courts have taken with regard to these kinds of protective orders.")

45. Some courts look to *Sibia* and focus on Federal Circuit precedent. *E.g., MedImmune, Inc. v. Centocor, Inc.*, 271 F. Supp. 2d 762, 773 (D. Md. 2003) ("As pronounced by the Federal Circuit, the policy underlying a restriction on counsel's access to confidential materials."). Others specifically abjure reliance on *In re Sibia. See supra* note 54 and accompanying text.

Once freed of adherence to *In re Sibia*, the district courts disagree on the approach.[46] A few find involvement by a litigator in patent prosecution to be enough to warrant a prosecution bar in a protective order.[47] For example, one district court stated that "advice on the scope of patent claims must also be defined as competitive decision-making."[48] What is significant here is the assumption underlying that conclusion. These courts tacitly assume that practitioners have tremendous freedom in crafting the scope of coverage of a patent during patent prosecution, attributing to practitioners abilities and capacities of inventors, not patent attorneys. For example, in a case decided by the influential Delaware district court, the court concluded that prosecuting litigators should be barred from prosecution because once they viewed the opponent's confidential information, they "would have to constantly

---

46. *See Avocent Redmond Corp. v. Rose Elec., Inc.*, 2007 WL 1549477 (W.D. Wash. May 24, 2007) (discussing split).

47. *E.g., SRU Biosystems, Inc. v. Hobbs*, 2005 Mass. Super. LEXIS 361 (Mass. Super. Ct. Aug 2, 2005) (requiring bar); *Chan v. Intuit, Inc.*, 218 F.R.D. 659, 662 (N.D. Cal. 2003) (entering protective order that precluded access to certain discoverable information by those engaged in patent prosecution and holding that "advice on the scope of patent claims must also be defined as competitive decision-making"); *In re Papst Licensing, GmbH, Patent Litig.*, 2000 U.S. Dist. LEXIS 6374 (E.D. La. May 4, 2000) (enjoining prosecution of patents related to patent-in-suit); *Medtronic, Inc. v. Guidant Corp.*, 2001 U.S. Dist. LEXIS 22805, at *13 (D. Minn. Dec. 19, 2001) ("prosecuting patents is distinct from other legal duties and presents unique opportunities for inadvertent disclosure"); *Motorola, Inc. v. Interdigital Tech. Corp.*, No. 93-488-LON, 1994 U.S. Dist. LEXIS 20714, at *13 (D. Del. Dec. 19, 1994) (in entering injunction against prosecuting related applications until one year after suit ended, court rejected attorneys' arguments that, though "theoretically possible for them to abuse the confidential information received, . . . they understand their ethical duty and will act in conformance with it"); *Ideal Toy Corp. v. Tyco Indus., Inc.*, 478 F. Supp. 1191, 1195 (D. Del. 1979) ("Weighing heavily against disclosure [of abandoned patent applications] is the fact that Tyco's counsel in this litigation is also actively engaged in the prosecution of other Tyco applications embracing the same subject matter . . . in the Patent and Trademark Office."); *see also Promega Corp. v. Applera Corp.*, No. 01-C-244-C, 2002 WL 32359938 (W.D. Wis. June 7, 2002) (discussing prosecution bars applicable to both house counsel and expert witnesses contained in protective order); *Semiconductor Energy Lab. Co. v. Sanyo N. Am. Corp.*, No. C.A. 00–018-GMS, 2001 WL 194303, at *1 n.5 (D. Del. Feb. 22, 2001) (noting disagreement among parties as to scope of prosecution bar in protective order); *Davis v. AT&T Corp.*, No. 98-CV-0189S(H), 1998 U.S. Dist. LEXIS 20471, 1998 WL 912012 (W.D.N.Y. Dec. 23, 1998) (discussing disclosure to plaintiff management-level employees); *Avery Dennison Corp. v. UCB SA*, No. 95 C 6351, 1996 U.S. Dist. LEXIS 16070, at *5, 1996 WL 633986, at *2 (N.D. Ill. Oct. 29, 1996) (In allowing discovery of abandoned applications, the court noted that "there has been no showing that counsel of record for UCB [the party seeking access to the abandoned applications] routinely advises UCB regarding patent matters or otherwise serves as UCB's chief patent counsel. In other words, there has been no adequate demonstration that disclosure to counsel is effectively disclosure to UCB.").

48. *Chan v. Intuit, Inc.*, 218 F.R.D. 659, 662 (N.D. Cal. 2003).

challenge the origin of every idea, every spark of genius."[49] As noted below, these assumptions are not correct in every instance.

Other courts also assume facts about patent prosecution, which may not be true in a given case. For example, one decision from the Northern District of Illinois concluded that patent prosecution by its nature constituted competitive decision-making based on the following assumptions about prosecution:

> [P]atent applications are not always fully formed and unchanging when they are filed. Patent applications may be revised in order to respond to a number of factors that may arise, such as concerns expressed by a USPTO examiner—or information about other products that have entered or are about to enter the market.
>
> We would expect patent prosecution counsel to be intimately involved in deciding how to shape the original application, or how later to revise it. It is that intimate involvement in the shaping and revision of patent applications that provides for the risk that patent counsel inadvertently will use information obtained from a party in patent litigation in shaping the application . . . .
>
> [T]heir roles—and not the mere label of "patent prosecutor"—brought them within the scope of what *U.S. Steel* referred to as competitive decision-making.[50]

Although the Northern District of Illinois purported to reject the conclusion that patent prosecution creates a per se bar,[51] the court *assumed* facts about patent prosecution that in effect make prosecution a per se bar: it assumed, for example, that attorneys will be "intimately involved" in shaping applications to cover specific products.[52] Indeed, the court held that if the lawyer had any "role in shaping [the client's] patent applications and how they are prosecuted," then the bar applied.[53] Thus, despite rejecting a per se bar, the court in effect adopted one: Any involvement in "shaping" how

---

49. *Motorola, Inc. v. Interdigital Tech. Corp.*, No. 93-488-LON, 1994 U.S. Dist. LEXIS 20714, at *15 (D. Del. Dec. 19, 1994). This approach was also adopted in *Commissariat a L'Energie Atomique v. Dell Computer Corp.*, No. 03-484-KAJ, 2004 U.S. Dist. LEXIS 12782, at *9 (D. Del. May 25, 2004).

50. *Cummins-Allison Corp. v. Glory Ltd.*, No. 02 C 7008, 2003 U.S. Dist. LEXIS 23653, at *23–24 (N.D. Ill. Jan. 2, 2004).

51. *Id.* at *26–27.

52. *Id.* at *23. Other courts have likewise made assumptions about patent prosecution which may, or may not, be true in a given case. *E.g.*, *Mikohn Gaming Corp. v. Acres Gaming, Inc.*, 1998 U.S. Dist. LEXIS 22251, at *12, 50 U.S.P.Q.2d 1783, 1786 (D. Nev. 1998) ("It therefore cannot be doubted that as patent prosecution counsel Mr. McCollum works very closely with and advises Acres on matters related to product design.").

53. *Cummins-Allison Corp.*, 2003 U.S. Dist. LEXIS 23653, at *28.

patents are prosecuted is enough to justify a bar. Other courts, in addition to the Northern District of Illinois, have reasoned precisely the same way.[54]

This is, of course, flatly contradicted by *In re Sibia*, which held that prosecution, alone, was insufficient to justify a bar. The obvious question is who is right?

4. A Suggested Analysis

The observations made by the courts explaining why patent attorneys should be denied access might justify denying access to putative *inventors—because* they clearly are in position to take information disclosed by an opposing party during litigation, turn around, and then apply for a patent derived from that information. But patent practitioners cannot "invent" subject matter, and cannot—except in unusual circumstances—even be named as inventors along with their clients on patent applications that they are prosecuting. Inventors have a "spark of genius" and file for patents on their inventions. In contrast, patent attorneys prosecute patent applications; they are usually not inventors or product design experts; and, as noted, they do not and generally cannot be inventors along with their clients. Absent facts establishing that a particular patent attorney is in fact involved in inventing or product design, courts should not assume that they are. Patent attorneys do not, solely by prosecuting applications, invent products or make design decisions. That can happen in particular cases, but it is not implicit in the nature of all patent prosecutions.

That said, there can be clear risks to the disclosing party raised by disclosure of sensitive information to a prosecuting litigator. Whether these risks are present in a particular case depends on the facts, not on a caricature of patent prosecution that assumes that patent practitioners are engaged in product design and development when they file an application. A reasoned analysis is required.

Misappropriation of trade secrets is the principal basis for a prosecution bar. For example, the prosecuting litigator can use information disclosed during discovery to draft claims in pending or new applications to cover products that the opposing party intends to bring to market.[55] Another

---

54. *In re Papst Licensing, GmbH, Patent Litig.*, 2000 U.S. Dist. LEXIS 6374 (E.D. La. May 4, 2000) ("advice and participation of the Papst parties' counsel in preparation and prosecution of patent applications related to the patents in suit is an intensely competitive decisionmaking activity").

55. *Papst Licensing, GmbH, Patent Litig.*, 2000 U.S. Dist. LEXIS 6374, at *12 (E.D. La. May 4, 2000) ("Counsel's ability to file new claims in existing and pending patents based on the confidential information discovered during the course of this litigation poses an unacceptable opportunity for inadvertent disclosure and misuse.").

example would be the risk that a litigator who sees draft patent applications of the other party will as a prosecutor "be better able to 'write around' [the disclosing party's] patents when drafting [his client's] own patent applications."[56]

Although these are legitimate concerns, the conclusion that every patent prosecutor is in position to misuse information disclosed during discovery in his role as litigator is not correct. For example, for practitioners only filing foreign applications here in the United States, there may be no direct contact with the ultimate client, with only indirect communications through the foreign associate providing instructions. Consequently, there may be no means of acquiring information that could disqualify the individual. Thus, instead of so presuming, courts should focus, as the Federal Circuit suggested, on the actual realities of the practice and the case.[57] Only by so doing can courts avoid disqualifying counsel in too broad a circumstance, thus unnecessarily driving up litigation costs and providing too much leverage to the opposing party or too often—keeping prosecuting attorneys from gaining access to information where they can misuse it.[58] Whether a prosecuting litigator should be denied discovery of sensitive information depends on the facts and circumstances of each case. Among other things, courts should inquire into whether the technology that the lawyer is prosecuting is sufficiently related to the patent-in-suit to create a reasonable likelihood that trade secrets could be misused. Courts also should consider the role the prosecuting attorney plays: Some companies, for example, do much of the drafting themselves, relying on outside patent counsel less so than others.

Finally, even if counsel is involved in competitive decision-making, courts also look to whether a prosecution bar, or denial of access, would result in

---

56. *Medtronic, Inc. v. Guidant Corp.*, 2001 U.S. Dist. LEXIS 22805, at *12 (D. Minn. Dec. 19, 2001). See *Andrx Pharm., LLC v. GlaxoSmithKline, PLC*, 236 F.R.D. 583 (S.D. Fla. 2006) (relying on similar notions to preclude adding outside counsel who prosecuted applications to protective order).

57. The correct resolution of this issue may depend on whose law controls: If the Federal Circuit's law controls, then *Sibia*, although not binding, suggests that unless outside counsel is involved in *something more than patent prosecution*—such as pricing or product design— counsel is not involved in competitive decision-making. If regional law applies, then whether a prosecuting litigator can be disqualified turns, apparently, on state trade secret law concerning the inevitable disclosure doctrine or other statutes or case law.

58. The choice of law issue discussed above is worth noting here. If a petition to disqualify were filed in the PTO, seeking to bar a practitioner from prosecuting applications because of his or her involvement in litigation, the PTO would look to the PTO Code; in contrast, the federal courts have based their decision not on any ethical rule but on concerns arising from the misuse of trade secrets; in their decisions they have focused almost entirely on jurisprudence developed under FED. R. CIV. P. 26(c).

hardship to the prosecuting litigator's client.[59] The length of time that counsel has been representing the client in either prosecution or litigation, or both, as well as the length of time the litigation has been pending are two obviously pertinent factors.[60]

C. A Proposed Prosecution Bar Raises Potential Conflicts and Liability

Where a prosecuting litigator is faced with the choice of whether to access confidential material from an opposing party during litigation, the decision is one that requires consideration of the interests of both the lawyer and the client. Also required is a recognition that liability can arise from the involvement of a prosecuting litigator. For example, the lawyer's own interests could conflict with, or differ from, the client's on the question of whether to seek a narrow or broad protective order.[61] A lawyer may want to avoid facing liability for exposure to confidences, and so will not want to oppose entry of a protective order. Or, the lawyer may not want to accept the ban on prosecuting applications because of his or her obligations to, and fees received from, the representation of other prosecution clients. In addition, the client may not appreciate that by having its prosecuting counsel litigate the case, it is risking having ownership of later-filed applications contested, and may not want to face that risk.

Where a concurrent conflict of interest exists, then the lawyer must obtain the informed consent of the client after consultation.[62] In consultation, the issues described above as well as other issues—including risk to the client of having a constructive trust asserted over any subsequent patents prosecuted by the lawyer-prosecutor—may need to be discussed with the client.

This section next discusses the risks—to client as well as lawyer—associated with refusing to accept a prosecution bar, or of remaining a prosecuting litigator in a case with a narrow bar in place.

---

59. *See, e.g., Motorola, Inc. v. Interdigital Tech. Corp.*, No. 93–488-LON, 1994 U.S. Dist. LEXIS 20714, at *15 (D. Del. Dec. 19, 1994).

60. *Id.* at *15–16.

61. *See* MODEL RULES Rule 1.7(a). *See generally* Lisa Dolak, *Risky Business: The Perils of Representing Competitors*, 30 AIPLA Q.J. 413 (2002) (analyzing Rule 1.7 and issues related to patent representations).

62. MODEL RULES Rule 1.7. *See generally* Lisa Dolak, *Risky Business: The Perils of Representing Competitors*, 30 AIPLA Q.J. 413, 417–18 (2002) (describing operation of Model Rule 1.7 in patent representations). Model Rule 1.7 will not control in most federal courts because of the choice of law issue discussed above.

The short-term benefit of avoiding the bar creates a difficulty for lawyer and client. The client is able to continue to enjoy the benefits of being represented by prosecution counsel, who presumably is knowledgeable in the technology. Yet, the short-term benefit may be outweighed by long-term costs—costs that the client may not recognize and appreciate absent consultation with the lawyer. The client may not understand that even if the lawyer succeeds in obtaining entry of a protective order, which does not preclude prosecution activities, doing so may place the lawyer, and perhaps the client as well, in a worse situation: The lawyer is now in a position of being accused of receiving confidential information of an opponent, and then turning around and using that information to benefit the client. Furthermore, the lawyer must be careful during prosecution to comply with PTO Code section 1.56—by disclosing information subject to a protective order to the extent required by that section, but in compliance with the procedures under MPEP section 724 (discussed below)—and to ensure that his or her client gives informed consent to the continued prosecution in light of the risks and the limitations created by access to its competitor's information.

Perhaps the central risk the prosecuting litigator faces is that by gaining access to information, he or she can be accused of having used the information for the benefit of this client *during* prosecution. The client, too, has been placed at similar risk because the opposing party can contend that the client received the patent only through the misconduct of the lawyer.[63] In the context of pure-prosecution practice, misuse of confidential information to obtain patents has already resulted in substantial liability. In two recent cases, for example, lawyers were sued for using one client's information to obtain patents for another client.[64] These cases arose in the context of firms prosecuting applications for multiple clients, and so the lawyers misused information gained through the attorney-client relationship, not through disclosure during discovery. However, because protective orders limit use to the litigation, use outside of that context will violate the protective order. Thus, the potential for the same sort of liability exists for prosecuting litigators,

---

63. See *Kaempe v. Myers*, 367 F.3d 958, 71 U.S.P.Q.2d 1147 (D.C. Cir. 2004) (affirming dismissal of malpractice claim against law firm based on conversion of patent rights); *Am. Stock Exchange, LLC v. Mopex, Inc.*, 230 F. Supp. 2d 333, 52 U.S.P.Q.2d 1385 (S.D.N.Y. 2002) (analyzing claim for constructive trust over patents based on misuse of trade secrets); *Bausch & Lomb Inc. v. Alcon Labs., Inc.*, 64 F. Supp. 2d 233 (W.D.N.Y. 1999) (analyzing claim on indefiniteness and counterclaims of misappropriation of trade secrets, unfair competition, and constructive trust).

64. Professor Lisa Dolak describes recently filed suits in which one client claimed that its lawyers used its proprietary information to obtain patents for another client. Lisa Dolak, *Conflicts of Interest: Guidance for the Intellectual Property Practitioner*, 42 IDEA 453, 468–71 (1999).

who acquire competitors' proprietary information while conducting discovery to use for the benefit of their clients during prosecution.

Prosecuting litigators have also been sanctioned for disclosing to the USPTO information produced by an opposing party during litigation that was material to a client's application. Specifically, in *Eagle Comtronics, Inc. v. Arrow Communication Laboratories, Inc.*,[65] lawyers for the defendant obtained a patent application from the plaintiff during discovery which, they believed, disclosed an invention which was actually conceived by one of plaintiff's employees, a former employee of the defendant (Lamb).[66] Even though a protective order in the case precluded using discovery materials for any purpose other than the litigation, the lawyers photocopied copies of the joint application and submitted them to the USPTO. Once part of the application listed only Lamb as the inventor, the other part listed both Lamb the plaintiff's employees (one of whom—Gould—was also a former employee of the defendant), as coinventors.[67]

On appeal, the Federal Circuit found that the district court had abused its discretion in finding the lawyer's conduct "not egregious enough to warrant an order to show cause" and so reversed the district court's denial of sanctions.[68] In doing so, the court stated:

> The conduct in this case was indeed egregious and amounted to much more than Eagle providing the PTO with material that it already possessed. . . . Patent applications are preserved in secrecy by both law and regulation for a reason. The integrity of the patent system is maintained in part by inventors' understanding that their patent applications will remain secret until either the patents issue or the applications are otherwise published by the PTO. Breaches of this secrecy undermine the integrity of the patent system.[69]

Thus, lawyers who obtain information during discovery that may be important to their client's prosecution activities may not use that information for purposes other than the litigation (if the protective order so provides).[70] Ignoring that obligation can—and in light of the Federal Circuit's finding of an abuse of discretion in *Eagle Comtronics*, often will—result in sanctions.

---

65. 305 F.3d 1303, 64 U.S.P.Q.2d 1481(Fed. Cir. 2002).
66. *Id.* at 1311, 64 U.S.P.Q.2d at 1485.
67. *Id.* 64 U.S.P.Q.2d at 1486.
68. *Id.* at 1312, 1314–15, 64 U.S.P.Q.2d at 1486–88.
69. *Id.* at 1314, 64 U.S.P.Q.2d at 1487–88 (citations omitted).
70. *See Damper Design, Inc. v. Cleveland Elec. Illuminating Co.*, No. 94-1223, 1995 U.S. App. LEXIS 3520, 1995 WL 71339 (Fed. Cir. Feb. 21, 1995) (reversing the trial court's decision that the prosecuting litigator had violated protective order by amending certain words in patent application after seeing those words in discovery responses of opponent because lawyer had previously used those same words).

Another risk of being exposed to information from an opposing party during litigation is the potential for inequitable conduct. It is clear that a lawyer who, as a result of entry of a protective order in a case, does not learn of material information cannot be held to have committed inequitable conduct by failing later to disclose that information to the USPTO.[71] Suppose, however, that a prosecuting litigator learns information through discovery from an opposing party that is material to patentability of an application he or she is prosecuting for a client, even if the client is different from the client in the litigation.

Inequitable conduct has been found where parties fail to advise the USPTO of information gleaned during discovery.[72] *Eagle Comtronics* shows that protective orders that restrict use to "this action" do not contemplate disclosure to the USPTO under the duty of candor.[73]

That raises a critical issue only recently addressed by the USPTO. Given that a practitioner who receives information subject to a protective order may not disclose it to the USPTO without violating the protective order, does the presence of the protective order provide justification for nondisclosure to the USPTO? If not, then may a lawyer withdraw from prosecution without disclosing the information?

The absence of well-developed authority on that issue provides another reason for prosecuting litigators to avoid exposure to discovery materials. Only in May 2004, the USPTO adopted revisions to the MPEP to provide a limited procedural path through this dilemma. Specifically, the MPEP permits practitioners under certain circumstances to disclose information that is subject to a protective order to the USPTO under seal.[74] The provision was added in light of the recognition that "[s]ituations arise in which it becomes necessary, or desirable, for parties to proceedings in the Patent and Trademark Office relating to pending patent applications or reexamination proceedings to submit to the Office trade secret, proprietary, and/or protective order materials."[75] However, the MPEP gives practitioners authority to submit materials under seal only in limited circumstances, and specifically exclude

---

71. *Arthrocare Corp. v. Smith & Nephew, Inc.*, 310 F. Supp. 2d 638, 676–77 (D. Del. 2004) (holding that a protective order entered in a prior case had shielded persons involved in prosecuting an application from learning of certain information, and so there was no inequitable conduct in their failure not to disclose that information), *vacated in part on other grounds*, 406 F.3d 1365, 74 U.S.P.Q.2d 1749 (Fed. Cir. 2005).

72. *See, e.g., ICU Med., Inc. v. B. Braun Med. Inc.*, 2005 WL 588341 (N.D. Cal. Mar. 14, 2005)

73. *Eagle Comtronics, Inc. v. Arrow Commc'n Labs., Inc.*, 305 F.3d 1303, 64 U.S.P.Q.2d 1481 (Fed. Cir. 2002).

74. Manual of Patent Examining Procedure (MPEP) § 724.01.

75. *Id.* § 724.

doing so with respect to information "submitted in amendments, arguments in favor of patentability, or affidavits under 37 C.F.R. 1.131 or 1.132."[76]

Despite its limitations, this new USPTO procedure provides a key, if partial, means to reduce controversies for prosecuting litigators. They should ensure that any protective order applicable to them provide that information be disclosed to the USPTO when it can be done so in accordance with the applicable MPEP sections. Including such a provision is important because protective orders that limit use of information to "this action" can be construed not to permit disclosure to the USPTO.[77] Thus, even if the procedure under MPEP section 724 is available, a lawyer who is subject to a protective order precluding any use other than for "this action" might not be able to take advantage of the MPEP procedure because doing so will violate the protective order.

D. Issues to Consider in Crafting Protective Orders

Including in a protective order a provision that permits disclosure to the USPTO when consistent with MPEP section 724 is merely one aspect of a properly executed protective order where a prosecuting litigator is involved. The scope of any protective order is subject to intense negotiation and, at times, substantial motion practice. The parties, when drafting a protective order, and the courts, when deciding whether and to what extent to include a bar on access, should address the following issues and do so in light of Federal Circuit law.[78]

---

76. *Id.* § 724.03. *See generally* USPTO OG Notice (May 18, 2004) (discussing operation of MPEP § 724.02)

77. *Eagle Comtronics, Inc. v. Arrow Commc'n Labs., Inc.*, 305 F.3d 1303, 64 U.S.P.Q.2d 1481 (Fed. Cir. 2002).

78. Federal Circuit law should apply to the question of whether lawyers should be denied access to discovery because of their representation of a client in patent prosecutions. By definition, that turns on issues "unique to patent law."

   Parties also seek to impose "licensing" bars in protective orders, whereby recipients of an opposing party's information are prohibited from engaging in licensing negotiations. *E.g.,* *Nazomi Commc'ns, Inc. v. Arm Holdings PLC*, No. C 02–02521-JF, 2002 U.S. Dist. LEXIS 21400, at *10, 2002 WL 32831822 (N.D. Cal. Oct. 11, 2002) ("As with patent prosecution, attorneys who both litigate and negotiate licenses for a client may be considered decision makers under a U.S. Steel analysis."), *vacated on other grounds,* 403 F.3d 1364, 74 U.S.P.Q.2d 1458 (Fed. Cir. 2005); *see also Intel Corp. v. VIA Techs., Inc.*, 198 F.R.D. 525, 530 (N.D. Cal. 2000) (involvement of in-house counsel "in licensing . . . constitutes competitive decisionmaking"); *Iams Co. v. Kaln Kan Foods, Inc.*, No. C-3-97-449, 1998 U.S. Dist. LEXIS

A threshold matter is whether the information truly is worth special, heightened protection. For example, if the information relates to products that could be reverse-engineered, this would suggest that a prosecution bar is more likely to be inappropriate.[79] Similarly, if the information is stale or quickly will become so, then a bar is less likely to be warranted.[80] For example, in biotechnology, decade-old technology provides little future competitive edge for product design. Thus, a careful examination of the market can provide the court and the parties with information on if the confidential information can be protected.

Another key issue is the length of time for which the litigator must refrain from prosecuting applications. Courts generally apply a one- or two-year bar. However, in several cases the bar ran not from the date of disclosure of the information or from any judgment, but from the exhaustion of any appeals.[81] Because of the one-year bar in the Patent Act,[82] the disclosing party should have to bear a substantial burden for imposition of a bar of longer than one year from the date of disclosure of the information.

The third issue is the breadth of the bar. There are several factors to consider in determining how broad a bar parties should negotiate or a court should impose. First, the court and parties must consider whether it can and should cover only inventions in either the exact same subject matter or for

---

19205, at *8–9 (S.D. Ohio Feb. 27, 1998) (addressing access by expert witness who was involved in product development); Louis S. Sorell, *In-House Access to Confidential Information Produced During Discovery in Intellectual Property Litigation*, 27 J. MARSHALL L. REV. 657 (1994).

79. *Davis v. AT&T Corp.*, No. 98-CV-0189S(H), 1998 U.S. Dist. LEXIS 20417, 1998 WL 912012 (W.D.N.Y. Dec. 23, 1998).

80. The court in *Papst Licensing, GmbH, Patent Litig.*, 2000 U.S. Dist. LEXIS 6374, at *14 (E.D. La. May 4, 2000) held that the only information which could be kept from the prosecuting litigator was "information that embodies product design." In some circumstances, for example where the litigator is tasked by the client in drafting claims to cover competitor's products, the scope of protection recognized by the *Papst* court may be too narrow. The Federal Circuit has held that there is nothing per se improper about drafting claims of a pending application to cover a competitor's product, *see* Lisa Dolak, *The Ethics of Delaying Prosecution*, 53 AM. U. L. REV. 739, 753, & n.82 (2004), but using nonpublic information obtained through discovery to do so presents a different question.

81. *Interactive Coupon Mktg. Group, Inc. v. H.O.T.! Coupons, LLC*, No. 98 C 7408, 1999 U.S. Dist. LEXIS 9004, 1999 WL 409990 (N.D. Ill. June 7, 1999), *modified*, 1999 U.S. Dist. LEXIS 12437, at *11, 1999 WL 618969, at *4 (N.D. Ill. Aug. 9, 1999) ("one year after the conclusion of this litigation, including appeals"); *Commissariat a L'Energie Atomique v. Dell Computer Corp.*, No. 03-484-KAJ, 2004 U.S. Dist. LEXIS 12782, at *7 (D. Del. May 25, 2004) (one year bar, including appeals).

82. *See, e.g.,* 35 U.S.C. §102(b) (2005) (conditioning issuance of patent on application being filed within one year after claimed invention is first sold or offered for sale in the United States).

any prosecution for the client.[83] A request for a bar that is broader than for the same subject matter should be viewed carefully. Another factor of appropriate breadth is whether the bar should cover only U.S. filings, or should the bar also prohibit prosecution of foreign filings.[84]

A fourth and related issue is whether the bar applies only to the client that the lawyer is represented in the case or whether it should prohibit a lawyer who is representing *any* client within the scope of the technological definition from prosecuting applications.[85] If the practitioner represents multiple clients in the same narrow field of technology, then a broad bar may seem appropriate. However, the obvious consequence of a broad bar is severe economic impact on the practitioner. Clearly, a court should weigh the parties' competing concerns in determining whether the bar should prohibit prosecution for any client other than the one which the lawyer is representing in the litigation.

Another aspect of the protective order is the definition of "prosecution." Incorporating into the protective order exactly which activities are prohibited and which are not is crucial. For example, some courts hold that the bar only applies to lawyers who "actually draft patent applications, claim language for patent applications or arguments made in support of patent applications related to" the disclosed materials.[86] Others may find that the reviewing attorney who is litigating the case may be the one to whom the bar

---

83. This issue was central to *Commissariat a L'Energie Atomique*. There, the court rejected a narrow bar:

    > I will not pick and choose which categories of LCD technology are fair game for CEA's patent prosecution attorneys and which are not. If CEA's patent prosecution attorneys have access to the Defendant's highly confidential information, they will be barred from prosecuting patents "relating to the broad subject matter of the patents in suit, that is, LCD technology."

    Commissariat a L'Energie Atomique, 2004 U.S. Dist. LEXIS 12782, at *10.
84. *Medtronic, Inc. v. Guidant Corp.*, 2001 U.S. Dist. LEXIS 22805, at *11 (D. Minn. Dec. 19, 2001) (seeking bar as to domestic and foreign filings).
85. See *Nazomi Commc'ns, Inc. v. Arm Holdings PLC*, No. C 02–02521-JF, 2002 U.S. Dist. LEXIS 21400, at *6, 2002 WL 32831822 (N.D. Cal. Oct. 11, 2002) (patentee argued that bar should be as to all clients that lawyer is representing in the technology area), *vacated on other grounds*, 403 F.3d 1364, 74 U.S.P.Q.2d 1458 (Fed. Cir. 2005); *Motorola, Inc. v. Interdigital Tech. Corp.*, No. 93-488-LON, 1994 U.S. Dist. LEXIS 20714, at *18 (D. Del. Dec. 19, 1994) (court prohibited prosecution only for the client involved in the litigation, ITC, not for any other clients). Interestingly, the *Motorola* court presumed that the ethical duty to its client, ITC would prevent the firm "from prosecuting patent applications for other clients that are of similar subject matter as ITC's patents in this case." *Id.* at *18 n.5.
86. *Medtronic, Inc. v. Guidant Corp.*, 2001 U.S. Dist. LEXIS 22805, at *15 (D. Minn. Dec. 19, 2001).

must be applied. The definition can be critical. For example, in *Chan v. Intuit, Inc.*,[87] the party seeking to bar the opposing party from access to information defined patent prosecution, or "patenting," as follows:

(a) "Patenting" shall mean and include:

(i) [P]reparing and/or prosecuting any patent application (or portion thereof), whether design or utility, and either in the United States or abroad, or participating in a reexamination or reissue proceeding . . . ;

(ii) [P]reparing patent claim(s) relating to any of the fields listed above;

(iii) [P]roviding advice, counsel or suggestion regarding, or in any other way influencing, claim scope and/or language, embodiment(s) for claim coverage, claim(s) for prosecution, or products or processes for coverage by claim(s) relating to the field(s) listed . . . above; and

(iv) [A]ssisting, supervising, and/or providing counsel to anyone in connection with doing any of the foregoing.[88]

The district court rejected plaintiff's challenge that paragraph 4(a)(iii) was overbroad, but held that paragraph 4(a)(iv) was "too broad and therefore overly restrictive."[89] Inclusion in a protective order of too broad a definition unnecessarily and perhaps unfairly restricts the prosecution activities of the prosecuting litigator, and with little actual, commensurate benefit to the opposing party.[90] An important issue to consider is whether the definition should include reexamination proceedings.[91]

Finally, as noted above, the prosecuting litigator should determine whether the protective order should make exception for disclosures appropriate under the new USPTO procedure under MPEP section 724.[92] By including such a provision, the prosecuting litigator can ensure that the protective order permits disclosure to the USPTO of material information in a manner that preserves the confidentiality of the information yet complies with the duty of disclosure under 1.56.

---

87. 218 F.R.D. 659 (N.D. Cal. 2003).

88. *Id.* at 660–61.

89. *Id.* at 662.

90. *See also Andrx Pharm., LLC v. GlaxoSmithKline, PLC*, 236 F.R.D. 583 (S.D. Fla. 2006) (advising with respect to scope of claims constituted competitive decision-making).

91. *See Microunity Sys., Eng'r., Inc. v. Dell, Inc.*, 2005 WL 2299440 (E.D. Tex. July 18, 2005) (party moved for clarification that protective order precluded participation in reexamination proceedings, but denying that scope of protection).

92. The public policy in ensuring that material information be disclosed to the PTO should, if it can be done in compliance with section 724, outweigh any need for withholding the information from the PTO. *Cf. Beckman Indus., Inc. v. Int'l Ins. Co.*, 966 F.2d 470, 475 (9th Cir. 1992) (analyzing modification of protective order to permit disclosure of information in other court proceedings).

The terms of the protective order on each of these issues can dramatically affect not just the client but the lawyer as well. For example, many patent practitioners develop expertise in narrow technologies,[93] and so a ban as to all clients in a "field" or "subject matter"—if broadly defined—could cost the lawyer significant revenue. Likewise, a client who relies on such a practitioner for prosecution and loses the lawyer's service because of entry of a protective order will face substantial costs in educating another lawyer on the technology and applications.[94]

The risks described above arise from *concurrently* prosecuting and litigating patents for a client. Engaging in these representations *successively* also creates its own risks, as the next section shows.

1. Liability and Disqualification of Prosecuting Litigators

There is no general requirement that the practitioner who prosecuted a patent be a witness in an infringement suit involving that patent. However, where an accused infringer makes a charge of inequitable conduct, and perhaps in other circumstances,[95] it may be necessary for the attorney to testify. An allegation of inequitable conduct by itself creates potential conflicts between the prosecuting litigator and the client, and also means that the lawyer will likely be deposed and could be called on to testify at trial. This section analyzes these issues arising from using the same lawyer successively, first as a prosecuting attorney, and then as a litigator.

---

93. The lawyer in *In re Sibia*, for example, prosecuted applications for 50 clients in the same general field. *In re Sibia Neurosciences, Inc.*, 1997 U.S. App. LEXIS 31828, at *2 (Fed. Cir. Oct. 22, 1997).

94. For this reason, protective orders should allow barred counsel time to educate replacement prosecution counsel. It may be useful, for example, for a litigator to delay having access to the highly confidential information to use that time to educate counsel, who will take over responsibility for prosecuting applications.

95. The admissibility of prosecuting counsel's testimony has become limited in recent years. For example, because the Federal Circuit has limited the use of so-called "extrinsic evidence" to determine claim meaning, it has become less likely that the testimony of a prosecuting attorney will be truly pertinent to many patent cases. *See Vitronics Corp. v. Conceptronic, Inc.*, 90 F.3d 1576, 1585, 39 U.S.P.Q.2d 1573, 1579 (Fed. Cir. 1996). *See generally Ruoyu Roy Wang, Texas Digital Systems v. Telegenix, Inc.: Toward a More Formalistic Patent Claim Construction Model*, 19 Berkeley Tech. L.J. 153 (2004) (describing increasing use of "objective" evidence to interpret claims, not subjective testimony).

E. Inequitable Conduct as a Conflict

Where lawyers litigate a patent that they or their firm obtained for the client (or its assignee), and the accused infringer makes an allegation of inequitable conduct arising out of the attorney's conduct, potential conflicts between lawyer and client arise.

Inequitable conduct is an affirmative defense to patent infringement that requires proof that a person substantively involved in prosecuting the patent intentionally misrepresented or failed to disclose material information to the USPTO and did so with an intent to deceive.[96] If inequitable conduct is found, then the patent (and perhaps even related patents) may be held by the court to be unenforceable, even though valid.[97] In addition, the patent owner may be required to pay the attorneys' fees of the accused infringer.[98]

An allegation of inequitable conduct based on the prosecuting attorney's misconduct is likely to create a significant risk that the lawyer's representation of the client will be materially limited by the lawyer's personal interests.[99] If the patent is unenforceable because of the attorney's misconduct, the client will have a claim against the lawyer for the harm caused.[100] Normally, of course, these allegations arise during litigation in which the trial counsel did not prosecute the patent, and so trial counsel can provide conflict-free advice to the client as to the strengths of the defense, the risks of continuing to assert the patent, and whether a malpractice claim against the prosecution counsel is appropriate. However, a prosecuting litigator faced with an allegation that a patent he or she prosecuted is unenforceable likely is not in position to provide the same candid advice in any detached manner. For example, the client may be best served by settling the case at a steep discount, or dismissing it altogether, but the lawyer—because his or her conduct may be the cause of the reduction in value of the case—may be unable to dispassionately give the client that advice because doing so highlights the fact that his or her own prior conduct was what harmed the client's case. The prosecuting

---

96. *See* Lisa Dolak, *As If You Didn't Have Enough to Worry About: Current Ethics Issues for Intellectual Property Practitioner*s, 82 J. Pat. & Trademark Off. Soc'y 235, 237–38 (2000).
97. *Consol. Aluminum Corp. v. Foseco Int'l Ltd.*, 910 F.2d 804, 809, 15 U.S.P.Q.2d 1481, 1487 (Fed. Cir. 1990).
98. *Brasseler, U.S.A. I, L.P. v. Stryker Sales Corp.*, 267 F.3d 1370, 1386, 60 U.S.P.Q.2d 1482, 1488 (Fed. Cir. 2001).
99. *See* Model Rules Rule 1.7(a)(2).
100. Clients whose patents have been held unenforceable have sued their lawyers for breach of fiduciary duty and malpractice. For example, in *Lex Tex Ltd. v. Skillman*, 579 F.2d 244, 16 U.S.P.Q.2d 1137 (D.C. 1990), the patents were held unenforceable by the Federal Circuit resulting in the reversal of a $9 million judgment in favor of the patentee. Lex Tex, the patentee, then sued the lawyers for having failed to disclose the pertinent prior art to the PTO nearly twenty years before.

litigator's personal interest in denying or downplaying the allegations may constitute a material limitation on his or her ability to provide competent legal advice to his or her client.

Again, the presence of a prosecuting litigator in cases with alleged inequitable conduct creates the risk of conflicts between counsel and client. A prosecuting litigator faced with a substantial allegation of inequitable conduct arising out of his or her own actions should, therefore, determine whether he or she may nonetheless competently and diligently represent the client in the lawsuit and, if so, obtain the client's informed consent to do so.[101]

F. Depositions of Prosecuting Litigators

Depositions of opposing trial counsel are "disfavored,"[102] because "'even a deposition of counsel limited to relevant and non-privileged information risks disrupting the attorney-client relationship and the impending litigation.'"[103] For this reason, the party seeking to depose opposing counsel usually must meet a substantial burden, though that burden varies among the courts.[104] However, litigating a patent that the lawyer prosecuted will risk disruption of trial preparation. Normally, attorneys who prosecute patents-in-suit are subject to deposition.[105] Although at times courts have denied the depositions of prosecuting attorneys who have been later named as trial counsel, normally they are subject to deposition even if they are trial counsel.[106] In addition, where trial counsel prosecuted the patent-in-suit and inequitable conduct

---

101. *See* MODEL RULES Rule 1.7(b)(1), (4).

102. *United States v. Bd. of Educ.*, 946 F.2d 180, 185 (2d. Cir. 1991).

103. *Alcon Labs., Inc. v. Pharmacia Corp.*, 225 F. Supp. 2d 340, 344 (S.D.N.Y. 2002) (quoting *Madanes v. Madanes*, 199 F.R.D. 135, 151 (S.D.N.Y. 2001)).

104. *Compare Shelton v. Am. Motors Corp.*, 805 F.2d 1323, 1327 (8th Cir. 1986) (requiring among other things that "[N]o other means exist to obtain the information than to depose opposing counsel."), with *In re Subpoena Issued to Dennis Friedman*, 350 F.3d 65, 67 (2d Cir. 2003) (rejecting the *Shelton* standard but requiring special showing). The issue was discussed at some length in *Simmons Foods, Inc. v. Willis*, 191 F.R.D. 625, 630–31 (D. Kan. 2000), where the court noted that the courts have generally agreed that *some* greater showing is necessary to depose opposing counsel, but have disagreed on how much.

105. "It is quite common for the attorney who prosecuted the patent application to be deposed." Jack L. Slobodin, *Overview of the Patent Infringement Lawsuit—From Appearance of the Case in the Official Unit Trial*, 423 PLI/Pat 197, 262 (1995) *see, e.g., Amicus Commc'ns, L.P. v. Hewlett-Packard Co.*, No. 99-0284 HHK/DAR, 1999 U.S. Dist. LEXIS 20901, at *5–8, 1999 WL 33117227, at *2 (D.D.C. Dec. 3, 1999) (collecting cases).

106. *Alcon Labs., Inc. v. Pharmacia Corp.*, 225 F. Supp. 2d 340, 344 (S.D.N.Y. 2002) ("[A] patent prosecution attorney cannot avoid being deposed simply because he is later selected to act as trial counsel in an infringement action concerning the very patent he helped to prosecute.").

is pled,[107] courts have almost without exception held that prosecuting attorneys must be made available for deposition—even though they are also trial counsel.[108]

Although the courts recognize that this makes litigation more difficult, they have for the most part not been forgiving of a client who chooses to have the prosecuting attorney represent him or her in litigation. "The retention of the same counsel to serve as both a prosecuting attorney for its patent and trial counsel in an action involving the validity of that patent presents a Hobson's choice to any litigant."[109] Courts that permit the deposition of the prosecuting litigator give litigants a choice between the risk arising from deposition of trial counsel and the benefit of retaining a lawyer who understands the underlying technology and who has already been paid by the client to gain that understanding.

Clearly, an attorney who is asked by a client to litigate a patent he or she prosecuted should advise the client of the risks of deposition versus the benefits of proceeding and should act accordingly. For example, the client may be unaware of the fact that trial counsel *could* be deposed. If lawyer and client decide to proceed, it may be wise for the prosecuting litigator to seek a court's order that his or her deposition be taken early in the case to avoid

---

107. There is a split on whether inequitable conduct must be pled in accordance with FED. R. CIV. P. 9(b). *See, e.g., ResQNet.com, Inc. v. Lansa, Inc.*, No. 01 Civ.3578(RWS), 2004 U.S. Dist. LEXIS 13579, 2004 WL 1627170 (S.D.N.Y. July 21, 2004) (quashing subpoena of prosecuting litigator in part because court held that no inequitable conduct defense had been pled in conformance with FED. R. CIV. P. 9(b)). This was arguably error because Rule 9(b) cannot be applied to require particularized pleading of most inequitable conduct defenses. *See* David Hricik, *Wrong About Everything: Application by the District Courts of Rule 9(b) to Inequitable Conduct*, 86 MARQ. L. REV. 895 (2003).

108. *Environ Prods. Inc. v. Total Containment Inc.*, 1996 U.S. Dist. LEXIS 12336, at *12, 41 U.S.P.Q.2d 1302, 1306 (E.D. Pa. 1995) (denying motion for protective order to preclude deposition of prosecuting litigator because the "affirmative defense of inequitable conduct makes [the prosecuting litigator's] mental impressions during the reexamination proceedings an issue in this litigation"); *Hay & Forage Indus. v. Ford New Holland, Inc.*, 132 F.R.D. 687, 690 (D. Kan. 1990) (in denying motion to quash subpoena of prosecuting litigator, court stated that attorney's "meetings with the patent examiner are relevant to the defense of inequitable conduct"); *see also Interactive Coupon Mktg. Group, Inc. v. H.O.T.! Coupons, LLC*, No. 98 C 7408, 1999 U.S. Dist. LEXIS 9004, 1999 WL 409990, at *4 (N.D. Ill. June 7, 1999) (denying motion to disqualifying trial counsel who had prosecuted patent-in-suit where counsel had not yet been deposed), *modified*, 1999 U.S. Dist. LEXIS 12437, 1999 WL 618969 (N.D. Ill. Aug. 9, 1999); *ResQNet.com, Inc. v. Lansa, Inc.*, No. 01 Civ. 3578(RWS), 2004 U.S. Dist. LEXIS 13579, 2004 WL 1627170 (S.D.N.Y. July 21, 2004) (quashing subpoena directed to trial counsel who had prosecuted patent-in-suit where no allegation of inequitable conduct had been pled and the other grounds for obtaining deposition were found to be insufficient); *aaiPharma, Inc. v. Kremers Urban Dev. Co.*, 361 F. Supp. 2d 770, 774 (N.D. Ill. 2005) (refusing to quash subpoenas served on trial counsel).

109. *Alcon Labs., Inc. v. Pharmacia Corp.*, 225 F. Supp. 2d 340, 344–45 (S.D.N.Y. 2002).

disclosure of trial strategy and to prevent interruption of trial preparation on the eve of trial.

1. Advocate-as-Witness Disqualification

District courts have reasoned that assertions of inequitable conduct can be used to disqualify counsel, believing that "if the attorneys representing the party accused of inequitable conduct are the same attorneys who represented the client in the patent prosecution, then the party asserting inequitable conduct will often move to disqualify those attorneys."[110] In fact, motions to disqualify trial counsel who prosecuted the application that led to the patent-in-suit are not uncommon, particularly when inequitable conduct is raised as a defense.[111] However, because of specialization of attorneys, it will seldom be the case that an attorney who prosecuted the patent-in-suit also serves as actual first-chair trial counsel—probably quite a rare event. Instead, as a practical matter the advocate-as-witness rule will matter only to the extent that counsel who prosecuted the patent-in-suit is precluded from acting in a pre-trial capacity in litigation.

Unfortunately, state court interpretations of the scope of the advocate-as-witness rule vary.[112] However, to the extent that federal courts addressing the ethical issue of the trial counsel testifying at trial about their role as having prosecuted the patent-in-suit follow the majority interpretation of the Model Rules, disqualification of the lawyers themselves should occur in few cases.[113] This is true for at least three reasons.

---

110. *Chiron Corp. v. Abbott Labs.*, 156 F.R.D. 219, 221, 31 U.S.P.Q.2d 1848 (N.D. Cal. 1994).

111. See *Coolsavings.com Inc. v. E-Centives, Inc.*, No. 98 C 4924, 2000 U.S. Dist. LEXIS 12985, 2000 WL 1262929 (N.D. Ill. Sept. 1, 2000) (denying motion to disqualify); *Sun Microsystems, Inc. v. Dataram Corp.*, No. CIV. 96–20708 SW, 1997 U.S. Dist. LEXIS 4557, at *12–13, 1997 WL 50272, at *4 (N.D. Cal. Feb. 4, 1997) (citing "inherent dangers" of inequitable conduct defense as including "attorney disqualification"); *Personalized Mass Media Corp. v. Weather Channel, Inc.*, 899 F. Supp. 239, 244–45 (E.D. Va. 1995) (disqualifying lawyer); *Summagraphics Corp. v. Sanders Assocs., Inc.*, 1991 U.S. Dist. LEXIS 16387, 19 U.S.P.Q.2d 1859, 1861–62 (D. Conn. 1991) (disqualifying lawyers whose testimony concerning validity would conflict with client's position at trial).

112. As shown above, in an infringement suit a federal court would apply its approach to determining ethics. In the typical case, the PTO Code would not preempt application of such rules, because it generally is not necessary for the PTO to achieve its federal objectives for practitioners to be able to act as advocates in suits involving issued patents where their testimony is required.

113. Under other sets of rules, disqualification may be more likely. *Personalized Mass Media Corp. v. Weather Channel, Inc.*, 899 F. Supp. 239, 244–45 (E.D. Va. 1995) (disqualifying lawyer). *Personalized Mass Media* was properly criticized, however, for applying the wrong definition of "prejudice" as the court reasoned that any charge of inequitable conduct meant that the attorney's testimony would be prejudicial—even if the attorney testified that

First, even if the prosecuting attorneys were witnesses at trial, only the attorneys who personally prosecuted the patent should be disqualified— not other members of their firm.[114] Only if there is a conflict under Model Rules 1.7 or 1.9 should members of the testifying attorney's firm be disqualified.[115]

Second, even those attorneys who were personally involved in prosecution and are disqualified under the advocate-as-witness rule are generally disqualified only from actually appearing before the jury at trial. When Model Rule 3.7(a) disqualifies a lawyer-witness, it does so only from "act[ing] as an advocate at trial."[116] The only disqualification that most courts now impose on lawyers who are disqualified under the lawyer-witness rule is that such lawyers may not serve as counsel *at trial*, and then, the proscription exists only where trial is to the jury—not before the bench. Accordingly, even a litigator disqualified from trying the case would be free to conduct discovery, argue dispositive motions, control and direct the lawsuit, and handle any appeal.

Further, assuming participation at trial by a lawyer who had prosecuted the patent was critical, inequitable conduct presents no jury issues.[117] Under this circumstance, a separate trial to the judge alone[118] may be used to obviate

---

he had not engaged in any misconduct. *See Coolsavings.com Inc. v. E-Centives, Inc.*, No. 98 C 4924, 2000 U.S. Dist. LEXIS 12985, at *10, 2000 WL 1262929 (N.D. Ill. Sept. 1, 2000) ("The Court finds the Personalized Mass Media case unpersuasive because the district court applied an incorrect prejudice standard.").

114. MODEL RULES Rule 3.7(b).

115. *Id. See generally Kubin v. Miller*, 801 F. Supp. 1101, 1114 (S.D.N.Y. 1992) (firm-wide disqualification is "extremely harsh" and should be limited); RESTATEMENT (THIRD) OF THE LAW GOVERNING LAWYERS § 108, cmt. i (a lawyer affiliated with the disqualified lawyer "may serve as advocate . . . so long as the representation would not involve a conflict of interest").

116. *See* A.B.A. Comm. on Ethics and Prof'l Responsibility, Informal Op. 89–1529 (1989) (lawyer may conduct pretrial proceedings); *see also* A.B.A. Comm. on Ethics and Prof'l Responsibility, Informal Op. 83–1503 (1983) (lawyer may handle appeal).

117. *Gardco Mfg., Inc. v. Herst Lighting Co.*, 820 F.2d 1209, 1212, 2 U.S.P.Q.2d 2015, 2018 (Fed. Cir. 1987) (holding there is no right to jury trial on any aspect of inequitable conduct). *See generally* Michael A. O'Shea, *A Changing Role for the* Markman *Hearing: In Light of* Festo IX, Markman *Hearings Could Become* M-F-G *Hearings Which Are Longer, More Complex, and Ripe for Appeal*, 37 CREIGHTON L. REV. 843, 849 (2004) (describing availability of bifurcation under FED. R. CIV. P. 42(b)).

118. *See generally Gardco Mfg., Inc.*, 820 F.2d at 1212, 2 U.S.P.Q.2d at 2018 (Fed. Cir. 1987) (noting availability of separate trials); *see also* Michael A. O'Shea, *A Changing Role for the* Markman *Hearing: In Light of* Festo IX, Markman *Hearings Could Become* M-F-G *Hearings Which Are Longer, More Complex, and Ripe for Appeal*, 37 CREIGHTON L. REV. 843, 843 (2004) (describing increasing role of pretrial, nonjury hearings to resolve many critical issues in patent cases).

any ethical issues since generally disqualification is not necessary when the fact-finder is a judge, not a jury.[119]

Finally, even in those few cases where the prosecuting attorney is also trial counsel and separate trials are not practicable, the fact is that it is extremely unlikely that the lawyer will ever testify in court. As in all civil cases, the vast majority of patent cases settle prior to trial.[120] Resolution of a motion to disqualify can, as a result, be delayed pending resolution of settlement negotiations or rulings on summary judgment.

For all these reasons, it is unlikely that the advocate-as-witness rule will often lead to disqualification at trial, at least in those jurisdictions following the ABA interpretation of Model Rule 3.7. However, there are also more subtle ethical issues that practitioners might face. For example, a lawyer who will be a witness and therefore recommends to the client a request for bifurcation could prejudice to the client. For example, bifurcation would allow the lawyer to remain in the case—but at additional expense to the client. Or, bifurcation might weaken the client's liability case because of admissibility issues or other reasons.[121] Thus, a lawyer who wants to seek bifurcation to avoid disqualification under the advocate-as-witness rule should discuss these issues with the client where they would affect the particular case, and to the extent necessary obtain informed consent.[122]

---

119. *See Interactive Coupon Mktg. Group, Inc. v. H.O.T.! Coupons, LLC*, No. 98 C 7408, 1999 U.S. Dist. LEXIS 9004, 1999 WL 409990, at *4 (N.D. Ill. June 7, 1999), *modified*, 1999 U.S. Dist. LEXIS 12437, 1999 WL 618969 (N.D. Ill. Aug. 9, 1999).

   However, some courts have stated that the fact that trial will be to the bench does not eliminate the possibility of disqualification, but instead the reasons for disqualification merely "'may be less persuasive.'" *See Coolsavings.com Inc. v. E-Centives, Inc.*, No. 98 C 4924, 2000 U.S. Dist. LEXIS 12985, at *15, 2000 WL 1262929 (N.D. Ill. Sept. 1, 2000) (*quoting United States v. Johnston*, 664 F.2d 152, 157 (7th Cir. 1981)); *see also Environ Prods., Inc. v. Total Containment, Inc.*, 41 U.S.P.Q.2d 1302, 1306 (E.D. Pa. 1996) (stating that prosecuting litigator "could rest assured that he will not be disqualified from this litigation if 'disqualification of the lawyer would work a substantial hardship on the client'") (quoting Pa. RULES OF PROFESSIONAL CONDUCT 3.7).

120. *See* Edward G. Poplawski, *Selection and Use of Experts in Patent Cases*, 27 AIPLA Q.J. 1, 3 (1999) (noting that more than 90% of patent cases settle prior to trial). This fact suggests that judges should in many cases delay deciding motions to disqualify based on the advocate-as-witness rule because any such ruling may be unnecessary. Conversely, a party that believes opposing counsel is disqualified under the advocate-as-witness rule cannot unduly delay raising the motion, for doing so risks waiver or accusation that the motion was raised on the "eve of trial" only as a litigation tactic. Clearly, providing timely notice, at least to the opposing party, of an objection to trial counsel's participation is needed.

121. *See* MODEL RULES Rule 1.7.

122. *See* MODEL RULES Rule 1.7(b).

G. Combining Opinion and Trial Representations

Companies marketing products or services in the United States will commonly obtain an "opinion of counsel" beforehand if the company is concerned that its product or service will be accused of infringing a patent owned by another party. Securing such an opinion both provides comfort to the client in knowing that it is not violating the law and also in reducing the likelihood of it being forced to pay "enhanced" damages if the opinion turns out to be incorrect.[123]

If an infringement suit is filed, then from the perspective of both lawyer and client, it would appear more efficient that the accused client rely on the same firm that provided it an opinion of counsel as its trial counsel—why, after all, educate two firms about what could be complex technology? Likewise, it may appear more efficient that a client sued for infringement that had not previously obtained an opinion of counsel obtain one during litigation from trial counsel.

This section shows that combining the attorney roles of opining and litigating creates risks for the client that may not arise as acutely when those roles are kept separate. In particular, it first shows that combining the roles of opinion and trial counsel increases the risk of disqualification under the advocate-as-witness rule, and then the risk of waiver of privilege or work product in communications with trial counsel as determined in the various approaches district courts have taken to the issue and of whether and to what degree combining the roles increases that risk. This section concludes by addressing whether obtaining an opinion from the same firm that serves as trial counsel may result in substantial harm to the client.

1. Advocate-as-Witness Disqualification

Model Rule 3.7 generally prohibits a lawyer from personally acting as an advocate at trial while also testifying as a necessary witness.[124] The rule also

---

123. Title 35 authorizes a trial court in its discretion to increase the damages awarded for patent infringement to a maximum of three times. 35 U.S.C. § 284 (2005); *see Mathis v. Spears*, 857 F.2d 749, 754, 8 U.S.P.Q.2d 1029, 8 U.S.P.Q.2d 1551, 1554 (Fed. Cir. 1988). One basis for awarding so-called "enhanced" damages is if the infringer "acted in wanton disregard of the patentee's patent rights, that is, where the infringement is willful." Read *Corp. v. Portec, Inc.*, 970 F.2d 816, 826, 23 U.S.P.Q.2d 1426, 1435 (Fed. Cir. 1992).

124. Model Rule 3.7 provides in full:

> (a) A lawyer shall not act as advocate at a trial in which the lawyer is likely to be a necessary witness unless:
>> (1) [T]he testimony relates to an uncontested issue;

"imputes" this conflict by sometimes preventing one lawyer at a firm from trying a case if another lawyer at the firm is disqualified.[125] Furthermore, as illustrated below, federal courts in many circuits are not bound by the strict limitations in the rule, and can impute disqualification even where that is unnecessary under the Model Rules.

A. The Courts Split on Advocate-as-Witness Disqualification

A lawyer who provides an opinion of counsel about a patent is likely to be subject to deposition,[126] and one who combines the opining role with a role in litigation may face a motion to disqualify based on the advocate-as-witness rule. The question of whether disqualification under the advocate-as-witness rule as trial counsel of a lawyer who provided an opinion is required has split the courts.

Some courts deny the motion because the attorney's role in preparing the opinion and the client's receipt of it are likely to be uncontested. These courts view the issue as one of the client's reliance on the opinion, which is not affected by the fact that trial and opinion counsel are from the same firm.[127]

Other courts disagree. Foremost, a Western District of Texas court disqualified an entire firm from litigating a case where lawyers had given an

---

    (2) [T]he testimony relates to the nature and value of legal services rendered in the case; or

    (3) [D]isqualification of the lawyer would work substantial hardship on the client.

  (b) A lawyer may act as advocate in trial in which another lawyer in the lawyer's firm is likely to be called as a witness unless precluded from doing so by Rule 1.7 or Rule 1.9.

125. MODEL RULES 3.7(b).

126. *E.g., Clinitec Nutrition Co. v. Baya Corp.,* No. 94 C 7050, 1996 WL 153881 (N.D. Ill. Mar. 28, 1996) (granting motion to compel deposition of opining-litigator).

127. The few courts that have analyzed whether an opining-litigator must be disqualified under the advocate-as-witness rule have split. *Compare Bristol-Myers Squibb Co. v. Rhone-Poulenc Rorer, Inc.,* No. 95 Civ. 8833(RPP), 2000 U.S. Dist. LEXIS 16015, 2000 WL 1655054, at *2 (S.D.N.Y. Nov. 3, 2000) (denying motion to disqualify opining-litigator on grounds that it was uncontested that he had provided the opinion and so disqualification was improper), *and Amsted Ind. Inc v. Nat'l Castings, Inc.,* 16 U.S.P.Q.2d 1737 (N.D. Ill. June 22, 1990) (holding that opining-litigator was not required to testify as to foundation of opinion), *with Rohm & Haas Co. v. Lonza, Inc.,* No. Civ. A. 96-5732, 1999 U.S. Dist. LEXIS 13919, at *1 1999 WL 718114, at *1 (E.D. Pa. Sept. 7, 1999) (granting motion to disqualify opining-litigator). Whether disqualification of an opining-litigator is appropriate would most typically turn on whether his testimony in the particular case would be necessary. Most often, for example, where the issue is the *reliance of the client* on the opinion and not the *preparation of the opinion,* disqualification would not be appropriate as the fact that the lawyer prepared the opinion would be an uncontested issue. Model Rule 3.7(a)(1) does not require disqualification where the lawyer's testimony "relates to an uncontested issue."

opinion of counsel. In *Crossroads Systems (Texas), Inc. v. Dot Hill Systems Corp.*,[128] lawyers from Morgan & Finnegan had given a noninfringement opinion to a client. Later, other Morgan & Finnegan lawyers represented the client when an infringement suit was filed against it over the same patent. The patentee, Crossroads, filed a motion to disqualify Morgan & Finnegan from acting as trial counsel for the accused infringer, Dot Hill. The trial court granted the motion, even though it recognized that the ethics rules generally did not require firm-wide disqualification under these circumstances. Explaining why firm-wide disqualification was required under the circumstances of this case, the court stated:

> The Court believes that . . . a strict prohibition on all members of the testifying lawyer's firm serving as trial counsel is appropriate. Crossroads will be seeking to attack the reasonableness of Dot Hill's reliance on the opinions given by Morgan & Finnegan attorneys, in part, by attacking the accuracy and validity of the opinions themselves as well as the work underlying the formulation of the opinions. Moreover, the reasonableness of Dot Hill's reliance on the opinions will necessarily raise other factual questions, such as what relevant, non-privileged facts (besides those contained in the opinion letters) were communicated between Dot Hill and its opinion counsel. Since both the credibility and legal acumen of Morgan & Finnegan attorneys will be in issue at the trial, if other Morgan & Finnegan attorneys were permitted to serve as trial counsel, they would be placed in the awkward and unseemly position of having to advocate for the credibility and reliability of the testimony of their law partners. Even worse, if the testifying Morgan & Finnegan attorneys were to give testimony that was adverse to Dot Hill's interests, the attorneys serving as trial counsel would be squarely confronted with a conflict of interest in grappling with competing duties to the client and to the firm.
>
> Other potential problems would be sure to arise in the course of a trial in which members of Morgan & Finnegan would be serving as trial counsel while others would be testifying as witnesses. The trial counsel would be put in the position of having to comment on and actively praise the work product of their own firm in the course of arguing the reasonable reliance on the opinion letters by Dot Hill. Another difficulty would be that numerous extraneous issues would likely be injected into the case if a Morgan & Finnegan witness is permitted to testify. Efforts at impeaching the Morgan & Finnegan witnesses may inquire into potential sources of bias, including the amount of fees that were generated in the production of the opinion letters and the amounts Morgan & Finnegan earned before the production of the letters and continues to earn to this day based on its work for Dot Hill. If Morgan & Finnegan were to continue to serve as trial counsel, these questions could potentially serve to impeach the credibility of Dot Hill's trial counsel at the same time as they affect the

---

128. 2006 U.S. Dist. LEXIS 36181, 2006 WL 1544621, 82 U.S.P.Q.2d 1517 (W.D. Tex. 2006).

credibility of the witnesses. The credibility of a party's trial counsel, however, clearly should not be an issue in the case.[129]

The court also rejected allowing the accused infringer to decide whether to call opinion counsel to the stand, explaining that it believed that such decision was tainted by the conflict faced by Morgan & Finnegan:

> Furthermore, so long as Morgan & Finnegan serves as trial counsel, the motivations behind the potential for a decision not to call the Morgan & Finnegan opinion attorneys as witnesses on behalf of Dot Hill becomes immediately suspect. So long as the Morgan & Finnegan trial attorneys are grappling with divided loyalties to their firm and to their client, there can be no assurance that their representation of Dot Hill would not be different if the credibility and competence of their partners were not in issue.[130]

Although this is an unusual case with somewhat distinct facts, some federal courts could continue to disqualify a firm from appearing at trial where another lawyer in the firm had given an opinion. Significantly, the *Crossroads Systems* court recognized that under Fifth Circuit precedent it was not bound to follow the more relaxed standards of the Model Rules and could impute the conflict even where it would not be imputed under those rules.[131] That was the result in a more recent case, *Landmark Graphics Corp. v. Seismic Micro Technology, Inc.*,[132] where the court held that the lawyer who had prosecuted the patent was not disqualified from pre- or post-trial activities even though he could not appear before the jury as trial counsel or serve as counsel during a bench trial on inequitable conduct.

B. What to Do

A firm that has already given an opinion of counsel to a client should investigate the district court's approach to advocate-as-witness disqualification before agreeing to represent the client in litigation. Likewise, trial counsel should refrain from providing such opinions after suit has been filed without

---

129. 2006 U.S. Dist. LEXIS 36181, at *30–34 (citations and footnote omitted).
130. *Id.* at *34. The court also noted: "Other issues that Morgan & Finnegan's service as trial counsel would tend to implicate include knowledge on the part of the Morgan & Finnegan attorneys concerning: (1) the reasons for the Chaparral [also an alleged infringer] purchase; (2) the development of products designed to defeat infringement; and (3) the economic benefit to Dot Hill with respect to the sale of potentially infringing products. In sum, there are simply too many potential rabbit trails and invitations to jury confusion if Morgan & Finnegan attorneys were permitted to serve as trial counsel when their partners will be taking the stand as witnesses." *Id.*
131. *Id.* at *27–28.
132. 2007 U.S. Dist. LEXIS 6897, at *19–20, 2007 WL 735007 (S.D. Tex. Jan. 31, 2007).

investigating first. Rules such as Model Rule 1.7(a)(2) or other applicable standards may require the lawyer to discuss potential disqualification with the client and seek the client's informed consent on how to proceed. Lawyer and client should discuss whether to seek bifurcation—to keep the lawyer in the case—or to have the case tried in one phase with new trial counsel, along with the advantages and disadvantages of either course.

Where roles are combined, there may be means to avoid disqualification. In some courts, for example, bifurcation or stay of the issue of willfulness may delay the need for disqualification.[133] However, on the question of whether or not to bifurcate, a lawyer's interests may conflict with those of the client. Lawyers may want to obtain bifurcation so that they can litigate at least part of the case. Bifurcation, however, may not be in the best interest of the client who may be better served by presentation of all issues in suit in a single proceeding before one fact-finder. Anticipation and discussion of the concurrent conflict of interest that could develop requires the informed consent of the client. This possible conflict, and needs for efficiency, led the *Crossroads* court to deny bifurcation.[134]

2. Enhanced Risk of Waiver of Work Product

Willful infringement, when proven, permits a court to award up to treble damages, costs, and attorneys' fees to the patentee.[135] Willful infringement occurs when the infringer acted with, at the least, "objective recklessness."[136] One factor in determining whether an accused infringer acted objectively recklessly is whether it relied on an opinion of counsel.[137] An alleged infringer can choose to waive privilege over an invalidity, noninfringement, or unenforceability opinion of counsel on which it relied in undertaking its activities.[138] When an accused infringer produces the opinion, it waives

---

133. *See generally* Edward Poplawski, *Effective Preparation of Patent Related Exculpatory Legal Opinions*, 29 AIPLA Q.J. 269, 288–91 (2001) (discussing means to reduce need for lawyer's testimony or otherwise stave off disqualification of opining-litigator); George M. Sirilla et al., *Advice of Counsel: Defense or Dilemma? Friend or Foe?*, 81 J. Pat. & Trademark Off. Soc'y 376 (1999) (discussing lawyer-witness rule and ability to bifurcate to avoid it).

134. 2006 U.S. Dist. LEXIS 36181, at *34–35.

135. *See Cohesive Techs., Inc. v. Waters Corp.*, 526 F. Supp. 2d 84 (D. Mass. 2007) (no enhanced damages or attorneys fees where infringement not willful).

136. *See id.*

137. *See id.*

138. *See, e.g., Carl Zeiss Jena GmgH v. Bio-Rad Labs. Inc.*, No. 98 CIV. 8012 RCC DFE, 2000 WL 1006371, at *1 (S.D.N.Y. July 19, 2000); *Saint-Gobain/Norton Indus. Ceramics Corp. v. Gen. Elec. Co.*, 884 F. Supp. 31, 33–34 (D. Mass. 1995).

privilege over that opinion and also, in many courts, on all communications on the "subject matter" of that opinion[139]

The scope of waiver of privilege or work product that accompanies production of an opinion of counsel has changed dramatically in just the last two years. Two recent Federal Circuit cases have become critical.

Changes began in a seminal May 2006 Federal Circuit case that addressed a petition for writ of mandamus challenging a district court's ruling on the scope of both the waiver of attorney-client privilege and work product immunity where the waivers resulted from the defendant's election to rely on the advice of counsel to rebut a charge of willful infringement.[140] For reasons that will become clear, the context of the observations made by the judges in deciding *EchoStar* is critically important because the court used broad language but was actually deciding a narrow issue.

In *EchoStar*, TiVo filed an infringement suit against EchoStar. EchoStar asserted the defense of reliance on the advice of two opinions of counsel, one from its in-house counsel and obtained before the suit had been filed, the other from its outside counsel, Merchant & Gould, obtained after the suit had been filed.[141] Both opinions addressed only noninfringement, not invalidity or unenforceability.[142] TiVo argued that the assertion of this defense triggered a broad subject matter waiver, and ultimately the district court largely agreed, ordering the production of privileged material and even work product created by Merchant & Gould that had not been communicated to EchoStar, excepting only "trial preparation or information unrelated to infringement."[143]

EchoStar sought review in the Federal Circuit with respect to the Merchant & Gould documents not provided to EchoStar by way of a petition for mandamus, and Merchant & Gould intervened.[144] Questions concerning the scope of waiver caused by reliance on both opinions were raised on appeal.

Concerning in-house counsel, the court quickly rejected EchoStar's attempt to characterize its reliance on its in-house counsel as not constituting reliance on *advice* of counsel. The court instead held that "[w]hether counsel

---

139. *See, e.g., Oxyn Telecomm., Inc. v. Onse Telecom*, No. 01 Civ. 1012(JSM), 2003 U.S. Dist. LEXIS 2671, at *21, 2003 WL 660848, at *6 (S.D.N.Y. Feb. 27, 2003) (if privileged communications are placed "in issue" by defenses in litigation, then a "broad" subject matter waiver [of privilege] is effected.").

140. *In re EchoStar Commc'ns Corp.*, 448 F.3d 1294, 78 U.S.P.Q.2d 1676 (Fed. Cir. 2006).

141. 448 F.3d at 1297, 78 U.S.P.Q.2d at 1677–78.

142. *Id.*, 78 U.S.P.Q.2d at 1678.

143. *Id.*

144. *Id.* In granting the petition, the court first held that Federal Circuit and not regional circuit law governs the extent to which a party waives attorney client privilege and work product by relying on advice of counsel to defend against willful infringement. *Id.* at 1298, 78 U.S.P.Q.2d at 1679.

is employed by the client or hired by outside contract, the offered advice or opinion is advice of counsel or an opinion of counsel."[145] The court stated that as a result Echostar waived "the attorney-client privilege with regard to any attorney-client communications relating to the same subject matter, including communications with counsel other than in-house counsel, which would include communications with Merchant & Gould."[146]

The preceding sentence bears examination. On appeal, there was no dispute concerning any in-house counsel documents.[147] Thus, the court's statement as to the scope of waiver was dicta as to in-house counsel because there was nothing to decide. In addition, the fact that nothing was in dispute also meant that there was nothing at issue in the case with respect to what "subject matter" was. In other words, the court did not decide whether by Echostar's reliance on a noninfringement opinion, the "subject matter" waived includes invalidity or unenforceability opinions. The sentence also bears examination as to the comment concerning Merchant & Gould. With respect to waiver of privileged communications with Merchant & Gould, the statement is also, seemingly, dicta because the issues on appeal related to work product of Merchant & Gould, not privilege. Further, the court did not decide whether communications made after suit was filed were waived because that issue was not presented either in the case. The context of the *EchoStar* quickly created a battleground for district courts and litigants.[148]

The court nonetheless turned to the scope of waiver concerning advice from Merchant & Gould that was, as noted above, received after the suit had been filed, and held that the district court had abused its discretion in ordering production of work product documents, whether they had been communicated to EchoStar, or not.[149] Noting that work product applied only to written or tangible communications, the court emphasized that the purpose of work product differed from attorney-client privilege and was designed to afford a "zone of privacy" around litigation to permit lawyers to commit thought to paper to prepare for trial.[150] As a result, there was no subject matter waiver of work product by reliance on work product; instead, protection only

---

145. *Id.*, 448 F.3d at 1299, 78 U.S.P.Q.2d 1679.
146. *Id.*
147. *Id.* at 1297 n.2, 78 U.S.P.Q.2d at 1678 n.2.
148. The Federal Circuit did not clarify matters by citing *Akeva LLC v. Mizuno Corp.*, 243 F. Supp. 2d 418, 423 (M.D.N.C. 2003). In that case, the district court held that privilege and work product were waived over an opinion obtained from trial counsel. That fact pattern was simply not present in *EchoStar*, and the policy issues implicated in *Akeva LLC* were not considered by the Federal Circuit. Why the court cited the decision is unclear, but the fact that it did so is causing confusion, as shown below.
149. *EchoStar*, 448 F.3d at 1300, 78 U.S.P.Q.2d at 1680.
150. *Id.* at 1301, 78 U.S.P.Q.2d at 1681.

over factual, not opinion, work product was waived by reliance on work product.[151]

In applying these principles to the context of reliance on an opinion of counsel defense against a charge of willful infringement, the Federal Circuit explained that the purpose of requiring subject matter waiver was to "prevent a party from using the advice he received as both a sword, by waiving privilege to favorable advice, and a shield, by asserting privilege to unfavorable advice."[152] To further that policy, the court reasoned that work product protection was waived to the extent it "could have such an effect."[153]

To guide courts in applying these principles, the court identified three categories of work product that generally would be implicated by reliance on advice of counsel:

(1) [D]ocuments that embody a communication between the attorney and client concerning the subject matter of the case, such as a traditional opinion letter;

(2) documents analyzing the law, facts, trial strategy, and so forth that reflect the attorney's mental impressions but were not given to the client; and

(3) documents that discuss a communication between attorney and client concerning the subject matter of the case but are not themselves communications to or from the client.[154]

With respect to the first category, the court reasoned that because privilege is waived when reliance on counsel is asserted, waiver extends to "any documentary communications such as opinion letters and memoranda."[155] Thus, in the court's view, work product was no different than privileged information: If either one is communicated to the client, protection is waived. That view is at odds with general principles governing work product. A lawyer does not waive work product protection by providing work product to a client, and a client cannot unilaterally choose to waive the lawyer's interest in the protection of work product.[156] Nonetheless, the *EchoStar* court reasoned

---

151. *Id.* at 1302, 78 U.S.P.Q.2d at 1681.
152. *Id.* at 1303, 78 U.S.P.Q.2d at 1682–83.
153. *Id.* 78 U.S.P.Q.2d at 1683.
154. *Id.* at 1302, 78 U.S.P.Q.2d at 1682.
155. *Id.*
156. Among other things, the work product privilege belongs also to the attorney, and the client cannot waive the attorney's interest in work product protection. *Hobley v. Burge*, 433 F.3d 946, 949 (7th Cir. 2006) ("An attorney has an independent interest in privacy, even when the client has waived its own claim, as long as invoking the privilege would not harm the client's interests." citing RESTATEMENT (THIRD) OF THE LAW GOVERNING LAWYERS § 90 cmt. c (2000)). The Federal Circuit reasoned that its holding was consistent with that principle: EchoStar had the right to waive attorney-client communications and that carried with it the

that when the privilege is waived by reliance on advice of counsel, disclosure "become[s] evidence of a non-privileged, relevant fact, namely what was communicated to the client. . . ."[157] If that were true, then any disclosure of work product to a client becomes evidence of a nonprivileged fact if privilege is otherwise waived. That proposition is startling.

With respect to the third category (the court placed it last, but recognized that it "falls admittedly somewhere interstitially between the first and second," and so logically ought to be examined second),[158] the court stated that work product documents that in effect memorialize or reflect a communication with the client are not protected.[159] "Though it is not a communication to the client directly nor does it contain a substantive reference to what was communicated, it will aid the parties in determining what communications were made to the client and protect against intentional or unintentional withholding of attorney-client communications from the court."[160] The court's holding makes sense because privilege over communications on the subject of the opinion has been waived, and the fact that a lawyer writes down a privileged communication does not convert the substance of the communication into a work product document. However, the court emphasized that information in such documents that had not been communicated could be redacted.[161]

With respect to the final category of documents (placed second in the court's analysis)—those that are work product but never communicated to the client—the court found work product protection still existed despite waiver of privilege.[162] "[I]f a legal opinion or mental impression was never communicated to the client, then it provides little if any assistance to the court in determining whether the accused knew it was infringing, and any relative value is outweighed by the policies supporting the work product doctrine."[163]

The three categories provide some framework for analysis, but, as noted, the *EchoStar* case has created multiple uncertainties, in part because the court used broad language in the context of a fairly narrow set of facts.

---

right to "waive privilege to evidence of those communications contained in Merchant & Gould's files." *EchoStar*, 448 F.3d at 1304 n.6, 78 U.S.P.Q.2d at 1683 n.6 (allowing, however, redaction of mental impressions). Thus, despite the language in *EchoStar*, the court clearly did not hold that a client has a right to waive work product protection; instead, a client has a right to waive protection over privileged communications even if they are memorialized in work product documents. The court's result was correct, but its language is difficult to reconcile with settled principles of work product.

157. *EchoStar*, 448 F.3d at 1303, 78 U.S.P.Q.2d at 1683.
158. *Id.* at 1304, 78 U.S.P.Q.2d at 1683.
159. *Id.*
160. *Id.*
161. *Id.*
162. *Id.* at 1303–04, 78 U.S.P.Q.2d at 1683.
163. *Id.* at 1304, 78 U.S.P.Q.2d at 1683.

First, for example, the question of what is the "subject matter" waived is obscured by the *EchoStar* decision. Although the case involved only noninfringement opinions received by the client, the court ultimately wrote that an accused infringer who asserts advice of counsel waived protection over communications "concerning whether that patent is valid, enforceable, and infringed by the accused."[164] This language suggests that reliance on an opinion of counsel for one defense waives protection for all. This was not an issue in the case, however, and the court's language is, at best, dicta.

After *EchoStar*, the district courts began to openly disagree on whether "subject matter" in such a context includes all opinions about any defense—whether or not mentioned in the opinion relied on by the defendant—or only opinions that relate to the same precise defense as in the opinion waived. Some courts hold that if an opinion concerning one defense is relied on, other opinions may be withheld. Thus, a defendant who relies on a noninfringement opinion waives protection over the subject matter of infringement, but not regarding opinions on invalidity or unenforceability.[165] Other courts, however, after closely parsing the precise context and language of the decision, hold that waiver does not extend beyond the precise subject matter; if an invalidity opinion is relied on, waiver of noninfringement advice does not occur.[166]

Second, the *EchoStar* court addressed temporal limitations in a footnote. It wrote:

> EchoStar contends that waiver of opinions does not extend to advice and work product given after litigation began. While this may be true when the work product is never communicated to the client, it is not the case when the advice is relevant to ongoing willful infringement, so long as that ongoing infringement is at issue in the litigation. *See Akeva LLC*, 243 F. Supp. 2d at 423 ("[O]nce a party asserts the defense of advice of counsel, this opens to inspection the advice received during the entire course of the alleged infringement."); *see also Crystal Semiconductor Corp. v. TriTech Microelectronics Int'l, Inc.*, 246 F.3d 1336, 1351–1353 (Fed. Cir. 2001) (noting that an infringer may continue its infringement after notification of the patent by filing suit and that the infringer has a duty of due care to avoid infringement after such notification).[167]

---

164. *Id.*
165. *Akeva LLC v. Mizuno Corp.*, 243 F. Supp. 2d 418, 422 (M.D.N.C. 2003).
166. *Intex Recreation Corp. v. Team Worldwide Corp.*, 439 F. Supp. 2d 46 (D.D.C. 2006); *Autobytel, Inc. v. Dealix Corp.*, 455 F. Supp. 2d 569 (E.D. Tex. 2006) (discussing split in the cases). *See also Genentech, Inc. v. Insmed Inc.*, 442 F. Supp. 2d 838, 847 (N.D. Cal. 2006) (waiver only applied to "documents and communications that contain opinions (formal or informal) and advice central and highly material to the ultimate questions of infringement and invalidity (the subject matter of the advice given by . . . opinion counsel").
167. *EchoStar*, 448 F.3d at 1302 n.4, 78 U.S.P.Q.2d at 1682 n.4.

This note, and in particular the citation to *Akeva*, was quickly followed by several district court opinions that took different views of the scope of waiver of work product with respect to post-suit communications with trial counsel. That issue was not involved in *EchoStar*.

Instead, the question of whether the subject matter waiver that accompanies reliance on an opinion of counsel extends to an accused infringer's communications with trial counsel was raised in and was decided by the Federal Circuit in the second critical case, the en banc decision in *In re Seagate Technology, LLC*.[168]

The *In re Seagate* court overruled its long-standing interpretation of what constituted "willful infringement." The court adopted a new interpretation of section 284 that authorizes imposition of up to treble damages only if the accused infringer acted at least in a manner of "objective recklessness."[169] In addition, the court held that a party aware of a patent that it might be infringing was not under an affirmative duty of care to obtain an opinion, and that its state of mind was irrelevant.[170] Objective recklessness is what matters.

Finally, but most pertinent here, the court held that waiver of an opinion of counsel did not by itself warrant the conclusion that protection over communications with trial counsel were also waived.[171] Instead, the Federal Circuit held that, absent "unique circumstances" such as party "chicanery," "as a general proposition" privilege was not waived over communications with trial counsel.[172] Likewise, the court held that "as a general proposition, relying on opinion counsel's work product does not waive work product immunity with respect to trial counsel."[173] The Federal Circuit's conclusions, however, rested on the fact that it was undisputed that opinion counsel had "operated separately and independently of trial counsel at all times."[174] Thus, so long as trial and opinion counsel operate "separately and independently . . . at all times," waiver of protection concerning the opinion from opinion counsel does not waive protection over communications relating to trial counsel.

It remains to be seen whether combining the roles of opinion and trial counsel will affect the likelihood of waiver of communications with trial counsel. Although there is a definite split, most courts hold that an accused infringer may rely on at least a pre-suit[175] opinion of counsel without waiving

---

168. 497 F.3d 1360, 83 U.S.P.Q.2d 1865 (Fed. Cir. 2007) (en banc).

169. *Id.* at 1371, 83 U.S.P.Q.2d 1870.

170. *Id.*

171. *Id.* at 1373, 83 U.S.P.Q.2d 1871–72.

172. *Id.* at 1374–75, 83 U.S.P.Q.2d 1873.

173. *Id.* at 1376, 83 U.S.P.Q.2d 1874.

174. *Id.* at 1366, 83 U.S.P.Q.2d 1866–67.

175. Where trial counsel provides a post-suit opinion—an unusual circumstance—there is an

trial counsel's work product, at least where the opinion comes from a different firm than trial counsel.[176]

The most certain lesson for now is that courts may continue to view the combination of roles as problematic. For example, in a district court decision decided before *In re Seagate, Novartis Pharmaceuticals Corp. v. Eon Labs Manufacturing, Inc.*,[177] the Cohen, Pontani firm defended accused infringer, Eon, at trial. In response to a charge of willful infringement, Eon had earlier procured an opinion from another member of Cohen, Pontani, Mr. Pontani. Judge Farnan held that Novartis was entitled to discover even work product information that Mr. Pontani never provided to Eon, Judge Farnan held that "Eon should be compelled to produce all legal advice it received from *any* member of the Cohen, Pontani law firm with regard to the subject matter of Mr. Pontani's opinion."[178] Judge Farnan seemed to view the decision to combine roles as risky:

> Eon has not only elected to engage in the unconventional and risky arrangement of having opinion and trial counsel from the same law firm, but Eon's opinion counsel, Mr. Pontani, has actually entered an appearance in this matter. Because the Court cannot differentiate between opinion and trial counsel, the Court will grant Novartis' Motion to Compel to the extent it seeks the production of all legal advice Eon received from the Cohen, Pontani law firm relating to the subject matter of Mr. Pontani's opinion.[179]

---

even greater risk of broader waiver. Explaining why, one court explained:

> Here, the opinions were rendered by trial counsel's firm after the litigation began. Although it is difficult to understand how there could be a defense to willful infringement based on an opinion rendered after the litigation began, defendants have raised such a defense. They cannot use their status as trial counsel to erect a barrier to discovery of documents to which plaintiff would otherwise be entitled. Neither can counsel play cute by carefully circumscribing information given to the lawyer in the firm who wrote the opinion, and funneling the information given him through other lawyers in the firm to avoid the concept of "communications between client and attorney." If a draft opinion is prepared and given to [the opining litigator] who reviews in light of trial strategy before it is given to the client and then sends it back for redrafting if it is a little weak or inconsistent with the trial strategy, plaintiffs have a right to know this. It bears on the independence, competence, analysis, credibility, and value of the opinion.

Michlin v. Canon, Inc., 208 F.R.D. 172, 174 (E.D. Mich. 2002).

176. See *Motorola, Inc. v. Vosi Techs., Inc.*, No. 01 C 4182, 2002 U.S. Dist. LEXIS 15655, at *6, 2002 WL 1917256 (N.D. Ill. Aug. 19, 2002) (holding that privilege over trial counsel's views of infringement or validity were not waived even though on same subject as pre-suit opinions by other lawyers).

177. 206 F.R.D. 396 (D. Del. 2002).

178. *Id.* at 399 (emphasis in original).

179. *Id.*

Other courts have made similar observations.[180] For example, one court reasoned that

> "the broad waiver rule requiring full disclosure of documents, even if they were not given to the client, is best suited to the situation where the opinion counsel is trial counsel. In that situation, the opinion counsel has a dual role in [advising] the client and, thus, there is a greater need to make sure the opinion is not tainted by bias or other influences."[181]

The court reasoned that where the opinion came from counsel separate and independent from trial counsel, then the reasons supporting broad waiver of work product are not implicated.[182]

For the time being, and absent further clarification from the Federal Circuit, combining the roles of opinion and trial counsel, although perhaps efficient, will be viewed as "unconventional" and "risky," even though there seems to be little reason for the distinction—after all, nothing prevents trial counsel, in one firm, from discussing its opinions with an accused infringer who received an opinion from another firm.

A. What to Do

Litigating cases involving opinions of counsel create numerous ethical issues for lawyers, and both the lawyer-as-witness issue and the question of waiver under *EchoStar* and *In re Seagate* have only begun to be litigated, and only by district courts. Many questions remain. The risk for now is obvious: A client who relies on the same firm may end up losing trial counsel, or facing such a broad waiver of privilege or work product as to end up with either the inability to rely on the opinion, or doing so but facing severe legal and practical restrictions on communications with trial counsel. In either event, the opinion of counsel may turn out to be a handful of sand.

H. Conclusion

Combining the role of prosecution of a patent with other forms of representation related to the subject matter of that patent, or concerning the patent itself, can create problems for both attorney and client. Whether combining forms of representation is in the best interest of the client, and practicable for the lawyer, must be determined on a case-by-case basis.

---

180. *Convolve, Inc. v. Compaq Computer Corp.*, 224 F.R.D. 98 (S.D.N.Y. 2004).
181. *Id.* at 106 (*quoting Akeva L.L.C. v. Mizuno Corp.*, 243 F. Supp. 2d 418, 424 (M.D.N.C. 2003)).
182. *Id.*

APPENDIX

1

Annotated Patent and Trademark Office Code of Professional Conduct

§ 10.1 Definitions

This part governs solely the practice of patent, trademark, and other law before the Patent and Trademark Office. Nothing in this part shall be construed to preempt the authority of each State to regulate the practice of law, except to the extent necessary for the Patent and Trademark Office to accomplish its federal objectives. Unless otherwise clear from the context, the following definitions apply to this part:

(a) *Affidavit* means affidavit, declaration under 35 U.S.C. 25 (see § 1.68 and § 2.20 of this subchapter), or statutory declaration under 28 U.S.C. 1746.

(b) *Application* includes an application for a design, plant, or utility patent, an application to reissue any patent, and an application to register a trademark.

(c) *Attorney* or *lawyer* means an individual who is a member in good standing of the bar of any United States court or the highest court of any State. A "non-lawyer" is a person who is not an attorney or lawyer.

(d) *Canon* is defined in § 10.20(a).

(e) *Confidence* is defined in § 10.57(a).

(f) *Differing interests* include every interest that may adversely affect either the judgment or the loyalty of a practitioner to a client, whether it be a conflicting, inconsistent, diverse, or other interest.

(g) *Director* means the Director of Enrollment and Discipline.

(h) *Disciplinary Rule* is defined in § 10.20(b).

(i) *Employee of a tribunal* includes all employees of courts, the Office, and other adjudicatory bodies.

(j) *Giving information* within the meaning of § 10.23(c) (2) includes making (1) a written statement or representation or (2) an oral statement or representation.

(k) *Law firm* includes a professional legal corporation or a partnership.

(1) *Legal counsel* means practitioner.

(m) *Legal profession* includes the individuals who are lawfully engaged in practice of patent, trademark, and other law before the Office.

(n) *Legal service* means any legal service which may lawfully be performed by a practitioner before the Office.

(o) *Legal System* includes the Office and courts and adjudicatory bodies which review matters on which the Office has acted.

(p) *Office* means Patent and Trademark Office.

(q) *Person* includes a corporation, an association, a trust, a partnership, and any other organization or legal entity.

(r) *Practitioner* means (1) an attorney or agent registered to practice before the Office in patent cases or (2) an individual authorized under 5 U.S.C. 500(b) or otherwise as provided by this subchapter, to practice before the Office in trademark cases or other non-patent cases. A "suspended or excluded practitioner" is a practitioner who is suspended or excluded under § 10.156. A "non-practitioner" is an individual who is not a practitioner.

(s) A *proceeding before the Office* includes an application, a reexamination, a protest, a public use proceeding, a patent interference, an *inter partes* trademark proceeding, or any other proceeding which is pending before the Office.

(t) *Professional legal corporation* means a corporation authorized by law to practice law for profit.

(u) *Registration* means registration to practice before the Office in patent cases.

(v) *Respondent* is defined in § 10.134(a)(1).

(w) *Secret* is defined in § 10.57(a).

(x) *Solicit* is defined in § 10.33.

(y) *State* includes the District of Columbia, Puerto Rico, and other federal territories and possessions.

(z) *Tribunal* includes courts, the Office, and other adjudicatory bodies.

(aa) *United States* means the United States of America, its territories and possessions.

[Added 50 FR 5172, Feb. 6, 1985, effective Mar. 8, 1985]

Meyer and Hricik Commentary

There are significant differences between several defined terms in the Patent and Trademark Office Code of Professional Conduct (PTO) Code and those in most state rules. Those differences are discussed in the main text. We again emphasize here that the following terms are defined significantly differently than most states:

- "Confidence"
- "Secret"

§ 10.2 [Reserved]

[Added 50 FR 5173, Feb. 6, 1985, effective Mar. 8, 1985; removed and reserved, 69 FR 35427, June 24, 2004, effective July 26, 2004] § 10.3 [Reserved]

[Added 50 FR 5173, Feb. 6, 1985, effective Mar. 8, 1985; removed and reserved, 69 FR 35427, June 24, 2004, effective July 26, 2004]

§ 10.4 Committee on Discipline

(a) The Commissioner shall appoint a Committee on Discipline. The Committee on Discipline shall consist of at least three employees of the Office, none of whom reports directly or indirectly to the Director or the Solicitor. Each member of the Committee on Discipline shall be a member in good standing of the bar of a State.

(b) The Committee on Discipline shall meet at the request of the Director and after reviewing evidence presented by the Director shall, by majority vote, determine whether there is probable cause to bring charges under § 10.132 against a practitioner. When charges are brought against a practitioner, no member of the Committee on Discipline, employee under the direction of the Director, or associate solicitor or assistant solicitor in the Office of Solicitor shall participate in rendering a decision on the charges.

(c) No discovery shall be authorized of, and no member of the Committee on Discipline shall be required to testify about, deliberations of the Committee on Discipline.

[Added 50 FR 5173, Feb. 6, 1985, effective Mar. 8, 1985]

Meyer and Hricik Commentary

The Committee on Discipline is obviously intended to serve, much like a grand jury, on a check on the authority of the Director of Enrollment and Discipline. Likewise, the prohibition against discovery of members and their deliberations in some respects is analogous to the grand jury process.

§ 10.5 [Reserved]

[Added 50 FR 5173, Feb. 6, 1985, effective Mar. 8, 1985; removed and reserved, 69 FR 35427, June 24, 2004, effective July 26, 2004]

§ 10.6 [Reserved]

[Added 50 FR 5173, Feb. 6, 1985, effective Mar. 8, 1985; paras. (d) & (e) removed 53 FR 38948, Oct. 4, 1988, effective Nov. 4, 1988; removed and reserved, 69 FR 35427, June 24, 2004, effective July 26, 2004]

§ 10.7 [Reserved]

[Added 50 FR 5174, Feb. 6, 1985, effective Mar. 8, 1985; removed and reserved, 69 FR 35427, June 24, 2004, effective July 26, 2004]

§ 10.8 [Reserved]

[Added 50 FR 5174, Feb. 6, 1985, effective Mar. 8, 1985; removed and reserved, 69 FR 35427, June 24, 2004, effective July 26, 2004]

§ 10.9 [Reserved]

[Added 50 FR 5174, Feb. 6, 1985, effective Mar. 8, 1985; para. (c) added, 58 FR 4335, Jan. 14, 1993, effective May 1, 1993; para. (c) amended, 60 FR 21438,

May 2, 1995, effective June 1, 1995; removed and reserved, 69 FR 35427, June 24, 2004, effective July 26, 2004]

§ 10.10 [Reserved]

[Added 50 FR 5175, Feb. 6, 1985, effective Mar. 8, 1985; revised 53 FR 38950, Oct. 4, 1988, effective Nov. 4, 1988; corrected 53 FR 41278, Oct. 20, 1988; removed and reserved, 69 FR 35427, June 24, 2004, effective July 26, 2004]

§ 10.11 Removing names from the register

A letter may be addressed to any individual on the register, at the address of which separate notice was last received by the Director, for the purpose of ascertaining whether such individual desires to remain on the register. The name of any individual failing to reply and give any information requested by the Director within a time limit specified will be removed from the register and the names of individuals so removed will be published in the Official Gazette. The name of any individual so removed may be reinstated on the register as may be appropriate and upon payment of the fee set forth in § 1.21(a)(3) of this subchapter.

[Added 50 FR 5175, Feb. 6, 1985, effective Mar. 8, 1985; revised, 69 FR 35427, June 24, 2004, effective July 26, 2004]

Meyer and Hricik Commentary

It is important for practitioners to keep the [Office of Enrollment and Discipline] OED apprised of address changes because notification will be sent to the last known address given to the OED. This may become automatic given the requirement of practitioner maintenance fees to be instituted in 2009. *See* 73 Fed. Reg. 67750 (Nov. 17, 2008).

§ 10.12–10.13 [Reserved]

§ 10.14 Individuals who may practice before the Office in trademark and other non-patent cases

(a) *Attorneys.* Any individual who is an attorney may represent others before the Office in trademark and other non-patent cases. An attorney is not required to apply for registration or recognition to practice before the Office in trademark and other non-patent cases.

(b) *Non-lawyers.* Individuals who are not attorneys are not recognized to practice before the Office in trademark and other non-patent cases, except that individuals not attorneys who were recognized to practice before the Office in trademark cases under this chapter prior to January 1, 1957, will be recognized as agents to continue practice before the Office in trademark cases.

(c) *Foreigners.* Any foreign attorney or agent not a resident of the United States who shall prove to the satisfaction of the Director that he or she is registered or in good standing before the patent or trademark office of the country in which he or she resides and practices, may be recognized for the limited purpose of representing parties located in such country before the Office in the presentation and prosecution of trademark cases, *provided:* The patent or trademark office of such country allows substantially reciprocal privileges to those permitted to practice in trademark cases before the United States Patent and Trademark Office. Recognition under this paragraph shall continue only during the period that the conditions specified in this paragraph obtain.

(d) Recognition of any individual under this section shall not be construed as sanctioning or authorizing the performance of any act regarded in the jurisdiction where performed as the unauthorized practice of law.

(e) No individual other than those specified in paragraphs (a), (b), and (c) of this section will be permitted to practice before the Office in trademark cases. Any individual may appear in a trademark or other non-patent case in his or her own behalf. Any individual may appear in a trademark case for (1) a firm of which he or she is a member or (2) a corporation or association of which he or she is an officer and which he or she is authorized to represent, if such firm, corporation, or association is a party to a trademark proceeding pending before the Office.

[Added 50 FR 5175, Feb. 6, 1985, effective Mar. 8, 1985]

Meyer and Hricik Commentary

The rule authorizes any attorney to represent others in non-patent cases, but only a registered patent practitioner may represent patent applicants.

As discussed in the text, the authority to represent others before the U.S. Patent and Trademark Office (USPTO) is not a general license to practice law. Here, section 10.14(d) reinforces that basic limitation on the authority of the office.

§ 10.15 Refusal to recognize a practitioner

Any practitioner authorized to appear before the Office may be suspended or excluded in accordance with the provisions of this part. Any practitioner who is suspended or excluded under this subpart or removed under § 10.11(b) shall not be entitled to practice before the Office.

[Added 50 FR 5175, Feb. 6, 1985, effective Mar. 8, 1985]

Meyer and Hricik Commentary

Significantly, this section limits the ability of the OED to suspend or exclude a practitioner who violates this part of the Code of Federal Regulations (CFR). Thus, proof of a violation of part of the PTO Code is required to suspend or exclude a practitioner from practicing before the PTO.

§ 10.16–10.17 [Reserved]

§ 10.18 Signature and certificate for correspondence filed in the Patent and Trademark Office

(a) For all documents filed in the Office in patent, trademark, and other non-patent matters, except for correspondence that is required to be signed by the applicant or party, each piece of correspondence filed by a practitioner in the Patent and Trademark Office must bear a signature by such practitioner complying with the provisions of § 1.4(d), § 1.4(e), or § 2.193(c)(1) of this chapter.

(b) By presenting to the Office (whether by signing, filing, submitting, or later advocating) any paper, the party presenting such paper, whether a practitioner or non-practitioner, is certifying that—

   (1) All statements made therein of the party's own knowledge are true, all statements made therein on information and belief are believed to be true, and all statements made therein are made with the knowledge that whoever, in any matter within the jurisdiction of the Patent and Trademark Office, knowingly and willfully falsifies, conceals, or covers up by any trick, scheme, or device a material fact, or makes any false, fictitious or fraudulent statements or representations, or makes or uses any false writing or document knowing the same to contain any false, fictitious or fraudulent statement or entry, shall be subject to the penalties set forth under 18 U.S.C. 1001, and that violations of this paragraph may jeopardize the validity of the application or document, or the validity or enforceability of any patent, trademark registration, or certificate resulting therefrom; and

   (2) To the best of the party's knowledge, information and belief, formed after an inquiry reasonable under the circumstances, that—

      (i) The paper is not being presented for any improper purpose, such as to harass someone or to cause unnecessary delay or needless increase in the cost of prosecution before the Office;

      (ii) The claims and other legal contentions therein are warranted by existing law or by a nonfrivolous argument for the extension, modification, or reversal of existing law or the establishment of new law;

      (iii) The allegations and other factual contentions have evidentiary support or, if specifically so identified, are likely to have evidentiary support after a reasonable opportunity for further investigation or discovery; and

      (iv) The denials of factual contentions are warranted on the evidence, or if specifically so identified, are reasonably based on a lack of information or belief.

(c) Violations of paragraph (b)(1) of this section by a practitioner or non-practitioner may jeopardize the validity of the application or document, or the validity or enforceability of any patent, trademark registration, or certificate resulting therefrom. Violations of any of paragraphs (b)(2)(i) through (iv) of this section are, after notice and reasonable opportunity to respond, subject to such sanctions as deemed appropriate by the Commissioner, or the Commissioner's designee, which may include, but are not limited to, any combination of—

   (1) Holding certain facts to have been established;

   (2) Returning papers;

(3) Precluding a party from filing a paper, or presenting or contesting an issue;
(4) Imposing a monetary sanction;
(5) Requiring a terminal disclaimer for the period of the delay; or
(6) Terminating the proceedings in the Patent and Trademark Office.

(d) Any practitioner violating the provisions of this section may also be subject to disciplinary action. *See* § 10.23(c)(15).

[Added 50 FR 5175, Feb. 6, 1985, effective Mar. 8, 1985; para. (a) revised, 58 FR 54494, Oct. 22, 1993, effective Nov. 22, 1993; paras. (a) & (b) revised, paras. (c) & (d) added, 62 FR 53131, Oct. 10, 1997, effective Dec. 1, 1997; para. (a) revised, 69 FR 56481, Sept. 21, 2004, effective Oct. 21, 2004]

Meyer and Hricik Commentary

This provision of the PTO Code is analogous to Fed. R. Civ. P. 11. *See also* section 10.85. In litigation, of course, both the opposing party and the court on its own motion may raise violations of Rule 11, whereas this PTO Code provision applies in *ex parte* prosecution and will only be raised by the examiner. In addition, the available sanctions differ significantly in form. In that regard, the section specifically states not only that discipline may be available, but that invalidity or unenforceability are also potential consequences of a violation.

§ 10.19 [Reserved]

PATENT AND TRADEMARK OFFICE CODE OF PROFESSIONAL RESPONSIBILITY

§ 10.20 Canons and Disciplinary Rules

(a) Canons are set out in §§ 10.21, 10.30, 10.46, 10.56, 10.61, 10.76, 10.83, 10.100, and 10.110. Canons are statements of axiomatic norms, expressing in general terms the standards of professional conduct expected of practitioners in their relationships with the public, with the legal system, and with the legal profession.

(b) Disciplinary Rules are set out in §§ 10.22–10.24, 10.31–10.40, 10.47–10.57, 10.62–10.68, 10.77, 10.78, 10.84, 10.85, 10.87–10.89,

10.92, 10.93, 10.101–10.103, 10.111, and 10.112. Disciplinary Rules are mandatory in character and state the minimum level of conduct below which no practitioner can fall without being subjected to disciplinary action.

[Added 50 FR 5175, Feb. 6, 1985, effective Mar. 8, 1985]

Meyer and Hricik Commentary

The PTO Code, like the Model Code, contained both mandatory "disciplinary rules" and hortatory "canons." Discipline can be based only on violation of a disciplinary rule, as is the case with the Model Code.

§ 10.21 Canon 1

A practitioner should assist in maintaining the integrity and competence of the legal profession.

[Added 50 FR 5175, Feb. 6, 1985, effective Mar. 8, 1985]

Meyer and Hricik Commentary

The duty of competency is a core ethical obligation. This hortatory canon recognizes its importance.

§ 10.22 Maintaining integrity and competence of the legal profession

(a) A practitioner is subject to discipline if the practitioner has made a materially false statement in, or if the practitioner has deliberately failed to disclose a material fact requested in connection with, the practitioner's application for registration or membership in the bar of any United States court or any State court or his or her authority to otherwise practice before the Office in trademark and other non-patent cases.

(b) A practitioner shall not further the application for registration or membership in the bar of any United States court, State court, or

(12) Knowingly filing, or causing to be filed, a frivolous complaint alleging a violation by a practitioner of the Patent and Trademark Office Code of Professional Responsibility.

(13) Knowingly preparing or prosecuting or providing assistance in the preparation or prosecution of a patent application in violation of an undertaking signed under § 10.10(b).

(14) Knowingly failing to advise the Director in writing of any change which would preclude continued registration under § 10.6.

(15) Signing a paper filed in the Office in violation of the provisions of § 10.18 or making a scandalous or indecent statement in a paper filed in the Office.

(16) Willfully refusing to reveal or report knowledge or evidence to the Director contrary to § 10.24 or paragraph (b) of § 10.131.

(17) Representing before the Office in a patent case either a joint venture comprising an inventor and an invention developer or an inventor referred to the registered practitioner by an invention developer when (i) the registered practitioner knows, or has been advised by the Office, that a formal complaint filed by a Federal or State agency, based on any violation of any law relating to securities, unfair methods of competition, unfair or deceptive acts or practices, mail fraud, or other civil or criminal conduct, is pending before a Federal or State court or Federal or State agency, or has been resolved unfavorably by such court or agency, against the invention developer in connection with invention development services and (ii) the registered practitioner fails to fully advise the inventor of the existence of the pending complaint or unfavorable resolution thereof prior to undertaking or continuing representation of the joint venture or inventor. "Invention developer" means any person, and any agent, employee, officer, partner, or independent contractor thereof, who is not a registered practitioner and who advertises invention development services in media of general circulation or who enters into contracts for invention development services with customers as a result of such advertisement. "Invention development services" means acts of invention development required or promised to be performed, or actually performed, or both, by an invention developer for a customer. "Invention development" means the evaluation, perfection, marketing, brokering, or promotion of an invention on behalf of a customer by an invention developer, including a patent search, preparation of a patent application, or any other act done by an invention developer for consideration toward the end of procuring or attempting to procure a license, buyer, or patent for an invention. "Customer" means any individual who has made an invention and who enters into a contract for invention

development services with an invention developer with respect to the invention by which the inventor becomes obligated to pay the invention developer less than $5,000 (not to include any additional sums which the invention developer is to receive as a result of successful development of the invention). "Contract for invention development services" means a contract for invention development services with an invention developer with respect to an invention made by a customer by which the inventor becomes obligated to pay the invention developer less than $5,000 (not to include any additional sums which the invention developer is to receive as a result of successful development of the invention).

(18) In the absence of information sufficient to establish a reasonable belief that fraud or inequitable conduct has occurred, alleging before a tribunal that anyone has committed a fraud on the Office or engaged in inequitable conduct in a proceeding before the Office.

(19) Action by an employee of the Office contrary to the provisions set forth in § 10.10(c).

(20) Knowing practice by a Government employee contrary to applicable Federal conflict of interest laws, or regulations of the Department, agency, or commission employing said individual.

(d) A practitioner who acts with reckless indifference to whether a representation is true or false is chargeable with knowledge of its falsity. Deceitful statements of half-truths or concealment of material facts shall be deemed actual fraud within the meaning of this part.

[Added 50 FR 5175, Feb. 6, 1985, effective Mar. 8, 1985; amended 50 FR 25073, June 17, 1985; 50 FR 25980, June 24, 1985; paras. (c)(13), (19) & (20), 53 FR 38950, Oct. 4, 1988, effective Nov. 4, 1988; corrected 53 FR 41278, Oct. 20, 1988; paras. (c)(10) & (c)(11), 57 FR 2021, Jan. 17, 1992, effective Mar. 16, 1992; para. (c)(9) amended, 58 FR 54494, Oct. 22, 1993, effective Nov. 22, 1993; para. (c)(9) amended, 61 FR 56439, Nov. 1, 1996, effective Dec. 2, 1996; para. (c)(15) amended, 62 FR 53131, Oct. 10, 1997, effective Dec. 1, 1997; para. (c)(11) revised, 65 FR 54604, Sept. 8, 2000, effective Nov. 7, 2000; para (c)(7) revised, 69 FR 49959, Aug. 12, 2004, effective Sept. 13, 2004]

Meyer and Hricik Commentary

This rule serves as a catchall provision and also prohibits several specific forms of conduct. The general provisions are designed in large measure to permit the USPTO to discipline practitioners for actions that occur outside the confines of practice before the USPTO that indicates a character or competency flaw demonstrating the need for discipline as well as to sanction conduct before the USPTO, in any context, which also indicates the same deficiencies.

The general provisions are relatively typical. First, they allow the USPTO to discipline practitioners who: (a) engage in disreputable or gross misconduct; (b) circumvent a disciplinary rule through the acts of another; (c) engage in illegal conduct involving moral turpitude, dishonesty, fraud, deceit, misrepresentation, or which either is prejudicial to the administration of justice or adversely reflects on the practitioner's fitness to practice before the USPTO; or (d) are suspended or disbarred by a state. *See Marinangeli v. Lehman,* 32 F. Supp. 2d 1 (D. D.C. 1998) (crime of moral turpitude of felony theft); *In re Rivera,* 67 U.S.P.Q.2d 1952 (Dir. PTO 2003) (reciprocal discipline based on state disciplinary action).

The specific prohibitions in the paragraph, although lumped in one long list, are each significant, although some are more intuitive than others. The specific prohibitions that are typical in ethical codes include:

- Misappropriating client funds that are due to the USPTO
- Improperly attempting to influence a USPTO employee
- Aiding the unauthorized practice of law before the USPTO
- Filing a frivolous ethics complaint against a practitioner
- Filing a scandalous paper or one that violates the Rule 11 of the USPTO, section 10.18
- Failing, "willfully," to disclose to the USPTO evidence of a violation of the PTO Code

Each of these sections is distinct from analogous provisions in the Model Code or state ethics rules, however, and the invention development provision is unique. *See generally Cichonski v. Am. Inventors Corp.,* 1995 WL 657107 (E.D. Pa. Nov. 3, 1995) (suit against invention development type corporation); *In re Cohen,* 66 U.S.Q.2d 1782 (Dir. PTO 2003) (disciplinary case involving same); *Moatz v. Colitz,* 68 U.S.Q.2d 1079 (Dir. PTO 2003) (same); *Bender v. Dudas,* 490 F.3d 1361 (Fed. Cir. 2007) (same). *See also Gugliotta v. Morano,* 829 N.E.2d 757 (Ct. App. Ohio 2005) (suit between invention development company and former attorney). In addition, the requirement that a lawyer avoid willfully disclosing a violation of the PTO Code is significantly different from most state rules.

The PTO Code in this section also includes some specific provisions that are unique to patent practice, not just in words, but in concept. These include:

- Failing to advise the USPTO that claims had been copied from another patent or application under 35 U.S.C. section 135
- Failing to advise a current or former client of the receipt of a paper that could significantly effect the client
- Misusing a certificate of mailing

- Committing inequitable conduct
- Materially altering an application after the oath is signed
- Prosecuting in violation of section 10.10(b)
- Representing so-called invention development entities
- Accusing another practitioner of having committed inequitable conduct without a reasonable belief
- Practicing before the office in violation of applicable law

Finally, this section has two other provisions. First, section 10.23(d) broadens the notion of knowledge of falsity to include the notion of reckless disregard and deceit by omission. Second, section 10.23(c)(5) allows the patent office to engage in "reciprocal discipline" when a practitioner is suspended or disbarred by certain jurisdictions.

§ 10.24 Disclosure of information to authorities

(a) A practitioner possessing unprivileged knowledge of a violation of a Disciplinary Rule shall report such knowledge to the Director.
(b) A practitioner possessing unprivileged knowledge or evidence concerning another practitioner, employee of the Office, or a judge shall reveal fully such knowledge or evidence upon proper request of a tribunal or other authority empowered to investigate or act upon the conduct of practitioners, employees of the Office, or judges.

[Added 50 FR 5176, Feb. 6, 1985, effective Mar. 8, 1985]

Meyer and Hricik Commentary

Section 10.24(a), if it means what it says, would impose an extraordinarily broad and likely unworkable reporting requirement on practitioners. Instead, it more likely requires reporting of a violation that calls into question the honesty or trustworthiness of another practitioner. There are no decisions giving the provision its literal meaning, and courts had to continue to reject reading analogous rules too broadly.

Section 10.24(b), less controversial, simply requires a practitioner to cooperate with the investigation of another practitioner.

§ 10.25–10.29 [Reserved]

§ 10.30 Canon 2

A practitioner should assist the legal profession in fulfilling its duty to make legal counsel available.

[Added 50 FR 5177, Feb. 6, 1985, effective Mar. 8, 1985]

Meyer and Hricik Commentary

This canon, hortatory in nature, has less significance in patent practice than, say, in other practice areas where significant needs for pro bono and reduced-rate legal representation go unmet.

§ 10.31 Communications concerning a practitioner's services

(a) No practitioner shall with respect to any prospective business before the Office, by word, circular, letter, or advertising, with intent to defraud in any manner, deceive, mislead, or threaten any prospective applicant or other person having immediate or prospective business before the Office.

(b) A practitioner may not use the name of a Member of either House of Congress or of an individual in the service of the United States in advertising the practitioner's practice before the Office.

(c) Unless authorized under § 10.14(b), a non-lawyer practitioner shall not hold himself or herself out as authorized to practice before the Office in trademark cases.

(d) Unless a practitioner is an attorney, the practitioner shall not hold himself or herself out:

  (1) To be an attorney or lawyer or

  (2) As authorized to practice before the Office in non-patent and trademark cases.

[Added 50 FR 5177, Feb. 6, 1985, effective Mar. 8, 1985]

Meyer and Hricik Commentary

These aspects of the PTO Code regulating solicitation are relatively straightforward and, with the exception of subsection (b), are common. Broadly, the section prohibits fraudulent, deceptive, or misleading communications as well as those that evidence the unauthorized practice of law. Those prohibitions are common. *See generally* Ill. St. B. Ass'n. Advisory Op. No. 96–08 (May 16, 1997) (holding that a firm that farms out patent prosecution work cannot advertise itself as doing patent prosecution); St. B. Mich. Op. RI-167 (July 29, 1993) (analyzing whether entity that would freely refer inventors to registered patent practitioners was a "lawyer referral service" in terms of state law).

§ 10.32 Advertising

(a) Subject to § 10.31, a practitioner may advertise services through public media, including a telephone directory, legal directory, newspaper, or other periodical, radio, or television, or through written communications not involving solicitation as defined by § 10.33.
(b) A practitioner shall not give anything of value to a person for recommending the practitioner's services, except that a practitioner may pay the reasonable cost of advertising or written communication permitted by this section and may pay the usual charges of a not-for-profit lawyer referral service or other legal service organization.
(c) Any communication made pursuant to this section shall include the name of at least one practitioner responsible for its content.

[Added 50 FR 5177, Feb. 6, 1985, effective Mar. 8, 1985]

Meyer and Hricik Commentary

These advertising rules are similar to analogous provisions in state rules. They incorporate the prohibitions in section 10.31 against fraudulent, deceptive, or misleading communications. Subsection (b) prohibits payment of referral fees for recommending the lawyer's services but permit commercial advertising costs. Significantly, in-person solicitation and mail are covered by section 10.33, not this section.

Although the USPTO has not addressed the issue, a noninteractive web site has generally been held to be an "advertisement" by most states, and so would be governed by this rule. E-mail and synchronous, real-time communications would be covered by section 10.33, not this section, for similar reasons.

§ 10.33 Direct contact with prospective clients

A practitioner may not solicit professional employment from a prospective client with whom the practitioner has no family or prior professional relationship, by mail, in-person, or otherwise, when a significant motive for the practitioner's doing so is the practitioner's pecuniary gain under circumstances evidencing undue influence, intimidation, or overreaching. The term "solicit" includes contact in person, by telephone or telegraph, by letter or other writing, or by other communication directed to a specific recipient, but does not include letters addressed or advertising circulars distributed generally to persons not specifically known to need legal services of the kind provided by the practitioner in a particular matter, but who are so situated that they might in general find such services useful.

[Added 50 FR 5177, Feb.6, 1985, effective Mar. 8, 1985]

Meyer and Hricik Commentary

Like most ethics codes, the PTO Code draws distinctions between synchronous communications such as letters, and public, asynchronous communications such as advertisements in bar journals. However, it permits greater communication than many state rules.

The rule does not apply to traditional advertisements, even if "targeted" to those in need of specific types of legal representation. Unlike some state ethics rules, it also specifically does not apply to private asynchronous communications, such as letters, if the recipient is not known by the practitioners to need legal services in a particular matter.

With respect to any in person or telephonic solicitation, or any asynchronous communication such as a letter or e-mail, the rule does apply. It prohibits such communications unless the practitioner has a familiar or prior professional relation, if the communication is for pecuniary gain (as opposed to a political purpose, for example) and the circumstances evidence under influence, intimidation, or overreaching. Thus, as written, it is broader than many states, which ban outright telephonic or in-person communications absent a familiar or prior professional relationship with the prospective client. (As written, it also seems to permit practitioners to mislead family members and former clients.)

§ 10.34 Communication of fields of practice

A registered practitioner may state or imply that the practitioner is a specialist as follows:

  (a) A registered practitioner who is an attorney may use the designation "Patents," "Patent Attorney," "Patent Lawyer," "Registered Patent Attorney," or a substantially similar designation.

  (b) A registered practitioner who is not an attorney may use the designation "Patents," "Patent Agent," "Registered Patent Agent," or a substantially similar designation, except that any practitioner who was registered prior to November 15, 1938, may refer to himself or herself as a "patent attorney."

[Added 50 FR 5177, Feb. 6, 1985, effective Mar. 8, 1985]

Meyer and Hricik Commentary

This rule reflects the historic ability of patent practitioners to advertise as such. Most state rules include a specific "safe harbor" for practitioners to accurately communicate this same information.

§ 10.35 Firm names and letterheads

  (a) A practitioner shall not use a firm name, letterhead, or other professional designation that violates § 10.31. A trade name may be used by a practitioner in private practice if it does not imply a current connection with a government agency or with a public or charitable legal services organization and is not otherwise in violation of § 10.31.

  (b) Practitioners may state or imply that they practice in a partnership or other organization only when that is the fact.

[Added 50 FR 5177, Feb. 6, 1985, effective Mar. 8, 1985]

Meyer and Hricik Commentary

Like most state rules, the PTO Code prohibits false or misleading firm names. Likewise, the safe harbor for certain trade names is also fairly common.

(b) In connection with the settlement of a controversy or suit, a practitioner shall not enter into an agreement that restricts the practitioner's right to practice before the Office.

[Added 50 FR 5177, Feb. 6, 1985, effective Mar. 8, 1985]

Meyer and Hricik Commentary

These common prohibitions are designed to protect both current and former clients. A settlement proposal that a lawyer forego representations can create a conflict between the lawyer and the current client and also restrict the ability of future clients to retain the practitioner.

§ 10.39 Acceptance of employment

A practitioner shall not accept employment on behalf of a person if the practitioner knows or it is obvious that such person wishes to:
(a) Bring a legal action, commence a proceeding before the Office, conduct a defense, assert a position in any proceeding pending before the Office, or otherwise have steps taken for the person, merely for the purpose of harassing or maliciously injuring any other person.
(b) Present a claim or defense in litigation or any proceeding before the Office that it is not warranted under existing law, unless it can be supported by good faith argument for an extension, modification, or reversal of existing law.

[Added 50 FR 5177, Feb. 6, 1985, effective Mar. 8, 1985]

Meyer and Hricik Commentary

Similar to and in some ways supplementing section 10.18(b)(2), this rule prohibits conduct that is merely to harass or maliciously injure a person or that is frivolous.

§ 10.40 Withdrawal from employment

(a) A practitioner shall not withdraw from employment in a proceeding before the Office without permission from the Office (*see* §§ 1.36 and

2.19 of this subchapter). In any event, a practitioner shall not withdraw from employment until the practitioner has taken reasonable steps to avoid foreseeable prejudice to the rights of the client, including giving due notice to his or her client, allowing time for employment of another practitioner, delivering to the client all papers and property to which the client is entitled, and complying with applicable laws and rules. A practitioner who withdraws from employment shall refund promptly any part of a fee paid in advance that has not been earned.

(b) Mandatory withdrawal. A practitioner representing a client before the Office shall withdraw from employment if:

　(1) The practitioner knows or it is obvious that the client is bringing a legal action, commencing a proceeding before the Office, conducting a defense, or asserting a position in litigation or any proceeding pending before the Office, or is otherwise having steps taken for the client, merely for the purpose of harassing or maliciously injuring any person;

　(2) The practitioner knows or it is obvious that the practitioner's continued employment will result in violation of a Disciplinary Rule;

　(3) The practitioner's mental or physical condition renders it unreasonably difficult for the practitioner to carry out the employment effectively; or

　(4) The practitioner is discharged by the client.

(c) *Permissive withdrawal.* If paragraph (b) of this section is not applicable, a practitioner may not request permission to withdraw in matters pending before the Office unless such request or such withdrawal is because:

　(1) The petitioner's client:

　　(i) Insists upon presenting a claim or defense that is not warranted under existing law and cannot be supported by good faith argument for an extension, modification, or reversal of existing law;

　　(ii) Personally seeks to pursue an illegal course of conduct;

　　(iii) Insists that the practitioner pursue a course of conduct that is illegal or that is prohibited under a Disciplinary Rule;

　　(iv) By other conduct renders it unreasonably difficult for the practitioner to carry out the employment effectively;

　　(v) Insists, in a matter not pending before a tribunal, that the practitioner engage in conduct that is contrary to the judgment and advice of the practitioner but not prohibited under the Disciplinary Rule; or

　　(vi) Has failed to pay one or more bills rendered by the practitioner for an unreasonable period of time or has failed to honor an agreement to pay a retainer in advance of the performance of legal services.

(2) The practitioner's continued employment is likely to result in a violation of a Disciplinary Rule;

(3) The practitioner's inability to work with co-counsel indicates that the best interests of the client likely will be served by withdrawal;

(4) The practitioner's mental or physical condition renders it difficult for the practitioner to carry out the employment effectively;

(5) The practitioner's client knowingly and freely assents to termination of the employment; or

(6) The practitioner believes in good faith, in a proceeding pending before the Office, that the Office will find the existence of other good cause for withdrawal.

[Added 50 FR 5178, Feb. 6, 1985, effective Mar. 8, 1985]

Meyer and Hricik Commentary

Like most state rules, the PTO Code permits withdrawal under some circumstances, requires it under a narrower circumstances—and in all events, requires approval before withdrawal can occur and requires that any withdrawal be done in a way that reasonably avoids prejudice to the client.

Withdrawal is required if: the client is acting merely to harass or maliciously injure a person; continued employment would violate a disciplinary rule; the lawyer is physically or mentally unable to continue; the client discharges the lawyer. Again, as explained below, the practitioner can withdraw only if permitted by the USPTO.

Permissive withdrawal is available under broader circumstances than analogous state rules. For example, if the client agrees freely, the lawyer may withdraw. Likewise, if the client fails to satisfy financial obligations or acts contrary to the advice of the practitioner to a matter not pending before the USPTO, the practitioner may withdraw. Finally, unlike most rules, the mere inability to work with co-counsel may be a basis for withdrawal.

The remainder of the permissive withdrawal provisions are in line with analogous state rules: withdrawal is permitted if the client pursues frivolous claims or defenses; engages in illegal conduct or that which violates a disciplinary rule; or makes it unreasonably difficult to carry out the representation. Likewise, the practitioner may withdraw if good cause likely exists or his or her mental or physical condition makes it difficult to continue.

Even where withdrawal is required or permitted, however, under section 10.40(a) the practitioner can withdraw only with any necessary permission from the USPTO. If permission is denied; the lawyer must continue the representation.

Finally, if withdrawal occurs, the lawyer must take reasonable steps to avoid foreseeable prejudice to the client. Obviously, any unearned fees or expense deposits must be returned. In addition, the lawyer is required to return "all papers and property to which the client is entitled." This may require the practitioner to return all papers to the client, all papers except internal accounting reports and the like. Most state rules have been interpreted to permit clients to own most of the file including, electronic files. Although some states authorize lawyers to exert retaining liens, care should be exercised any time papers are withheld on that basis.

§ 10.41–10.45 [Reserved]

§ 10.46 Canon 3

A practitioner should assist in preventing the unauthorized practice of law.

[Added 50 FR 5178, Feb. 6, 1985, effective Mar. 8, 1985]

Meyer and Hricik Commentary

This hortatory canon is of particular concern in patent practice because nonlawyer patent agents practice law along with lawyers. As the text of the book points out, this creates uncertainties in patent practice that do not arise in other areas.

§ 10.47 Aiding unauthorized practice of law

(a) A practitioner shall not aid a non-practitioner in the unauthorized practice of law before the Office.
(b) A practitioner shall not aid a suspended or excluded practitioner in the practice of law before the Office.
(c) A practitioner shall not aid a non-lawyer in the unauthorized practice of law.

[Added 50 FR 5178, Feb. 6, 1985, effective Mar. 8, 1985]

Meyer and Hricik Commentary

These prohibitions are common and straightforward. As the text of the book points out, however, patent agents create unique issues concerning the unauthorized practice of law.

Generally, to avoid aiding nonlawyers to practice law, the practitioner must both supervise the nonlawyer's work and be responsible for it. Nothing, in other words, prevents a practitioner from having a secretary draft a patent application. The practitioner, however, must supervise the work and remains ultimately responsible for it.

§ 10.48 Sharing legal fees

A practitioner or a firm of practitioners shall not share legal fees with a non-practitioner except that:
- (a) An agreement by a practitioner with the practitioner's firm, partner, or associate may provide for the payment of money, over a reasonable period of time after the practitioner's death, to the practitioner's estate or to one or more specified persons.
- (b) A practitioner who undertakes to complete unfinished legal business of a deceased practitioner may pay to the estate of the deceased practitioner that proportion of the total compensation which fairly represents the services rendered by the deceased practitioner.
- (c) A practitioner or firm of practitioners may include non-practitioner employees in a compensation or retirement plan, even though the plan is based in whole or in part on a profit-sharing arrangement, providing such plan does not circumvent another Disciplinary Rule.

[Added 50 FR 5178, Feb. 6, 1985, effective Mar. 8, 1985; para. (b) revised, 58 FR 54511, Oct. 22, 1993, effective June 3, 1994]

Meyer and Hricik Commentary

The introductory prohibition against sharing legal fees with a nonpractitioner is as important as the three narrow exceptions that follow. As a general rule, it is improper to "share legal fees" with nonpractitioners. Although read literally this would preclude a practitioner from employing a secretary, obviously it does not reach that far.

§ 10.49 Forming a partnership with a non-practitioner

A practitioner shall not form a partnership with a non-practitioner if any of the activities of the partnership consist of the practice of patent, trademark, or other law before the Office.

[Added 50 FR 5178, Feb. 6, 1985, effective Mar. 8, 1985]

Meyer and Hricik Commentary

Lawyers and patent agents are "practitioners." Thus, this section prohibits forming partnerships between lawyers or patent agents, on the one hand, and those who are not lawyers or patent agents, on the other.

§ 10.50–10.55 [Reserved]

§ 10.56 Canon 4

A practitioner should preserve the confidences and secrets of a client.

[Added 50 FR 5178, Feb. 6, 1985, effective Mar. 8, 1985]

Meyer and Hricik Commentary

Like the duty of competency, the duty of confidentiality expressed in this hortatory canon is one of the core duties in the practitioner-client relationship.

§ 10.57 Preservation of confidences and secrets of a client

(a) "Confidence" refers to information protected by the attorney-client or agent-client privilege under applicable law. "Secret" refers to other information gained in the professional relationship that the client has requested be held inviolate or the disclosure of which would be embarrassing or would be likely to be detrimental to the client.

(b) Except when permitted under paragraph (c) of this section, a practitioner shall not knowingly:

(1) Reveal a confidence or secret of a client.

(2) Use a confidence or secret of a client to the disadvantage of the client.

(3) Use a confidence or secret of a client for the advantage of the practitioner or of a third person, unless the client consents after full disclosure.

(c) A practitioner may reveal:

(1) Confidences or secrets with the consent of the client affected but only after a full disclosure to the client.

(2) Confidences or secrets when permitted under Disciplinary Rules or required by law or court order.

(3) The intention of a client to commit a crime and the information necessary to prevent the crime.

(4) Confidences or secrets necessary to establish or collect the practitioner's fee or to defend the practitioner or the practitioner's employees or associates against an accusation of wrongful conduct.

(d) A practitioner shall exercise reasonable care to prevent the practitioner's employees, associates, and others whose services are utilized by the practitioner from disclosing or using confidences or secrets of a client, except that a practitioner may reveal the information allowed by paragraph (c) of this section through an employee.

[Added 50 FR 5178, Feb. 6, 1985, effective Mar. 8, 1985]

Meyer and Hricik Commentary

States have historically disagreed more widely on the breadth of the duty of confidentiality and the scope of its exceptions than perhaps any other ethical issue. The PTO Code probably overall falls somewhere in the middle of these varied approaches.

With respect to breadth, section 10.57(a) does not reach as broadly as some state rules, which define "confidences" to include all information relating to the representation of the client. Instead, the PTO Code protects attorney or agent-client privileged information as well as information that either the client requested to be kept confidential or which would embarrass or be detrimental to the client if disclosed. In this respect, it is narrower than probably a majority of the states.

The scope of the exceptions are narrower, however, unlike many state rules, for example, there are no mandatory exceptions to confidentiality.

Other rules do require revelation. section 10.24 requires disclosure of violation of the PTO Code, and also in connection with investigations of violations. Also section 10.85 requires lawyers to reveal information to prevent or rectify client fraud, under some circumstances.

Like most rules, the PTO Code distinguishes between revelation and use. Adverse use is prohibited. Use that is not adverse but which benefits the practitioner or a third party is permitted only after informed consent.

Revelation is prohibited: absent consent unless either revelation is permitted by a disciplinary rule or required by law; necessary to prevent the client from committing a crime; to establish or collect a fee; or to defend the practitioner from a claim of wrongful conduct.

Some state rules permit lawyers to disclose client confidences when any crime is intended. Some states limit permission disclosure to crimes that will cause bodily harm, or in which the lawyer's services were involved. A few states require disclosure of confidences under some circumstances.

Similarly, the exception in the PTO Code that permits disclosure to defend against a charge of wrongful conduct is broader than in some states, including those that require that the client be making the charge against the lawyer. The PTO Code is not so limited.

Finally, like most state rules, the PTO Code imposes a duty of reasonable care with respect to employees. Requiring incoming and departing employees to sign forms that acknowledge the obligations of confidentiality may be necessary.

§ 10.58–10.60 [Reserved]

§ 10.61 Canon 5

A practitioner should exercise independent professional judgment on behalf of a client.

[Added 50 FR 5179, Feb. 6, 1985, effective Mar. 8, 1985]

Meyer and Hricik Commentary

Loyalty, like competency and confidentiality, is another core obligation. The exercise of independent professional judgment on behalf of a client, as expressed in this hortatory canon, is loyalty's central component.

§ 10.62 Refusing employment when the interest of the practitioner may impair the practitioner's independent professional judgment

(a) Except with the consent of a client after full disclosure, a practitioner shall not accept employment if the exercise of the practitioner's professional judgment on behalf of the client will be or reasonably may be affected by the practitioner's own financial, business, property, or personal interests.

(b) A practitioner shall not accept employment in a proceeding before the Office if the practitioner knows or it is obvious that the practitioner or another practitioner in the practitioner's firm ought to sign an affidavit to be filed in the Office or be called as a witness, except that the practitioner may undertake the employment and the practitioner or another practitioner in the practitioner's firm may testify:

(1) If the testimony will relate solely to an uncontested matter.

(2) If the testimony will relate solely to a matter of formality and there is no reason to believe that substantial evidence will be offered in opposition to the testimony.

(3) If the testimony will relate solely to the nature and value of legal services rendered in the case by the practitioner or the practitioner's firm to the client.

(4) As to any matter, if refusal would work a substantial hardship on the client because of the distinctive value of the practitioner or the practitioner's firm as counsel in the particular case.

[Added 50 FR 5179, Feb. 6, 1985, effective Mar. 8, 1985]

Meyer and Hricik Commentary

This section contains two distinct prohibitions.

Subsection (a) prohibits undertaking a representation where the practitioner's own interests will or reasonably may effect the practitioner's exercise of professional judgment on behalf of a client. These issues can arise where, for example, a practitioner refers a client to a business owned by the practitioner. Absent consent after disclosure, certain representations are prohibited.

Subsection (b) express the "advocate as witness" rule. This subsection addresses a practitioner's obligation to decline employment: § 10.63 addresses the practitioner's obligation to withdraw from already existing representations. This is a common prohibition, designed to avoid blurring the rules of advocate and witness at and during jury trials. Somewhat surprisingly—as the PTO does not use juries—subsection (b) adopts a common version of the advocate as witness rule and, further, broadens it to include submission of affidavits. Further, subsection (b) applies imputed disqualification—if any practitioner must sign an affidavit or testify, every practitioner is disqualified.

This approach is unusually broad, and is perhaps unnecessarily broad given the purpose of the advocate-as-witness rule is generally agreed to be to avoid jury confusion. Further, subsection (b)(4) is a much narrower exception than is allowed in many states.

§ 10.63 Withdrawal when the practitioner becomes a witness

(a) If, after undertaking employment in a proceeding in the Office, a practitioner learns or it is obvious that the practitioner or another practitioner in the practitioner's firm ought to sign an affidavit to be filed in the Office or be called as a witness on behalf of a practitioner's client, the practitioner shall withdraw from the conduct of the proceeding and the practitioner's firm, if any, shall not continue representation in the proceeding, except that the practitioner may continue the representation and the practitioner or another practitioner in the practitioner's firm may testify in the circumstances enumerated in paragraphs (1) through (4) of § 10.62(b).

(b) If, after undertaking employment in a proceeding before the Office, a practitioner learns or it is obvious that the practitioner or another practitioner in the practitioner's firm may be asked to sign an affidavit to be filed in the Office or be called as a witness other than on behalf of the practitioner's client, the practitioner may continue the representation until it is apparent that the practitioner's affidavit or testimony is or may be prejudicial to the practitioner's client.

[Added 50 FR 5179, Feb. 6, 1985, effective Mar. 8, 1985]

Meyer and Hricik Commentary

Section 10.62 addresses the practitioner's obligation to decline a representation based on the advocate-as-witness rule. This rule addresses the practitioner's obligations to withdraw from certain ongoing representations.

The obligations of practitioners under this rule turn first on whether the practitioners will be called by their client or someone else. If they are to be called by someone other than their client, then the practitioners may continue

Most state rules are less restrictive. In many states, rule 1.8(a) provides:

(a) A lawyer shall not enter into a business transaction with a client or knowingly acquire an ownership, possessory, security, or other pecuniary interest adverse to the client unless:

    (1) [T]he transaction and terms on which the lawyer acquires the interest are fair and reasonable to the client and are fully disclosed and transmitted in writing to the client in a manner which can reasonably be understood by the client;

    (2) [T]he client is given reasonable opportunity to seek the advice of independent counsel in the transaction; and

    (3) [T]he client consents in writing thereto.

Because the PTO Code requires arguably less disclosure than these state rules, the question of which applies can be critical. The only court to have addressed the question of which rules apply to determining whether adequate disclosure was made in the context of determining the enforceability of an attorney-client contract held that state law, not the PTO Code, applied. *Buechel v. Bain,* 2000 WL 142598 (N.Y. App. Div. Sept. 28, 2000); *see also* D.C. Bar Op. 195 (Dec. 13, 1988) (without addressing PTO Code, opinion reasoned that a lawyer could not take an assignment of patent to secure payment of fees due for prosecuting application). *See also, Monco v. Janus,* 583 N.E.2d 575, 581 (Ill. App. 1991) (applying state disclosure requirements, although again without addressing PTO Code, in analyzing business transaction between client and practitioner).

Thus, a practitioner prosecuting an application for a client may, under section 10.64(a)(3), take an interest in the application to the extent allowed thereby. However, the disclosures the lawyer must make to obtain an enforceable agreement are probably measured by state law. In any event, compliance with the more strict disclosure obligation is obviously the safest course because it best protects the client, and as a consequence, the lawyer.

The second paragraph expresses the common prohibition against providing financial assistance to clients with expected exceptions for prosecution-related fees and expenses.

§ 10.65 Limiting business relations with a client

A practitioner shall not enter into a business transaction with a client if they have differing interests therein and if the client expects the practitioner to exercise professional judgment therein for the protection of the client, unless the client has consented after full disclosure.

[Added 50 FR 5179, Feb. 6, 1985, effective Mar. 8, 1985]

Meyer and Hricik Commentary

This rule follows many state rules designed to prohibit conflicts of interest from developing between lawyers and their clients. Obviously, the rule does not apply to general commercial transactions between practitioner and client that are available on the same terms to the general public.

§ 10.66 Refusing to accept or continue employment if the interests of another client may impair the independent professional judgment of the practitioner

(a) A practitioner shall decline proffered employment if the exercise of the practitioner's independent professional judgment in behalf of a client will be or is likely to be adversely affected by the acceptance of the proffered employment, or if it would be likely to involve the practitioner in representing differing interests, except to the extent permitted under paragraph (c) of this section.

(b) A practitioner shall not continue multiple employment if the exercise of the practitioner's independent professional judgment in behalf of a client will be or is likely to be adversely affected by the practitioner's representation of another client, or if it would be likely to involve the practitioner in representing differing interests, except to the extent permitted under paragraph (c) of this section.

(c) In the situations covered by paragraphs (a) and (b) of this section, a practitioner may represent multiple clients if it is obvious that the practitioner can adequately represent the interest of each and if each consents to the representation after full disclosure of the possible effect of such representation on the exercise of the practitioner's independent professional judgment on behalf of each.

(d) If a practitioner is required to decline employment or to withdraw from employment under a Disciplinary Rule, no partner, or associate, or any other practitioner affiliated with the practitioner or the practitioner's firm, may accept or continue such employment unless otherwise ordered by the Director or Commissioner.

[Added 50 FR 5179, Feb. 6, 1985, effective Mar. 8, 1985]

Meyer and Hricik Commentary

This is the general provision in the PTO Code governing current client conflicts of interest. By its express terms, it relates only to concurrent representations.

Subsection (a) requires practitioners to decline a representation if either (i) the exercise of his or her independent professional judgment will or is likely to be adversely affected; or (2) it would involve the lawyer in representing differing interests, unless in either circumstances, it is obvious the practitioner can adequately represent the client(s) and each affected client consents after full disclosure.

Subsection (b) applies when a practitioner represents more than one client in the same matter (for example, multiple inventors not under an obligation to assign to a common assignee). He or she may not continue such representations if either (1) his or her exercise of independent professional judgment will or likely will be adversely affected; or (2) it would be likely to involve the practitioner in representing differing interests, unless, in either circumstance, it is obvious the practitioner can adequately represent each client and each affected client consents after full disclosure.

Subsection (d) imputes a practitioner's disqualification under either subsection (a) or (b) to all parties, associates, or practitioners affiliated with the affected practitioner. Obviously, this requires firms to establish reasonable conflicts checking procedures.

§ 10.67 Settling similar claims of clients

A practitioner who represents two or more clients shall not make or participate in the making of an aggregate settlement of the claims of or against the practitioner's clients, unless each client has consented to the settlement after being advised of the existence and nature of all the claims involved in the proposed settlement, of the total amount of the settlement, and of the participation of each person in the settlement.

[Added 50 FR 5179, Feb. 6, 1985, effective Mar. 8, 1985]

Meyer and Hricik Commentary

This is a common rule but one that will seldom be implicated in practice before the USPTO. Significantly, and unlike some state rules, this section applies both to the making *or* participation in an aggregate settlement unless the clients are advised as required by the rule.

§ 10.68 Avoiding influence by others than the client

(a) Except with the consent of the practitioner's client after full disclosure, a practitioner shall not:
  (1) Accept compensation from one other than the practitioner's client for the practitioner's legal services to or for the client.
  (2) Accept from one other than the practitioner's client any thing of value related to the practitioner's representation of or the practitioner's employment by the client.
(b) A practitioner shall not permit a person who recommends, employs, or pays the practitioner to render legal services for another, to direct or regulate the practitioner's professional judgment in rendering such legal services.
(c) A practitioner shall not practice with or in the form of a professional corporation or association authorized to practice law for a profit, if a non-practitioner has the right to direct or control the professional judgment of a practitioner.

[Added 50 FR 5180, Feb. 6, 1985, effective Mar. 8, 1985]

Meyer and Hricik Commentary

Payment of legal fees by someone other than the client is a well-known source of possible conflict. The payer may want, for example, to limit the ability of the lawyer to pursue certain avenues because of cost, whereas the lawyer in his or her professional judgment may believe those actions to be required. This provision is essentially identical to state rules on this subject.

Significantly, the practitioner can be paid by a third party, but only with the client's consent. However, the third party cannot direct or regulate the practitioner's professional judgment in providing the services.

§ 10.69–10.75 [Reserved]

§ 10.76 Canon 6

A practitioner should represent a client competently.

[Added 50 FR 5180, Feb. 6, 1985, effective Mar. 8, 1985]

Meyer and Hricik Commentary

Competency, like confidentiality and loyalty, is a core obligation expressed in a hortatory canon.

§ 10.77 Failing to act competently

A practitioner shall not:
- (a) Handle a legal matter which the practitioner knows or should know that the practitioner is not competent to handle, without associating with the practitioner another practitioner who is competent to handle it.
- (b) Handle a legal matter without preparation adequate in the circumstances.
- (c) Neglect a legal matter entrusted to the practitioner.

[Added 50 FR 5180, Feb. 6, 1985, effective Mar. 8, 1985]

Meyer and Hricik Commentary

These basic principles no doubt form the basis of the bulk of complaints and claims against practitioners. Missed deadlines, failure to draft properly, and other violations of the duty are noted in the cases cited in this Appendix, Appendix 3, as well as in the text of the book.

§ 10.78 Limiting liability to client

A practitioner shall not attempt to exonerate himself or herself from, or limit his or her liability to, a client for his or her personal malpractice.

[Added 50 FR 5180, Feb. 6, 1985, effective Mar. 8, 1985]

Meyer and Hricik Commentary

This is a common prohibition. Generally, states recognize that it does not prohibit a lawyer from using an arbitration provision in an engagement letter. Obviously state law must be consulted to ensure any applicable requirements are met. Second, it does not prohibit in-house counsel from being indemnified by the corporate employer for claims against in-house counsel by third parties, such as inventors or joint ventures or joint venturers.

§ 10.79–10.82 [Reserved]

§ 10.83 Canon 7

A practitioner should represent a client zealously within the bounds of the law.

[Added 50 FR 5180, Feb. 6, 1985, effective Mar. 8, 1985]

Meyer and Hricik Commentary

The duty of warm zeal is an oft-expressed value but one, which in fact, is generally not recognized by many states. Nonetheless, this hortatory canon states the goal.

§ 10.84 Representing a client zealously

(a) A practitioner shall not intentionally:
  (1) Fail to seek the lawful objectives of a client through reasonable available means permitted by law and the Disciplinary Rules, except as provided by paragraph (b) of this section. A practitioner does not violate the provisions of this section, however, by acceding to reasonable requests of opposing counsel which do not prejudice the rights of the client, by being punctual in fulfilling all professional commitments, by avoiding offensive tactics, or by treating with courtesy and consideration all persons involved in the legal process.
  (2) Fail to carry out a contract of employment entered into with a client for professional services, but a practitioner may withdraw as permitted under §§ 10.40, 10.63, and 10.66.
  (3) Prejudice or damage a client during the course of a professional relationship, except as required under this part.
(b) In representation of a client, a practitioner may:
  (1) Where permissible, exercise professional judgment to waive or fail to assert a right or position of the client.

(2) Refuse to aid or participate in conduct that the practitioner believes to be unlawful, even though there is some support for an argument that the conduct is legal.

[Added 50 FR 5180, Feb. 6, 1985, effective Mar. 8, 1985]

Meyer and Hricik Commentary

Although many state rules divide the allocation of authority between lawyer and client based on whether it is an objective (a decision for the client) or a means to achieve the client's objective (a decision for the lawyer), the PTO Code takes the approach in this section. Obviously, whether to file an application, and which countries to file in are matters for the client, whereas the strategy for responding to an office action when directed to do so by a client is for the lawyer to formulate.

Section 10.84 does limit the power of both practitioner and client. The practitioner must continue to represent a client unless withdrawal is permitted. Likewise, the practitioner may not prejudice or damage the client unless the PTO Code requires him or her to do so. The practitioner, conversely, has the freedom to waive rights or positions of the client and to refuse to out where legality is questionable.

§ 10.85 Representing a client within the bounds of the law

(a) In representation of a client, a practitioner shall not:
   (1) Initiate or defend any proceeding before the Office, assert a position, conduct a defense, delay a trial or proceeding before the Office, or take other action on behalf of the practitioner's client when the practitioner knows or when it is obvious that such action would serve merely to harass or maliciously injure another.
   (2) Knowingly advance a claim or defense that is unwarranted under existing law, except that a practitioner may advance such claim or defense if it can be supported by good faith argument for an extension, modification, or reversal of existing law.
   (3) Conceal or knowingly fail to disclose that which the practitioner is required by law to reveal.
   (4) Knowingly use perjured testimony or false evidence.
   (5) Knowingly make a false statement of law or fact.

(6) Participate in the creation or preservation of evidence when the practitioner knows or it is obvious that the evidence is false.

(7) Counsel or assist a client in conduct that the practitioner knows to be illegal or fraudulent.

(8) Knowingly engage in other illegal conduct or conduct contrary to a Disciplinary Rule.

(b) A practitioner who receives information clearly establishing that:

(1) A client has, in the course of the representation, perpetrated a fraud upon a person or tribunal shall promptly call upon the client to rectify the same, and if the client refuses or is unable to do so the practitioner shall reveal the fraud to the affected person or tribunal.

(2) A person other than a client has perpetrated a fraud upon a tribunal shall promptly reveal the fraud to the tribunal.

[Added 50 FR 5180, Feb. 6, 1985, effective Mar. 8, 1985]

Meyer and Hricik Commentary

Sections 10.24, 10.57, and this section together address exceptions to the lawyer's duty of confidentiality. This section also addresses other obligations.

With respect to confidentiality, a practitioner is required to reveal even confidential information if: (a) required by law to do so, (b) to rectify a fraud perpetrated on a client in the course of a representation, and (c) when any non-client has perpetrated fraud on a tribunal.

The other obligations in many ways further the obligations of § 10.18. Obviously, claims that involve the use of perjured testimony or false evidence lack merit.

§ 10.86 [Reserved]

§ 10.87 Communicating with one of adverse interest

During the course of representation of a client, a practitioner shall not:

(a) Communicate or cause another to communicate on the subject of the representation with a party the practitioner knows to be represented by another practitioner in that matter unless the practitioner has the prior consent of the other practitioner representing such other party or is authorized by law to do so. It is not improper, however, for a practitioner to encourage a client to meet with an opposing party for settlement discussions.

(b) Give advice to a person who is not represented by a practitioner other than the advice to secure counsel, if the interests of such person are or have a reasonable possibility of being in conflict with the interests of the practitioner's client.

[Added 50 FR 5180, Feb. 6, 1985, effective Mar. 8, 1985]

Meyer and Hricik Commentary

Subsection (a) prohibits *ex parte* contact with a person known to be "represented by counsel" in a matter; if the person is unrepresented. Subsection (b) limits the ability of the practitioner to communicate with the person.

§ 10.88 Threatening criminal prosecution

A practitioner shall not present, participate in presenting, or threaten to present criminal charges solely to obtain an advantage in any prospective or pending proceeding before the Office.

[Added 50 FR 5180, Feb. 6, 1985, effective Mar. 8, 1985]

Meyer and Hricik Commentary

Most states have this prohibition. In most states, it is not violated unless the threat seeks an advantage that could not be gained through the criminal, the threat is frivolous, or the lawyer has no intent of carrying it out.

§ 10.89 Conduct in proceedings

(a) A practitioner shall not disregard or advise a client to disregard any provision of this Subchapter or a decision of the Office made in the course of a proceeding before the Office, but the practitioner may take appropriate steps in good faith to test the validity of such provision or decision.

(b) In presenting a matter to the Office, a practitioner shall disclose:
  (1) Controlling legal authority known to the practitioner to be directly adverse to the position of the client and which is not disclosed by opposing counsel or an employee of the Office.
  (2) Unless privileged or irrelevant, the identities of the client the practitioner represents and of the persons who employed the practitioner.
(c) In appearing in a professional capacity before a tribunal, a practitioner shall not:
  (1) State or allude to any matter that the practitioner has no reasonable basis to believe is relevant to the case or that will not be supported by admissible evidence.
  (2) Ask any question that the practitioner has no reasonable basis to believe is relevant to the case and that is intended to degrade a witness or other person.
  (3) Assert the practitioner's personal knowledge of the facts in issue, except when testifying as a witness.
  (4) Assert the practitioner's personal opinion as to the justness of a cause, as to the credibility of a witness, as to the culpability of a civil litigant, or as to the guilt or innocence of an accused; but the practitioner may argue, on the practitioner's analysis of the evidence, for any position or conclusion with respect to the matters stated herein.
  (5) Engage in undignified or discourteous conduct before the Office (*see* § 1.3 of the subchapter).
  (6) Intentionally or habitually violate any provision of this subchapter or established rule of evidence.

[Added 50 FR 5180, Feb. 6, 1985, effective Mar. 8, 1985]

Meyer and Hricik Commentary

Subsection (a) recognizes the right of a client to test the validity of a rule but prohibits counseling a client to disregard a provision. It is uncommon.

In contrast, Subsection (b)(1) is a near-universal requirement. This subsection would require during prosecution disclosure of on-point directly adverse authority from the PTO, the Federal Circuit, and the United States Supreme Court. Subsection (b)(2) is uncommon but probably seldom controversial.

Subsection (c) is common but will rarely be implicated in patent prosecution, and almost as rarely in *inter partes* proceedings. It may occasionally occur during *pro se* arguments made during *ex parte* appeals of rejected applications and also during *pro se* arguments made in *inter partes* cases.

§ 10.90–10.91 [Reserved]

§ 10.92 Contact with witnesses

(a) A practitioner shall not suppress any evidence that the practitioner or the practitioner's client has a legal obligation to reveal or produce.

(b) A practitioner shall not advise or cause a person to be secreted or to leave the jurisdiction of a tribunal for the purpose of making the person unavailable as a witness therein.

(c) A practitioner shall not pay, offer to pay, or acquiesce in payment of compensation to a witness contingent upon the content of the witness' affidavit, testimony or the outcome of the case. But a practitioner may advance, guarantee, or acquiesce in the payment of:

    (1) Expenses reasonably incurred by a witness in attending, testifying, or making an affidavit.

    (2) Reasonable compensation to a witness for the witness' loss of time in attending, testifying, or making an affidavit.

    (3) A reasonable fee for the professional services of an expert witness.

[Added 50 FR 5181, Feb. 6, 1985, effective Mar. 8, 1985]

Meyer and Hricik Commentary

Like the prior section, these are common among state ethical rules but will rarely be an issue in patent prosecution. In interference proceedings and other *inter partes* proceedings, they would control, especially regarding expert witness declarations.

§ 10.93 Contact with officials

(a) A practitioner shall not give or lend anything of value to a judge, official, or employee of a tribunal under circumstances which might give the appearance that the gift or loan is made to influence official action.

(b) In an adversary proceeding, including any inter partes proceeding before the Office, a practitioner shall not communicate, or cause another to communicate, as to the merits of the cause with a judge, official, or Office employee before whom the proceeding is pending, except:

(1) In the course of official proceedings in the cause.

(2) In writing if the practitioner promptly delivers a copy of the writing to opposing counsel or to the adverse party if the adverse party is not represented by a practitioner.

(3) Orally upon adequate notice to opposing counsel or to the adverse party if the adverse party is not represented by a practitioner.

(4) As otherwise authorized by law.

[Added 50 FR 5181, Feb. 6, 1985, effective Mar. 8, 1985]

Meyer and Hricik Commentary

Paragraph (a) prohibits not all gifts, but only those that "might give the appearance" of attempting to curry favor. PTO officials have rules limiting their ability to accept gifts, and, obviously, a wise course to forego any gifts.

Paragraph (b) prohibits *ex parte* contacts about the merits of a matter unless excepted. It does not apply to *ex parte* prosecution. In *inter partes* proceedings, the Standing Order for Interferences provides useful guidance as to acceptable *ex parte* contacts with the administrative judge.

§ 10.94–10.99 [Reserved]

§ 10.100 Canon 8

A practitioner should assist in improving the legal system.

[Added 50 FR 5181, Feb. 6, 1985, effective Mar. 8, 1985]

Meyer and Hricik Commentary

This is a hortatory goal.

§ 10.101 Action as a public official

(a) A practitioner who holds public office shall not:

    (1) Use the practitioner's public position to obtain, or attempt to obtain, a special advantage in legislative matters for the practitioner or for a client under circumstances where the practitioner knows or it is obvious that such action is not in the public interest.

    (2) Use the practitioner's public position to influence, or attempt to influence, a tribunal to act in favor of the practitioner or of a client.

    (3) Accept any thing of value from any person when the practitioner knows or it is obvious that the offer is for the purpose of influencing the practitioner's action as a public official.

(b) A practitioner who is an officer or employee of the United States shall not practice before the Office in patent cases except as provided in § 10.10(c) and (d).

[Added 50 FR 5181, Feb. 6, 1985, effective Mar. 8, 1985; para. (b) amended, 54 FR 6520, Feb. 13, 1989]

Meyer and Hricik Commentary

These prohibitions apply only to practitioners who currently hold public office. Usually, conflict of interest rules of the agency will define any prohibitions applicable after government employment has ended.

§ 10.102 Statements concerning officials

(a) A practitioner shall not knowingly make false statements of fact concerning the qualifications of a candidate for election or appointment to a judicial office or to a position in the Office.

(b) A practitioner shall not knowingly make false accusations against a judge, other adjudicatory officer, or employee of the Office.

[Added 50 FR 5181, Feb. 6, 1985, effective Mar. 8, 1985]

Meyer and Hricik Commentary

These are common and fairly rarely in issue in the USPTO, for obvious reasons.

§ 10.103 Practitioner candidate for judicial office

A practitioner who is a candidate for judicial office shall comply with applicable provisions of law.

[Added 50 FR 5181, Feb. 6, 1985, effective Mar. 8, 1985]

Meyer and Hricik Commentary

The obvious implication of this rule is that a practitioner-candidate can be disciplined for violating a law governing judicial election.

§ 10.104–10.109 [Reserved]

§ 10.110 Canon 9

A practitioner should avoid even the appearance of professional impropriety.

[Added 50 FR 5181, Feb. 6, 1985, effective Mar. 8, 1985]

Meyer and Hricik Commentary

It is important to emphasize that Canon 9 is hortatory. A practitioner cannot violate it. Nonetheless, courts sometimes find "violations" of section 10.110. *See, e.g., Friedman v. Lehman,* 40 U.S.Q.2d 1206 (D. D.C. 1996); *Kearney & Trecker Corp. v. Giddigns & Lewis, Inc.,* 452 F.2d 579 (7th Cir. 1971).

§ 10.111 Avoiding even the appearance of impropriety

(a) A practitioner shall not accept private employment in a matter upon the merits of which he or she has acted in a judicial capacity.
(b) A practitioner shall not accept private employment in a matter in which he or she had personal responsibility while a public employee.
(c) A practitioner shall not state or imply that the practitioner is able to influence improperly or upon irrelevant grounds any tribunal, legislative body, or public official.

[Added 50 FR 5181, Feb. 6, 1985, effective Mar. 8, 1985]

Meyer and Hricik Commentary

This section addresses the limitations on practice facing former government employees and officials. *See generally Moatz v. Kersey,* 67 U.S.Q.2d 1291 (Dir. PTO 2002); *In re Thomas Atheridge,* 1984 Commr. Pat. LEXIS 6 (July 2, 1986) *McCandlish v. Doe,* 1992 Commr. Pat. LEXIS 1 (Feb. 11, 1992); *see also* Va. Legal Eth. Op. 1520 (addressing propriety of a former examiner who signed a restriction requirement and then served as an expert witness in connection with the patent arising from the application he oversaw).

With respect to subsection (b), the PTO has generally interpreted "matter" in section 10.111(b) quite broadly. *See Friedman v. Lehman,* 40 U.S.Q.2d 1206 (D. D.C. 1996) (noting that the PTO had interpreted "matter" to include "most procedures required in completing patent applications . . . including placing a restriction on the patent . . . regardless of how isolated or incidental the step may be."). Likewise, "personal responsibility" has been held to include placing restrictions in a case as well as signing a notice of allowance. *Id.,* citing *Kearney & Trecker Corp. v. Giddigns & Lewis, Inc.,* 452 F.2d 579 (7th Cir. 1971).

Significantly, under section 10.66(d), a conflict under this rule is imputed to all practitioners in the firm. Unlike many state rules that permit unilateral screening of the former government employee to avoid imputations, the PTO Code does not do so.

§ 10.112 Preserving identity of funds and property of client

(a) All funds of clients paid to a practitioner or a practitioner's firm, other than advances for costs and expenses, shall be deposited in one or more identifiable bank accounts maintained in the United States or, in the case of a practitioner having an office in a foreign country or registered under § 11.6(c), in the United States or the foreign country.

(b) No funds belonging to the practitioner or the practitioner's firm shall be deposited in the bank accounts required by paragraph (a) of this section except as follows:

   (1) Funds reasonably sufficient to pay bank charges may be deposited therein.

   (2) Funds belonging in part to a client and in part presently or potentially to the practitioner or the practitioner's firm must be deposited therein, but the portion belonging to the practitioner or the practitioner's firm may be withdrawn when due unless the right of the practitioner or the practitioner's firm to receive it is disputed by the client, in which event the disputed portion shall not be withdrawn until the dispute is finally resolved.

(c) A practitioner shall:

   (1) Promptly notify a client of the receipt of the client's funds, securities, or other properties.

   (2) Identify and label securities and properties of a client promptly upon receipt and place them in a safe deposit box or other place of safekeeping as soon as practicable.

   (3) Maintain complete records of all funds, securities, and other properties of a client coming into the possession of the practitioner and render appropriate accounts to the client regarding the funds, securities, or other properties.

   (4) Promptly pay or deliver to the client as requested by a client the funds, securities, or other properties in the possession of the practitioner which the client is entitled to receive.

[Added 50 FR 5181, Feb. 6, 1985, effective Mar. 8, 1985; para. (a) revised, 70 FR 56119, Sept. 26, 2005, effective Nov. 25, 2005]

Meyer and Hricik Commentary

As the cases in this Appendix and Appendix 3 show, commingling funds, misappropriation, and failure to account are common bases for discipline or complaint.

The critical question that all rules respecting client funds turns on is: Who owns the money? If the funds are earned, they cannot be kept in trust. If the funds are not earned, they must be kept in trust. The PTO Code allows the practitioner to keep in the trust account funds sufficient to avoid bank charges.

A practitioner, finally, must notify a client when in receipt of client properties and keep complete records of all transactions.

§ 10.113–10.129 [Reserved]

INVESTIGATIONS AND DISCIPLINARY PROCEEDINGS
Note: The following sections of Title 37 are provided for completeness but without commentary, as they are principally procedural, not substantive. Nonetheless, we felt that it was necessary to include them because of their importance to understanding operation of the OED.

§ 10.130 Reprimand, suspension or exclusion

(a) The Commissioner may, after notice and opportunity for a hearing, (1) reprimand or (2) suspend or exclude, either generally or in any particular case, any individual, attorney, or agent shown to be incompetent or disreputable, who is guilty of gross misconduct, or who violates a Disciplinary Rule.
(b) Petitions to disqualify a practitioner in ex parte or inter partes cases in the Office are not governed by §§ 10.130 through 10.170 and will be handled on a case-by-case basis under such conditions as the Commissioner deems appropriate.

[Added 50 FR 5181, Feb. 6, 1985, effective Mar. 8, 1985]

§ 10.131 Investigations

(a) The Director is authorized to investigate possible violations of Disciplinary Rules by practitioners. See § 10.2(b)(2).
(b) Practitioners shall report and reveal to the Director any knowledge or evidence required by § 10.24. A practitioner shall cooperate with the Director in connection with any investigation under paragraph (a) of this section and with officials of the Office in connection with any disciplinary proceeding instituted under § 10.132(b).

(c) Any nonpractitioner possessing knowledge or information concerning a violation of a Disciplinary Rule by a practitioner may report the violation to the Director. The Director may require that the report be presented in the form of an affidavit.

[Added 50 FR 5181, Feb. 6, 1985, effective Mar. 8, 1985]

§ 10.132 Initiating a disciplinary proceeding; reference to an administrative law judge

(a) If after conducting an investigation under § 10.131(a) the Director is of the opinion that a practitioner has violated a Disciplinary Rule, the Director shall, after complying where necessary with the provisions of 5 U.S.C. 558(c), call a meeting of the Committee on Discipline. The Committee on Discipline shall then determine as specified in § 10.4(b) whether a disciplinary proceeding shall be instituted under paragraph (b) of this section.
(b) If the Committee on Discipline determines that probable cause exists to believe that a practitioner has violated a Disciplinary Rule, the Director shall institute a disciplinary proceeding by filing a complaint under § 10.134. The complaint shall be filed in the Office of the Director. A disciplinary proceeding may result in:
(1) A reprimand, or
(2) Suspension or exclusion of a practitioner from practice before the Office.
(c) Upon the filing of a complaint under § 10.134, the Commissioner will refer the disciplinary proceeding to an administrative law judge.

[Added 50 FR 5181, Feb. 6, 1985, effective Mar. 8, 1985]

§ 10.133 Conference between Director and practitioner; resignation

(a) General. The Director may confer with a practitioner concerning possible violations by the practitioner of a Disciplinary Rule whether or not a disciplinary proceeding has been instituted.
(b) Resignation. Any practitioner who is the subject of an investigation under § 10.131 or against whom a complaint has been filed under

§ 10.134 may resign from practice before the Office only by submitting with the Director an affidavit stating his or her desire to resign.

(c) If filed prior to the date set by the administrative law judge for a hearing, the affidavit shall state that:

(1) The resignation is freely and voluntarily proffered;

(2) The practitioner is not acting under duress or coercion from the Office;

(3) The practitioner is fully aware of the implications of filing the resignation;

(4) The practitioner is aware (i) of a pending investigation or (ii) of charges arising from the complaint alleging that he or she is guilty of a violation of the Patent and Trademark Office Code of Professional Responsibility, the nature of which shall be set forth by the practitioner to the satisfaction of the Director;

(5) The practitioner acknowledges that, if and when he or she applies for reinstatement under § 10.160, the Director will conclusively presume, for the limited purpose of determining the application for reinstatement, that:

(i) The facts upon which the complaint is based are true and

(ii) The practitioner could not have successfully defended himself or herself against (A) charges predicated on the violation under investigation or (B) charges set out in the complaint filed against the practitioner.

(d) If filed on or after the date set by the administrative law judge for a hearing, the affidavit shall make the statements required by paragraphs (b) (1) through (4) of this section and shall state that:

(1) The practitioner acknowledges the facts upon which the complaint is based are true; and

(2) The resignation is being submitted because the practitioner could not successfully defend himself or herself against (i) charges predicated on the violation under investigation or (ii) charges set out in the complaint.

(e) When an affidavit under paragraphs (b) or (c) of this section is received while an investigation is pending, the Commissioner shall enter an order excluding the practitioner "on consent." When an affidavit under paragraphs (b) or (c) of this section is received after a complaint under § 10.134 has been filed, the Director shall notify the administrative law judge. The administrative law judge shall enter an order transferring the disciplinary proceeding to the Commissioner and the Commissioner shall enter an order excluding the practitioner "on consent."

(f) Any practitioner who resigns from practice before the Office under this section and who intends to reapply for admission to practice before the Office must comply with the provisions of § 10.158.

(g) Settlement. Before or after a complaint is filed under § 10.134, a settlement conference may occur between the Director and a practitioner for the purpose of settling any disciplinary matter. If an offer of settlement is made by the Director or the practitioner and is not accepted by the other, no reference to the offer of settlement or its refusal shall be admissible in evidence in the disciplinary proceeding unless both the Director and the practitioner agree in writing.

[Added 50 FR 5181, Feb. 6, 1985, effective Mar. 8, 1985]

§ 10.134 Complaint

(a) A complaint instituting a disciplinary proceeding shall:
   (1) Name the practitioner, who may then be referred to as the "respondent."
   (2) Give a plain and concise description of the alleged violations of the Disciplinary Rules by the practitioner.
   (3) State the place and time for filing an answer by the respondent.
   (4) State that a decision by default may be entered against the respondent if an answer is not timely filed.
   (5) Be signed by the Director.
(b) A complaint will be deemed sufficient if it fairly informs the respondent of any violation of the Disciplinary Rules which form the basis for the disciplinary proceeding so that the respondent is able to adequately prepare a defense.

[Added 50 FR 5182, Feb. 6, 1985, effective Mar. 8, 1985]

§ 10.135 Service of complaint

(a) A complaint may be served on a respondent in any of the following methods:
   (1) By handing a copy of the complaint personally to the respondent, in which case the individual handing the complaint to the respondent shall file an affidavit with the Director indicating the time and place the complaint was handed to the respondent.
   (2) By mailing a copy of the complaint by "Express Mail" or first-class mail to:
      (i) A registered practitioner at the address for which separate notice was last received by the Director or

        (ii) A nonregistered practitioner at the last address for the respondent known to the Director.

    (3) By any method mutually agreeable to the Director and the respondent.

(b) If a complaint served by mail under paragraph (a)(2) of this section is returned by the U.S. Postal Service, the Director shall mail a second copy of the complaint to the respondent. If the second copy of the complaint is also returned by the U.S. Postal Service, the Director shall serve the respondent by publishing an appropriate notice in the Official Gazette for four consecutive weeks, in which case the time for answer shall be at least thirty days from the fourth publication of the notice.

(c) If a respondent is a registered practitioner, the Director may serve simultaneously with the complaint a letter under § 10.11(b). The Director may require the respondent to answer the § 10.11(b) letter within a period of not less than 15 days. An answer to the § 10.11(b) letter shall constitute proof of service. If the respondent fails to answer the § 10.11(b) letter, his or her name will be removed from the register as provided by § 10.11(b).

(d) If the respondent is represented by an attorney under § 10.140(a), a copy of the complaint shall also be served on the attorney.

[Added 50 FR 5183, Feb. 6, 1985, effective Mar. 8, 1985]

§ 10.136 Answer to complaint

(a) Time for answer. An answer to a complaint shall be filed within a time set in the complaint which shall be not less than thirty days.

(b) With whom filed. The answer shall be filed in writing with the administrative law judge. The time for filing an answer may be extended once for a period of no more than thirty days by the administrative law judge upon a showing of good cause provided a motion requesting an extension of time is filed within thirty days after the date the complaint is filed by the Director. A copy of the answer shall be served on the Director.

(c) Content. The respondent shall include in the answer a statement of the facts which constitute the grounds of defense and shall specifically admit or deny each allegation set forth in the complaint. The respondent shall not deny a material allegation in the complaint which the respondent knows to be true or state that respondent is without sufficient information to form a belief as to the truth of an allegation when in fact the respondent possesses that information. The respondent shall also state affirmatively special matters of defense.

(d) Failure to deny allegations in complaint. Every allegation in the complaint which is not denied by a respondent in the answer is deemed to be admitted and may be considered proven. No further evidence in respect of that allegation need be received by the administrative law judge at any hearing. Failure to timely file an answer will constitute an admission of the allegations in the complaint.

(e) Reply by the Director. No reply to an answer is required by the Director and any affirmative defense in the answer shall be deemed to be denied. The Director may, however, file a reply if he or she chooses or if ordered by the administrative law judge.

[Added 50 FR 5183, Feb. 6, 1985, effective Mar. 8, 1985; amended 50 FR 25073, June 17, 1985]

§ 10.137 Supplemental complaint

False statements in an answer may be made the basis of a supplemental complaint.

[Added 50 FR 5183, Feb. 6, 1985, effective Mar. 8, 1985]

§ 10.138 Contested case

Upon the filing of an answer by the respondent, a disciplinary proceeding shall be regarded as a contested case within the meaning of 35 U.S.C. 24. Evidence obtained by a subpoena issued under 35 U.S.C. 24 shall not be admitted into the record or considered unless leave to proceed under 35 U.S.C. 24 was previously authorized by the administrative law judge.

[Added 50 FR 5183, Feb. 6, 1985, effective Mar. 8, 1985]

§ 10.139 Administrative law judge; appointment; responsibilities; review of interlocutory orders; stays

(a) Appointment. An administrative law judge, appointed under 5 U.S.C. 3105, shall conduct disciplinary proceedings as provided by this part.

(b) Responsibilities. The administrative law judge shall have authority to:

    (1) Administer oaths and affirmations;

    (2) Make rulings upon motions and other requests;

    (3) Rule upon offers of proof, receive relevant evidence, and examine witnesses;

    (4) Authorize the taking of a deposition of a witness in lieu of personal appearance of the witness before the administrative law judge;

    (5) Determine the time and place of any hearing and regulate its course and conduct;

    (6) Hold or provide for the holding of conferences to settle or simplify the issues;

    (7) Receive and consider oral or written arguments on facts or law;

    (8) Adopt procedures and modify procedures from time to time as occasion requires for the orderly disposition of proceedings;

    (9) Make initial decisions under § 10.154; and

    (10) Perform acts and take measures as necessary to promote the efficient and timely conduct of any disciplinary proceeding.

(c) Time for making initial decision. The administrative law judge shall set times and exercise control over a disciplinary proceeding such that an initial decision under § 10.154 is normally issued within six months of the date a complaint is filed. The administrative law judge may, however, issue an initial decision more than six months after a complaint is filed if in his or her opinion there exist unusual circumstances which preclude issuance of an initial decision within six months of the filing of the complaint.

(d) Review of interlocutory orders. An interlocutory order of an administrative law judge will not be reviewed by the Commissioner except:

    (1) When the administrative law judge shall be of the opinion (i) that the interlocutory order involves a controlling question of procedure or law as to which there is a substantial ground for a difference of opinion and (ii) that an immediate decision by the Commissioner may materially advance the ultimate termination of the disciplinary proceeding or

    (2) In an extraordinary situation where justice requires review.

(e) Stays pending review of interlocutory order. If the Director or a respondent seeks review of an interlocutory order of an administrative law judge under paragraph (b)(2) of this section, any time period set for taking action by the administrative law judge shall not be stayed unless ordered by the Commissioner or the administrative law judge.

[Added 50 FR 5183, Feb. 6, 1985, effective Mar. 8, 1985; amended 50 FR 25073, June 17, 1985]

§ 10.140 Representative for Director or respondent

(a) A respondent may be represented before the Office in connection with an investigation or disciplinary proceeding by an attorney. The attorney shall file a written declaration that he or she is an attorney within the meaning of § 10.1(c) and shall state:
  (1) The address to which the attorney wants correspondence related to the investigation or disciplinary proceeding sent and
  (2) A telephone number where the attorney may be reached during normal business hours.
(b) The Commissioner shall designate at least two associate solicitors in the Office of the Solicitor to act as representatives for the Director in disciplinary proceedings. In prosecuting disciplinary proceedings, the designated associate solicitors shall not involve the Solicitor or the Deputy Solicitor. The Solicitor and the Deputy Solicitor shall remain insulated from the investigation and prosecution of all disciplinary proceedings in order that they shall be available as counsel to the Commissioner in deciding disciplinary proceedings.

[Added 50 FR 5183, Feb. 6, 1985, effective Mar. 8, 1985]

§ 10.141 Filing of papers

(a) The provisions of § 1.8 of this subchapter do not apply to disciplinary proceedings.
(b) All papers filed after the complaint and prior to entry of an initial decision by the administrative law judge shall be filed with the administrative law judge at an address or place designated by the administrative law judge. All papers filed after entry of an initial decision by the administrative law judge shall be filed with the Director. The Director shall promptly forward to the Commissioner any paper which requires action under this part by the Commissioner.
(c) The administrative law judge or the Director may provide for filing papers and other matters by hand or by "Express Mail."

[Added 50 FR 5184, Feb. 6, 1985, effective Mar. 8, 1985]

§ 10.142 Service of papers

(a) All papers other than a complaint shall be served on a respondent represented by an attorney by:
    (1) Delivering a copy of the paper to the office of the attorney; or
    (2) Mailing a copy of the paper by first-class mail or "Express Mail" to the attorney at the address provided by the attorney under § 10.140(a)(1); or
    (3) Any other method mutually agreeable to the attorney and a representative for the Director.
(b) All papers other than a complaint shall be served on a respondent who is not represented by an attorney by:
    (1) Delivering a copy of the paper to the respondent; or
    (2) Mailing a copy of the paper by first-class mail or "Express Mail" to the respondent at the address to which a complaint may be served or such other address as may be designated in writing by the respondent; or
    (3) Any other method mutually agreeable to the respondent and a representative of the Director.
(c) A respondent shall serve on the representative for the Director one copy of each paper filed with the administrative law judge or the Director. A paper may be served on the representative for the Director by:
    (1) Delivering a copy of the paper to the representative; or
    (2) Mailing a copy of the paper by first-class mail or "Express Mail" to an address designated in writing by the representative; or
    (3) Any other method mutually agreeable to the respondent and the representative.
(d) Each paper filed in a disciplinary proceeding shall contain therein a certificate of service indicating:
    (1) The date of which service was made and
    (2) The method by which service was made.
(e) The administrative law judge or the Commissioner may require that a paper be served by hand or by "Express Mail."
(f) Service by mail is completed when the paper mailed in the United States is placed into the custody of the U.S. Postal Service.

[Added 50 FR 5184, Feb. 6, 1985, effective Mar. 8, 1985]

§ 10.143 Motions

Motions may be filed with the administrative law judge. The administrative law judge will determine on a case-by-case basis the time period for response to a motion and whether replies to responses will be authorized. No motion shall be filed with the administrative law judge unless such motion is supported by a written statement by the moving party that the moving party or attorney for the moving party has conferred with the opposing party or attorney for the opposing party in an effort in good faith to resolve by agreement the issues raised by the motion and has been unable to reach agreement. If issues raised by a motion are resolved by the parties prior to a decision on the motion by the administrative law judge, the parties shall promptly notify the administrative law judge.

[Added 50 FR 5184, Feb. 6, 1985, effective Mar. 8, 1985]

§ 10.144 Hearings

(a) The administrative law judge shall preside at hearings in disciplinary proceedings. Hearings will be stenographically recorded and transcribed and the testimony of witnesses will be received under oath or affirmation. The administrative law judge shall conduct hearings in accordance with 5 U.S.C. 556. A copy of the transcript of the hearing shall become part of the record. A copy of the transcript shall be provided to the Director and the respondent at the expense of the Office.

(b) If the respondent to a disciplinary proceeding fails to appear at the hearing after a notice of hearing has been given by the administrative law judge, the administrative law judge may deem the respondent to have waived the right to a hearing and may proceed with the hearing in the absence of the respondent.

(c) A hearing under this section will not be open to the public except that the Director may grant a request by a respondent to open his or her hearing to the public and make the record of the disciplinary proceeding available for public inspection, provided, Agreement is reached in advance to exclude from public disclosure information which is privileged or confidential under applicable laws or regulations. If a disciplinary proceeding results in disciplinary action against a practitioner, and subject to § 10.159(c), the record of the entire disciplinary proceeding, including any settlement agreement, will be available for public inspection.

[Added 50 FR 5184, Feb. 6, 1985, effective Mar. 8, 1985]

§ 10.145 Proof; variance;
amendment of pleadings

In case of a variance between the evidence and the allegations in a complaint, answer, or reply, if any, the administrative law judge may order or authorize amendment of the complaint, answer, or reply to conform to the evidence. Any party who would otherwise be prejudiced by the amendment will be given reasonable opportunity to meet the allegations in the complaint, answer, or reply, as amended, and the administrative law judge shall make findings on any issue presented by the complaint, answer, or reply as amended.

[Added 50 FR 5184, Feb. 6, 1985, effective Mar. 8, 1985]

§ 10.146–10.148 [Reserved]

§ 10.149 Burden of proof

In a disciplinary proceeding, the Director shall have the burden of proving his or her case by clear and convincing evidence and a respondent shall have the burden of proving any affirmative defense by clear and convincing evidence.

[Added 50 FR 5184, Feb. 6, 1985, effective Mar. 8, 1985]

§ 10.150 Evidence

(a) Rules of evidence. The rules of evidence prevailing in courts of law and equity are not controlling in hearings in disciplinary proceedings. However, the administrative law judge shall exclude evidence which is irrelevant, immaterial, or unduly repetitious.

(b) Depositions. Depositions of witnesses taken pursuant to § 10.151 may be admitted as evidence.

(c) Government documents. Official documents, records, and papers of the Office are admissible without extrinsic evidence of authenticity. These documents, records, and papers may be evidenced by a copy certified as correct by an employee of the Office.

(d) Exhibits. If any document, record, or other paper is introduced in evidence as an exhibit, the administrative law judge may authorize the withdrawal of the exhibit subject to any conditions the administrative law judge deems appropriate.

(e) Objections. Objections to evidence will be in short form, stating the grounds of objection. Objections and rulings on objections will be a part of the record. No exception to the ruling is necessary to preserve the rights of the parties.

[Added 50 FR 5184, Feb. 6, 1985, effective Mar. 8, 1985]

§ 10.151 Depositions

(a) Depositions for use at the hearing in lieu of personal appearance of a witness before the administrative law judge may be taken by respondent or the Director upon a showing of good cause and with the approval of, and under such conditions as may be deemed appropriate by, the administrative law judge. Depositions may be taken upon oral or written questions, upon not less than ten days written notice to the other party, before any officer authorized to administer an oath or affirmation in the place where the deposition is to be taken. The requirement of ten days notice may be waived by the parties and depositions may then be taken of a witness at a time and place mutually agreed to by the parties. When a deposition is taken upon written questions, copies of the written questions will be served upon the other party with the notice and copies of any written cross-questions will be served by hand or "Express Mail" not less than five days before the date of the taking of the deposition unless the parties mutually agree otherwise. A party on whose behalf a deposition is taken shall file a copy of a transcript of the deposition signed by a court reporter with the administrative law judge and shall serve one copy upon the opposing party. Expenses for a court reporter and preparing, serving, and filing depositions shall be borne by the party at whose instance the deposition is taken.

(b) When the Director and the respondent agree in writing, a deposition of any witness who will appear voluntarily may be taken under such terms and conditions as may be mutually agreeable to the Director and the respondent. The deposition shall not be filed with the administrative law judge and may not be admitted in evidence before the administrative law judge unless he or she orders the deposition admitted in evidence. The admissibility of the deposition shall lie within the discretion of the administrative law judge who may reject the deposition on any reasonable basis including the fact that demeanor is involved and that the witness should have been called to appear personally before the administrative law judge.

[Added 50 FR 5185, Feb. 6, 1985, effective Mar. 8, 1985]

§ 10.152 Discovery

Discovery shall not be authorized except as follows:
- (a) After an answer is filed under § 10.136 and when a party establishes in a clear and convincing manner that discovery is necessary and relevant, the administrative law judge, under such conditions as he or she deems appropriate, may order an opposing party to:
  - (1) Answer a reasonable number of written requests for admission or interrogatories;
  - (2) Produce for inspection and copying a reasonable number of documents; and
  - (3) Produce for inspection a reasonable number of things other than documents.
- (b) Discovery shall not be authorized under paragraph (a) of this section of any matter which:
  - (1) Will be used by another party solely for impeachment or cross-examination;
  - (2) Is not available to the party under 35 U.S.C. § 122;
  - (3) Relates to any disciplinary proceeding commenced in the Patent and Trademark Office prior to March 8, 1985;
  - (4) Relates to experts except as the administrative law judge may require under paragraph (e) of this section.
  - (5) Is privileged; or
  - (6) Relates to mental impressions, conclusions, opinions, or legal theories of any attorney or other representative of a party.
- (c) The administrative law judge may deny discovery requested under paragraph (a) of this section if the discovery sought:
  - (1) Will unduly delay the disciplinary proceeding;
  - (2) Will place an undue burden on the party required to produce the discovery sought; or
  - (3) Is available (i) generally to the public, (ii) equally to the parties; or (iii) to the party seeking the discovery through another source.
- (d) Prior to authorizing discovery under paragraph (a) of this section, the administrative law judge shall require the party seeking discovery to file a motion (§ 10.143) and explain in detail for each request made how the discovery sought is necessary and relevant to an issue actually raised in the complaint or the answer.

(e) The administrative law judge may require parties to file and serve, prior to any hearing, a pre-hearing statement which contains:

  (1) A list (together with a copy) of all proposed exhibits to be used in connection with a party's case-in-chief,

  (2) A list of proposed witnesses,

  (3) As to each proposed expert witness:

    (i) An identification of the field in which the individual will be qualified as an expert;

    (ii) A statement as to the subject matter on which the expert is expected to testify; and

    (iii) A statement of the substance of the facts and opinions to which the expert is expected to testify,

  (4) The identity of government employees who have investigated the case, and

  (5) Copies of memoranda reflecting respondent's own statements to administrative representatives.

(f) After a witness testifies for a party, if the opposing party requests, the party may be required to produce, prior to cross-examination, any written statement made by the witness.

[Added 50 FR 5185, Feb. 6, 1985, effective Mar. 8, 1985]

§ 10.153 Proposed findings and conclusions; post-hearing memorandum

Except in cases when the respondent has failed to answer the complaint, the administrative law judge, prior to making an initial decision, shall afford the parties a reasonable opportunity to submit proposed findings and conclusions and a post-hearing memorandum in support of the proposed findings and conclusions.

[Added 50 FR 5185, Feb. 6, 1985, effective Mar. 8, 1985]

§ 10.154 Initial decision of administrative law judge

(a) The administrative law judge shall make an initial decision in the case. The decision will include (1) a statement of findings and conclusions, as well as the reasons or basis therefore with appropriate references to the record, upon all the material issues of fact, law, or discretion presented on the record, and (2) an order of suspension or exclusion from practice, an order of reprimand, or an order dismissing the complaint. The administrative law judge shall file the decision with the Director and shall transmit a copy to the representative of the Director and to the respondent. In the absence of an appeal to the Commissioner, the decision of the administrative law judge will, without further proceedings, become the decision of the Commissioner of Patents and Trademarks thirty (30) days from the date of the decision of the administrative law judge.

(b) The initial decision of the administrative law judge shall explain the reason for any penalty or reprimand, suspension or exclusion. In determining any penalty, the following should normally be considered:
   (1) The public interest;
   (2) The seriousness of the violation of the Disciplinary Rule;
   (3) The deterrent effects deemed necessary;
   (4) The integrity of the legal profession; and
   (5) Any extenuating circumstances.

[Added 50 FR 5185, Feb. 6, 1985, effective Mar. 8, 1985; amended 50 FR 25073, June 17, 1985]

§ 10.155 Appeal to the Commissioner

(a) Within thirty (30) days from the date of the initial decision of the administrative law judge under § 10.154, either party may appeal to the Commissioner. If an appeal is taken, the time for filing a cross-appeal expires 14 days after the date of service of the appeal pursuant to § 10.142 or 30 days after the date of the initial decision of the administrative law judge, whichever is later. An appeal or cross-appeal by the respondent will be filed and served with the Director in duplicate and will include exceptions to the decisions of the administrative law judge and supporting reasons for those exceptions. If the Director files the appeal or cross-appeal, the Director shall serve on the other party a copy of the appeal or cross-appeal. The other party to an appeal or cross-appeal may file a reply brief. A respondent's reply brief shall be filed and served in duplicate with the Director. The time for filing any reply brief expires thirty (30) days after the date of service pursuant to § 10.142 of an appeal, cross-appeal or copy thereof. If the Director files a reply brief, the Director shall serve on the other party a copy of the reply brief. Upon the filing of an appeal, cross-appeal, if any, and reply briefs, if any, the Director shall transmit the entire record to the Commissioner.

(b) The appeal will be decided by the Commissioner on the record made before the administrative law judge.

(c) The Commissioner may order reopening of a disciplinary proceeding in accordance with the principles which govern the granting of new trials. Any request to reopen a disciplinary proceeding on the basis of newly discovered evidence must demonstrate that the newly discovered evidence could not have been discovered by due diligence.

(d) In the absence of an appeal by the Director, failure by the respondent to appeal under the provisions of this section shall be deemed to be both acceptance by the respondent of the initial decision and waiver by the respondent of the right to further administrative or judicial review.

[Added 50 FR 5185, Feb. 6, 1985, effective Mar. 8, 1985; para. (d) added, 54 FR 26026, June 21, 1989, effective Aug. 1, 1989; para. (a) amended, 60 FR 64125, Dec. 14, 1995, effective Jan. 16, 1996]

§ 10.156 Decision of the Commissioner

(a) An appeal from an initial decision of the administrative law judge shall be decided by the Commissioner. The Commissioner may affirm, reverse, or modify the initial decision or remand the matter to the administrative law judge for such further proceedings as the Commissioner may deem appropriate. Subject to paragraph (c) of this section, a decision by the Commissioner does not become a final agency action in a disciplinary proceeding until 20 days after it is entered. In making a final decision, the Commissioner shall review the record or those portions of the record as may be cited by the parties in order to limit the issues. The Commissioner shall transmit a copy of the final decision to the Director and to the respondent.

(b) A final decision of the Commissioner may dismiss a disciplinary proceeding, reprimand a practitioner, or may suspend or exclude the practitioner from practice before the Office.

(c) A single request for reconsideration or modification of the Commissioner's decision may be made by the respondent or the Director if filed within 20 days from the date of entry of the decision. Such a request shall have the effect of staying the effective date of the decision. The decision by the Commissioner on the request is a final agency action in a disciplinary proceeding and is effective on its date of entry.

[Added 50 FR 5186, Feb. 6, 1985, effective Mar. 8, 1985; para. (a) amended and para. (c) added, 54 FR 6660, Feb. 14, 1989]

§ 10.157 Review of Commissioner's final decision

(a) Review of the Commissioner's final decision in a disciplinary case may be had, subject to § 10.155(d), by a petition filed in the United States District Court for the District of Columbia. *See* 35 U.S.C. 32 and Local Rule 213 of the United States District Court for the District of Columbia.
(b) The Commissioner may stay a final decision pending review of the Commissioner's final decision.

[Added 50 FR 5186, Feb. 6, 1985, effective Mar. 8, 1985; amended 53 FR 13120, Apr. 21, 1988; para. (a) amended, 54 FR 26026, June 21, 1989, effective Aug. 1, 1989]

§ 10.158 Suspended or excluded practitioner

(a) A practitioner who is suspended or excluded from practice before the Office under § 10.156(b) shall not engage in unauthorized practice of patent, trademark and other non patent law before the Office.
(b) Unless otherwise ordered by the Commissioner, any practitioner who is suspended or excluded from practice before the Office under § 10.156(b) shall:
 (1) Within 30 days of entry of the order of suspension or exclusion, notify all bars of which he or she is a member and all clients of the practitioner for whom he or she is handling matters before the Office in separate written communications of the suspension or exclusion and shall file a copy of each written communication with the Director.
 (2) Within 30 days of entry of the order of suspension or exclusion, surrender a client's active Office case files to (i) the client or (ii) another practitioner designated by the client.
 (3) Not hold himself or herself out as authorized to practice law before the Office.
 (4) Promptly take any necessary and appropriate steps to remove from any telephone, legal, or other directory any advertisement,

statement, or representation which would reasonably suggest that the practitioner is authorized to practice patent, trademark, or other non-patent law before the Office, and within 30 days of taking those steps, file with the Director an affidavit describing the precise nature of the steps taken.

(5) Not advertise the practitioner's availability or ability to perform or render legal services for any person having immediate, prospective, or pending business before the Office.

(6) Not render legal advice or services to any person having immediate, prospective, or pending business before the Office as to that business.

(7) Promptly take steps to change any sign identifying a practitioner's or the practitioner's firm's office and the practitioner's or the practitioner's firm's stationery to delete therefrom any advertisement, statement, or representation which would reasonably suggest that the practitioner is authorized to practice law before the Office.

(8) Within 30 days, return to any client any unearned funds, including any unearned retainer fee, and any securities and property of the client.

(c) A practitioner who is suspended or excluded from practice before the Office and who aids another practitioner in any way in the other practitioner's practice of law before the Office, may, under the direct supervision of the other practitioner, act as a paralegal for the other practitioner or perform other services for the other practitioner which are normally performed by lay-persons, provided:

(1) The practitioner who is suspended or excluded is:
   (i) A salaried employee of:

(A) The other practitioner;

(B) The other practitioner's law firm; or

(C) A client-employer who employs the other practitioner as a salaried employee;

(2) The other practitioner assumes full professional responsibility to any client and the Office for any work performed by the suspended or excluded practitioner for the other practitioner;

(3) The suspended or excluded practitioner, in connection with any immediate, prospective, or pending business before the Office, does not:
   (i) Communicate directly in writing, orally, or otherwise with a client of the other practitioner;
   (ii) Render any legal advice or any legal services to a client of the other practitioner; or
   (iii) Meet in person or in the presence of the other practitioner with:

(A) Any Office official in connection with the prosecution of any patent, trademark, or other case;

(B) Any client of the other practitioner, the other practitioner's law firm, or the client-employer of the other practitioner;

(C) Any witness or potential witness which the other practitioner, the other practitioner's law firm, or the other practitioner's client-employer may or intends to call as a witness in any proceeding before the Office. The term "witness" includes individuals who will testify orally in a proceeding before, or sign an affidavit or any other document to be filed in, the Office.

(d) When a suspended or excluded practitioner acts as a paralegal or performs services under paragraph (c) of this section, the suspended or excluded practitioner shall not thereafter be reinstated to practice before the Office unless:

(1) The suspended or excluded practitioner shall have filed with the Director an affidavit which (i) explains in detail the precise nature of all paralegal or other services performed by the suspended or excluded practitioner and (ii) shows by clear and convincing evidence that the suspended or excluded practitioner has complied with the provisions of this section and all Disciplinary Rules, and

(2) The other practitioner shall have filed with the Director a written statement which (i) shows that the other practitioner has read the affidavit required by subparagraph (d)(1) of this section and that the other practitioner believes every statement in the affidavit to be true and (ii) states why the other practitioner believes that the suspended or excluded practitioner has complied with paragraph (c) of this section.

[Added 50 FR 5186, Feb. 6, 1985, effective Mar. 8, 1985]

§ 10.159 Notice of suspension or exclusion

(a) Upon issuance of a final decision reprimanding a practitioner or suspending or excluding a practitioner from practice before the Office, the Director shall give notice of the final decision to appropriate employees of the Office and to interested departments, agencies, and courts of the United States. The Director shall also give notice to appropriate authorities of any State in which a practitioner is known to be a member of the bar and any appropriate bar association.

(b) The Director shall cause to be published in the Official Gazette the name of any practitioner suspended or excluded from practice. Unless otherwise ordered by the Commissioner, the Director shall publish in the Official Gazette the name of any practitioner reprimanded by the Commissioner.

(c) The Director shall maintain records, which shall be available for public inspection, of every disciplinary proceeding where practitioner is reprimanded, suspended, or excluded unless the Commissioner orders that the proceeding be kept confidential.

[Added 50 FR 5186, Feb. 6, 1985, effective Mar. 8, 1985]

§ 10.160 Petition for reinstatement

(a) A petition for reinstatement of a practitioner suspended for a period of less than five years will not be considered until the period of suspension has passed.

(b) A petition for reinstatement of a practitioner excluded from practice will not be considered until five years after the effective date of the exclusion.

(c) An individual who has resigned under § 10.133 or who has been suspended or excluded may file a petition for reinstatement. The Director may grant a petition for reinstatement when the individual makes a clear and convincing showing that the individual will conduct himself or herself in accordance with the regulations of this part and that granting a petition for reinstatement is not contrary to the public interest. As a condition to reinstatement, the Director may require the individual to:

    (1) Meet the requirements of § 10.7, including taking and passing an examination under § 10.7(b) and

    (2) Pay all or a portion of the costs and expenses, not to exceed $1,500, of the disciplinary proceeding which led to suspension or exclusion.

(d) Any suspended or excluded practitioner who has violated the provisions of § 10.158 during his or her period of suspension or exclusion shall not be entitled to reinstatement until such time as the Director is satisfied that a period of suspension equal in time to that ordered by the Commissioner or exclusion for five years has passed during which the suspended or excluded practitioner has complied with the provisions of § 10.158.

(e) Proceedings on any petition for reinstatement shall be open to the public. Before reinstating any suspended or excluded practitioner, the Director shall publish in the Official Gazette a notice of the suspended or excluded practitioner's petition for reinstatement and shall permit the public a reasonable opportunity to comment or submit evidence with respect to the petition for reinstatement.

[Added 50 FR 5186, Feb. 6, 1985, effective Mar. 8, 1985]

§ 10.161 Savings clause

(a) A disciplinary proceeding based on conduct engaged in prior to the effective date of these regulations may be instituted subsequent to such effective date, if such conduct would continue to justify suspension or exclusion under the provisions of this part.
(b) No practitioner shall be subject to a disciplinary proceeding under this part based on conduct engaged in before the effective date hereof if such conduct would not have been subject to disciplinary action before such effective date.

[Added 50 FR 5186, Feb. 6, 1985, effective Mar. 8, 1985]

§ 10.162–10.169 [Reserved]

§ 10.170 Suspension of rules

(a) In an extraordinary situation, when justice requires, any requirement of the regulations of this part which is not a requirement of the statutes may be suspended or waived by the Commissioner or the Commissioner's designee, sua sponte, or on petition of any party, including the Director or the Director's representative, subject to such other requirements as may be imposed.
(b) Any petition under this section will not stay a disciplinary proceeding unless ordered by the Commissioner or an administrative law judge.

[Added 50 FR 5186, Feb. 6, 1985, effective Mar. 8, 1985]

APPENDIX
2

Forms and Checklists

File Intake Procedure

- Any file or group of files coming in to the firm should be directed to docketing. Records and the partner whose case or client is coming in should immediately be notified.
- An inventory of identified cases should be made and compared to any provided inventory (i.e., the files listed as sent to us are the files received by us). If no inventory came with the files, a list of cases that have been received should be made.
  - Depending on size of the intake, records or docketing can handle this step.
  - If the intake is large, records should handle this step, but docketing can easily manage a few files at a time.
- If the intake involves matters for a new client, the partner or assistant does the conflict on the client and gets a new client number. This is provided to docketing.
  - The files should then go to docketing for initial review and docket numbers.
- Docket numbers need to be assigned to each case and then submitted to client intake for a matter number. The new docket numbers should be handwritten on the actual file jacket until labels are made.
- The files are entered, that is, docketed into docketing software (e.g., CPi, PATTSY CPA, etc.) and an initial review of the files is done to prioritize for further review by attorney or assistant (i.e., check for immediate due dates). Screen prints from CPi should be attached to each file for reference.

NEW U.S. UTILITY (NONPROVISIONAL) APPLICATION CHECKLIST[1]	YES	NO	N/A

Are all pages of the **specification** present, legible, and running numerically?

Is the specification more than 100 pages with abstract, claims, and figures?

If Yes, add page fees. _____
(no. of pages)

Is there a certified translation of the application?

Are claim count, multiple dependency, numerical order checked? Complete the fee calculation sheet on the back of the file.

Is the **Abstract** present—less than 150 words?

Are there **formal/informal drawings**, and are they labeled?

Are all figures listed in the specification present and correctly identified?

If this is a national stage off a Patent Cooperation Treaty (PCT), do not submit color drawings as this would be new matter. Are there color figures?
If Yes, amend the specification and add a petition as necessary under 37 C.F.R. § 1.84(a)(2).

Is there a **Sequence Listing**?

If Yes, is a fully labeled disk/CD-ROM and paper copy or 2 CD-ROM equivalents (also labeled) being provided?

Is the sequence listing incorporated by reference into the specification?

Is there a **biological deposit**?

If YES, is a certificate of deposit (and translations if necessary) provided? Is the biological deposit recited in the specification?

Is a **Preliminary Amendment** required?

Are all pages of preliminary amendment present and running numerically?

Does preliminary amendment change the number of claims present in application?

---

1. The form should be modified for the practice. For example, mechanical and electrical devices do not require the presence of sequence listings and biological deposits.

NEW U.S. UTILITY (NONPROVISIONAL)
APPLICATION CHECKLIST   YES   NO   N/A

Has the **cross reference to related applications** been
    updated for priority?

Is there a **title** change?

Is an **Application Data Sheet** (ADS) being filed?

Does the information in the ADS correspond with
    the Declaration, Assignment, and information in
    the instruction letter?

Is there an **Information Disclosure Statement**?

If Yes, has the International Search Report (ISR) and
    all references in the ISR been provided, including
    translations?

If Yes, have all the references in the specification
    been provided? If no, add paragraph requesting
    from for company or foreign associate.

Is there a properly executed **Declaration**?

Does Declaration correctly identify the application?

If there is no executed Declaration, is an unexecuted
    Declaration attached?

Is there an **Assignment**?

Does the Assignment properly identify the
    application?

Is Assignment Recordation Coversheet properly
    completed? (Address/Corporate Entity/Individual
    Names—see checklist)

Are all attachments checked off on Application
    Transmittal Form present?

Are all the fees properly calculated, taking into
    account small entity if applicable, assignment if
    applicable, multiple dependent claim fee or
    additional fees, if applicable?

Have you attached postcards in duplicate, and are
    the fees listed on the postcard if not filed EFS?

If filing via EFS, has the attorney checked that
    everything has been correctly uploaded?

Is the docket number listed correctly on all pages?

Are the inventors' names, addresses, and nationality
    correct on all papers including Assignment,
    Assignment Recordation, and Declaration.

Is the title of the application correct on all papers?

NEW U.S. UTILITY (NONPROVISIONAL)
APPLICATION CHECKLIST   YES   NO   N/A

Are all issues in the Order Letter addressed?
Is the correspondence address correct?
List all papers being submitted:

1.   4.   7.
2.   5.   8.
3.   6.   9.

Client Name: _____   Client Number: _____

Reviewed by: _____   Date: _____

SUGGESTED NEW PCT APPLICATION CHECKLIST
(cont'd)   YES   NO   N/A

Are all pages of the **specification** present, legible, and
running numerically?
Number of pages of specification: _____
Number of pages of claims: _____
Priority/benefit applications claimed:
No. _____ Filed _____
No. _____ Filed _____
No. _____ Filed _____

Is there a corporate applicant?
If Yes, please provide:
Corporate Name:
Corporate Address:
How many inventors are there?
Is at least one inventor a citizen/resident of the United
States? (required)
Is the **Abstract** present—less than 150 words?
Are there **formal/informal drawings,** and are they
labeled?
Are all figures listed in the specification present?
Has a figure been designated to be published on the
face of the application?
Are there color figures? If Yes, obtain black and white
copies.
Is there a **Sequence Listing**?
If Yes, is a fully labeled disk/CD-ROM and paper copy
or 2 CD-ROM equivalents (also labeled) being
provided in PCT format?
If sequence listing is long, file on CD-ROM to avoid
page fee. Must enclose declaration stating electronic
copy is identical to CRF copy. See 37 C.F.R. 1.821.
Is the sequence listing incorporated by reference into
the specification?
Is there a **biological deposit**?
If YES, has certificate of deposit (and translations if
necessary) been provided?
Is there a reference in the specification to incorporate
by reference all the priority applications?

SUGGESTED NEW PCT APPLICATION CHECKLIST
  (cont'd)   YES   NO   N/A

Has a **Search Authority** been designated?[2]
EPO, KPO or U.S.: _____
  Is there a completed PCT safe with disk?

Is there an Assignment?
Does the Assignment properly identify the application?
Is Assignment Recordation Coversheet properly
  completed? (Address/Corporate Entity/Individual
  Names—see checklist)
Are all attachments checked off on Application
  Transmittal Form present?

Have you attached postcards in duplicate, and are the
  fees listed on the postcard?
Is the docket number listed correctly on all pages?

Client Name: _____   Client Number: _____

Reviewed by: _____   Date: _____

---

2. Different search authorities cost different amounts. Although the Korean Search Office (KPO) is recommended for electrical and mechanical searches, another ISA, such as US or EP, may be better for chemical and biotechnical cases.

SUGGESTED[3] APPLICATION CHECKLIST

Firm ref. no.:   Group Art:

Client ref. no.:   _____   Confirmation No.:

Application no.:   Examiner:

Responsible attorney:

Billing attorney   _____

Filing date: _____

PCT filing date: _____

Priority date: _____

Expiration date: _____

Title: _____

Inventors/Addresses Citizenship:

1. _____   _____
2. _____   _____
3. _____   _____
4. _____   _____
5. _____   _____

If a divisional application, have we confirmed that all listed inventors should remain inventors on the divisional application. YES ☐ NO ☐ N/A ☐

Document Retrieval Information:

As-filed application reference no.:   _____

As-filed figure(s) reference no(s).:   _____

As-filed sequence listing reference no.:   _____

Claim for Priority:

Foreign Priority/Provisional Application: Serial No.: _____

    Filing Date: _____

Line of Parent Applications:

This application is a _____ (CON/DIV/371) of _____

    filed _____.

1. Has the specification been amended to reflect the claim   YES ☐ NO ☐
   for priority in the cross reference to related applications?

Official Filing Receipt:
1. Is the filing date correct?   YES ☐   NO ☐
2. Are the inventors names and addresses correctly listed?   YES ☐   NO ☐
3. Is the title correct?   YES ☐   NO ☐
4. Is the claim for priority correct?   YES ☐   NO ☐
5. Has foreign filing license been granted?   YES ☐   NO ☐

Information Disclosure Statements (*All IDSs should be checked to make sure that all references are acknowledged by the USPTO on receipt of acknowledged copies.*)

1. Have all the IDSs from the parent application/patent been submitted?   YES ☐   NO ☐
2. Has the ISR (210) been cited in a 1449?   YES ☐   NO ☐
3. Has the Written Opinion and IPRP been cited?   YES ☐   NO ☐

ISR listed on PTO-1449 _____   Acknowledged _____
IPRP listed on PTO-1449 _____   Acknowledged _____
IDS filed _____   Acknowledged _____
IDS filed _____   Acknowledged _____
IDS filed _____   Acknowledged _____
IDS filed _____   Acknowledged _____
IDS filed _____   Acknowledged _____
IDS filed _____   Acknowledged _____
References listed in specification filed _____
Comments_____
Related References: (If handling filings around the world, make sure PTO-892 forms and their Office Actions are supplied to jurisdictions requiring such disclosure.[4]
PTO-892/SR dated in OA _____ Sent to CA ___; IL___; US ___
PTO-892/SR dated in OA _____ Sent to CA ___; IL___; US ___
PTO-892/SR dated in OA _____ Sent to CA ___; IL___; US ___
PTO-892/SR dated in OA _____ Sent to CA ___; IL___; US ___

Power of Attorney
Declaration executed on _____ Filed on _____
Power of Attorney executed on _____ Filed on _____
Revocation Power of Attorney executed on _____
   Filed On _____

---

4. We note that although new Australian applications no longer require this degree of reporting, for older applications the requirement may still apply.

Assignment
Assignment sent to client on _____
Assignment executed on _____
Assignment recorded on _____
Reel/Frame Number _____/_____
Assignee Name (1)_____ (2)
Assignee Address (1)_____ (2)

Sequence Listing
Sequence Listing stored at: _____
Sequence Listing copy to use:_____

1. Specification amended to incorporate any sequence listing?   YES ☐   NO ☐
2. Statement regarding identity of CRF and paper copy?   YES ☐   NO ☐

Biological Deposit
Is a biological deposit necessary?   _____
If Yes, where is it deposited: _____
What is the accession no.? _____

Notice of Allowance/Notice of Allowability Checklist

1. Application no. correct?   YES ☐   NO ☐
2. Filing date correct?   YES ☐   NO ☐
3. Title correct? Has the title been amended during prosecution?   YES ☐   NO ☐
4. Inventor name(s) correct?   YES ☐   NO ☐
5. Claim count correct? Claims as allowed _____   YES ☐   NO ☐

Application and Prosecution History

1. Was application allowed as originally filed? (i.e., there were no amendments or office actions, and application is not a rewrite)   YES ☐   NO ☐
   If Yes, note to applicant.
2. Was **convention priority** claimed?   YES ☐   NO ☐
   If Yes: Have all certified copies been filed?   YES ☐   NO ☐
   If No, note to applicant.
   Receipt acknowledged by PTO?   YES ☐   NO ☐
   If No: Request acknowledgement at this time.
3. Have **acceptable drawings** been filed?   YES ☐   NO ☐
   If No, contact Examiner.

4. Did Examiner require restriction or an **election of species**? YES ☐ NO ☐
   If Yes:
   a. Has client provided instructions regarding filing of a divisional application? YES ☐ NO ☐
   b. Is a divisional application required? YES ☐ NO ☐
   c. Has a divisional been filed? YES ☐ NO ☐
   d. What group was elected if a restriction? _____?
   e. What groups remain? _____
   f. What is the class/subclass category for the elected group? Class_____ Subclass _____.
   g. Is rejoinder possible? If Yes, what claims can be rejoined with the elected prosecuted group? _____
   h. Has rejoinder been requested? _____
   (Remember the claims to be rejoined must have consistent amendments. Such rejoinder will generally require an requesting/request continued examination (RCE) to pursue the rejoined claims.)
5. Have all client requests and correspondence been answered? YES ☐ NO ☐
6. Is an **Assignment** required in this application? (If this is a continuation—see parent file) YES ☐ NO ☐
   If Yes: Has it been filed? YES ☐ NO ☐
   If No: File or request from client at this time.
   Has recorded Assignment been returned from PTO? YES ☐ NO ☐
   If No: Request from PTO at this time.
   Has recorded Assignment been returned to client? YES ☐ NO ☐
   If No: Return with Allowance letter, unless instructed otherwise.
7. Did Examiner require a new **declaration** or has one been requested from the client by attorney? YES ☐ NO ☐
   If Yes: Has it been filed in PTO? YES ☐ NO ☐
   If no: File at this time. YES ☐ NO ☐
8. Have all prior art/references brought to our attention by the client been filed in the PTO? YES ☐ NO ☐
   If Yes: Has Examiner returned initialed PTO-1449 for each reference in each IDS filed? YES ☐ NO ☐
   If No: a. Request return of initialed PTO-1449s at this time; and/or
   b. Bring any unfiled references to the attention of the Working Attorney immediately.
9. Did Examiner attach an Examiner's Amendment and/or Reasons for Allowance? YES ☐ NO ☐
   If Yes: Should Comments on Reasons for Allowance be filed? If Yes: File Comments at this time. YES ☐ NO ☐

10. Patent Term Adjustment—Number of Days:_____
    Has the adjustment period been?   YES ☐ NO ☐
11. Is it necessary to file a Maintenance Fee Address
    Change?   YES ☐ NO ☐
12. Has the Correspondence Address been changed to
    include our Customer No.?   YES ☐ NO ☐

Current Assignee(s):_(Enter carefully as this information will be entered on the Issue Fee Transmittal form.)

_____

_____

Address: _____
(City, State or Country)
This file has been reviewed by: _____   on _____
   (filing specialist)   (date)

Below For Attorney Use Only
I have reviewed this checklist and file, and the following applies:

☐ This case is in condition for payment of the issue fee subject to any specific client instructions for payment. Please check for client correspondence before attending to payment, as clients will sometimes give instructions not to pay an issue fee after the completion and signing of this Notice of Allowance checklist.

☐ DO NOT PAY ISSUE FEE until the following comments have been addressed and or actions taken.

Comments:

Attorney Signature   Date

SUGGESTED FILED PCT CHECKLIST

Firm Ref. No.:_____.
Client Ref. No.:_____.
SUBMITTED WITH APPLICATION:
Title of Application: _____
_____ (1) **Filing Fees**
_____ Paid on Filing: _____
If No, deadline date to pay fees: _____
Application No.: **PCT/**   (2) **Priority Information**
No. of priorities claimed: _____
Filing Date: _____ a) Serial No. of first priority appl.: ____
Submitted on filing: _____
Earliest Priority   If No, date submitted: _____
Appl. No.: _____
b) Serial No. of second priority appl.: ____
Earliest Filing Date: _____ Submitted on filing: _____
If No, date submitted: _____
Searching Authority: _____
c) Serial No. of third priority appl.: _____
Submitted on filing: _____
Client Ref. No.:   If No, date submitted: _____
Contact Person: _____ (3) **Deposits Receipt:** _____
No. of Deposits: _____
Title: _____ All submitted? _____
If No, date submitted: _____
Licensees: _____
(4) **Sequence Listing:** _____
If No, date submitted: _____
16-Month Deadline: (5) **Formal Drawings:** _____
_____ If No, date submitted: _____
6) **Powers of Attorney**
No. Required: _____
First Applicant POA filed with appl.? ____
If No, date filed: _____
Second Applicant POA filed with appl.? ___
If No, date filed: _____
Third Applicant POA filed with appl.? ____
If No, date filed: _____

Application filed in the name of: **SPECIAL NOTES**

Applicant: _____   _____

_____

Applicant/Inventors: _____   _____

_____   _____

_____   _____

_____

Applicants for US only: _____   _____

Assignment in Priority Case: ____   _____

_____

If No assignment is executed at the time   _____

of filing of the PCT, check with the attorney   _____

about the assignment. Make sure the case is   _____

docketed for periodic checks to see if the

priority assignment has been executed. Once

the assignment has been executed,

the applicant in the international case must be

changed.

Docket dates for check of priority case: _____

Deadline date for submission of change in

PCT case: _____

Date Request for Change of Status of Inventor/Applicant

Submitted to the IB: _____

Date of PCT/IB/306 acknowledging change: _____

ASSIGNMENT INFORMATION:

_____

_____

_____

_____

_____

PCT CHAPTER I CHECKLIST   Date Received

Notification of Receipt of Search Copy (PCT/ISA/202): _____

Notification of the Int'l Appl. No. and of the Int'l Filing Date (PCT/IB/105):

_____

Notification Concerning Payment of Prescribed Fees (PCT/RO/102): _____

_____

Notification of Receipt of Record Copy (PCT/IB/301): _____

Notification Concerning Submission of Priority Document (PCT/IB/304):

_____

Invitation to Correct Defects: _____

Due date to respond:_____   _____

PCT CRITICAL DATES

Formalities Check (to be completed by 16 months)   SPECIAL NOTES

Powers of Attorney (date submitted): _____   _____

Declarations (date submitted): _____   _____

Priority Document (date submitted): _____   _____

Formal Drawings (date submitted): _____   _____

Change of Applicant(s): _____   _____

International Search Report   Chapter I National/Regional Phase:

Due: _____   **20-Month Date:** _____

Received: _____   **30-Month Date:** _____

Article 19 Amdts due: _____   Countries: _____

Response filed: _____   _____

Date of CRL: _____   _____

By: _____   _____

PCT Chapter II Demand (19 or 22 months)

Due: _____

Reminder CRL: _____

Instructions received: _____

Demand filed: _____

Article 34 filed: _____

IPEA: _____

PCT CHAPTER I/II CHECKLIST   Date Received

Acknowledgment Forms

First Notice Informing the Applicant of the Communication
of the Int'l Application (PCT/IB/308): _____

Notification of Receipt of Demand (PCT/IPEA/402):   _____

Second Notice Informing the Applicant of the Communication
of the Int'l Application (PCT/IB/308): _____

Information Concerning Elected Offices Notified of Their
Election (PCT/IB/332):   _____

PCT CRITICAL DATES

Published Document

Due: _____   **SPECIAL NOTES**

Received: _____   _____

Published with ISR: _____   _____

Published with Formals: _____   _____

Date of CRL: _____   _____

By: _____   _____

Written Opinion (PCT/ISA/237)

Due: _____

Received: _____

Deadline: _____

Response filed: _____

Date of CRL: _____

By: _____

IPRP—International Report on Patentability (PCT/IB/373)

Due: _____

Received: _____

No. of Annexes: _____

Date of CRL: _____

By: _____

Chapter II National/Regional Phase Deadline (30 months)

Due: _____

Reminder CRL: _____

Instructions Received: _____

Countries: _____

_____

SUGGESTED LIST FOR TRANSFER OF PATENT FILES
FROM A DIFFERENT FIRM

Issue	YES	NO	N/A
Docketing & Filing			

1. Has a prepared letter to the client to request transfer of electronic copies of all materials and transfer of docketing data from other firm (transferring party) been sent?

2. Is client file list here?
File Arrival Date: _____

3. Is file list from the transferring party here?

4. Do the lists correspond? If No, follow up with client.

5. Have electronic copies been requested of all applications, sequence listings, tables, and figures?

5a. Have electronic copies of all information been received?

5b. If request for electronic copies was sent, but copies have not been received, has client been asked probability of receipt?

6. Are files missing? Please detail on attached sheet.

7. Docket of due dates from the transferring party (for immediate due dates and a 12-month docket) received?

7a. If No, please review ALL files immediately and triage for 1-month due dates and 3-month due dates.

7b. Are there any 1-month due dates?

7c. Are there any 3-month due dates?

8. Have all cases been docketed within 2 weeks of receipt/after triage?
Date Docket Entry Completed: _____

8a. Has an electronic docket been uploaded into docketing system?

8b. If not capable of transfer to our docket, what measures have been instituted to make sure data is entered into our system?

9. Have all the cases been run through conflicts? (usually done by family) Date: _____

10. Have all the cases been assigned docket numbers?

11. Have all the cases been re-jacketed and labeled?
Date Completed: _____

Issue	YES	NO	N/A

Attorneys/Agents/Administrative Assistants

13. Have Revocations and new Powers of Attorney been filed in the cases? (Within 3 months of file transfer)

13a. Has a 2-month status check been put in place to check PAIR on all cases prior to acceptance of revocation?

14. Do all the provisional applications have assignments?

14a. If No, prepare a letter to client recommending that provisionals, even if expired, be assigned to the entity.

15. Have all the U.S. utility applications been assigned?

16. Are there foreign cases?

16a. If Yes, have letters been sent to foreign counsel indicating change of counsel (within 3 months of file transfer)?

Letters Completed On: _____

17. Are there PCT cases pending?

17a. If Yes, prepare Rule 92bis changes of attorney for the case. Have they been filed? Filed with RO on: _____

Responsible/Billing Attorney: _____ Dated: _____

Docketer: _____

Foreign Filing Specialist: _____

INITIAL DISCLOSURE MEMO

Date:
To: [LIST ALL RECIPIENTS]
From:
Subject: Duty of Disclosure Requirements for U.S. Patent Applications

Each applicant and every other person substantively involved in prosecution of a U.S. patent application must deal with the U.S. Patent and Trademark Office (PTO) with candor and good faith. One aspect of this obligation is that all information material to patentability of any claimed invention, including relevant "prior art" (as defined below), must be disclosed to the PTO if it is known to any person who is under a duty of disclosure. This memorandum summarizes this important duty. Please ask if anything is unclear.

Who Must Comply with the Duty of Disclosure?
Individuals under a duty of disclosure include:

- Each inventor named in the application;
- Each attorney or agent who prepares or prosecutes the patent application;
- Every other person who is substantively involved in the preparation or prosecution of the application and who is associated with any one of
  o An inventor
  o The assignee of the patent application or
  o Anyone to whom there is an obligation to assign the patent application.

We are providing this notice to you because we believe you are substantively involved. If you know of people who you think were substantively involved in prosecution, but who are not listed recipients of this notice, please let us know.

What Must be Disclosed?
At the outset, you are required to disclose only information you already know about. We are not asking you to do any research and do not want you to do any. If we have not already done so, we will soon forward to you an Information Disclosure Statement (IDS) on which we will list all relevant prior art that we know of, as we have our own independent duty of disclosure. Just as we will disclose art to you, you should disclose to us all relevant prior art and other information that you're aware of and, as noted below, give us a copy of it if you already have it.

   "Prior art" refers to several different types of information. In every case, determining whether something is "prior" turns on one of two dates: (a) the effective filing date of the U.S. patent application, or (b) the date the invention was made. Here, for purposes of this letter, you should consider _____ to be the effective filing date. Here, for purposes of this letter, you should consider _____ to be the date the invention was made.

Some examples of information and prior art that you should disclose to us for us to at least evaluate includes:

(1)   Facts about any public use, sale, or offer for sale of the invention (even if experimental) made more than one year before the filing of the application, i.e., before _____, 2008, which is based on the filing date of _____, 2009;

(2)   Facts about any prototypes of the invention obtained from anyone not employed by your employer and made more than a year before the filing of the application, i.e., before _____, 2008, which is based on the filing date of _____, 2009.

(3)   Any description of the invention you published more than a year before filing the patent application, i.e., before _____, 2008, which is based on the filing date of _____, 2009;

(4)   Any device or design disclosed in any kind of article (e.g., magazine articles, web pages, books, scientific papers, advertisements, etc.) published before the filing of the patent application (which was _____, 2009) and that show the same or closely related designs or technology;

(5)   Information on the same or related designs/technology you obtained prior to filing the application (i.e., _____, 2009) at seminars, conventions, plant visits, in-house reviews, confidential or nonconfidential disclosures to your employer from others, etc.;

(6)   Any dispute or potential dispute about inventorship of even one claim of the application;

(7)   Articles or other information (whenever published) that reasonably can be construed to state a position by you or your employer that is inconsistent with patentability, including any article that suggests the invention does not work as described, that it is not new or would have been obvious, or that the application does not contain the best mode known to any inventor to carry out the invention, etc.

(8)   Prior art cited in related foreign patent application search reports, the search reports and office actions, issued in foreign applications, as well as cited in oppositions to a foreign application.

(9)   Information discovered or generated in litigation, interference, or other *inter partes* proceeding, relating to the subject matter for which patent protection is sought.

(10) Failed tests of the prior invention, so that we can determine whether those tests must or should be disclosed, or can document the reason for not turning them over.

(11) Translations of foreign language documents can create issues for us to consider. Please advise me if you know of any translation of any foreign document that you believe is material to patentability.

(12) Information concerning the "best mode" of practicing the claimed invention. If there are particular methods or inputs you prefer in making or using the claimed invention, please let me know.

(13) Co-pending applications also create issues for us to consider if the co-pending application is closely related to the application we are filing for you or another has filed on your behalf. Please advise us of related co-pending applications, and do not assume that the examiner(s) will determine, on their own, that one application you have filed is relevant to this application.

(14) Prior office actions by an examiner concerning identical, or substantially identical, claims (e.g., in instances where an obviousness-type double patenting rejection has been asserted). If you have related applications pending, and an examiner has considered them and issued an office action, please let us know.

(15) The publicly available information that any inventor believes to be "closest" to the invention.

Materiality: Would a Reasonable Examiner Think It Important?

Not all prior art or other information must be disclosed; only that which is material to patentability. Although we would rather than you err on the side of disclosing information to us, so that we can determine whether the information is "material," you should know that information is considered "relevant" if a reasonable examiner would consider it important to patentability. It is important you understand that this includes *but is not limited to* the following information:

1. Information that establishes, by itself or in combination with other information, the non-patentability of any of the pending claims when each term of the claim is given its broadest reasonable interpretation consistent with the specification;

2. Information that refutes, or is inconsistent with, a position we take with regard to an argument about patentability offered by either the PTO or the applicant; *or*

3. Information that relates to whether any named inventor is the true, and only, inventor.

Again, we realize that determining whether information is "material" can be complicated, and the answer sometimes unclear or subject to judgment calls. It is important you understand that there are significant benefits to disclosure. Conversely, we do not want to bury the PTO with too much repetitious or tangential information. You should keep in mind, also, that all prior art provided to the PTO will ordinarily become part of the publicly available record. Again, please contact us with any questions.

If you have a copy of any patent, article, or other document, send it to me. If it is not in English but you have a translation already, then the translation must be provided. But, if you don't have an English translation, let me know who is most knowledgeable about what it says and why it arguably is material.

Information we submit normally becomes available to the public at the same time the application file does. Thus, if the application issues as a patent or is published, the application file will be available for public inspection. So, let us know if any information you provide to us is not proper for public release, so we can determine what to do.

How Long Does the Duty Last?

The duty lasts so long as the application is pending. If you later learn of information, please let us know. We'll also remind you about the duty if we are advised that a patent will be issued. But you should know that it is never too early to advise us of material information. Please do so promptly, even if you learn about it after we file the application. You can avoid certain fees by submitting information early in the process. Likewise, late submissions can reduce any extension of term to which any patent might otherwise be entitled.

Once a patent has been allowed, submission of material information to the USPTO can delay issuance. Whereas relevant prior art can, but need not, be submitted to the USPTO after issuance of a application as a patent, any information submitted after issuance will be placed in the patent file without review or comment by the PTO.

Why Disclose Information to the PTO?

If the information is submitted within the time limits and with any necessary fees, then the information will be considered by the patent examiner. The fact that the examiner allows a patent after giving the information consideration is given significant weight in law suits alleging invalidity of the patent. It can be difficult to convince a court that a patent should be invalidated over information that the examiner took into account. Therefore, disclosure can be to your advantage.

Holding back information can have severe consequences. A patent can be held to be unenforceable if a court holds that a person to whom the duty of disclosure applies failed to provide the PTO with material information he or she knew of and with the intent to deceive the PTO. Furthermore, if one patent is held unenforceable, it can affect related patents, too.

For these reasons, please disclose to us all information which you believe may be relevant to the patentability of any claimed invention. If you are in doubt, please ask us whether particular information may be considered important, or how public disclosure might be avoided.

Questions?

Patent prosecution is not simple, and the duty of candor is only summarized in this memo. If you have questions, just ask.

Post Notice of Allowance Letter

Dear_____:

I am pleased to enclose a Notice of Allowance for the subject patent application. This means that the U.S. Patent and Trademark Office (PTO) has reviewed your application and has found no objections to it. Therefore, a patent likely will be issued to you if certain conditions are met.

Please Provide the Issue Fee

The patent will not issue unless you pay an issue fee of $_____. It must be paid by _____. Please send your payment to me by _____ date, or we will not pay the issue fee, and the patent will not issue.

Has Full Disclosure of Material Information Been Made?

We also are writing because this is the last opportunity to be sure that we have disclosed to the PTO all information that you know of that is material to patentability of any claimed invention. Please see my earlier memo, a copy of which is attached. Now that we have a Notice of Allowance, I need you to review this issue again to make sure nothing was overlooked. *Failure to bring this information to the attention of the PTO could cause any patent to be unenforceable and, as a result, worthless.*

At this stage, it is not too late to bring such information to the attention of the PTO. Again, please advise me by telephone immediately if you are aware of any information that might fall into any of the above categories, so that we can discuss the information.

Is Inventorship Correct?

It is my understanding that the inventor(s) are _____. If, on reflection, you believe that there are other inventors, please immediately advise me. This is very important because failing to accurately list every inventor—even an inventor who contributed only to one claim in the patent—can under some circumstances result in invalidity.

Can You Still Claim Small Entity Status?

An applicant who can claim "small entity" status may pay reduced fees. Although _____ held this small entity status at the time of filing of the patent application, you need to confirm that your status has not changed.

Please carefully read the enclosed Small Entity Certification. If it is still accurate, please sign it and return it to me if you want to claim this status. However, if you have any question as to whether it is still a "small entity," call me. Improperly claiming small entity status can result in invalidity of the patent.

Is the Patent Term Adjustment Correct?

We recommend that you review the PTO's determination of patent term. We note that the PTO awarded ___ days term under 35 U.S.C. § 154. If you dispute the patent term, we must file the request for reconsideration with or before payment of the issue fee. *See* 37 C.F.R. §1.705.

What are your Instructions Regarding Continuation/Divisional Applications?

We note that the application was subject to a restriction requirement that was made final. Please provide instructions on whether a divisional application should be filed on any of remaining groups _____ listed in the Restriction Requirement mailed _____.

Additionally or alternatively, please let us know whether a continuation application is to be filed on any unclaimed embodiment or previously cancelled subject matter.

Finally, please don't hesitate to call me if you have any questions about the enclosed.

Sincerely,
Enc.

3

U.S. Patent and Trademark Office—Office of Enrollment and Discipline Decisions

OED Discipline Final Decisions

The Office of Enrollment and Discipline (OED) final decisions can be found *at* http://www.uspto.gov/web/offices/com/sol/foia/oed/disc/disc.htm.

Abdallah, Iman A.	D2000–08

In re Abdallah, No. D00–08 (Dep't Comm. June 11, 2001), *available at* http://www.uspto.gov/web/offices/com/sol/foia/oed/disc/D26.pdf (practitioner was in default for failing to file an Answer to the Complaint with various allegations, including violation of 37 C.F.R. §§ 10.23(b)(1), 10.23(b)(4), 10.23(b)(6), 10.23(c)(5), 10.23(c)(14), 10.23(c)(2)(i), 10.23(c)(16), 10.77(c), 10.84(a)(1), 10.84(a)(2), 10.84(a)(3), 10.112(c)(4), and 10.131(b); excluded from practice before the U.S. Patent and Trademark Office [USPTO]).

Anonymous 1	D1996–01

Bovard v. Respondent, No. D96–01 (Comm'r Pat. Aug. 28, 1997), *available at* http://www.uspto.gov/web/offices/com/sol/foia/oed/disc/D01.pdf (practitioner violated 37 C.F.R. § 10.23(c)(7) by (1) failing to inform the examiner that claims of a patent application had been copied from a U.S. patent, and (2) repeatedly arguing that the copied claims were patentable; privately reprimanded).

Anonymous 2	August 6, 1999

In re Anonymous (Comm'r Pat. Aug. 6, 1999), *available at* http://www.uspto.gov/web/offices/com/sol/foia/oed/disc/D07.pdf (practitioner was privately reprimanded for backdating a certificate of mailing).

Anonymous 3	August 23, 2000

In re Anonymous (USPTO Dir. Aug. 23, 2000), *available at* http://www.uspto.
gov/web/offices/com/sol/foia/oed/disc/D16.pdf (practitioner was privately
reprimanded "for engaging in conduct that resulted in a no-contest plea to
causing bodily injury to a child through criminal negligence").

Anonymous	March 14, 2001

In re Anonymous (USPTO Dir. Mar. 14, 2001), *available at* http://www.uspto.
gov/web/offices/com/sol/foia/oed/disc/D19.pdf (practitioner was suspended for
an indeterminate period from practice before the USPTO).

Anonymous 5	D2003–13

In re Respondent, No. D2003–13 (USPTO Dir. Feb. 9, 2004), *available at*
http://www.uspto.gov/web/offices/com/sol/foia/oed/disc/D2003–13.pdf
(practitioner violated (1) 37 C.F.R. § 10.36 by charging "$73,368.80 for work
valued at no more than $18,000," (2) 37 C.F.R. § 10.23(c)(2)(i) by blatantly
misrepresenting misleading information to the client in numerous instances
regarding dates and nature of services provided, and (3) 37 C.F.R. § 10.23(b)(4)
by engaging in conduct involving dishonesty, deceit, or misrepresentation;
privately reprimanded).

Anonymous 6	D2004–10

In re Anonymous, No. D2004–10 (USPTO Dir. Aug. 19, 2004), *available at*
http://www.uspto.gov/web/offices/com/sol/foia/oed/disc/D2004–10.pdf
(practitioner violated (1) 37 C.F.R. § 10.23(a) by having been convicted for
possession of marijuana and paraphernalia, and, (2) 37 C.F.R. § 10.23(b)(6) by
engaging in disreputable or gross conduct that adversely reflects on his fitness
to practice; privately reprimanded).

Anonymous 7	March 27, 1998

In re Anonymous (Comm'r Pat. Mar. 27, 1998), *available at* http://www.uspto.
gov/web/offices/com/sol/foia/oed/disc/anonymous6.pdf (petition to reconsider
the OED director's decision was denied because petitioner failed to present
evidence that he had sufficient technical expertise, either by formal education

Cohen, Jonathan M.	D2002–09

In re Cohen, No. D2002–09 (USPTO Dir.), *available at* http://www.uspto.gov/
web/offices/com/sol/foia/oed/disc/C2001–65_Cohen_Jonathan_Final_Order.
pdf (practitioner violated 37 C.F.R. §§ 10.40(a), 10.66(b), and 10.77(c) by
representing two conflicted clients; publicly reprimanded by the director of the
USPTO).

Cohen, Matthew J.	D2002–15

In re Cohen, 66 U.S.P.Q.2d 1782 (USPTO Dir. 2002), *available at* http://www.
uspto.gov/web/offices/com/sol/foia/oed/disc/Cohen_Matthew.pdf
(practitioner violated (1) 37 C.F.R. §§ 10.77(b) and (c) by failing to respond to
office action, pay issue fees, and respond to non-fee publication requirements,
causing five patent applications to go abandoned, failing to inform clients of
issued Notice of Abandonment, and failing to seek to revive abandoned
applications, (2) 37 C.F.R. §§ 10.112(c)(2) and (c)(3) by failing to maintain
complete records of at least one client's application file, and allowing fees
paid by clients be deposited in a nonpractitioner's bank account, (3) 37 C.F.R.
§ 10.48 by sharing legal fees with a nonpractitioner, (4) 37 C.F.R. § 10.68(a)
by accepting at least once compensation, without consent of client after full
disclosure, from someone other than the client for legal services to or for that
client, (5) 37 C.F.R. § 10.23(b)(4) by engaging in conduct that involved
misrepresentation, and (6) 37 C.F.R. § 10.23(b)(6) by engaging in conduct that
adversely reflects on his fitness to practice before the USPTO; suspended for
18 months from practice before the USPTO).

Colitz, Michael J. Jr	D1999–04

Moatz v. Colitz, 68 U.S.P.Q.2d (USPTO Dir. 2003), *available at* http://www.
uspto.gov/web/offices/com/sol/foia/oed/disc/colitz_final_decision_recon.pdf
(practitioner violated (1) 37 C.F.R. §§ 10.47(a) and/or (c) "by aiding non-
practitioner invention development companies in the unauthorized practice of
law before the USPTO and/or by aiding the non-lawyer invention development
companies in the unauthorized practice of law," (2) 37 C.F.R. §§ 10.48 and/or
10.49 "by sharing legal fees with a non-practitioner and/or forming a
partnership with a non-practitioner to practice patent law before the USPTO,"
(3) 37 C.F.R. §§ 10.77(b) and/or (c) "by handling a legal matter without
preparation adequate under the circumstances and/or by neglecting a legal
matter entrusted to the practitioner," (4) 37 C.F.R. § 10.40(a) "by withdrawing
from employment without taking reasonable steps to avoid foreseeable

prejudice to the rights of his client(s)," and (5) 37 C.F.R. § 10.68 by permitting a nonpractitioner, who recommended and/or paid practitioner to render legal services to others, to direct and/or regulate practitioner's professional judgment in rendering such legal services; suspended from practice before the USPTO for five years, with the final two years to be stayed).

Combs, E. Michael	D1999–11

Moatz v. Combs, No. D99–11 (Dep't Comm. Feb. 16, 2000), *available at* http://www.uspto.gov/web/offices/com/sol/foia/oed/disc/D11.pdf (practitioner's Affidavit of Resignation was approved and entered; excluded on consent from practice before the USPTO).

Cooper, Byron W.	D2001–02

In re Cooper, No. D2001–02 (USPTO Dir. Feb. 13, 2001), *available at* http://www.uspto.gov/web/offices/com/sol/foia/oed/disc/D22.pdf (practitioner suspended from practice before the USPTO for 2 years, with an actual suspension time of 30 days because the 2-year suspension is stayed, and the practitioner is placed on probation for 2 years).

Corbin, Charles C.	D2000–12

In re Corbin, No. D2000–12 (Dep't Comm. Aug. 14, 2001), *available at* http://www.uspto.gov/web/offices/com/sol/foia/oed/disc/D28.pdf (practitioner violated (1) 37 C.F.R. §§ 10.23(b)(1) and (c)(5) by engaging in conduct resulting in suspension from practice as an attorney on ethical grounds in Colorado and Ohio, (2) 37 C.F.R. §§ 10.23(c)(16) and 10.131(b) "by failing to cooperate with OED's investigation concerning complaints and allegations" made against practitioner, (3) 37 C.F.R. §§ 10.23(b)(1), 10.23(b)(6), 10.77(c), 10.84(a)(1), and 10.84(a)(3) by failing to file the patent issue fee and the formal drawing within required time, causing an patent application to go abandoned, and failing to seek to revive the abandoned patent application, and (4) 37 C.F.R. §§ 10.23(b) (6) and 10.23(c)(14) by failing to notify the director of the suspension in two states, which would preclude continued registration with the USPTO, suspended for an indeterminate period from practice before the USPTO).

Corbin, Charles C.	D2001–14

In re Corbin, No. D2001–14 (Dep't Comm. Aug. 1, 2002), *available at* http://www.uspto.gov/web/offices/com/sol/foia/oed/disc/D2001–14.pdf (practitioner violated (1) 37 C.F.R. §§ 10.23(b)(4)-(6) by practicing before the USPTO in trademark cases while not being a licensed attorney, (2) 37 C.F.R. §§ 10.77(c), 10.84(a)(1), and 10.84(a)(3) by failing to inform a client of pertinent events and papers filed in a trademark opposition proceeding and causing a default judgment entered against the client in the proceeding; excluded from practice before the USPTO).

Dabney, Tami A	D2007–03

In re Dabney, No. D2007–03 (USPTO Dir. Mar. 27, 2007), *available at* http://www.uspto.gov/web/offices/com/sol/foia/oed/disc/d2007–03.pdf (practitioner violated 37 C.F.R. § 10.23(c)(5) by having her license to practice law in Ohio revoked for not disclosing past criminal convictions during applications to the Ohio Bar; suspended from practice before the USPTO for three months).

Davis, F. Eugene	D2001–10

In re Davis, No. D2001–10 (Dep't Comm. Jan. 28, 2002), *available at* http://www.uspto.gov/web/offices/com/sol/foia/oed/disc/D2001–10.pdf (practitioner in default violated 37 C.F.R. §§ 10.23(b)(1), 10.23(b)(6), 10.23(c)(5), 10.23(c)(14, 10.23(c)(16), and 10.131(b) by engaging in professional misconduct; excluded from practice before the USPTO).

Denenberg, David W.	D2006–20

In re Denenberg, No. D2006–20 (USPTO Dir. Dec. 18, 2006), *available at* http://www.uspto.gov/web/offices/com/sol/foia/oed/disc/d2006–20.pdf (practitioner violated 37 C.F.R. § 10.23(c)(5) by having been suspended from the practice of law in the State of New York for ninety days for (1) being convicted of "misconduct in relation to nominating petitions in violation of Election Law," and sentenced to a conditional discharge; suspended from practicing before the USPTO for three months).

DeSha, Michael J.	D2004–01

In re DeSha, No. D2004–01 (USPTO Dir. Dec. 24, 2003), *available at* http://www.uspto.gov/web/offices/com/sol/foia/oed/disc/D2004–01.pdf (practitioner was excluded on consent from practice before the USPTO).

| Dix, Brendan B. | D2001–15 |

In re Dix, No. D01–15 (Dep't Comm. Aug. 19, 2002), *available at* http://www.uspto.gov/web/offices/com/sol/foia/oed/disc/D2001–15.pdf (practitioner was suspended from practice before the USPTO for six months, with the six-month suspension stayed, and placed on probation for five years).

| Drake, Malik N. | D2006–08 Final Order |

In re Drake, No. D2006–08 (USPTO Dir. Nov. 27, 2006), *available at* http://www.uspto.gov/web/offices/com/sol/foia/oed/disc/d2006–08.pdf (practitioner violated 37 C.F.R. § 10.23(b)(4) by using government equipment to engage in activities related to practitioner's law practice; reprimanded).

| Dunsmuir, George H. | D2000–11 |

In re Dunsmuir, No. D2000–11 (Dep't Comm. Dec. 3, 2001), *available at* http://www.uspto.gov/web/offices/com/sol/foia/oed/disc/D2000–11.pdf (practitioner in default violated 37 C.F.R. § 10.23(c)(5); suspended from practice before the USPTO for five years).

| Eslinger, Lewis | D2004–03 |

In re Eslinger, No. D04–03 (Dep't Comm. July 30, 2004), *available at* http://www.uspto.gov/web/offices/com/sol/foia/oed/disc/D2004–03.pdf (practitioner was excluded on consent from practice before the USPTO).

| Flagg, Rodger H. | D2002–07 |

In re Flagg, No. D02–07 (Dep't Comm. July 7, 2002), *available at* http://www.uspto.gov/web/offices/com/sol/foia/oed/disc/D2002–07.pdf (practitioner's Affidavit of Resignation was approved and entered; excluded on consent from practice before the USPTO).

| Flynn, William C. | D2005–10 |

In re Flynn, No. D05–10 (USPTO Dir. Dec. 20, 2005), *available at* http://www.uspto.gov/web/offices/com/sol/foia/oed/disc/D05–10.pdf (practitioner violated

37 C.F.R. § 10.23(c)(5) by having been suspended from practice of law for five years by the Supreme Court of Minnesota for his criminal conviction related to possession of pornographic work involving minors; suspended for five years from practice before the USPTO).

Frease, John B.	D2000–02

Moatz v. Frease, No. D2000–02 (Dep't Comm. Aug. 22, 2000), *available at* http://www.uspto.gov/web/offices/com/sol/foia/oed/disc/D06.pdf (practitioner in default violated (1) 37 C.F.R. §§ 10.23(b)(1), (b)(6) and (c)(5) by having been suspended indefinitely from the practice of law in Ohio for violating its ethical rules of conduct, (2) 37 C.F.R. § 10.23(c)(14) by knowingly failing to advise the director of practitioner's suspension by the Supreme Court of Ohio, and (3) 37 C.F.R. §§ 10.23(c)(16) and 10.131(b) by willfully failing to reveal or report knowledge or evidence to the director in connection with investigations; suspended for an indeterminate period from practice before the USPTO).

Frederiksen, Mark D.	D2002–08

In re Frederiksen, No. D02–08 (USPTO Dir. Sept. 23, 2002), *available at* http://www.uspto.gov/web/offices/com/sol/foia/oed/disc/D2002–08.pdf (practitioner was publicly reprimanded by the Iowa Supreme Court and suspended by the Nebraska Supreme Court for misappropriating $15,000 from his own law firm, engaging conducts involving dishonesty, fraud, deceit, or misrepresentation, and failing to maintain complete records of all funds of a client coming into his possession; suspended for five years from practice before the USPTO).

Garmon, Judith E.	D1999–05

In re Garmon, No. D99–14 (USPTO Dir. July 28, 2000), *available at* http://www.uspto.gov/web/offices/com/sol/foia/oed/disc/D14.pdf (practitioner in default was excluded from practice before the USPTO).

Gernstein, Terry M.	D1999–06

In re Gernstein, No. D99–06 USPTO Dir. Apr. 9, 2001), *available at* http://www.uspto.gov/web/offices/com/sol/foia/oed/disc/D23.pdf (practitioner in a settlement of a disciplinary matter was suspended for three months from practice before the USPTO).

Gilliam, Steven Dale	D2002–04

Moatz v. Gilliam, No. D02–04 (Dep't Comm. Nov. 25, 2002), *available at*
http://www.uspto.gov/web/offices/com/sol/foia/oed/disc/D2002–04.pdf
(practitioner in default violated (1) 37 C.F.R. § 10.77(c) by failing to return a
client's phone calls and failing to file the client's patent application
while being paid more than $4,000 for services rendered, and (2) 37 C.F.R.
§§ 10.23(b)(5) and (c)(16) by failing to cooperate with the Director in
connection with an investigation and engaging in conduct prejudicial to
the administration of justice; excluded from practice before the USPTO).

Goates, Gary B.	D2000–03

Moatz v. Goates, No. D00–03 (Comm'r Pat. July 28, 2000), *available at* http://
www.uspto.gov/web/offices/com/sol/foia/oed/disc/D15.pdf (practitioner in a
settlement of a disciplinary matter was (1) suspended for one year from
practice before the USPTO, with the suspension stayed, and (2) publicly
reprimanded for conduct in violation of a rule in Patent and Trademark
Office Code of Professional Conduct [PTO Code]).

Gould, David F.	D1996–02

Bovard v. Gould, No. D96–02 (Dep't Comm. May 6, 1997), *available at*
http://www.uspto.gov/web/offices/com/sol/foia/oed/disc/D02.pdf (practitioner
in default violated (1) 37 C.F.R. §§ 10.23(a), 10.23(b)(6), 10.77(a), and
10.77(c) by failing to pursue the filing of a patent application for a client and
failing to keep the client informed regarding the status of the application,
(2) 37 C.F.R. §§ 10.23(a), 10.23(b)(6), 10.77(c), and 10.112(c)(4) by causing a
client to sign a declaration for a design patent application without providing a
typed specification, a claim, and necessary drawings to review before
signing the declaration, failing to conduct proper patent and trademark
searches for the client, failing to properly advise the client regarding legal
considerations bearing on client's efforts to obtain a patent and trademark,
and failing to return money paid by the client, (3) 37 C.F.R. §§ 10.23(b)(5),
10.23(c)(16), and 10.24(a) by failing to respond to communications from
the OED, which was investigating him, and (4) 37 C.F.R. §§ 10.23(a),
10.23(b)(4), 10.23(b)(6), and 10.23(d) by giving false testimony in a
disciplinary proceeding brought against him by the Board of Overseers of
the Bar of Maine; excluded from practice before the USPTO, with
practitioner's registration to practice as a patent attorney before the
PTO revoked).

Greenberg, Alan G.	D2000–05

In re Greenberg, No. D00–05 (Dep't Comm. Aug. 21, 2001), *available at* http://www.uspto.gov/web/offices/com/sol/foia/oed/disc/D2000–05.pdf (practitioner in default violated (1) 37 C.F.R. § 1023(c)(5) by having been disbarred by the Supreme Court of Minnesota on ethical grounds, (2) 37 C.F.R. § 1023(c)(5) by having been disbarred by the Supreme Court of the United States based on his disbarment in Minnesota, and (3) 37 C.F.R. §§ 10.23(b)(1), 10.23(b)(6), 10.23(c)(16), 10.24(a), and 10.131(b) by engaging in "conduct that adversely reflects on his fitness to practice before the USPTO," willfully refusing to "reveal or report knowledge or evidence to the Director," failing to "report to the Director unprivileged knowledge of a violation of a Disciplinary Rule," and failing to "cooperate with the Director in connection with any disciplinary proceeding"; excluded from practice before the USPTO).

Halvonik, John P.	D1995–03 Final Decision
	D1995–03 Petition

Bovard v. Halvonik, No. D96–03 (Comm'r Pat. Mar. 4, 1999), *available at* http://www.uspto.gov/web/offices/com/sol/foia/oed/disc/d1996–03.pdf (practitioner violated (1) 37 C.F.R. §§ 10.23(a) and 10.23(b)(6) "by filing a client's draft patent application without making the client's requested changes," (2) 37 C.F.R. § 10.77(c) "by delaying to determine which version of that patent application had been filed with the PTO," (3) 37 C.F.R. §§ 10.112(c)(4), 10.23(b)(6), 10.23(a) "by failing to pay back $500 to a client," and (4) 37 C.F.R. §§ 10.112(c)(4) and 10.23(b)(6) "by failing to return a client's disclosure materials"; suspended for seven months from practice before the USPTO, with three months vacated if the practitioner "completes and passes the Multi-State Bar Examination section on Professional Responsibility and enrolls in and completes a state or local bar association course(s) regarding the management of a sole practitioner office").

Bovard v. Halvonik, No. D96–03 (Comm'r Pat. Mar. 26, 1999), *available at* http://www.uspto.gov/web/offices/com/sol/foia/oed/disc/d1996–03pet.pdf (the final decision in disciplinary case D96–03 is stayed because practitioner filed petition stating his intention to seek judicial review of the decision).

Herring, Joseph C.	D2002–16

In re Herring, No. D02–16 (USPTO Dir. Sept. 20, 2002), *available at* http://www.uspto.gov/web/offices/com/sol/foia/oed/disc/D2002–16.pdf (practitioner was suspended for six months from practice before the USPTO in a settlement of disciplinary matter).

Hilke, Charles N.	D1999–13

In re Hilke, No. D99–13 (Comm'r Pat. Nov. 9, 1999), *available at* http://www. uspto.gov/web/offices/com/sol/foia/oed/disc/D09.pdf (practitioner's Affidavit of Resignation was approved and entered; excluded on consent from practice before the USPTO).

Hillman, Val Jean F.	D2002–17

In re Hillman, No. D2002–17 (USPTO Dir. May 31, 2002), *available at* http:// www.uspto.gov/web/offices/com/sol/foia/oed/disc/Hillmanredacted.pdf (practitioner's Affidavit of Resignation was approved and entered; excluded on consent from practice before the USPTO).

Hill, Kenneth E.	D2001–06

Moatz v. Hill, No. D2001–06 (USPTO Dir. July 26, 2004), *available at* http:// www.uspto.gov/web/offices/com/sol/foia/oed/disc/D2001–06.pdf (practitioner violated 37 C.F.R. § 10.77(c) by failing to file timely responses for office actions in 24 patent applications and causing the applications abandoned; reprimanded).

Ho, Lawrence Y.D.	D2006–18

In re Ho, No. D2006–18 (USPTO Dir. Jan. 17, 2007), *available at* http://www. uspto.gov/web/offices/com/sol/foia/oed/disc/D2006–18.pdf (practitioner violated 37 C.F.R. § 10.31(a) "by attempting to defraud, deceive and/or mislead prospective applications or other person having immediate or prospective business before the Office by advertising on the Firm's web site that he is registered with the USPTO, knowing that he was not registered"; reprimanded).

Hoffman, Bernard S.	D1999–01

Moatz v. Hoffman, No. D99–01 (Comm'r Pat. Oct. 13, 1999), *available at* http://www.uspto.gov/web/offices/com/sol/foia/oed/disc/D05.pdf (practitioner in a settlement agreement was suspended from practice before the USPTO for three months).

In re Hoffman (Comm'r Pat. Feb. 16, 2000), *available at* http://www.uspto.gov/web/offices/com/sol/foia/oed/disc/D12.pdf (practitioner's petition to seal the administrative record was denied because the "request is overly-broad and offers no showing why his desire to have the entire record kept confidential outweighs the public's right to access").

Hurey, Michael	D2000–06

In re Hurey, No. D00–06 (Dep't Comm. May 3, 2001), *available at* http://www.uspto.gov/web/offices/com/sol/foia/oed/disc/D24.pdf (practitioner in a settlement agreement was suspended from practice before the USPTO for four years).

Illich, Russell	D2000–13

In re Illich, No. D00–13 (Dep't Comm. June 28, 2001), *available at* http://www.uspto.gov/web/offices/com/sol/foia/oed/disc/D27.pdf (practitioner in default violated (1) 37 C.F.R. § 10.23(c)(16) by willfully refusing to reveal or report knowledge or evidence to the director, and/or (2) 37 C.F.R. § 10.131(b) by failing to cooperate with the director in connection with investigation; excluded from practice before the USPTO).

Jennings, Larry M	D2004–12

In re Jennings, No. D04–12 (USPTO Dir. Oct. 5, 2005), *available at* http://www.uspto.gov/web/offices/com/sol/foia/oed/disc/D04–12.pdf (practitioner violated (1) 37 C.F.R. § 10.23(b)(4) by representing in at least one letter to a client that an application was pending when the application was actually abandoned, (2) 37 C.F.R. § 10.23(c)(8) by failing to notify a client of the Notice of Abandonment in an application, (3) 37 C.F.R. § 10.77(c) by allowing an application to go abandoned while failing to notify the client of the Notice of Abandonment, (4) 37 C.F.R. § 10.23(c)(8) by failing to notify the client of the Notice of Abandonment in a second application, (5) 37 C.F.R. § 10.77(c) by allowing the second application to be come abandoned while failing to notify the client of the Notice of Abandonment, (6) 37 C.F.R. § 10.77(c) by "failing to deliver the PCT application to the U.S. Postal service before the deadline," and (7) 37 C.F.R. § 10.112(a) by failing to deposit the client's funds in an identifiable bank account and separately preserve the identity of the client's funds; suspended for one year from practice before the USPTO).

Johnson, Larry D.	D2001–09

In re Johnson, No. D2001–09 (USPTO Dir. July 9, 2001), *available at* http://
www.uspto.gov/web/offices/com/sol/foia/oed/disc/D25.pdf (practitioner
violated 37 C.F.R. § 10.23(b)(5) by settling a malpractice suit with a former
client on condition that the former client not "make, file, solicit or induce the
making of a complaint to" the USPTO; publicly reprimanded).

Kaardal, Ivar M.	D2003–08

In re Kaardal, No. D03–08 (USPTO Dir. Feb 24, 2004), *available at* http://
www.uspto.gov/web/offices/com/sol/foia/oed/disc/D2003–08.pdf (practitioner
violated (1) 37 C.F.R. § 10.23(b)(4) by engaging conduct involving dishonesty,
fraud, deceit, or misrepresentation, (2) § 10.23(b)(5) by engaging in conduct
prejudicial to the administration of justice, (3) § 10.23(c)(16) by willfully
refusing to reveal or report knowledge or evidence to the director of OED,
(4) § 10.23(c)(17) by failing to inform the inventor/client of the Federal Trade
Commission (FTC) consent decree, (5) §§ 10.47(a) and (c) by aiding a
nonpractitioner in the unauthorized practice of law and in practice before the
USPTO, (6) § 10.48 by sharing legal fees with a nonpractitioner, (7) § 10.62(a)
by accepting employment, without first giving the client full disclosure and
then getting the client's consent, when his professional judgment have been
affected by his own financial or business interests, (8) § 10.68(a)(1) by
accepting compensation "from someone other than his client without first
giving the client full disclosure and then getting the client's consent," and
(9) §§ 10.77(b) and (c) by handling "a legal matter without adequate
preparation or neglecting the legal matter entrusted to him"; excluded on
consent from practice before the USPTO).

Kearns, Jerry T.	D2001–07

In re Kearns, No. D2001–07 (USPTO Dir. June 8, 2001), *available at* http://
www.uspto.gov/web/offices/com/sol/foia/oed/disc/D21.pdf (practitioner was
reprimanded and voluntarily agreed "not to practice before the USPTO on any
matter whatsoever, and not to represent any client directly or indirectly in
any matter pending in the USPTO, for the duration of his disability from
practicing law in Colorado").

| Kersey, George E. | D2000–07 |

Moatz v. Kersey, 67 U.S.P.Q. 1291 (USPTO Dir. 2002), *available at* http://www.uspto.gov/web/offices/com/sol/foia/oed/disc/kersey_redacted.pdf (practitioner violated (1) 37 C.F.R. § 10.23(c)(20) by "representing private clients while employed by the U.S. Air Force," and (2) 37 C.F.R. §§ 10.23(c)(5) and 10.24 by "failing to report suspensions from the practice of law in two jurisdictions"; suspended from practice before the USPTO for six months).

| Kersey, George E. | D2004–05 |

Moatz v. Kersey, No. D2004–05, (USPTO Dir. June 27, 2007), *available at* http://www.uspto.gov/web/offices/com/sol/foia/oed/disc/D2004–05.pdf (practitioner violated (1) 37 C.F.R. § 10.23(c)(5) by "continuing to practice law while disbarred by the state of New Hampshire," and (2) 37 C.F.R. §§ 10.23(b) (5) and 10.24 by "failing to return client files and continuing to practice before the USPTO while under a suspension"; excluded from practice before the USPTO).

| Krause, Dean Luca | D2002–03 |

In re Krause, No. D2002–03 (May 14, 2002), *available at* http://www.uspto.gov/web/offices/com/sol/foia/oed/disc/D2002–03.pdf (practitioner violated 37 C.F.R. §§ 10.23(b)(6), 10.77(a), 10.77(b) and 10.77(c); privately reprimanded in a settlement of disciplinary action).

| Kroll, Michael I. | D2003–07 |

Moatz v. Kroll, No. D03–97 (USPTO Dir. Feb. 24, 2004), *available at* http://www.uspto.gov/web/offices/com/sol/foia/oed/disc/D2003–07.pdf (practitioner violated 37 C.F.R. §§ 10.36(a)(1), 10.23(c)(2)(ii), and 10.85(a)(6); suspended for three years from practice before the USPTO, with suspension stayed if practitioner complies with the terms of the agreement).

| Liniak, Thomas Paul | D2006–03A |

In re Liniak, No. D06–03 (USPTO Dir. Oct. 18, 2005), *available at* http://www.uspto.gov/web/offices/com/sol/foia/oed/disc/d06–03a.pdf (practitioner was excluded on consent from practice before the USPTO).

Lobato, Emmanuel J.	D2002–02

In re Lobato, No. D2002–02 (USPTO Dir. Feb. 4, 2002), *available at* http://www.uspto.gov/web/offices/com/sol/foia/oed/disc/D2002–02.pdf (practitioner was excluded on consent from practice before the USPTO).

Lynt, Christopher H.	D2005–08

In re Lynt, No. D05–08 (USPTO Dir.), *available at* http://www.uspto.gov/web/offices/com/sol/foia/oed/disc/D05–08.pdf (practitioner violated 37 C.F.R. § 10.23(c)(5) by having been suspended on ethical grounds by the Commonwealth of Virginia for coinventing and claiming the client's invention as the practitioner's own invention; suspended from practice for two years before the USPTO).

Maiorino, Salvatore J.	D2004–11

In re Maiorino, No. D2004–11 (USPTO Dir. Aug. 9, 2004), *available at* http://www.uspto.gov/web/offices/com/sol/foia/oed/disc/D2004–11.pdf (practitioner violated 37 C.F.R. §§ 10.23(a), (b)(3), (b)(6), and (c)(1) by having been convicted "on charges of Sexual Assault in the Fourth Degree in the Connecticut Superior Court for the Judicial District of New Haven at Meriden"; publicly reprimanded).

	D1995–03
Marinangeli, Michael G.	D1995–03 Reconsideration
	D1995–03 Petition

Bovard v. Marinangeli, No. D95–03 (Comm'r Pat. Apr. 24, 1997), *available at* http://www.uspto.gov/web/offices/com/sol/foia/oed/disc/D1995–03.pdf (practitioner violated 37 C.F.R. § 10.23(b)(3) by having been convicted for stealing credit cards and bank checks; suspended from practice before the USPTO for two years).

Bovard v. Marinangeli, No. D95–03 (Comm'r Pat. Sept. 5, 1997), *available at* http://www.uspto.gov/web/offices/com/sol/foia/oed/disc/D1995–03_recon.pdf (practitioner's request for reconsideration of the final decision was denied).

Bovard v. Marinangeli, No. D95–03 (Comm'r Pat. Oct. 7, 1997), *available at* (the final decision was stayed because of practitioner's intention to seek judicial review).

Marks, Andrew S.	D2005–05

In re Marks, No. D05–05 (USPTO Dir. July 7, 2005), *available at* http://www.
uspto.gov/web/offices/com/sol/foia/oed/disc/D05–05.pdf (practitioner violated
37 C.F.R. §§ 10.23(b)(4), 10.23(b)(6), 10.23(c)(1), 10.23(c)(5), and 10.57(b)(3)
by having been convicted for insider trading securities fraud and disbarred
from practice on ethical ground by the State Bar of New York; excluded for
five years from practice before the USPTO).

Marzocco, Ralph L.	D2000–04

In re Marzocco, No. D00–04 (Dep't Comm. Oct. 25, 2000), *available at* http://
www.uspto.gov/web/offices/com/sol/foia/oed/disc/D17.pdf (practitioner in
default violated (1) 37 C.F.R. §§ 10.23(b)(1), 10.23(b)(6), and 10.23(c)(5) by
having been disbarred by the Supreme Court of Ohio on ethical grounds,
(2) 37 C.F.R. §§ 10.23(b)(1), 10.23(b)(6), and 10.23(c)(14) by failing to "report
his disbarment by the Supreme Court of Ohio to the Director of the OED in a
timely manner," (3) 37 C.F.R. §§ 10.23(b)(1), 10.23(b)(6), and 10.23(c)(5) by
failing to "report his disbarment by the U.S. District Court for the Southern
District of Ohio on ethical grounds to the Director of OED in a timely
manner," and (4) 37 C.F.R. §§ 10.23(b)(1), 10.23(b)(6), 10.23(c)(16), and
10.131(b) by failing to respond in a timely manner to a Requirement for
Information issued by the OED; suspended for an indetermination period
from practice before the USPTO).

Maxwell, Micheal D.	D2006–10

In re Maxwell, No. D2006–10 (USPTO Dir. May 21, 2007), *available at* http://
www.uspto.gov/web/offices/com/sol/foia/oed/disc/d2006–10.pdf (practitioner
violated (1) 37 C.F.R. § 10.23(c)(5) by having been "suspended from the
practice of law on ethical grounds by the Supreme Court of Iowa," and
(2) 37 C.F.R. § 10.23(c)(14) by knowingly failing "to inform OED director of
his suspension before the Supreme Court of Iowa"; suspended for one year
from practice before the USPTO).

Morton, Richard F.	D2004–08

In re Morton, No. D04–08 (Dep't Comm. Mar. 22, 2005), *available at* http://
www.uspto.gov/web/offices/com/sol/foia/oed/disc/D2004–08.pdf (practitioner
violated (1) 37.C.F.R. § 10.23(b)(5) by prosecuting "a trademark application
while suspended from the practice of law," (2) 37 C.F.R. § 10.23(b)(6) by

engaging in conduct that adversely reflects his fitness to practice before the USPTO, and (3) 37 C.F.R. § 10.23(c)(5) by having been "suspended from practice as an attorney on ethical grounds by the Supreme Court of Illinois"; suspended from practice for one year after being readmitted by the Supreme Court of Illinois).

Mullen, Martin G.	D2001–13

In re Mullen, No. D2001–13 (USPTO Dir. Oct. 4, 2001), *available at* http://www.uspto.gov/web/offices/com/sol/foia/oed/disc/mullenredacted.pdf (practitioner was suspended from practice before the USPTO for four years in a settlement with OED director).

Reciprocal discipline by the State of Virginia was entered in this case in February 2002. *See In re Martin G. Mullen*, VSB Dkt. No. 02–000–1877.

Mybeck, II, Walter R.	D2001–05

In re Mybeck, No. D01–05 (Dep't Comm. Aug. 15, 2002), *available at* http://www.uspto.gov/web/offices/com/sol/foia/oed/disc/D2001–05.pdf (practitioner in default violated 37 C.F.R. §§ 10.23(b)(1), 10.23(c)(5), 10.23(c)(14), 10.23(c)(16), 10.77(c), 10.84(a)(1), and 10.84(a)(2) by having engaged in professional misconduct; excluded from practice before the USPTO).

Osredkar, Peter J.	D2006–03B

In re Osredkar, No. D06–03 (USPTO Dir. Mar. 28, 2006), *available at* http://www.uspto.gov/web/offices/com/sol/foia/oed/disc/d06–03b.pdf (practitioner violated (1) 37 C.F.R. § 10.23(b)(4) by presenting a forged letter of recommendation during job interviews with two law firms, by presenting to a law firm an altered law school transcript, by misrepresenting dates of his previous law firm employment on resumes submitted to two law firms, and by falsely representing prior employment on resumes submitted to law firms, (2) 37 C.F.R. § 10.23(c)(2)(ii) by giving false or misleading information to the OED regarding his knowledge about a forged letter of recommendation and an altered law school transcript, and (3) 37 C.F.R. § 10.23(c)(5) by having been disbarred in the State of New York; excluded from practice before the USPTO).

Peirce, Matthew J.	D2004–04

In re Peirce, No. D04–04 (USPTO Dir. Apr. 8, 2005), *available at* http://www.uspto.gov/web/offices/com/sol/foia/oed/disc/D2004–04.pdf (practitioner violated (1) 37 C.F.R. § 10.68(a)(1) by accepting "compensation from someone other than his client without first giving the client full disclosure and then getting the client's consent," and (2) 37 C.F.R. § 10.77 by failing to inform a client in a patentability opinion that the client's previous disclosure could potentially bar the client from obtaining a patent on the invention, filing a patent application five days after the deadline for claiming priority to the provisional application, failing to respond to the Notice to File corrected application papers for multiple patent applications, and causing the applications abandoned; suspended for two years from practice before the USPTO).

Reichmanis, Maria	D2001–04

In re Reichmanis, No. D2001–04 (Dep't Comm. Nov. 8, 2001), *available at* http://www.uspto.gov/web/offices/com/sol/foia/oed/disc/D29.pdf (practitioner violated (1) 37 C.F.R. § 10.77(c) by neglecting a legal matter entrusted to her, (2) 37 C.F.R. § 10.23(c)(16) by willfully refusing "to reveal or report knowledge or evidence to the Director," and (3) 37 C.F.R. § 10.131(b) by failing to "cooperate with an investigation by the Director"; excluded from practice before the USPTO).

Reynolds, David Duncan	D1999–12

Moatz v. Reynolds, No. D99–12 (Dep't Comm. Apr. 4, 2001), *available at* http://www.uspto.gov/web/offices/com/sol/foia/oed/disc/D20.pdf (practitioner violated (1) 37 C.F.R. §§ 10.23 (b)(6) and (c)(1) by having been convicted for hit and run, eluding, and DWI, all of which involve breach of trust, dishonesty and/or moral turpitude, and (2) 37 C.F.R. § 10.24(a) by failing to report the convictions to the USPTO; suspended for two years from practice before the USPTO).

Rivera, Chrispin M.	D2002–06

In re Rivera, 67 U.S.P.Q.2d 1952 (USPTO Dir. 2003), *available at* http://www. uspto.gov/web/offices/com/sol/foia/oed/disc/Riveraredacted.pdf (practitioner violated 37 C.F.R. § 10.23(c)(5) by having been suspended by the State Bar of Nevada "for violating ethical rules involving competence, diligence, communication, safekeeping property, and engaging in conduct involving dishonesty, fraud, deceit or misrepresentation"; suspended for two years from practice before the USPTO).

Rose, Stuart W.	D2006–16

Moazt v. Rose, No. D06–16 (Dep't Comm. June 14, 2007), *available at* http://
www.uspto.gov/web/offices/com/sol/foia/oed/disc/d2006–16.pdf (practitioner
violated 37 C.F.R. §§ 10.23(b)(3)-(4), (b)(6) and (c)(1) by having been convicted
of a felony, intent to manufacture a controlled substance, and sentenced to 14
years; excluded from practice before the USPTO).

Rosenberg, Marshall E.	D2006–07

Moatz v. Rosenberg, No. D06–07 (Dep't Comm. Mar. 7, 2007), *available at*
http://www.uspto.gov/web/offices/com/sol/foia/oed/disc/d2006–07.pdf
(practitioner violated (1) 37 C.F.R. §§ 10.23(b)(4), 10.23(c)(2)(i)–(ii), 10.23(c)
(3), 10.23(c)(8), 10.23(c)(15), 10.40(a), 10.77(b)–(c), 10.84(a)–(3), 10.85(4)–(6),
10.112(a), and 10.112(c)(3) by having been paid by a client for $4,000 plus
filing fee while filing the application without paying the filing fee, failing to
respond to PTO's notice, and causing the application to be abandoned,
(2) 37 C.F.R. §§ 10.77(b) and (c) by filing the application without paying the
filing fee, failing to respond to PTO's Notice to File Missing Parts, and
causing the application to be abandoned in other four separate occasions;
excluded from practice before the USPTO).

Rostoker, Michael David	D2004–15
	Attachment to Initial Decision

In re Rostoker, No. D04–15 (Dep't Comm. May 31, 2006), *available at* http://
www.uspto.gov/web/offices/com/sol/foia/oed/disc/d2004–15.pdf (practitioner
violated 37 C.F.R. §§ 10.23(b)(3)–(4), (b)(6), and (c)(1) by having been
convicted of eleven felony counts, and (2) 37 C.F.R. §§ 10.23(b)(1), (b)(6), and
(c)(5) for having been disbarred on ethical grounds by the Commonwealth of
Massachusetts; excluded from practice before the USPTO).

Ryznic, John E.	D2001–16

In re Ryznic, 67 U.S.P.Q.2d 1115 (USPTO Dir. 2003), *available at*
http://www.uspto.gov/web/offices/com/sol/foia/oed/disc/ryznicfinalorder.pdf
(practitioner violated (1) 37 C.F.R. § 10.23(b)(6) by "being a practitioner
who, as an employee of the Office, prosecuted or aided in any manner in the

prosecution of a patent application before the Office in violation of" 37 C.F.R. § 10.10(c), (2) § 10.23(c)(16) by failing to cooperate with "the Director in connection with an investigation," (3) § 10.23(c)(19) by aiding "in the prosecution of a patent application while employed by the USPTO," (4) § 10.23(c)(20) by knowingly engaging in "practice as a Government employee contrary to the applicable Federal conflict of interests laws, or regulations of the Department of Commerce and the USPTO," (5) § 10.40(b)(2) by failing to withdraw when it was obvious that practitioner's "continued representation would result in violation of the a Disciplinary Rule," (6) § 10.77(b) "by remaining agent of record when he entered on duty at the USPTO," (7) § 10.77(c) by failing to correct omissions in the specification that were "the best mode contemplated by the inventor of carrying out his invention," and (8) § 10.112(c)(3) by failing to "maintain at least one client's property in a safe matter" and "maintain and preserve complete records of at least one client's property"; suspended for two years from practice before the USPTO).

Schaefer, Kenneth R.	D2007–01

In re Schaefer, No. D2007–01 (USPTO Dir. Apr. 30, 2007), *available at* http://www.uspto.gov/web/offices/com/sol/foia/oed/disc/d2007–01.pdf (practitioner violated (1) 37 C.F.R. § 10.23(b)(5) by allowing an application to become abandoned without the client's consent, (2) 37 C.F.R. § 10.77(c) by allowing an application to become abandoned, failing to report to the client the substance of a call from the patent examiner, failing to notify the client the Notice of Abandonment of an application, failing to revive the application that had become abandoned, and failing to notify the client of the opportunity to revive the application, and (3) 37 C.F.R. § 10.40(a) by failing to withdraw from the application and failing to deliver to the client papers and other property belonging to the client, including the application file; suspended for three months from practice before the USPTO).

Schwartz, Stanley D.	D2008–01

In re Schwartz, No. D2008–01 (USPTO Dir. Oct. 29, 2007), *available at* http://www.uspto.gov/web/offices/com/sol/foia/oed/disc/D2008–01.pdf (practitioner violated 37 C.F.R. §§ 10.23(b)(3) and (5)–(6) by having been found guilty by a Maryland Circuit Court for (1) sexual abuse of a minor, (2) sexual offense in the fourth degree, and (3) sexual offense in the third degree; excluded from practice before the USPTO).

Sheinbein, Sol	D2003–14
	D03–14 Reconsideration
	D03–14 Stay

Moatz v. Sheinbein, No. D03–14 (USPTO Dir. May 5, 2005), *available at* http://www.uspto.gov/web/offices/com/sol/foia/oed/disc/D03–14.pdf (practitioner violated 37 C.F.R. §§ 10.23(a), (b), and (c)(5) by having been disbarred on ethical grounds from practice law in Maryland and District of Columbia for sending his son to Israel after (1) being told by his son that he killed another person, and (2) knowing that his son was being investigated by homicide detectives; excluded from practice before the USPTO).

Moatz v. Sheinbein, No. D03–14 (USPTO Dir. June 23, 2005), *available at* http://www.uspto.gov/web/offices/com/sol/foia/oed/disc/D03–14RH.pdf (practitioner's petition for reconsideration of the Final Decision D03–14 was denied).

Moatz v. Sheinbein, No. D03–14 (PTO, Dir. June 23, 2005), *available at* (practitioner's petition for stay of a final decision was denied because the petition "does not raise sufficient basis for a stay").

Spangler, Jeffrey Thomas	D2005–03

In re Spangler, No. D05–03 (Dep't Comm. Oct. 18, 2005), *available at* http://www.uspto.gov/web/offices/com/sol/foia/oed/disc/D05–03.pdf (practitioner violated 37 C.F.R. § 10.23(c)(5) by having been suspended on ethical grounds by the Supreme Court of Pennsylvania for his assault and reckless endangerment convictions; suspended for 18 months from practice before the USPTO).

Stanback, Jr., Clarence F.	D2000–14

In re Stanback, No. D00–14 (USPTO Dir. Apr. 2, 2001), *available at* http://www.uspto.gov/web/offices/com/sol/foia/oed/disc/D18.pdf (practitioner was suspended for five years from practice before the USPTO in a settlement agreement).

Sturges, Hiram	D1999–09

Moatz v. Sturges, No. D99–09 (Comm'r Pat. Feb. 2, 2000), *available at* http://www.uspto.gov/web/offices/com/sol/foia/oed/disc/D10.pdf (practitioner was excluded on consent from practice before USPTO).

Sylvester, Bradley P.	D2005–06

In re Sylvester, No. D05–06 (USPTO Dir. Mar. 15, 2006), *available at* http://www.uspto.gov/web/offices/com/sol/foia/oed/disc/d05–06.pdf (practitioner violated (1) 37 C.F.R. § 10.23(c)(8) by failing to inform a client of "the Notice of Abandonment received from the USPTO when the correspondence (i) could have a significant effect on a matter pending before the Office, (ii) was received by the practitioner on behalf of a client, and (iii) was correspondence of which a reasonable practitioner would believe under the circumstances the client should be notified," (2) 37 C.F.R. § 10.77(c) by "neglecting the patent application that was entrusted to him" by a client, (3) 37 C.F.R. § 10.84(a)(2) "by failing to carry out the contract of employment with" a client to prosecute a patent application, (4) 37 C.F.R. § 10.84(3) by prejudicing and damaging a client during the attorney-client relationship, and (5) 37 C.F.R. § 10.112(c)(4) by failing to promptly deliver a client's property as requested; suspended for six months from practice before the USPTO).

Tassan, Bruce A.	D2003–10

In re Tassan, No. D03–10 (USPTO Dir. Sept. 8, 2003), *available at* http://www.uspto.gov/web/offices/com/sol/foia/oed/disc/tassan_bruce_a.pdf (practitioner violated 37 C.F.R. §§ 10.23(b)(5), (b)(6), (c)(5), and 10.93(b) by (1) communicating orally as to the merits of the cause with Trademark Trial and Appeal Board (TTAB) judges in an *inter partes* proceeding without notice to the opposing counsel, and (2) leaving improper voice mails to TTAB judges; publicly reprimanded, prohibited for two years from "communicating personally by telephone or in-person with the TTAB regarding any matter in which he is representing a client," except that he "may participate fully on behalf of clients in hearings before the TTAB," and required to "complete a course of treatment for anger management," completion of which shall "be confirmed in a letter signed by his counselor to the OED Director").

Teplitz, Jerome M.	D2000–10

Moatz v. Teplitz, No. D2000–10 (USPTO Dir. May 6, 2002), *available at*
http://www.uspto.gov/web/offices/com/sol/foia/oed/disc/teplitz_final_order_
and_recon.pdf (practitioner violated 37 C.F.R. §§ 10.23(b)(1), (b)(6), and
(c)(5) by having been suspended by both the Supreme Court of Illinois and
the U.S. District Court for the Northern District of Illinois for breaching the
attorney-client relationship; suspended for three years from practice
before the USPTO).

Uland, Larry L.	D1999–03

Bovard v. Uland, 56 U.S.P.Q.2d 1531 (Dep't Comm. 1999), *available at*
http://www.uspto.gov/web/offices/com/sol/foia/oed/disc/D04.pdf
(practitioner violated (1) 37 C.F.R. §§ 10.23(a), 10.23(b)(6), 10.77(a),
10.77(c), 10.84(a)(2), 10.84(a)(3), 10.112(c)(3), and 10.112(c)(4) by failing
to file a responsive amendment in a patent application at a client's request
and failing to repay the client $500 for service he did not render, and
(2) 37 C.F.R. §§ 10.23(a), 10.23(b)(6), 10.77(a), 10.77(c), 10.84(a)(2),
10.84(a)(3), and 10.112(c)(4) by failing to file a patent application 18 months
after being retained and failing to repay a client $2,500 for service he did
not render; suspended for an indeterminate period from practice before
the USPTO).

Van Der Wall, Robert J.	D2004–02

In re Van Der Wall, No. D04–02 (USPTO Dir. May 27, 2004), *available at*
http://www.uspto.gov/web/offices/com/sol/foia/oed/disc/D2004–02.pdf
(practitioner violated (1) 37 C.F.R. § 10.23(b)(8) by failing to inform a client of
a Notice of Abandonment, and (2) 37 C.F.R. § 10.77(c) by neglecting to
"communicate with his client before adding an inventor to a PCT application";
reprimanded).

Vander Weit, John, Jr.	D2006–11

In re Vander Weit, No. D06–11 (Dep't Comm. July 31, 2007), *available at*
http://www.uspto.gov/web/offices/com/sol/foia/oed/disc/D2006–11.pdf
(practitioner violated 37 C.F.R. § 10.23(c)(5) by having been suspended by
the Supreme Court of Illinois; suspended indefinitely from practice before
the USPTO).

Volk, David L.	D1999–14

In re Volk, No. C97–53 and C97–75 (Comm'r Pat. Aug. 6, 1999), *available at* http://www.uspto.gov/web/offices/com/sol/foia/oed/disc/D08.pdf (practitioner was excluded on consent from practice before the USPTO).

Wengrovsky, Todd	D2003–09
	Addendum A
	Addendum B

In re Wengrovsky, No. D03–09 (USPTO Dir.), *available at* http://www.uspto. gov/web/offices/com/sol/foia/oed/disc/D2003–09.pdf (practitioner, "a person not registered to practice patent law before the USPTO," violated (1) 37 C.F.R. § 10.23(b)(2) by circumventing 37 C.F.R. §§ 10.112(b) and (c) through the acts of another, (2) 37 C.F.R. § 10.23(b)(4) by "engaging in conduct involving misrepresentation before the USPTO," (3) 37 C.F.R. § 10.23(b)(5) by engaging in conduct prejudicial to the administration of justice for failing to cooperate in an investigation, (4) 37 C.F.R. § 10.23(b)(6) by engaging in conduct reflecting adversely on his fitness to practice, (5) 37 C.F.R. § 10.24 by failing to cooperate in an investigation, (6) 37 C.F.R. § 10.32(c) by "advertising in a telephone directory without including the name of at least one registered practitioner responsible for the advertisement's content," (7) 37 C.F.R. § 10.47 by "assisting another in the unauthorized practice of law before the USPTO," (8) 37 C.F.R. § 10.48 by sharing legal fees with a nonpractitioner, (9) 37 C.F.R. § 10.49 by "forming a partnership with a nonpractitioner, and through this partnership practicing patent, trademark, or other law before the USPTO," (10) 37 C.F.R. §§ 10.57(c)–(d) by failing to obtain, after full disclosure by practitioner, "consent from the clients to disclose their inventions and patent applications to a non-practitioner," (11) 37 C.F.R. § 10.68(a)(1) by failing to obtain consent from the client after full disclosure by practitioner of all conflicts arising from his compensation from the partnership, (12) 37 C.F.R. § 10.77(a) by "failing to associate with someone registered to practice patent law before the USPTO," and (13) 37 C.F.R. §§ 10.112(a)–(c) by maintaining client legal fees in the partnership's business checking account; reprimanded, "prohibited from practicing and/or aiding others in the practice of patent law before the USPTO," and placed on probation subject to terms).

Wittenberg, Malcom B.	D2003–12

Moatz v. Wittenberg, No. D2003–12 (USPTO Dir. June 16, 2004), *available at* http://www.uspto.gov/web/offices/com/sol/foia/oed/disc/D2003–12.pdf (practitioner violated (1) 37 C.F.R. §§ 10.23(b)(4), (b)(6), (c)(1), and 10.57(b)(3) by trading in a client's stock on inside information and by having been convicted for insider trading, and (2) 37 C.F.R. §§ 10.23(b)(6) and (c)(5) by having been disbarred on ethical grounds by Virginia State Bar; excluded on consent from practice before the USPTO).

Ziegler, Thomas K.	D2000–09

In re Ziegler, No. D00–09 (USPTO Dir. Aug. 29, 2001), *available at* http://www.uspto.gov/web/offices/com/sol/foia/oed/disc/D2000–09.pdf (practitioner was suspended for 179 days from practice before the USPTO).

Correlation Tables

The following tables, from the U.S. Patent and Trademark Office (PTO), correlates the Patent and Trademark Office Code of Professional Conduct (PTO Code) with other ethical codes. *See also* Timir Chheda, *A Handy List: Comparison of the ABA Model Rules of Professional Conduct with the Patent Rules of Ethics,* 5 J. Marshall Rev. Intell. Prop. L. 477 (2006).

Table 1 Principal Source Of Sections 11.1 through 11.18

Section	Source	Part 10 Concordance
§ 11.1	37 C.F.R. 10.1	§ 10.1
MRPR		
§ 11.2	37 C.F.R. 10.2	§ 10.2
DC RULE XI, § 6		
§ 11.3	37 C.F.R. 10.170	§ 10.170
§ 11.4	37 C.F.R. 10.3	§ 10.3
§ 11.5	37 C.F.R. 10.5	§ 10.5
§ 11.6	37 C.F.R. 10.6	§ 10.6
§ 11.7(a)(b)	37 C.F.R. 10.7(a)	§ 10.7(a)
§ 11.7(b)(1)	37 C.F.R. 10.7(b)	§ 10.7(b)
§ 11.7(b)(2)	New	None
37 C.F.R. 1.8 and 1.10	None	
§ 11.7(c)	Case law	None
RDCCA 46(12)(ii), third sentence		
§ 11.7(d)	New	§ 10.7(b)
§ 11.7(e)	New	None
§ 11.7(f)	37 C.F.R. 10.6(c)	§ 10.6(c)
37 C.F.R. 10.7(b)	§ 10.7(b)	
§ 11.7(g)	37 C.F.R. 10.7(a)	§ 10.7(a)
§ 11.7(h)	Case law	None
California State Bar Policy	None	
FlaRSC 2–13	None	
GaSCR Part A, § 11	None	
MoSCR 8.05	None	

§ 11.7(i) .... California State Bar Policy .... None
§ 11.7(j) .... RDCCA 46(f)–(g) .... None

Willner v. Comm. on Character & Fitness, 373 U.S. 96 (1963)
§ 11.7(k) .... Colo. Rule 201.12 .... None
§ 11.8(a) .... RDCCA 46(b)(10) .... None
§ 11.8(b)–(c) .... RDCCA 46(h)(2), (3) .... None
§ 11.8(d) .... OGVSB Rule 11 .... None
§ 11.9(a)–(c) .... 37 C.F.R. 10.9(a)–(c) .... § 10.9
§ 11.10(a) .... 37 C.F.R. 10.10(a) .... § 10.10
§ 11.10(b) .... 5 C.F.R. 2637.201 .... § 10.10(b)
5 C.F.R. 2637.202 .... § 10.10(b)
§ 11.10(c) .... 5 C.F.R. 2637.201 .... None
5 C.F.R. 2637.202 .... None
§ 11.10(d)–(e) .... 37 C.F.R. 10.10(c)–(d) .... § 10.10(c)–(d)
§ 11.11(a) .... 37 C.F.R. 10.11(a) .... § 10.11(a)
§ 11.11(b) .... OGVSB Rule 19 .... None
§ 11.11(c) .... New .... None
§ 11.11(d) .... New .... None
§ 11.11(e)–(f) .... 1064 Off.Gaz.12 .... None
§ 11.12(a)–(d) .... OGVSB Rule 17 .... None
§ 11.12(e) .... OGVSB Rule 19 .... None
§ 11.13 .... OGVSB Rule 17 .... None
§ 11.14 .... 37 C.F.R. 10.14 .... § 10.14
§ 11.15 .... 37 C.F.R. 10.15 .... § 10.15
§ 11.16 .... New .... None

§ 11.17 [Reserved]
§ 11.18 .... 37 C.F.R. 10.18 .... § 10.18

Abbreviations:
Colo. Rule = Rules Governing Admission to the Bar of the State of Colorado (Mar. 23, 2000).
DC RULE XI = Rule XI of the Rules Governing the District of Columbia Bar.
FlaLRSC 2–13 = Rule 2–13 of the Florida Rules of the Supreme Court Relating to Admissions to the Bar.
Fed. R. Civ. P. 11
GaSCR Part A, § 11 = Part A, Rule 11 of the Georgia Supreme Court Rules Governing Admission to the Practice of Law.
MoSCR 8.05 = Rule 8.05 of the Missouri Supreme Court Rules Governing Admission to the Bar in Missouri.
OGVSB = Organization & Government of the Virginia State Bar.
RDCCA = Rules of the District of Columbia Court of Appeals.

Table 2 Principal Source of Sections 11.19 through 11.62

Section	Source	Part 10 Concordance
§ 11.19	DC RULE XI	§ 10.1, 10.2
37 C.F.R. 10.130	§ 10.130	
§ 11.20	DC RULE XI, § 3	None
§ 11.21	DC BPR Chap. 6	None
§ 11.22	DC BPR Chap. 2	None
§ 11.23	37 C.F.R. 10.4	§ 10.4
§ 11.24	DC BPR Chap. 10	None
§ 11.25	DC BPR Chap. 8	None
Calif. § 6102(d)	None	
§ 11.26	DC BPR Chap	None
§ 11.27	37 C.F.R. 10.133	§ 10.133

DC BPR Chap.15

§ 11.28	DC BPR Chap. 14	None

DC RULE XI, §13
§§ 11.29–11.31 [Reserved]

§ 11.32	37 C.F.R. 10.132	§ 10.132

§ 11.33 [Reserved]

§ 11.34	37 C.F.R. 10.134	§ 10.134
§ 11.35	37 C.F.R. 10.135	§ 10.135
§ 11.36	37 C.F.R. 10.136	§ 10.136
§ 11.37	37 C.F.R. 10.137	§ 10.137
§ 11.38	37 C.F.R. 10.138	§ 10.138
§ 11.39	37 C.F.R. 10.139	§ 10.139
§ 11.40	37 C.F.R. 10.140	§ 10.140
§ 11.41	37 C.F.R. 10.141	§ 10.141
§ 11.42	37 C.F.R. 10.142	§ 10.142
§ 11.43	37 C.F.R. 10.143	§ 10.143
§ 11.44	37 C.F.R. 10.144	§ 10.144
§ 11.45	37 C.F.R. 10.145	§ 10.145

§§ 11.46–11.48 [Reserved]

§ 11.49	37 C.F.R. 10.149	§ 10.149
§ 11.50	37 C.F.R. 10.150	§ 10.150
§ 11.51	37 C.F.R. 10.151	§ 10.151
§ 11.52	37 C.F.R. 10.152	§ 10.152
§ 11.53	37 C.F.R. 10.153	§ 10.153
§ 11.54	37 C.F.R. 10.154	§ 10.154
§ 11.55(a)	37 C.F.R. 10.155(a)	§ 10.155(a)

FRAP Rule 28

§ 11.55(b)	FRAP Rule 28	None

FRAP Rule 32(a)(4), and (7)
FRAP Rule 32(a)(4), (5) and (6)
§ 11.55(c)–(e) .... 37 C.F.R. 10.155(b)–(d) .... § 10.155(b)–(d)
§ 11.56 .... 37 C.F.R. 10.157 .... § 10.157
§ 11.58 .... 37 C.F.R. 10.158 .... § 10.158

DC Rule XI, §14
Calif. Rule 955
§ 11.59 .... 37 C.F.R. 10.159 .... § 10.159
§ 11.60 .... 37 C.F.R. 10.160 .... § 10.160

DC RULE XI, §16
DC BPR Chap. 9
§ 11.61 .... 37 C.F.R. 10.161 .... § 10.161
§ 11.62 .... New

Abbreviations:
Calif § 6102(d) = Article 6, § 6102(d) of the California State Bar Act.
Calif. Rule = California Bar Rule.
DC BPR = Rules of the District of Columbia Court of Appeals Board of Professional Conduct (1999).
DC RULE XI = Rule XI of the Rules Governing the District of Columbia Bar (1999).
FRAP = Federal Rules of Appellate Procedure.

Table 3 Principal Source of Sections 11.100 through 11.806

Section Source Part 10 Concordance

Competence
§ 11.101(a) .... MRPR 1.1 .... § 10.77(a)
§ 11.101(b) .... DCRPR 1.1b .... None
§ 11.101(c)(1) .... § 10.23(c)(7) .... § 10.23(c)(7)
§ 11.101(c)(2) .... § 10.23(c)(13) .... § 10.23(c)(13)
§ 11.101(c)(3) .... § 10.23(c)(19) .... § 10.23(c)(19)
§ 11.101(c)(4) .... § 10.23(c)(20) .... § 10.23(c)(20)

Scope of Representation
§ 11.102(a) .... MRPR 1.2(a) .... § 10.84(a)(1)
§ 11.102(b) .... MRPR 1.2(b) .... None
§ 11.102(c) .... MRPR 1.2(c) .... § 10.84(b)
§ 11.102(d) .... MRPR 1.2(d) .... § 10.85(a)(6)(7)(8)
§ 10.89
§ 11.102(e) .... MRPR 1.2(e) .... § 10.40(c)(1)(iii)
§ 10.111(c)
§ 11.102(f) .... DCRPR 1.2(d) .... None

Diligence
§ 11.103(a) .... MRPR 1.3 .... § 10.77(c)
§ 10.84(a)(1), (3)
§ 11.103(b)–(c) .... New .... § 10.77(c)
§ 10.84(a)(1), (3)

Communication
§ 11.104(a) .... MRPR 1.4(a) .... § 10.77(c)
§ 10.84(a)(1)(3)
§ 11.104(b) .... MRPR 1.4(b) .... None
§ 11.104(c) .... DCRPR 1.4(c) .... None
§ 11.104(d)(1) .... 10.23(c)(8) .... § 10.23(c)(8)

Fees
§ 11.105(a) .... MRPR 1.5(a) .... § 10.36(a)(b)
§ 11.105(b)–(c) .... MRPR 1.5(b)–(c) .... None
§ 11.105(e)(1) .... MRPR 1.5(e)(1) .... § 10.37(a)
§ 11.105(e)(2)–(4) .... DCRPR 1.5(e)(2)–(4) .... § 10.37(a)
§ 11.105(f) .... MRPR 1.5(f) .... None

Confidentiality
§ 11.106(a)(1) .... MRPR 1.6(a) .... § 10.57(a)(b)(c)
§ 11.106(a)(2)–(3) .... DCRPR 1.6 .... § 10.57(a)(b)(c)
§ 11.106(b)(1) .... MRPR 1.6(b)(2) .... § 10.57(c)(4)
§ 11.106(b)(2) .... MRPR 1.6(b)(2) .... None
§ 11.106(c) .... 37 C.F.R. 1.56 .... None
§ 11.106(d)–(h) .... DCRPR 1.6 .... None

Conflicts of Interest
§ 11.107(a) .... MRPR 1.7 .... § 10.62(a)
§ 10.66(a)(b)
§ 10.68(b)
§ 11.107(b)&(b)(1) .... MRPR 1.7 .... § 10.62(a)(b)
§ 10.63
§ 10.65(a)
§ 10.66(a)(b)(c)
§ 10.68(a)
§ 11.107(b)(2) .... MRPR 1.7 .... None

Prohibited Transactions
§ 11.108(a) .... MRPR 1.8(a) .... § 10.65(a)
§ 11.108(b) .... MRPR 1.8(b) .... § 10.57(b)
§ 11.108(c) .... MRPR 1.8(c) .... None
§ 11.108(d) .... MRPR 1.8(d) .... None
§ 11.108(e) .... MRPR 1.8(e) .... § 10.64(b)
§ 11.108(f) .... MRPR 1.8(f) .... § 10.68(a)(b)

§ 11.108(f)(1)(ii) .... New .... None
§ 11.108(g) .... MRPR 1.8(g) .... § 10.67(a)
§ 11.108(h) .... MRPR 1.8(h) .... § 10.63(a)
§ 11.108(i) .... MRPR 1.8(i) .... None
§ 11.108(j) .... MRPR 1.8(j) .... § 10.62(a)
§ 10.64(a)
35 U.S.C. 4
§ 11.108(k) .... New .... None

Former Client
§ 11.109(a) .... MRPR 1.9(a) .... § 10.66(c)
§ 11.109 (b) .... MRPR 1.9(b) .... None
§ 11.109 (c) .... MRPR 1.9(c) .... None

Imputed Disqualification
§ 11.110(a) .... MRPR 1.10(a) .... § 10.66(d)
§ 11.110(b) .... MRPR 1.10(b) .... § 10.66(d)
§ 11.110(c) .... MRPR 1.10(c) .... § 10.66(a)

Government/Private
§ 11.111(a) .... MRPR 1.11(a) .... § 10.111(b)
§ 11.111(b) .... MRPR 1.11(b) .... None
§ 11.111(c) .... MRPR 1.11(c) .... None
§ 11.111(d) .... MRPR 1.11(d) .... None
§ 11.111(e) .... MRPR 1.11(e) .... None

Former Judge
§ 11.112(a)(b) .... MRPR 1.12(a)(b) .... § 10.111(a)(b)
§ 11.112(c) .... MRPR 1.12(c) .... § 10.66(d)
§ 11.112(d) .... MRPR 1.12(d) .... None

Organization as Client
§ 11.113(a) .... MRPR 1.13(a) .... None
§ 11.113(b) .... MRPR 13(b) .... § 10.68(b)
§ 11.113(c) .... MRPR 1.13(c) .... § 10.66(d)
§ 10.68(b)
§ 11.113(d) .... MRPR 1.13(d) .... None
§ 11.113(e) .... MRPR 13(e) .... § 10.66(b)(c)

Disabled Client
§ 11.114............................ MRPR 1.14 .... None

Safekeeping of Property
§ 11.115(a) .... VRPC 1.15(a) .... § 10.112(a)
§ 11.115(b) .... New .... None
§ 11.115(c) .... VRPC 1.15(b) .... § 10.112(b)(2)
§ 11.115(d) .... VRPC 1.15(c) .... § 10.112(c)
§ 11.115(e)–(f) .... VRPC 1.15(d)–(e) .... § 10.112(c)(3)

§ 11.115(g) .... VRCP 1.15(f) .... None
§ 11.115(h)–(i) .... § 10.23(c)(3) .... § 10.23(c)(3)

Declining/Terminating Representation
§ 11.116(a)(1) .... MRPR 1.16(a)(1) .... § 10.39
§ 10.40(b)(1)(2)
§ 11.116(a)(2) .... MRPR 1.16(a)(2) .... § 10.40(b)(3)
§ 10.40(c)(4)
§ 11.116(a)(3) .... MRPR 1.16(a)(3) .... § 10.40(b)(4)
§ 11.116(b)(1) .... MRPR 1.16(b)(1) .... § 10.40(c)(1)(ii)(iii)
§ 10.40(c)(2)
§ 11.116(b)(2) .... MRPR 1.16(b)(2) .... § 10.40(c)(1)(iv)
§ 11.116(b)(3) .... MRPR 1.16(b)(3) .... § 10.40(c)(1)(vi)(ix)(x)
§ 11.116(b)(5) .... MRPR 1.16(b)(5) .... § 10.40(c)(1)(iv)(v)
§ 11.116(b)(6) .... MRPR 1.16(b)(6) .... § 10.40(c)(6)
§ 11.116(c) .... MRPR 1.16(c) .... § 10.40(a)
§ 11.116(d) .... MRPR 1.16(d) .... § 10.40(a)

Sale of Practice
§ 11.117 .... MRPR 1.17 .... None
§§ 11.118–11.200 [Reserved]

Advisor
§ 11.201(a) .... MRPR 2.1(a) .... § 10.68(b)
§ 11.201(b) .... New .... None

Intermediary
§ 11.202(a)(1) .... MRPR 2.2(a)(1) .... § 10.66(a)(c)
§ 11.202(a)(2) .... MRPR 2.2(a)(2) .... § 10.66(a)(c)
§ 11.202(a)(3) .... MRPR 2.2(a)(3) .... § 10.66(a)(c)
§ 11.202(b) .... New .... None
§ 11.202(c) .... MRPR 2.2(b) .... None
§ 11.202(c) .... MRPR 2.2(c) .... § 10.66(b)(c)

Evaluation for Third Party
§ 11.203 .... MRPR 2.3 .... None
§§ 11.204–11.300 [Reserved]

Meritorious Claim
§ 11.301 .... MRPR 3.1 .... § 10.63(a)(b)
§ 10.39(a)(b)
§ 10.85(a)(1)(2)

Expediting Litigation
§ 11.302(a) .... MRPR 3.2 .... § 10.23(b)(5)
§ 10.84(a)(1)(2)
§ 11.302(b) .... DCRPR 3.2(a) .... None

Candor
§ 11.303(a)(1) .... MRPR 3.3(a)(1) .... § 10.23(b)(4)(5)
§ 10.85(a)(4)(5)
§ 11.303(a)(2) .... MRPR 3.3(a)(2) .... § 10.23(b)(4)(5)
§ 10.85(a)(3)
§ 10.85(b)(1)
§ 10.92(a)
§ 11.303(a)(3) .... MRPR 3.3(a)(3) .... § 10.85(a)(5)
§ 10.89(b)(1)
§ 11.303(a)(4) .... MRPR 3.3(a)(4) .... § 10.23(b)(4)(5)
§ 10.85(a)(7)
§ 10.85(b)(1)
§ 11.303(b) .... MRPR 3.3(b) .... § 10.85(b)
§ 11.303(c)(d) .... MRPR 3.3(c)(d) .... None
§ 11.303(e)(1) .... § 10.23(c)(9) .... § 10.23(c)(9)
§ 11.303(e)(2) .... § 10.23(c)(10) .... § 10.23(c)(10)
§ 11.303(e)(3) .... § 10.23(c)(11) .... § 10.23(c)(11)
§ 11.303(e)(4) .... § 10.23(c)(15) .... § 10.23(c)(15)
§ 11.303(c)(5) .... § 10.23(c)(2)(ii) .... § 10.23(c)(2)(ii)
Fairness
§ 11.304(a) .... MRPR 3.4(a) .... § 10.23(b)(4)(5)
§ 10.89(c)(6)
MRPR 3.4(b) .... § 10.23(b)(4)(5)(6)
§ 10.85(a)(6)
§ 10.92(c)
§ 11.304(c) .... MRPR 3.4(c) .... § 10.23(b)(5)
§ 10.89(a)
§ 10.89(c)(5)(7)
§ 11.304(d) .... MRPR 3.4(d) .... § 10.23(b)(5)
§ 10.89(a)
§ 10.89(c)(6)
§ 11.304(e) .... MRPR 3.4(e) .... § 10.23(b)(5)
§ 10.89(c)(1)(2)(3)(4)

Impartiality
§ 11.305(a) .... MRPR 3.5(a) .... § 10.89
§ 10.92
§ 10.101(a)
§ 11.305(b) .... MRPR 3.5(b) .... None
§ 11.305(c) .... MRPR 3.5(c) .... § 10.84(a)
§ 10.89(c)(5)
§ 11.305(d)(1) .... § 10.23(c)(4) .... § 10.23(c)(4)

Trial Publicity
§ 11.306 [Reserved]

Practitioner as Witness
§ 11.307(a) .... MRPR 3.7(a) .... § 10.62(b)(1)(2)
§ 10.63
§ 11.307(b) .... MRPR 3.7(b) .... § 10.62(b)
§ 10.63
§ 11.308 [Reserved]

Advocate on Nonjudicial Proceeding
§ 11.309 .... MRPR 3.9 .... § 10.89(b)(2)
§ 10.111(c)
§§ 11.310–11.400 [Reserved]

Truthfulness to Others
§ 11.401 .... MRPR 4.1 .... § 10.85(a)(3)(4)(5)(7)
§ 10.85(b)

Communication Between Practitioner and Opposing Parties
§ 11.402(a) .... MRPR 4.2(a) .... § 10.87(a)
§ 11.402(b)–(d) .... DCRPR 4.2(b)–(d) .... None

Dealing with Unrepresented Person
§ 11.403 .... MRPR 4.3 .... § 10.87(a)

Respect for Rights of Third Persons
§ 11.404 .... MRPR 4.4 .... § 10.84(a)(1)
§ 10.85(a)(1)
§ 10.89(c)(2)
§§ 11.405–11.500 [Reserved]

Responsibilities of a Partner or Supervisory Practitioner
§ 11.501(a)–(b) .... MRPR 5.1(a)–(b) .... § 10.57(d)
§ 11.501(c) .... MRPR 5.1(c) .... § 10.23(b)(2)

Responsibilities of a Subordinate Practitioner
§ 11.502 .... MRPR 5.2 .... None

Responsibilities Regarding Nonpractitioner Assistants
§ 11.503(a) .... MRPR 5.3(a) .... § 10.57(d)
§ 11.503(b) .... MRPR 5.3(b) .... § 10.23(b)
§ 11.503(c) .... MRPR 5.3(c) .... None

Professional Independence of a Practitioner
§ 11.504(a) .... MRPR 5.4(a) .... § 10.48(a)
§ 11.504(b) .... MRPR 5.4(c) .... § 10.68(b)
§ 11.504(d) .... MRPR 5.4(d) .... § 10.68(c)

Unauthorized Practice of Law
§ 11.505(a) .... MRPR 5.5(a) .... § 10.47(a)
§ 10.14(d)
§ 11.505(b) .... MRPR 5.5(b) .... § 10.47(a)
§ 11.505(c) .... § 10.47(a) .... § 10.47(a)
§ 11.505(d) .... § 10.47(b) .... § 10.47(b)
§ 10.23(c)(6)
§ 11.505(e) .... New .... § 10.14(b)
§ 11.505(f) .... § 10.47(b) .... § 10.47(b)

Restrictions on Right to Practice
§ 11.506(a)–(b) .... MRPR 5.6 .... § 10.38

Responsibilities Regarding Law-Related Services
§ 11.507(a)(1)(2) .... MRPR 5.7(a)(1)(2) .... None
§ 11.507(a)(3) .... New .... None
§ 11.507(b) .... MRPR 5.7(b) .... None
§§ 11.508–11.600 [Reserved]

Pro Bono Publico Service
§ 11.601 .... DCRPR 6.1 .... None

Accepting Appointments
§ 11.602 .... MRPR 6.2 .... None

Membership in Legal Services Organization
§ 11.603 .... MRPR 6.3 .... None
§ 11.604 .... § 10.32(a)
§§ 11.605–11.700 [Reserved]

Law Reform Activities
§ 11.701(b)(1)–(4) .... DCRPR 7.1(b) .... § 10.111(c)
§ 11.701(b)(5) .... New .... None
§ 11.701(c) .... DCRPR 7.1(c) .... § 10.33
§ 11.701(d)–(e) .... New .... § 10.31(a)–(b)

Advertising
§ 11.702(a) .... MRPR 7.2(a) .... § 10.32(a)
§ 11.702(b) .... MRPR 7.2(b) .... None
§ 11.702(c) .... MRPR 7.2(c) .... § 10.32(b)
§ 11.702(d) .... MRPR 7.2(d) .... None
§ 11.702(e) .... New .... § 10.32(c)

Direct Contact with Prospective Clients
§ 11.703(a) .... MRPR 7.3(a) .... § 10.33
§ 11.703(b)–(d) .... MRPR 7.3(b)–(d) .... None

Communication of Fields of Practice and Certification

§ 11.704 .... MRPR 7.4 .... None
§ 11.704(a)–(c) .... § 10.32(c)–(d) .... § 10.31(c)–(d)
§ 10.34(a)–(b) .... § 10.34(a)–(b)
§ 11.704(d) .... New .... None
§ 11.704(e) .... MRPR 7.4(b) .... None

Firm Names and Letterheads

§ 11.705(a) .... MRPR 7.5(a) .... § 10.35(a)
§ 11.705(b) .... MRPR 7.5(b) .... None
§ 11.705(c) .... MRPR 7.5(c) .... § 10.31(b)
§ 11.705(d) .... MRPR 7.5(d) .... § 10.35(b)
§§ 11.706–11.800 [Reserved]

Bar Admission and Disciplinary Matters

§ 11.801(a) .... MRPR 8.1(a) .... § 10.22(a)(b)
§ 11.801(b) .... MRPR 8.1(b) .... § 10.23(b)(5)
§ 10.24(b)
§ 11.801(c) .... § 10.23(c)(16) .... § 10.23(c)(16)

Judicial and Legal Officials

§ 11.802(a) .... MRPR 8.2(a) .... § 10.102
§ 11.802(b) .... MRPR 8.2(b) .... § 10.103

Reporting Professional Misconduct

§ 11.803(a) .... MRPR 8.3(a) .... § 10.24(a)
§ 11.803(b) .... MRPR 8.3(b) .... § 10.24(a)
§ 11.803(c) .... MRPR 8.3(c) .... None
§ 11.803(d) .... New .... None
§ 11.803(f)(1) .... § 10.23(c)(5) .... § 10.23(c)(5)
§ 11.803(f)(2) .... § 10.23(c)(14) .... § 10.23(c)(14)
§ 11.803(f)(3) .... § 10.23(c)(12) .... § 10.23(c)(12)
§ 11.803(f)(4) .... § 10.23(c)(18) .... § 10.23(c)(18)

Misconduct

§ 11.804(a) .... MRPR 8.4(a) .... § 10.23(b)(1)(2)
§ 11.804(b) .... MRPR 8.4(b) .... § 10.23(c)(1)
§ 11.804(d) .... MRPR 8.4(d) .... § 10.23(b)(5)
§ 11.804(e) .... MRPR 8.4(e) .... § 10.23(c)(5)
§ 11.804(f) .... MRPR 8.4(f) .... None
§ 11.804(g) .... MRPR 8.4(g) .... 35 U.S.C. 32
§ 10.23(a)
§ 11.804(h)(1) .... § 10.23(c)(2) .... § 10.23(c)(2)
§ 11.804(h)(2) .... § 10.23(c)(17) .... § 10.23(c)(17)
§ 11.804(h)(3) .... § 10.23(c)(17) .... § 10.23(c)(17)
§ 11.804(h)(4) .... 31 C.F.R. 8.35(c) .... None

§ 11.804(h)(5) .... New .... None
§ 11.804(h)(6) .... 31 C.F.R. 8.36...................... None
§ 11.804(h)(7) .... 18 U.S.C. 205(a) and (b) ..... None
18 U.S.C. 209(a)
§ 11.804(h)(8) .... 18 U.S.C. 205 .... None
§ 11.804(h)(9) .... New .... None
§ 11.804(h)(10) .... § 10.23(c)(16) .... § 10.23(c)(16)
§ 11.804(i) .... § 10.23(d) .... § 10.23(d)

Disciplinary Authority: Choice of Law
§ 11.805 .... MRPR 8.5 .... None

Sexual Relations with Clients and Third Persons
§ 11.806 .... NYADSD 200.29–a .... None

Abbreviations:
DCRPR = District of Columbia Court of Appeals Rules of Professional Conduct (1999).
MRPR = Model Rules of Professional Conduct of the American Bar Association (1999).
NYADSD = Official Court Rules of the New York Appellate Division, Second Department (2000).
VRPC = Virginia Rules of Professional Conduct (1999).

Table of Cases

aaiPharma, Inc. v. Kremers Urban Dev. Co., 361 F. Supp. 2d
  770 (N.D. Ill. 2005). 193*n*108
Abbott Labs. v. Brennan, 952 F.2d 1346 (Fed. Cir. 1991). 109*n*26
Abbott Labs. v. Torpharm, Inc., 300 F.3d 1367, 63 U.S.P.Q.2d
  (BNA) 1929 (Fed. Cir. 2002). 126*n*81
Accuweb, Inc. v. Foley & Lardner, 2007 WL 259829
  (Wis. App. 2007). 100*n*63
Adamasu v. Gifford, Krass, Groh, Sprinkle, Anderson & Citkowski,
  PC, 409 F. Supp. 2d 788 (E.D. Mich. 2005) 102*n*67
Adams, United States v., 383 U.S. 39 (1966). 82*n*16
Affymetrix, Inc. v. Illumina, Inc., 2005 U.S. Dist. LEXIS 15482
  (D. Del. 2005) 171*n*8
Air Measurement Tech., Inc. v. Hamilton, 2005 WL 425411
  (W.D. Tex. Feb. 22, 2005) 75*n*3
Akeva LLC v. Mizuno Corp., 243 F. Supp. 2d 418
  (M.D.N.C. 2003). 203*n*148, 206–207, 206*n*165, 209*n*181
Akron Polymer Container Corp. v. Exxel Container, Inc.,
  148 F.3d 1380, 47 U.S.P.Q.2d (BNA) 1533 (Fed. Cir. 1998). 149, 149*n*161
Alcon Labs., Inc. v. Pharmacia Corp., 225 F. Supp. 2d 340
  (S.D.N.Y. 2002). 192*n*103, 192*n*106, 193*n*109
Allen Eng'g Corp. v. Bartell Indus., Inc., 299 F.3d 1336, 63
  U.S.P.Q.2d (BNA) 1769 (Fed. Cir. 2002). 146*n*148, 147*n*154
Allied Tube & Conduit Corp. v. John Maneely Corp., 125 F.
  Supp. 2d 987 (D. Ariz. 2000). 160*n*196
Amalgamated Dev. Co., In re, 375 A.2d 494 (D.C. 1977). 23*n*66
American Airlines, Inc., In re, 972 F.2d 605 (5th Cir. 1992). 20*n*54
American Sigma, Inc. v. QED Envtl. Sys., Inc., 1989 Commr.
  Pat. LEXIS 18 (July 31, 1989) 16*n*37
American Silver LLC v. Gen. Resonance LLC, 2007 WL 4828352
  (D. Md. Dec. 21, 2007). 60*n*34
American Stock Exch., LLC v. Mopex, Inc., 230 F. Supp. 2d 333,
  52 U.S.P.Q.2d (BNA) 1385 (S.D.N.Y. 2002). 26*n*1, 183*n*63
Amsted Ind. Inc v. Nat'l Castings, Inc., 16 U.S.P.Q.2d 1737
  (N.D. Ill. June 22, 1990). 198*n*127
Anderson v. Eppstein, 2001 Pat. App. LEXIS 1, 59 U.S.P.Q.2d (BNA)
  1280 (Bd. App. & Inter. 2001). 16*n*36, 19*n*46, 67–68, 69–70, 110*n*30

Anderson's-Black Rock, Inc. v. Pavement Salvage Co., 396 U.S.
305 (1969) 82*n*16
Andrx Pharm., LLC v. GlaxoSmithKline, PLC, 236 F.R.D. 583
(S.D. Fla. 2006) 181*n*56, 189*n*90
Argus Chem. Corp. v. Fibre Glass-Evercoat Co., 759 F.2d 10,
225 U.S.P.Q. (BNA) 1100 (Fed. Cir. 1985) 119*n*65
Aristocrat Tech. Australia Pty Ltd. v. Int'l Game Tech., 2008 WL
819764 (Mar. 28, 2008) 80*n*9
Arthrocare Corp. v. Smith & Nephew, Inc., 310 F. Supp. 2d 638
(D. Del. 2004), *vacated*, 406 F.3d 1365, 74 U.S.P.Q.2d (BNA)
1749 (Fed. Cir. 2005) 185*n*71
Atheridge, In re, 1984 Commr. Pat. LEXIS 6 (July 2, 1986) 259
Atofina v. Great Lakes Chem. Corp., 78 U.S.P.Q.2d (BNA) 1417
(Fed. Cir. 2006) 136, 136*nn*112–113
Autobytel, Inc. v. Dealix Corp., 455 F. Supp. 2d 569
(E.D. Tex. 2006) 206*n*166
Avocent Redmond Corp. v. Rose Elec., Inc., 2007 WL 1549477
(W.D. Wash. May 24, 2007) 174*n*31, 178*n*46
Avocent Redmond Corp. v. Rose Elec., 2007 U.S. Dist.
LEXIS 39736 (W.D. Wash. May 30, 2007) 37*n*28
Avco Corp. v. PPG Indus., Inc., 867 F. Supp. 84, 34 U.S.P.Q.2d
(BNA) 1026 (D. Mass. 1994) 141*n*127
Avery Dennison Corp. v. UCB SA, No. 95 C 6351, 1996 U.S. Dist.
LEXIS 16070, 1996 WL 633986 (N.D. Ill. Oct. 29, 1996) 178*n*47

Basco, In re, 221 S.W.3d 637 (Tex. 2007) 70*n*16
BASF Corp. v. United States, 321 F. Supp. 2d 1373
(Ct. Int'l Trade 2004) 170*n*3
Bausch & Lomb Inc. v. Alcon Labs., Inc., 64 F. Supp. 2d 233
(W.D.N.Y. 1999) 26*n*1, 183*n*63
Baxter Diagnostics, Inc. v. AVL Scientific Corp., 798 F.
Supp. 612 (C.D. Cal. 1992) 36*n*26
Baxter Int'l Inc. v. McGaw, Inc., 149 F.3d 1321, 47 U.S.P.Q.2d
(BNA) 1225 (Fed. Cir. 1998) 130
Beasley v. Avery Dennison Corp., 2005 WL 1719222
(W.D. Tex. July 22, 2005) 75*n*3
Beckman Indus., Inc. v. Int'l Ins. Co., 966 F.2d 470
(9th Cir. 1992) 189*n*92
Beech Aircraft Corp. v. EDO Corp., 990 F.2d 1237 (Fed. Cir. 1993) 26*n*3
Bender v. Dudas, 490 F.3d 1361 (Fed. Cir. 2007) 96–97, 225
Berkeley Ltd. P'ship v. Arnold, White & Durkee. 118 F.
Supp. 2d 668 (D. Md. 2000) 52*n*18
Biax Corp. v. Fujitsu Computer Sys. Corp., 2007 U.S. Dist.
LEXIS 35770 (E.D. Tex. May 16, 2007) 66–67
Black v. Missouri, 492 F. Supp. 848 (W.D. Mo. 1980) 96*n*57
Board of Educ., United States v., 946 F.2d 180 (2d. Cir. 1991) 192*n*102
Board of Educ. v. Am. Bioscience, Inc., 333 F.3d 1330, 67
U.S.P.Q.2d (BNA) 1252 (Fed. Cir. 2003) 155*n*179

Board of Educ. ex rel. Fla. v. Am. Bioscience, Inc., 333 F.3d 1330
  (Fed. Cir. 2003) 90n45
Boehm v. Wheeler, 223 N.W.2d 536 (Wis. 1975) 99n61
Boehringer Ingelheim Yetmedica, Inc. v. Schering-Plough Corp.,
  68 F. Supp. 2d 508 (D.N.J. 1999) 132n103
Bogese, In re, 303 F.3d 1362 (Fed. Cir. 2002) 100n62
Boivin, In re, 533 P.2d 971, 974 (Or. 1975) 43
Bose Corp. v. JBL, Inc., 274 F.3d 1354, 61 U.S.P.Q.2d (BNA)
  1216 (Fed. Cir. 2001) 20n52
Brasseler, U.S.A. I, L.P. v. Stryker Sales Corp., 267 F.3d 1370, 60
  U.S.P.Q.2d (BNA) 1482 (Fed. Cir. 2001) 13n19, 105n5, 111n37,
                                              118–119, 121, 123n73, 124nn75–77,
                                                       127n87, 147, 191n98
Brasseler U.S.A., I, L.P. v. Stryker Sales Corp., 93 F. Supp. 2d
  1255 (S.D. Ga. 1999) 147n154
Bristol-Myers Squibb Co. v. Ben Venue Labs., 90 F. Supp. 2d 522
  (D.N.J. 2000) 13n18
Bristol-Myers Squibb Co. v. Rhone-Poulenc Rorer, Inc., 326
  F.3d 1226, 66 U.S.P.Q.2d (BNA) 1481 (Fed. Cir. 2003) 126n81, 144–145
Bristol-Myers Squibb Co. v. Rhone-Poulenc Rorer, Inc., No. 95
  Civ. 8833 (RPP), 2000 U.S. Dist. LEXIS 16015, 2000 WL
  1655054 (S.D.N.Y. Nov. 3, 2000) 198n127
Brown v. Regents of the Univ. of Cal., 866 F. Supp. 439
  (N.D. Cal. 1994) 97n59
Bruno Indep. Living Aids, Inc. v. Acorn Mobility Serv., Ltd.,
  277 F. Supp. 2d 965, 69 U.S.P.Q.2d (BNA) 1229 (W.D. Wis. 2003) 123n73
Buechel v. Bain, 713 N.Y.S.2d 332 (N.Y. 2000) (App. Div. 2000) 18n42, 23n65
Buechel v. Bain, 2000 WL 142598 (N.Y. App. Div. Sept. 28, 2000) 245

Cabinet Vision v. Cabnetware, 129 F.3d 595, 44 U.S.P.Q.2d
  (BNA) 1683 (Fed. Cir. 1997) 112n39
Cal. Med. Prods. Inc. v. Tecnol Med. Prods. Inc., 921 F. Supp. 1219
  (D. Del. 1995) 160n196
C&F Packing Co. v. IBP, Inc., 916 F. Supp 735 (N.D. Ill. 1995) 132n103
Cardiac Pacemakers, Inc. v. St. Jude Med., Inc., 381 F.3d 1371
  (Fed. Cir. 2004) 87n30
CardioGrip Corp. v. Mueller & Smith, LP, 2008 U.S. Dist.
  LEXIS 2627 (S.D. Ohio Jan. 14, 2008) 38n32, 163n1
Cargill, Inc. v. Canbra Foods, Ltd., 476 F.3d 1359
  (Fed. Cir. 2007) 141n129, 142n132
Carlson v. Fredrikson & Byron, P.A., 475 N.W.2d 882
  (Minn. Ct. App. 1991) 31n19
Carl Zeiss Jena GmgH v. Bio-Rad Labs. Inc., No. 98 CIV. 8012
  RCC DFE, 2000 WL 1006371 (S.D.N.Y. July 19, 2000) 201n138
Catalina Lighting, Inc. v. Lamps Plus, Inc., 295 F.3d 1277,
  63 U.S.P.Q.2d (BNA) 1545 (Fed. Cir. 2002) 126n82
Catalina Mktg. Int'l, Inc. v. Coolsavings.com, Inc., 289 F.3d 801
  (Fed. Cir. 2002) 79n8

CCS Fitness, Inc. v. Brunswick Corp., 288 F.3d 1359 (Fed. Cir. 2002) 86*n*27
Certain Magnetic Switches for Coaxial Transmission Lines & Products
    Containing Same, In re, No. 337-TA-346, 1993 ITC LEXIS 143
    (Int'l Trade Comm'n Mar. 2, 1993). 174–175*n*31
CFMT, Inc. v. YieldUP Int'l Corp., 144 F. Supp. 2d 305
    (D. Del. 2001), *rev'd*, 349 F.3d 1333 (Fed. Cir. 2003) 144–145, 145*n*144
Chan v. Intuit, Inc., 218 F.R.D. 659 (N.D. Cal. 2003) 178*nn*47–48, 189–190
Chiron Corp. v. Abbott Labs., 156 F.R.D. 219, 31 U.S.P.Q.2d
    1848 (N.D. Cal. 1994) 194*n*110
Chopra v. Townsend, Townsend and Crew, LLP, 2008 WL 413944
    (D. Colo. Feb. 13, 2008). 99*n*61
Cichonski v. Am. Inventors Corp., 1995 WL 657107
    (E.D. Pa. Nov. 3, 1995) 225
Clinitec Nutrition Co. v. Baya Corp., No. 94 C 7050, 1996 WL 153881
    (N.D. Ill. Mar. 28, 1996) 198*n*126
Cohen, In re, 66 U.S.Q.2d 1782 (Dir. PTO 2003) 225
Cohesive Techs., Inc. v. Waters Corp., 526 F. Supp. 2d 84
    (D. Mass. 2007). 201*n*135
Collard & Roe, P.C. v. Vlacancich, 2004 WL 2453219
    (N.Y. Sup. Ct. App. Oct. 29, 2004). 81*n*14
Colorpix Sys. of Am. v. Broan Mfg. Co., 131 F. Supp. 2d 1499
    (D. Conn. 2001) 36*n*26
Commissariat a L'Energie Atomique v. Dell Computer Corp.,
    No. 03-484-KAJ, 2004 U.S. Dist. LEXIS 12782
    (D. Del. May 25, 2004). 170*n*5, 179*n*49, 187*n*81, 188*n*83
Comtech, Inc. v. Reuter, 1986 WL 6829 (E.D.N.Y.
    Mar. 18, 1986). 26*n*2, 28–29*n*11
Consolidated Aluminum Corp. v. Foseco Int'l Ltd., 910 F.2d 804,
    15 U.S.P.Q.2d (BNA) 1481, 1483-1484,1487
    (Fed. Cir. 1990). 112*n*42, 146*n*146, 191*n*97
Consolidated Kinetics Corp. v. Marshall, Neil & Pauley, Inc.,
    521 P.2d 1209 (Wash. Ct. App. 1974) 109*n*26
Convolve, Inc. v. Compaq Computer Corp., 224 F.R.D. 98
    (S.D.N.Y. 2004). 208*n*180
Coolsavings.com Inc. v. E-Centives, Inc., No. 98 C 4924, 2000
    U.S. Dist. LEXIS 12985, 2000 WL 1262929
    (N.D. Ill. Sept. 1, 2000) 194*n*111, 194*n*113, 196*n*119
Critikon Inc. v. Becton Dickinson Vascular Access Inc., 120
    F.3d 1253, 43 U.S.P.Q.2d (BNA) 1666 (Fed. Cir. 1997) 111*n*34, 154*n*175
Crossroads Sys. (Texas), Inc. v. Dot Hill Sys. Corp., 2006
    U.S. Dist. LEXIS 36181, 2006 WL 1544621, 82 U.S.P.Q.2d
    (BNA) 1517 (W.D. Tex. 2006) 199–200
Crystal Semiconductor Corp. v. TriTech Microelectronics Int'l, Inc.,
    246 F.3d 1336 (Fed. Cir. 2001) 206
Cummins-Allison Corp. v. Glory Ltd., No. 02 C 7008, 2003 U.S.
    Dist. LEXIS 23653 (N.D. Ill. Jan. 2, 2004). 172*n*14, 179*n*50, 179*n*53
Curtis v. Radio Representatives, Inc., 696 F. Supp. 729 (D.D.C. 1988) 50–51

Damper Design, Inc. v. Cleveland Elec. Illuminating Co.,
    No. 94-1223, 1995 U.S. App. LEXIS 3520, 1995 WL 71339
    (Fed. Cir. Feb. 21, 1995) 184*n*70
Dann v. Johnston, 425 U.S. 219 (1976) 82*n*16
Davis v. AT&T Corp., No. 98-CV-0189S(H), 1998 U.S. Dist.
    LEXIS 20471, 1998 WL 912012 (W.D.N.Y. Dec. 23, 1998) 178*n*47, 187*n*79
Dayco Prods., Inc. v. Total Containment, Inc., 329
    F.3d 1358, 66 U.S.P.Q.2d (BNA) 1801
    (Fed. Cir. 2003). 112*n*43, 113*n*47, 114*n*53, 123*n*73,
                                                                    148–149, 149*n*161, 150*n*163
Delta Process Equip., Inc. v. New England Ins. Co.,
    560 So.2d 923 (La. App. 1990) 99*n*61
Digital Control Inc. v. Charles Mach. Works, 437 F.3d 1309
    (Fed. Cir. 2006). 140*n*123
Dippin' Dots, Inc v. Mosey, 476 F.3d 1337 (Fed. Cir. 2007) 146*n*149
Dippin' Dots Patent Litig., In re, 249 F. Supp. 2d 1346
    (N.D. Ga. 2003). 147*n*151
Discotrade Ltd. v. Wyeth-Ayerst Int'l Inc., 200 F. Supp. 2d 355
    (S.D.N.Y. 2002). 36*n*26
Dow Chem. Co. v. Exxon Corp., 139 F.3d 1470
    (Fed. Cir. 1998). 108*n*24, 109*n*26
Dresser Indus., In re, 972 F.2d 540
    (5th Cir. 1992). 16*n*37, 20*n*54, 21*n*56, 50*n*12
Ducane Gas Grills, Inc., In re, 320 B.R. 312 (Bankr. D. S.C. 2004) 28*n*11
Dunbar v. Baylor College of Med., 984 S.W.2d 338 (Tex. Ct. App. 1998). 28*n*6

Eagle Comtronics, Inc. v. Arrow Commc'n Lab., Inc., 305
    F.3d 1303, 64 U.S.P.Q.2d (BNA) 1481 (Fed. Cir. 2002) 184–185, 186*n*77
EchoStar Commc'ns Corp., In re, 448 F.3d 1294, 78 U.S.P.Q.2d
    (BNA) 1676 (Fed. Cir. 2006). 202–209, 202*n*140, 203*n*148, 204*n*156, 206*n*167
Eli Lilly & Co. v. Zenith Goldline Pharm. Inc., 81, U.S.P.Q.2d
    (BNA) 1369 (Fed. Cir. 2006). 141*n*130
Elmwood Liquid Prods., Inc. v. Singleton Packing Corp., 328
    F. Supp. 974, 170 U.S.P.Q. (BNA) 398 (M.D. Fla. 1971). 128*n*90
Emory Univ. v. Nova Biogenetics, Inc., 2006 WL 2708635
    (N.D. Ga. Sept. 20, 2006). 29*n*12
Englishtown Sportswear, Ltd. v. Tuttle, 547 F. Supp. 700, 216
    U.S.P.Q. (BNA) 486 (S.D.N.Y. 1982) 17*n*39
Environ Prods., Inc. v. Total Containment, Inc., 41 U.S.P.Q.2d
    (BNA) 1302 (E.D. Pa. 1996) 196*n*119
Environ Prods., Inc. v. Total Containment, Inc., 43 U.S.P.Q.2d
    (BNA) 1288 (E.D. Pa. 1997) 153*n*174, 193*n*108
Enzo Biochem, Inc. v. Applera Corp., 2007 WL 30338 (D. Conn.
    Jan. 5, 2007). 57–59
eSpeed, Inc. v. Brokertec USA, LLC, 480 F.3d 1129 (Fed. Cir. 2007). 140*n*123
Ex parte. See name of party
Ex rel. See name of related party

Faughn v. Perez, 145 Cal. App. 4th 592 (Cal. App. 2006)................... 36*n*26

Fawer, Brian, Hardy & Zatzkis v. Howes, 639 So. 2d 329
  (Ct. App. La. 1994)... 55*n*28

Ferguson Beauregard/Logic Controls v. Mega Sys., LLC, 2001
  WL 34771614 (E.D. Tex. Dec. 13, 2001), *aff'd in part, rev'd in*
  part, 350 F.3d 1327 (Fed. Cir. 2003) 160*n*196

Ferring B.V. v. Aventis Pharm, Inc. 437 F.3d 1181
  (Fed. Cir. 2006)..126*n*84, 143*n*136

Ferring B.V. v. Barr Labs., Inc., 437 F.3d 1181 (Fed. Cir. 2006) 140*n*123

Festo Corp. v. Shoketsu Kinzoko Kogyo Kabushiki Co., 535
  U.S. 722 (2002) 84–85

Fina Oil & Chem. Co. v. Ewen, 123 F.3d 1466, 43 U.S.P.Q.2d
  (BNA) 1935 (Fed. Cir. 1997)..........................92*n*50, 155*n*180

Finger Furniture Co. v. Finger Interests No. 1, Ltd., 71 U.S.P.Q.2d
  (BNA) 1287 (TTAB 2004)............................16*n*37, 42–44, 44*n*40

Fisons Corp. v. Atochem N. Am., Inc., 1990 WL 180551
  (S.D.N.Y. 1990)... 41*n*37

Flex-Rest, LLC v. Steelcase, Inc., 455 F.3d 1351 (Fed. Cir. 2006)............ 121*n*72

Flo-Con Sys., Inc. v. Servsteel, Inc., 759 F. Supp. 456 (N.D. Ind. 1990).......... 66*n*1

FMC Corp v. Manitowoc Co., 835 F.2d 1411, 5 U.S.P.Q.2d
  (BNA) 1112 (Fed. Cir. 1987)....................... 105*n*6, 124*n*76, 141*n*130

Fortson v. Winstead, McGuire, Secrest & Minick, 961 F.2d 469
  (4th Cir. 1992).. 31*n*20

Fotodyne, Inc. v. Barry, 1989 WL 142846 (Wis. App. Sept. 26, 1989) 99*n*61

Frank's Casing Crew & Rental Tools, Inc. v. PMR Techs., Ltd., 292
  F.3d 1363, 63 U.S.P.Q.2d (BNA) 1065 (Fed. Cir. 2002)..........91*n*46, 155–156

Friedman, In re Subpoena Issued to, 350 F.3d 65 (2d Cir. 2003)............ 192*n*104

Friedman v. Lehman, 40 U.S.Q.2d 1206 (D.D.C. 1996) 258, 259

Furnace Brook LLC v. Overstock.com, Inc., 2006 WL 2337208
  (S.D.N.Y. Aug. 10, 2006)... 160*n*196

Futures Tech. Ltd. v. Quigg, 684 F. Supp. 430 (E.D. Va. 1988) 158*n*189

Galarowicz v. Comm'r of Patents & Trademarks, 848 F.2d 1245
  (Fed. Cir. 1988).. 13*n*17

Gambro Lundia AB v. Baxter Healthcare Corp., 110 F.3d 1573, 42
  U.S.P.Q.2d (BNA) 1378 (Fed. Cir. 1997) 132*nn*106–107

Gardco Mfg., Inc. v. Herst Lighting Co., 820 F.2d 1209,
  2 U.S.P.Q.2d (BNA) 2015 (Fed. Cir. 1987).....................195*nn*117–118

GD Searle & Co. v. Pennie & Edmonds, LLP, 2004 WL 3270190
  (N.Y. Sup. Ct. Jan. 14, 2004)... 60*n*33

GD Searle & Co. v. Nutrapharm, Inc., 1999 WL 249725
  (S.D.N.Y. Apr. 28, 1999) 38*n*30

Gen-Cor, LLC v. Buckeye Corrugated, Inc., 111 F. Supp. 2d 1049
  (S.D. Ind. 2000)... 36*n*26

Genentech, Inc. v. Insmed Inc., 442 F. Supp. 2d 838 (N.D. Cal. 2006) 206*n*166

GFI, Inc. v. Franklin Corp., 265 F.3d 1268 (Fed. Cir. 2001)..........123*n*74, 126*n*83

Glaxo Inc. v. Novopharm Ltd., 52 F.3d 1043 (Fed. Cir. 1995) 146*n*145

Golden Valley Microwave Foods Inc. v. Weaver Popcorn Co.,
   837 F. Supp. 1444, 24 U.S.P.Q.2d (BNA) 1801
   (N.D. Ind. 1992) 128*n*91, 132*n*103, 134*n*107, 141*n*128, 150*nn*163–164
Goldstein, In re, 16 U.S.P.Q.2d (BNA) 1963 (Comm'r. Pat. 1988) 93*n*52
Graham v. John Deere Co., 383 U.S. 1 (1966). 82*n*16
Gugliotta v. Morano, 829 N.E.2d 757 (Ct. App. Ohio 2005) 225
Gursky & Ederer, LLP v. GMT Corp., 2004 WL 2793174
   (N.Y. Sup. Ct. Oct. 5, 2004). 50*n*14

Hackett v. Village Court Assocs., 602 F. Supp. 856 (E.D. Wis. 1985) 31*n*20
Halcon Int'l, Inc. v. Werbow, 228 U.S.P.Q. (BNA) 611
   (Comm'r Pat. 1985). 69*n*10
Haworth, Inc. v. Steelcase, Inc., 685 F. Supp. 1422, 8 U.S.P.Q.2d
   (BNA) 1001 (W.D. Mich. 1988). 120*n*68
Hay & Forage Indus. v. Ford New Holland, Inc., 132 F.R.D. 687
   (D. Kan. 1990). 193*n*108
Hebert v. Lisle Corp., 99 F.3d 1109, 40 U.S.P.Q.2d (BNA) 1611
   (Fed. Cir. 1996). 112*n*39
Henry Filters, Inc. v. Peabody Barnes, Inc., 611 N.E.2d 873
   (Ct. App. Ohio 1992). 29*n*13, 30*n*15
Herring, People v., 2001 WL 1161242 (Colo. O.P.D.J. 2001). 99*n*61
Hilleby v. FMC Corp., 25 U.S.P.Q.2d (BNA) 1413 (N.D. Cal. 1992) 66*n*1
Hizey v. Carpenter, 830 P.2d 646 (Wash. 1992). 168*n*1
Hoar Constr. Co., In re, 2008 WL 2262087 (Tex. App.–Houston
   [14th Dist.] 2008. . . . . 70*n*14
Hobley v. Burge, 433 F.3d 946 (7th Cir. 2006) 204*n*156
Hoeksema, In re, 399 F.2d 269, 158 U.S.P.Q. (BNA) 596
   (CCPA 1968). 89*n*39
Hoffmann-La Roche, Inc. v. Promega Corp., 323 F.3d 1354, 66
   U.S.P.Q.2d (BNA) 1385 (Fed. Cir. 2003) 140*n*125
Holmes Group, Inc. v. Vornado Air Circulation Sys., Inc.,
   535 U.S. 826, 62 U.S.P.Q.2d (BNA) 1801 (2002). 20*n*48
Hopper v. Frank, 16 F.3d 92 (5th Cir. 1994). 31*n*20, 36, 36*n*27
Hutchins v. Fish & Richardson, PC, Civ. A. No. 05-30062-MAP
   (Filed Mar. 4, 2005) 60*n*34

Iams Co. v. Kaln Kan Foods, Inc., No. C-3-97-449, 1998 U.S. Dist.
   LEXIS 19205 (S.D. Ohio Feb. 27, 1998) 186*n*78
ICU Med., Inc. v. B. Braun Med. Inc., 2005 WL 588341
   (N.D. Cal. Mar. 14, 2005) 185*n*72
Ideal Toy Corp. v. Tyco Indus., Inc., 478 F. Supp. 1191
   (D. Del. 1979) 178*n*47
Igen, Inc. v. White, 672 N.Y.S.2d 867 (N.Y. Sup. Ct. App. Div. 1998) 99*n*61
Immunocept, LLC v. Fulbright & Jaworski, LLP, 504 F.3d 1281
   (Fed. Cir. 2007). 85*n*25
Impax Labs., Inc. v. Aventis Pharm. Inc., 468 F.3d 1366
   (Fed. Cir. 2006). 143*n*133

Imperial Chem. Indus., PLC v. Barr Labs., 795 F. Supp. 619,
22 U.S.P.Q.2d (BNA) 1906 (S.D.N.Y. 1992), *vacated,* 991 F.2d 811
(Fed. Cir. 1993)... 146n146
IMT, Inc. v. Haynes & Boone, LLP, 1999 WL 58838
(N.D. Tex. Feb. 1, 1999) 102n67
Independent Serv. Orgs. Antitrust Litig., In re, No. CIV. A. MDL-1021,
1995 U.S. Dist. LEXIS 4698, 1995 WL 151739 (D. Kan. Mar. 9, 1995) 171n8
Indianapolis Podiatry, P.C. v. Efroymson, 720 N.E.2d 376
(Ind. App. 1999)... 41n37
Infosint S.A. v. H. Lundbeck A.S., 2007 U.S. Dist. LEXIS 36678,
2007 WL 1467784 (S.D.N.Y. May 16, 2007).................... 171n8, 174n31
Inkine Pharma. Co. v. Coleman, 759 N.Y.S.2d 62
(N.Y. Sup. Ct. App. Div. 2003)....................................... 99n61
In re. See name of party
Insultherm, Inc. v. Tank Insulation Int'l, Inc., 64 F.3d 671, 36
U.S.P.Q.2d (BNA) 1271 (Fed. Cir. 1995) 119n64
Intel Corp. v. VIA Techs., Inc., 198 F.R.D. 525 (N.D. Cal. 2000)....... 171n8, 186n78
Interactive Coupon Mktg. Group, Inc. v. H.O.T.! Coupons, LLC,
No. 98 C 7408, 1999 U.S. Dist. LEXIS 9004, 1999 WL 409990
(N.D. Ill. June 7, 1999), *modified,* 1999 U.S. Dist. LEXIS 12437,
1999 WL 618969 (N.D. Ill. Aug. 9, 1999) 174n31, 175, 176n38,
187n81, 193n108, 196n119
International Bus. Mach. Corp. v. Levin, 579 F.2d 271 (7th Cir. 1978)......... 38n30
International Tele-Marine v. Malone & Assocs., 845 F. Supp. 1427
(D. Colo. 1994)... 33n22
Intervet, Inc. v. Merial Ltd., 241 F.R.D. 55 (D.D.C. 2007) 171n10
Intex Recreation Corp. v. Team Worldwide Corp., 439 F. Supp. 2d 46
(D.D.C. 2006) 206n166

Jack Eckerd Corp. v. Dart Group Corp. 621 F. Supp. 725 (D. Del. 1985) 33n22
Jackson Jordan, Inc. v. Leydig, Voit & Mayer, 633 N.E.2d 627 (Ill. 1994) 75n3
Jazz Photo Corp. v. Dreier, 2005 WL 3542468 (D.N.J. Dec. 23, 2005) 2n11
Johnston, United States v., 664 F.2d 152 (7th Cir. 1981)................... 196n119
J. P. Stevens & Co. v. Lex Tex Ltd., 747 F.2d 1553, 223 U.S.P.Q.
(BNA) 1089 (Fed. Cir. 1984)....................................... 111n34
Juicy Whip, Inc. v. Orange Bang, Inc., 292 F.3d 728, 63
U.S.P.Q.2d (BNA) 1251 (Fed. Cir. 2002)....................112n39, 143n135

Kabi Pharmacia AB v. Alcon Surgical Inc., 25 U.S.P.Q.2d (BNA)
1030 (D. Del. 1992) 38n30, 39n33
Kaempe v. Myers, 367 F.3d 958, 71 U.S.P.Q.2d (BNA) 1147
(D.C. Cir. 2004) 26n1, 183n63
Kairos Scientific Inc. v. Fish & Richardson, P.C., 2006 Cal. App. Unpub.
LEXIS 667 (2006) 2n10
Kairos Scientific Inc. v. Fish & Richardson, P.C., 2006 Cal. App. Unpub.
LEXIS 667 (2006) 99n61
Kansas v. Mayes, 531 P.2d 102, 185 U.S.P.Q. (BNA) 624 (Kan. 1975)......... 15n30

Kearney & Trecker Corp. v. Giddigns & Lewis, Inc., 452 F.2d 579
  (7th Cir. 1971).. 258, 259
Keller v. Clark Equip. Co., 715 F.2d 1280 (8th Cir. 1983)................... 99*n*61
Kersey v. Dennison Mfg. Co., 1992 WL 71390 (D. Mass. 1992)............... 28*n*11
Key Pharm. v. Hercon Labs. Corp., 161 F.3d 709, 48 U.S.P.Q.2d
  (BNA) 1911 (Fed. Cir. 1998)...................................... 138*n*118
Kingsdown Med. Consultants, Ltd. v. Hollister, Inc.,
  863 F.2d 867, 9 U.S.P.Q.2d (BNA) 1384 (Fed. Cir. 1988)......... 111*n*33, 112*n*41,
                                                            125–127, 141*n*130
Kirsh, In re, 973 F.2d 1454 (9th Cir. 1992)................................. 18*n*44
Koehring Co. v. Manitowoc Co., 418 F. Supp. 1133 (E.D. Wis. 1976)........... 66*n*1
KSR Int'l Co. v. Telefl ex Inc., 127 S. Ct. 1727 (2007) 82*n*16
K-2 Corp. v. Salomon S.A., 191 F.3d 1356 (Fed. Cir. 1999) 80*n*10
Kubin v. Miller, 801 F. Supp. 1101 (S.D.N.Y. 1992) 195*n*115

Landmark Graphics Corp. v. Seismic Micro Tech., Inc., 2007 U.S.
  Dist. LEXIS 6897, 2007 WL 735007 (S.D. Tex. Jan. 31, 2007)................200
Levenger Co. v. Feldman, 516 F. Supp. 2d 1272 (S.D. Fla. 2007).............. 105*n*7
Levin v. Ripple Twist Mills, Inc., 416 F. Supp. 876 (E.D. Pa. 1976)............. 66*n*1
Lex Tex Ltd. v. Skillman, 579 A.2d 244, 16 U.S.P.Q.2d (BNA) 1137
  (D.C. App. 1990)......................................105*n*8, 191*n*100
Link v. Wabash R.R. Co., 370 U.S. 626 (1962) 165*n*5
Lipman v. Dickinson, 174 F.3d 1363 (Fed. Cir. 1999).........................221
Li Second Family Ltd. P'ship v. Toshiba Corp., 231 F.3d 1373, 56
  U.S.P.Q.2d (BNA) 1681 (Fed. Cir. 2000) 146*n*147
Litton Sys., Inc. v. Honeywell, Inc., No. CV.90–93 MRP, 1995
  WL 366468 (C.D. Cal. Jan. 6, 1995)................................ 120*n*68
LNP Eng'g Plastics, Inc. v. Miller Waste Mills, Inc., 2000
  WL 33341185 (D. Del. 2000) 138*n*118
Lockwood v. Am. Airlines, Inc., 107 F.3d 1565 (Fed. Cir. 1997) 88*n*35
Lumenyte Int'l Corp. v. Cable Lite Corp., Nos. 96-1011, 1996 U.S.
  App. LEXIS 16400, 1996 WL 383927 (Fed. Cir. July 9, 1996) 159*n*195

Madanes v. Madanes, 199 F.R.D. 135 (S.D.N.Y. 2001)................... 192*n*103
Mahoning Cty. Bar Ass'n v. Harpman, 608 N.E.2d 872 (Ohio Bd.
  Unauth. Prac. 1993).. 10*n*6
Manoir-Electroalloys Corp. v. Amalloy Corp., 711 F. Supp. 188
  (D.N.J. 1989)... 38*n*30, 44
Marinangeli v. Lehman, 32 F. Supp. 2d 1 (D.D.C. 1998) 225
Markush, Ex parte, 1925 Dec. Comm'r Pat. 126 (1924)........................79
Marlow Indus., Inc., v. Igloo Prods. Corp., 2003 WL 21212626
  (Fed. Cir. 2003)... 154*n*177
Marshall v. Quinn-L Equities, Inc., 704 F. Supp. 1384 (N.D. Tex. 1988)....... 31*n*20
Mathis v. Spears, 857 F.2d 749, 8 U.S.P.Q.2d (BNA) 1029, 8
  U.S.P.Q.2d (BNA) 1551 (Fed. Cir. 1988) 197*n*123
Matsushita Elec. Indus. Co. v. United States, 929 F.2d 1577
  (Fed. Cir. 1991).. 174*n*30

McCandlish v. Doe, LEXIS 1, 22 U.S.P.Q.2d (BNA) 1223
(Comm'r Pat. 1992) 2*n*7, 15*n*27, 259
McCarthy v. John T. Henderson Inc., 587 A.2d 280
(N.J. Super. Ct. App. Div. 1991) 31*n*19
McKesson Info. Solutions, Inc. v. Bridge Med., Inc., 487
F.3d 897, 82 U.S.P.Q.2d (BNA) 1873-75
(Fed. Cir. 2007) 151–153, 151*n*167, 153*n*170
MedImmune, Inc. v. Centocor, Inc., 271 F. Supp. 2d 762
(D. Md. 2003) 174*n*31, 175*n*32, 176*n*38, 177*n*45
Medtronic, Inc. v. Guidant Corp., 2001 U.S. Dist. LEXIS 22805
(D. Minn. Dec. 19, 2001) 178*n*47, 181*n*56, 188*n*84, 188*n*86
*Messing, Rudavsky & Weliky, P.C. v. President & Fellows of Harvard
Coll.*, 764 N.E.2d 825 (Mass. 2002) 13*n*22
Meyerland Cmty. Improvement Ass'n v. Temple, 700 S.W.2d 263
(Tex. App.-Houston [1st Dist.] 1985, writ ref'd n.r.e.) 31*n*20
MGP Ingredients, Inc. v. Mars, Inc., 245 F.R.D. 497 (D. Kan. 2007) 174*n*31
Michlin v. Canon, Inc., 208 F.R.D. 172 (E.D. Mich. 2002) 207*n*175
Microunity Sys., Eng'g, Inc. v. Dell, Inc., 2005 WL 2299440
(E.D. Tex. July 18, 2005) 189*n*91
Midwest Indus., Inc. v. Karavan Trailers, Inc., 175 F.3d 1356,
50 U.S.P.Q.2d (BNA) 1672 (Fed. Cir. 1999) 20*n*49
Mikohn Gaming Corp. v. Acres Gaming, Inc., 1998 U.S. Dist. LEXIS 22251,
50 U.S.P.Q.2d (BNA) 1783 (D. Nev. 1998) 176*n*40, 177*n*42, 179*n*52
Minatronics Corp. v. Buchanan Ingersoll PC, 1996 WL 76508
(Pa. Comm. Pl. Feb. 7, 1996) 99*n*61
Mindscape, Inc. v. Media Depot, Inc., 973 F. Supp. 1130
(N.D. Cal. 1997) 163*n*1
MMTC, Inc. v. Rogan, 369 F. Supp. 2d 675 (E.D. Va. 2004) 158*n*189
Moatz v. Colitz, 68 U.S.Q.2d 1079 (Dir. PTO 2003) 225
Moatz v. Kersey, 67 U.S.Q.2d 1291 (Dir. PTO 2002) 259
Moha, B.V. v. Diamond Automation, Inc., 325 F.3d 1306, 66 U.S.P.Q.2d
(BNA) 1429 (Fed. Cir. 2003). 144*n*140
Mold-Masters Ltd. v. Husky Injection Molding Sys., Ltd., 01 C 1576,
2001 WL 1268587 (N.D. Ill. Nov. 15, 2001) 23*n*65
Molins PLC v. Textron, Inc., 48 F.3d 1172, 33 U.S.P.Q.2d (BNA)
1823 (Fed. Cir. 1995) 113*n*44, 124*n*76, 131*n*99, 132*n*101, 149
Monco v. Janus, 583 N.E.2d 575 (Ill. App. 1991). 13*n*20, 245
Monon Corp. v. Wabash Nat'l Corp., 764 F. Supp. 1320
(N.D. Ind. 1991) 66*n*1
Monsanto Co. v. Bayer Bioscience, N.V., 264 F. Supp. 2d 852
(E.D. Mo. Dec. 27, 2002), *rev'd*, 2004 WL 612877
(Fed. Cir. 2004). 139*n*121, 141*n*128
Monsanto Co. v. Bayer Bioscience N.V., 514 F.3d 1229, 85
U.S.P.Q.2d (BNA) 1582 (Fed. Cir. 2008) 112*n*42, 114*n*48, 139*n*119
Morin v. Trupin, 711 F. Supp. 97 (S.D.N.Y. 1989) 31*n*20
Morphosys AG v. CAT, 158 F. Supp. 2d 84 (D.D.C. 2001) 86*n*28
*Morrison Knudsen Corp. v. Hancock, Rothert & Bunshoft,
LLP*, 81 Cal. Rptr. 2d 425 (Cal. App. 1999) 17*n*39

Morton Int'l Inc. v. Cardinal Chem. Co., 5 F.3d 1464 (Fed Cir. 1993) 80*n*13
Motorola, Inc. v. Interdigital Tech. Corp., No. 93-488-LON,
   1994 U.S. Dist. LEXIS 20714
   (D. Del. Dec. 19, 1994). 173*n*26, 178*n*47, 179*n*49, 182*n*59, 188*n*85
Motorola, Inc. v. Vosi Techs., Inc., No. 01 C 4182, 2002
   U.S. Dist. LEXIS 15655, 2002 WL 1917256
   (N.D. Ill. Aug. 19, 2002) 208*n*176
Moyroud v. Itek Corp., 528 F. Supp. 707 (S.D. Fla. 1981). 67*n*3

National Recovery Techs., Inc. v. Magnetic Separation Sys., Inc.,
   166 F.3d 1190 (Fed. Cir. 1999) 89*n*38
National Steel Car, Ltd. v. Canadian Pac. Ry., Ltd., 254
   F. Supp. 2d 527 (E.D. Pa. 2003) 160*n*196
Nazomi Commc'ns, Inc. v. Arm Holdings PLC, No. C 02-02521-JF,
   2002 U.S. Dist. LEXIS 21400, 2002 WL 32831822 (N.D. Cal. Oct. 11, 2002),
   vacated, 403 F.3d 1364, 74 U.S.P.Q.2d (BNA) 1458
   (Fed. Cir. 2005). 169*n*2, 174*n*31, 176, 186*n*78, 188*n*85
Nebraska v. Flores, 622 N.W.2d 632 (Neb. 2001) 28*n*7
News Am. v. Marquis, No. CV 000177440S, 27 Conn. L. Rptr. 195,
   2000 Conn. Super. LEXIS 1273, 2000 WL 726821
   (Conn. Super. Ct. May 3, 2000) 171*n*8
New Tek Mfg. Inc. v. Beehner, 702 N.W.2d 336 (Neb. 2005) 38*n*31, 101*n*64
New York Inst. of Tech. v. Biosound, Inc., 658 F. Supp. 759
   (S.D.N.Y. 1987). 66*n*1
New York Marine & Gen. Ins. Co. v. Tradeline and Deepak Fertilizers and
   Petrochemicals Corp., 186 F.R.D. 317 (S.D.N.Y. 1999). 68*n*6
Nilssen v. Osram Sylvania, Inc., 504 F.3d 1223
   (Fed. Cir. 2007). 28*n*11, 126*n*84, 143*n*135, 153*n*171, 157*n*186, 158*n*190
Nisus Corp. v. Perma-Chink Sys., Inc., 497 F.3d 1316
   (Fed. Cir. 2007). 132*n*105, 153*n*173
Nobelpharma AB v. Implant Innovations, Inc., 141 F.3d 1054
   (Fed. Cir. 1998). 144*n*141
Nordberg, Inc. v. Telsmith, Inc., 82 F.3d 394, 38 U.S.P.Q.2d
   (BNA) 1593 (Fed. Cir. 1996). 116*n*59, 123*n*73
Norton v. Curtiss, 433 F.2d 779, 167 U.S.P.Q. (BNA) 532
   (C.C.P.A. 1970). 115*n*57
Novadigm, Inc. v. Marimba, Inc., 2000 WL 228356
   (N.D. Cal. 2000) 147*n*154
Novartis Pharm. Corp. v. Eon Labs Mfg., Inc., 206 F.R.D. 396
   (D. Del. 2002) 208–209
Novo Nordisk Pharm. Inc. v. Bio-Tech. Gen. Corp., 76 U.S.P.Q.2d
   (BNA) 1811, 424 F.3d 1347 (Fed. Cir. 2005) 90*n*43, 140–141, 141*n*126

Oxford Sys., Inc. v. Cellpro, Inc., 45 F. Supp. 2d 1055
   (W.D. Wash. 1999). 38*n*30
Oxyn Telecomm., Inc. v. Onse Telecom, No. 01 Civ. 1012(JSM),
   2003 U.S. Dist. LEXIS 2671, 2003 WL 660848
   (S.D.N.Y. Feb. 27, 2003) 202*n*139

Panduit Corp. v. All States Plastic Mfg. Co., 744 F.2d 1564,
   223 U.S.P.Q. (BNA) 465 (Fed. Cir. 1984) 20*n*50
Papst Licensing, GmbH, Patent Litig., In re, 2000 U.S.
   Dist. LEXIS 6374 (E.D. La. May 4, 2000) 178*n*47, 180*nn*54–55, 187*n*80
Paragon Podiatry Lab., Inc. v. KLM Lab., Inc., 984 F.2d 1182, 25
   U.S.P.Q.2d (BNA) 1561 (Fed. Cir. 1993) 117*n*61, 146*n*150
Parker v. Carnahan, 772 S.W.2d 151
   (Tex. App.-Texarkana 1989, writ denied). 30*n*16
Patent No. 4,409,763, In re, 7 U.S.P.Q.2d (BNA) 1798
   (Comm'r Pat. 1988) 165*n*7
Paul E. Iancono Structural Eng'r, Inc. v. Humphrey, 722 F.2d 435
   (9th Cir. 1983). 21*n*58
Penn Yan Boats, Inc., v. Sea Lark Boats, Inc., 359 F. Supp. 948,
   175 U.S.P.Q. (BNA) 260 (S.D. Fla. 1972) 132*n*103
People v. See opposing party
PerSeptive Biosystems, Inc. v. Pharmacia Biotech, Inc., 225
   F.3d 1315, 56 U.S.P.Q.2d (BNA) 1001
   (Fed. Cir. 2000). 155*n*178, 156–157
Personalized Mass Media Corp. v. Weather Channel, Inc., 899
   F. Supp. 239 (E.D. Va. 1995). 194*n*111, 194*n*113
Personalized Media Commc'ns, LLC v. Int'l Trade Comm'n,
   161 F.3d 696 (Fed. Cir. 1998) 80*n*10
Poly-America, Inc. v. GSE Lining Tech., Inc., 1998 WL 355477
   (N.D. Tex. 1998). 136*n*111
Premysler v. Lehman, 71 F.3d 387 (Fed. Cir. 1996). 22*n*64
Presidio Components, Inc. v. Am. Tech. Ceramics Corp., 2008
   WL 608407 (S.D. Cal. Mar. 4, 2008) 176*n*38
Procter & Gamble Co. v. Kimberly-Clark Corp., 740 F. Supp. 1177
   (D.S.C. 1989). 140*n*123
Promega Corp. v. Applera Corp., No. 01-C-244-C, 2002
   WL 32359938 (W.D. Wis. June 7, 2002). 178*n*47
Purdue Pharma LP v. Faulding Inc., 20 F.3d 1320 (Fed. Cir. 2000) 88*n*34

Quintel Corp. v. Citibank, 589 F. Supp. 1235 (S.D.N.Y. 1984) 31*n*20

Read Corp. v. Portec, Inc., 970 F.2d 816, 23 U.S.P.Q.2d (BNA) 1426
   (Fed. Cir. 1992). 197*n*123
Red Eagle Res. Corp. v. Baker Hughes, No. H-91-0627, 1992 WL 170614
   (S.D. Tex. Mar. 4, 1992). 20–21, 20*n*55
Refac Int'l, Ltd. v. Lotus Dev. Corp., 81 F.3d 1576, 38 U.S.P.Q.2d
   (BNA) 1665 (Fed. Cir. 1993). 104*n*3, 140*n*123, 143*n*135
Reiffin v. Microsoft Corp., 214 F.3d 1342 (Fed. Cir. 2000) 88*n*32
Rembrandt Techs., LP v. Comcast Corp. 2007 WL 470631
   (E.D. Tex. Feb. 8, 2007) 57–59
Resolution Trust Corp. v. Bright, 6 F.3d 336 (5th Cir. 1993) 20*n*54
ResQNet.com, Inc. v. Lansa, Inc., No. 01 Civ.3578(RWS) ......2004 U.S. Dist. LEXIS
   13579, 2004 WL 1627170 (S.D.N.Y. July 21, 2004) 193*nn*107–108

Rivera, In re, 67 U.S.P.Q.2d (BNA) 1952 (Dir. PTO 2003) .225
Rohm & Haas Co. v. Crystal Chem. Co., 722 F.2d 1556,
   220 U.S.P.Q. (BNA) 289 (Fed. Cir. 1983) 140*n*123
Rohm & Haas Co. v. Lonza, Inc., No. Civ. A. 96-5732, 1999
   U.S. Dist. LEXIS 13919, 1999 WL 718114 (E.D. Pa. Sept. 7, 1999) 198*n*127
Rose v. Summers, Compton, Wells & Hamburg P.C., 887 S.W.2d 683
   (Mo. Ct. App. 1994) 31*n*20
Rosenberg v. Carr Fastener Co., 51 F.2d 1014, 10 U.S.P.Q.
   (BNA) 448 (2d Cir. 1931) 164*n*3
R.R. Donnelly & Sons Co. v. Quark, Inc., 2007 U.S. Dist.
   LEXIS 424, 2007 WL 61885 (D. Del. Jan. 4, 2007) 171*n*10

Safe Flight Instrument Corp. v. Sundstrand Data Control Inc.,
   682 F. Supp. 20, 7 U.S.P.Q.2d (BNA) 1823 (D. Del. 1988) 170*n*5
Saint-Gobain/Norton Indus. Ceramics Corp. v. Gen. Elec.
   Co., 884 F. Supp. 31 (D. Mass. 1995) 201*n*138
Sakraida v. Ag Pro, Inc., 425 U.S. 273 (1976) 82*n*16
Schering Corp. v. Roussel-UCLAF SA, 104 F.3d 341 (Fed. Cir. 1997) 94*n*53
Schloetter v. Railoc of Ind., Inc., 546 F.2d 706 (7th Cir. 1976) 66*n*1
Seagate Tech., LLC., In re, 497 F.3d 1360, 83 U.S.P.Q.2d (BNA)
   1865 (Fed. Cir. 2007) (en banc) 207–209
Security Bank v. Klicker, 418 N.W.2d 27 (Wis. Ct. App. 1987) 31*n*19
Semiconductor Energy Lab. Co. v. Samsung Elec. Co., 4 F.
   Supp. 2d 477 (E.D. Va. 1998) 109*n*27
Semiconductor Energy Lab. Co. v. Samsung Elec. Co.,
   204 F.3d 1368, 54 U.S.P.Q.2d (BNA) 1001
   (Fed. Cir. 2000) 130*n*95, 136*n*112, 136*n*115, 137–138, 137*nn*116–117
Semiconductor Energy Lab. Co. v. Sanyo N. Am. Corp., No.
   C.A. 00–018-GMS, 2001 WL 194303 (D. Del. Feb. 22, 2001) 178*n*47
Sentinel Prods. Corp v. Platt, 64 U.S.P.Q.2d (BNA) 1536
   (D. Mass. 2002) 53–54
Shannon v. Gordon, 670 N.Y.S.2d 887 (N.Y. Sup. Ct. 1998) 28*n*11, 29*n*12
Shelton v. Am. Motors Corp., 805 F.2d 1323 (8th Cir. 1986) 192*n*104
Sibia Neurosciences, Inc., v. Cadus Pharm. Corp., In re,
   No. 96-1231-IEG (POR), 1997 U.S. Dist. LEXIS 24130
   (S.D. Cal. July 15, 1997) 172–180, 176*n*41, 177*n*45, 190*n*93
Sigma-tau Industrie Farmaceutiche Riunite, S.p.A. v. Lonza, Ltd.,
   62 F. Supp. 2d 70 (D.D.C. 1999) 141*n*128
Simmons Foods, Inc. v. Willis, 191 F.R.D. 625 (D. Kan. 2000) 192*n*104
Sinorgchem Co., Shandong v. Int'l Trade Comm'n., 511 F.3d 1132
   (Fed. Cir. 2007) 86*n*27
Small v. Weiffenbach, 10 U.S.P.Q.2d (BNA) 1898
   (Comm'r Pat. 1989) 2*n*7, 15*n*27
Smith v. Diamond, 209 U.S.P.Q. (BNA) 1091 (D.D.C. 1981) 165*n*5
Sperry v. Fla. ex rel. Florida Bar, 373 U.S. 379 (1963) 5*n*1, 107–108*n*17
SRU Biosystems, Inc. v. Hobbs, 2005 Mass. Super. LEXIS 361
   (Mass. Super. Ct. Aug 2, 2005) 178*n*47

State St. Assocs., L.P., In re, B.R. 2005 WL 887151
(Bankr. N.D.N.Y. Mar. 23, 2005) 28*n*9
Strausbourger Pearson Tulcin Wolff, Inc. v. Wiz Tech., Inc. 82 Cal.
Rptr. 2d 326 (Cal. App. 1999). 33*n*22
Strojirenstvi v. Seisakusho, 2 U.S.P.Q.2d (BNA) 1222
(Comm'r Pat. & Trademarks Aug. 29, 1986) 38*n*32
Strojirenstvi v. Toyoda, 1986 Commr. Pat. LEXIS 14
(Comm'r. Pat. Aug. 29, 1986). 66*n*1, 68*n*8, 71*n*18
Sullivan County Reg'l Refuse Disposal Dist. v. Town of Acworth,
686 A.2d 755 (N.H. 1996) 70*n*17
Summagraphics Corp. v. Sanders Assocs., Inc., 1991 U.S. Dist.
LEXIS 16387, 19 U.S.P.Q.2d (BNA) 1859 (D. Conn. 1991). 194*n*111
Sun Microsystems, Inc. v. Dataram Corp., No. CIV. 96–20708 SW,
1997 U.S. Dist. LEXIS 4557, 1997 WL 50272
(N.D. Cal. Feb. 4, 1997). 194*n*111
Sunrise Med. HHG, Inc. v. AirSep Corp., 95 F. Supp. 2d 348
(W.D. Pa. 2000) 132*n*100, 132*n*103
Sun Studs, Inc. v. Applied Theory Assocs., Inc., 772 F.2d 1557,
227 U.S.P.Q. (BNA) 81 (Fed. Cir. 1985) 20*n*53, 28–30, 28*n*10, 66*n*1
Svedala Indus., Inc. v. Winston & Strawn, 1993 WL 198918
(N.D. Ill. June 10, 1993). 163*n*1
Symbol Tech., Inc. v. Lemelson Med., 277 F.3d 1361 (Fed. Cir. 2002) 100*n*62
Synergy Tech & Design Inc. v. Terry, 2007 U.S. Dist. LEXIS 34463
(N.D. Cal. May 2, 2007). 28*n*11

Techno Corp. v. Kenkco USA, Inc., 515 F. Supp. 2d 1086
(N.D. Cal. 2007) 140*n*125
Telectronics Proprietary, Ltd. v. Medtronic, Inc., 836 F.2d 1332
(Fed. Cir. 1988). 28*n*11, 66*n*1
Texarkana College Bowl, Inc. v. Phillips, 408 S.W.2d 537
(Tex. Civ. App.-Texarkana 1966, no writ) 50*n*14
Trading Techs. Int'l, Inc. v. eSpeed, Inc., No. 04 C 5312, 2004
U.S. Dist. LEXIS 19429, 2004 WL 2534389 (N.D. Ill. Sept. 24, 2004). 174*n*31
Transamerica Ins. Fin. Corp. v. Pennmed Consultants, Inc.,
1996 WL 605131 (Oct. 18, 1996) 28*n*9
Transitron Elec. Corp. v. Hughes Aircraft Co., 487 F. Supp. 885, 205
U.S.P.Q. (BNA) 799 (D. Mass. 1980). 119*n*64
Trinity Indus., Inc. v. Road Sys., Inc., 235 F. Supp. 2d 536
(E.D. Tex. 2002) 115*n*55
Two Thirty Nine Joint Venture v. Joe, 60 S.W.3d 896
(Tex. Ct. App. 2001), *rev'd,* 145 S.W.3d 150 (Tex. 2004) 21*n*60, 168*n*1

Ulead Sys., Inc. v. Lex Computer Mgmt Corp., 351 F.3d 1139
(Fed. Cir. 2003). 158*n*190
Ultimax Cement Mfg. Corp. v. CTS Cement Mfg. Corp., 2007 US
Dist. LEXIS 44096 (May 7, 2007). 28*n*11
Union Pac. Res. Co. v. Chesapeake Energy Corp., 236 F.3d 684
(Fed. Cir. 2001). 80*n*12, 89*n*37

United States v. See name of opposing party
Universal Mfg. Co. v. Gardner, Carton & Douglas, 207 F.
  Supp. 2d 830 (N.D. Ill. 2002) 60n33
University of Iowa Research Found. v. Beveridge, DeGrandi,
  Weilacher & Young LLP, 50 U.S.P.Q.2d (BNA) 1620
  (S.D. Iowa 1998). 165n6
University of N.M. v. Fordham, No. 104,761, 2002 WL 529661
  (Bd. Pat. App. & Interf. Apr. 2, 2002) 14n24, 17, 17n38, 18, 49, 49n9, 49n11
University of Rochester v. G.D. Searle & Co., 358 F.3d 916
  (Fed. Cir. 2004). 88n31
University of W.Va. Bd. of Trustees v. VanVoorhies, 33 F.
  Supp. 2d 519 (N.D. W. Va. 1998). 28n11, 29n12
Upjohn Co. v. Mova Pharm. Corp., 225 F.3d 1306, 56
  U.S.P.Q.2d (BNA) 1286 (Fed. Cir. 2000) 141n128
U.S. Steel Corp. v. United States, 730 F.2d 1465
  (Fed. Cir. 1984). 171n8, 174, 179

Vas-Cath Inc. v. Mahurkar, 935 F.2d 1555 (Fed. Cir. 1991) 88n33
Vehicle Techs. Corp. v. Titan Wheel Int'l, 212 F.3d 1377
  (Fed. Cir. 2000). 85n24
Visa U.S.A., Inc. v. First Data Corp., 241 F. Supp. 2d 1100
  (N.D. Cal. 2003) 41n37
Vitronics Corp. v. Conceptronic, Inc., 90 F.3d 1576, 39 U.S.P.Q.2d
  (BNA) 1573 (Fed. Cir. 1996). 86n27, 190n95
Voight v. Kraf, 342 F. Supp. 821 (D. Idaho 1972) 74n1
Voith Sulzer Paper Tech. of Heidenheim Germany, In re,
  No. 506, 1997 U.S. App. LEXIS 12854, 1997 WL 264842
  (Fed. Cir. May 6, 1997) 176n41
Volvo Penta of the Ams., Inc. v. Brunswick Corp., 187 F.R.D. 240
  (E.D. Va. 1999) 171n8

Wands, In re, 858 F.2d 731 (Fed. Cir. 1988). 89–90
Warner-Lambert Co. v. Teva Pharm. USA, Inc., 418 F.3d 1326
  (Fed. Cir. 2005). 89n40
Warren v. Eckert Seamans Cherin & Mellott, 2000 WL 1060652
  (Pa. Com. Pl. Apr. 25, 2000) 81n14
Weiffenbach v. Frank, 18 U.S.P.Q.2d (BNA) 1397
  (Comm'r Pat. 1991) 2n7, 15n27
Weiffenbach v. Gould, 14 U.S.P.Q.2d (BNA) 1331
  (Comm'r Pat. 1989) 2n7, 15n27
Weiffenbach v. Logan, 27 U.S.P.Q.2d (BNA) 1870
  (Comm'r Pat. 1993) 2n7, 15n27
We're Talkin' Mardi Gras, LLC v. Davis, 192 F. Supp. 2d 635
  (E.D. La. 2002) 26n1
Wiener, Ex parte, 125 U.S.P.Q. (BNA) 594 (Comm'r Pat. 1958) 101n66
Williams, People v., 915 P.2d 669 (Colo. 1996) 99n61
W.R. Grace & Co. v. Western U.S. Indus., Inc., 608 F.2d 1214, 203
  U.S.P.Q. (BNA) 721 (9th Cir. 1979) 119–120, 119n64

Wycoff v. Motorola, Inc., 502 F. Supp. 77, 209 U.S.P.Q. (BNA) 115
   (N.D. Ill. 1980) 120*n*68

Young Dental Mfg. Co. v. Q3 Special Prods, Inc., 112 F.3d 1137
   (Fed. Cir. 1997)... 87*n*29

Zletz, In re, 893 F.2d 319, 13 U.S.P.Q.2d (BNA) 1320
   (Fed. Cir. 1989)... 139*n*122

Index

ABA Model Code of Professional
 Responsibility.
Abandonment, patent
 on-sale bar, 147
 unavoidable, 159, 164
 unintentional, 38*n*31, 159, 159*n*195, 164
Acquisition of interest, in patent or
 application avoidance of, 243–45
Administrative law judges, 266–67
Adversity, conflict of interest, 48–51, 48*n*7,
 50*nn*13–14, 51*n*17
Advertising, disciplinary rules, 228–29
Advocate-as-witness disqualification
 depositions of prosecuting litigators,
  194–96, 194*nn*111–113, 195*nn*115–118,
  196*nn*119–120
 Model Rules, 196
 opinion and trial representations, 197–
  201, 197*n*124, 198*nn*126–127, 200*n*130
 state law, 198–200
Agents
 communications with USPTO, 27
 conflict of interest, 3, 3*n*12
 death of, 177
 ethical rules, 1–2
 exclusion, 261–62, 275, 279–81
 lateral hiring of, 63–64
 patent attorneys vs., 22–23, 23*nn*65–66
 registration, 5–9, 10*n*6
 suspension of, 222, 261, 262, 275, 277–81
 unauthorized practice of law,
  7–9, 10*n*6, 75
 unregistered, 7–9, 10*n*6
 use of opinions, 9–10
 withdrawal, 19*n*46, 33*n*22, 45–47, 45*n*1,
  109, 109*n*29, 233–36, 242–43, 251
Akeva LLC v. Mizuno Corp., 203*n*148,
 206–7, 206*n*165, 209*n*181
*Akron Polymer Container Corp. v. Exxel
 Container, Inc.,* 149, 149*n*161

Allen Eng'g Corp. v. Bartell Indus., Inc.,
 146*n*148, 147*n*154
Amendments, avoidance of unnecessary,
 83–84, 84*n*18
American Bar Association (ABA). *See* Model
 Code; Model Rules
Anderson v. Eppstein, 16*n*36, 19*n*46, 67–68,
 69–70, 110*n*30
Annuities, 163, 165–66. *See also*
 Maintenance fees
Appeal
 improper claim rejections, 84–85
 PTO Code disciplinary rules, 275–76
Applications, co-pending, 148–50, 149*n*161
Atofina v. Great Lakes Chem. Corp., 136,
 136*nn*112–13
Attorneys
 death of, 177
 exclusion of, 261–62, 275, 279–81
 lateral hiring of, 63–64
 patent agents vs., 22–23, 23*nn*65–66
 registration, 5–7, 10*n*6
 suspension of, 222, 261, 262, 275, 277–81
 unregistered, 6–7
 use of opinions, 9–10
 withdrawal, 19*n*46, 33*n*22, 45–47, 45*n*1,
  109, 109*n*29, 233–36, 242–43, 251

Bender v. Dudas, 96–97, 225
Best mode requirement, 87, 144,
 144*n*139, 146
Biax Corp. v. Fujitsu Computer Sys. Corp.,
 66–67
Black's Law Dictionary, 117
Board of Patent Appeals and Interferences,
 15, 67–70
Boivin, In re, 43
Brasseler, U.S.A. I, L.P. v. Stryker Sales Corp.,
 13*n*19, 105*n*5, 111*n*37, 118–19, 121,
 123*n*73, 124*nn*75–77, 127*n*87, 147, 191*n*98

Bristol-Myers Squibb Co. v. Rhone-Poulenc Rorer, Inc., 126n81, 144–45
Brooks and Kushman firm, 29–30
Buried material information, 131–33, 132n103, 132nn105–107
Business entities. *See also* Corporations
   client identity issues, 31–37, 31nn19–20, 36n26

Candor. *See* Duty of candor
CFMT, Inc. v. YieldUP Int'l Corp., 144–45, 145n144
C.F.R. *See* Code of Federal Regulations
Chan v. Intuit, Inc., 178nn47–48, 189–90
Checklists. *See* Forms and checklists
Choice of law
   applicable standards, 11–23
      Federal Circuit, 19–21, 20n54
      patent agents' special issues, 22–23, 23nn65–66
      professional conduct code, 17–19, 17n39, 18n42, 18n45
      during prosecution, 14–17, 14n24, 17n39
CIP (continuation-in-part) applications, 101–2, 101n66, 102n67
Claims
   amendments, avoidance of unnecessary, 83–84, 84n18
   appeals of improper rejections, 84–85
   broad scope of, 81–83, 81n14, 82nn15–16, 83n17
   compliance specifications
      best mode, 87, 144, 144n139, 146
      enabling disclosure, 89–90, 89n39
      written description, 88, 88nn35–36
   deadlines, 99–100, 99n60, 99n61
   definiteness, 80
   filing dates, 101–2, 101n66, 102n67
   inventors
      joint, 92–98
      verification of, 90–92, 91n47, 92n49, 93n52
   Jepson claims, 79
   language, 85–87, 85n24, 86nn26–27
   maintenance fees, 100–101
   Markush claims, 79
   process, 81–83
   product, 81–83
   product-by-process, 81–83
   responding to Office Actions, 54–59, 98–99

Client identity, 25–31
   business entities, 31–37, 31n19, 31n20, 36n26
   corporate family conflicts, 32–35, 33n22
   inventors, 26–31, 26n1, 26n4, 28n11, 29nn12–14
   representation, 30, 30n17
   PTO Code, 260–61
Client interactions, PTO Code, 229, 238–40, 245–47, 249–52, 260–61
Clients, former, 65–71
   conflict examples, 71
   possession of confidences, 69–70, 69n10
   prohibitions, 65–72
   substantial relationship test, 66–68, 66n1, 67n5, 68n8
   work product, 70–71, 70n17, 71n18
Code of Federal Regulations (C.F.R.)
   Section 37, 26–27, 91, 93, 95–96, 120, 155–57, 159–61, 165, 185–86, 217, 244
   Rule 1.56, 91, 105, 105n9, 106n10, 106nn12–13, 109, 109n25, 111n33, 112–15, 112n43, 113n45, 113n47, 114nn50–53, 115n55, 115n57, 120, 127–30, 135, 155–56, 155n181, 159–61, 183, 189–90
Cohen, Pontani firm, 208–9
Combined Declaration and Power of Attorney, 26–28
Committee on Discipline, 213–15
Communications, 227–28, 230, 252–53
Competency, 220–21. *See also under* Prosecution
Complaints, 264–66
Compliance specifications
   best mode, 87, 144, 144n139, 146
   enabling disclosure, 89–90, 89n39
   written description, 88, 88nn35–36
Computer Packages, Inc. (CPi), 63–64
Computer Patent Annuities, 163, 165–66
Conduct codes. *See specific codes*
Confidential information
   conflict of interest, 60, 60n34
   Model Rules, 70
   PTO Code, 238–40
Conflict of interest, 45–64
   adversity, 48–51, 48n7, 50nn13–14, 51n17
   confidential information, 60, 60n34
   corporate affiliate intellectual property, 63
   differing interests, 48–51, 48n7, 50nn13–14, 51n17
   lateral hires, 63–64

material limitations, 51–52, 52*n*18
Model Rules, 48–50, 48*n*7, 50*nn*13–14, 51*n*17
patent agents, 3, 3*n*12
professional conduct code, 45*n*1, 47–48, 47*n*2
property rights
    priority, 52–59, 54*n*26, 56*n*29
prosecution issues, 61–64
right to exclude, 59–60, 60*n*33
state law, 47–48
Consent, prospective, 40–44, 40*n*34
Contested cases, 266
Continuation-in-part (CIP) applications, 101–2, 101*n*66, 102*n*67
Co-pending applications
inequitable conduct doctrine, 148–50
    different client and same lawyer, 149
    different client of other firm lawyers, 149–50, 149*n*161
    same client and same lawyer, 148–49
Copyright, as form of protection, 75–78, 76*n*6
Corporations
conflict of interest, 63
as employer of inventors, 26–31, 28*n*11, 29*nn*12–14
intellectual property of affiliates, 63
Corporate family conflicts, 32–35, 33*n*22
sales of business units, 61–62
Correlation tables of ethical codes, 333–44
CPi (Computer Packages, Inc.), 63–64
Crossroads Sys. (Texas), Inc. v. Dot Hill Sys. Corp., 199–200
Crystal Semiconductor Corp. v. TriTech Microelectronics Int'l, Inc., 206
Curtis v. Radio Representatives, Inc., 50–51

Damages
enhanced, 197, 197*n*123
lapsed maintenance fees, 38, 38*n*31
malpractice claims, 2
willful infringement, 201, 207
Database keywords, 61–62, 122
Dayco Prods., Inc. v. Total Containment, Inc., 112*n*43, 113*n*47, 114*n*53, 123*n*73, 148–49, 149*n*161, 150*n*163
Deadlines, 99–100, 99*nn*60–61, 101–2, 101*n*66, 102*n*67
Declarant and application relationships, inequitable conduct doctrine, 143–44, 143*n*135, 144*n*138
Declarations, 26–28

Definiteness, 80
Depositions
of prosecuting litigators, 192–96
    advocate-as-witness disqualification, 194–96
PTO Code, 272–73
Design patents, 76, 77–78
Disclosure. *See* Duty of disclosure
Discovery, 273–74
Disqualification petitions, 16–17, 16*n*37, 17*n*39
Double patenting, 148–49, 151–52
Duty of candor, 103–61
client v. practitioner, 118
co-pending applications, 149
definition, 111
disqualification petitions, 16, 16*n*37
duty of confidentiality, 60
duty of disclosure, 106–8, 106*n*13
imputation of knowledge, 120
materiality, 113, 113*n*45, 114*n*52, 115
nondelegability of, 105
prior art, nondisclosure of, 129–31
protective orders, 185–86
state confidentiality law, 3, 106–10, 106*n*13
verification of inventors, 91
Duty of disclosure. *See also* Information disclosure statement (IDS)
after patent grant, 39, 104–5
definition, 106, 106*n*12
enablement, 89–90, 89*n*39
foreign language references, 135–39
litigation information, 153–55
maintenance fee reminders, 39
MPEP, 120–21, 127–28, 153, 189
Office Actions-foreign, 121–23
Office Actions-U.S., 54–59, 98–99
prior art, 129–31
during prosecution, 14
protective orders, 189
PTO Code, 108–9, 109*n*25, 114, 114*n*53, 226
reexamination proceedings, 154–55
reissue proceedings, 55, 153*n*174, 154–55, 154*n*175, 189
state law, 108–9

Eagle Comtronics, Inc. v. Arrow Commc'n Lab., Inc., 184–85, 186*n*77
EchoStar Commc'ns Corp., In re, 202–9, 202*n*140, 203*n*148, 204*n*156, 206*n*167

Employees, as inventors, 26–31, 28n11,
29nn12–14
Employers. *See* Corporations
Employment, PTO Code, 232–36, 233,
241–42, 246–47
Enablement, inequitable conduct doctrine,
144–45, 144n139, 146nn146–147
Enabling disclosure, 89–90, 89n39
Engagement letters
client identity, 30, 32, 36–38
ending dates of representation, 38–39
joint inventorship, 94–98
prospective consent, 40–44
Entity approach, 31–37, 31nn19–20, 36n26
Enzo Biochem, Inc. v. Applera Corp., 57–59
Estoppel, 81–85, 83n17
Ethical codes, correlation tables, 333–44
Ethics 2000 (Model Rules), 1, 42
European claims, 85, 85n22
Evidence, 271–72
Examiner, former, 70–71, 70n17, 259
Exclusion, attorney/agent, 261–62, 275,
279–81
Ex parte. See name of party
Ex parte contacts, 253, 256
Ex parte prosecution, 16–17, 219, 254–55,
256, 261
Ex parte reexamination proceedings, 160–61
Ex rel. See name of related party

Federal Circuit Court of Appeals
choice of law, 19–21, 20n54
regional circuit law vs., 13
Federal Rules of Civil Procedure, 13, 22, 168
Fees. *See also* Maintenance fees
annuities, 163, 165–66
division of among practitioners, 232
for legal services, 231
sharing legal, 237
Festo Corp. v. Shoketsu Kinzoko Kogyo
Kabushiki Co., 84–85
File wrapper estoppel, 84
Filing dates, (CIP) applications, 101–2,
101n66, 102n67
Finger Furniture Co. v. Finger Interests No. 1,
Ltd., 16n37, 42–44, 44n40
Foreign annuities, 163–66
Foreign language document, prior art, 135
Foreign language translations
misleading, 135–39, 136nn111–113,
136n115
omitting material information, 136–38

partial, 135–36, 138–39
mischaracterization of, 138–39
Forms and checklists
file intake procedure, 283–89
Filed PCT Checklist, 294–95
New PCT Application Checklist,
287–93
PCT Chapter 1 Checklist, 296
PCT Chapter 1/II Checklist, 297
Transfer of Patent Files to a Different
Firm, 298–99
U.S. Utility (Nonprovisional)
Application Checklist, 284–86
Initial Disclosure Memo, 300–305
Frank's Casing Crew & Rental Tools, Inc. v.
PMR Techs., Ltd., 91n46, 155–56
Fried, Frank, Harris, Shriver & Jacobson
firm, 34n22

Geographical siloing, 123
Gump, Akin, 42–44

Hiring practices, 63–64. *See also*
Employment, PTO Code
Hopper v. Frank, 31n20, 36, 36n27
Hunton firm, 57–58

IDS. *See* Information disclosure statement
Inequitable conduct
reissue, 55, 153n174, 154–55,
154n175, 189
Inequitable conduct doctrine, 103–61
background, 104–5, 105n4,
105n6, 105n8
first principles, 111–12, 111nn33–35,
111n37, 112n39
materiality and Rule 1.56, 112–15,
112n43, 113n45, 113n47,
114nn50–53, 115n55, 115n57
preemption of state law,
105–10, 105n9, 106n10,
106n12, 106n13, 108nn24–27,
109nn29–31
intent to deceive
inference of, 125–29, 126n81, 127n85,
127n87, 128nn91–92, 130n95
knowledge of information, 116–23,
116n59, 117n61
duty to investigate, 121–22, 121n72
imputation, 118–23, 118n63,
119n64–65, 120nn68–69
materiality, 123–25, 124n76

protest, 212
recurrent fact patterns
    buried material information, 131–33,
        132*n*103, 132*nn*105–107
    contradictory information,
        withholding of, 139
    co-pending applications, 148–50,
        149*n*161
    declarant and applicant relationships,
        143–44, 143*n*135, 144*n*138
    information from ongoing litigation,
        153–55, 154*n*175
    maintenance fees, 158–59
    McKesson disclosure statements,
        151–53
    mischaracterization of references,
        133–35
    misclaiming priority of disclosure,
        157–58, 157*n*187
    misleading foreign language
        translation, 135–39, 136*nn*111–113,
        136*n*115
    misrepresentation of information,
        155–57, 155*n*179, 155*n*181
    petitions to make special, 160
    petitions to reinstate, 159–60,
        159*n*195
    prior art, nondisclosure of, 129–31
    prior sales, 146–47, 147*n*151, 147*n*154
    reexamination, 154–55, 160–61
    rejection of similar claims, 150–51,
        150*nn*163–164
    Section 112 requirements, 144–46,
        144*n*139, 146*nn*146–147
    test data, 139–43, 140*n*123, 140*n*125,
        141*nn*127–128, 141*n*130, 142*n*132,
        143*n*133
Information disclosure statement (IDS),
    55, 115, 122, 124, 132–35, 135*n*110,
    151, 290
    Office Actions-foreign, 121–23
    Office Actions-U.S., 54–59, 98–99
In re. See name of party
Intellectual property
    conflict of interest, 63
    forms of protection, 75–78, 76*n*6
Intent to deceive, inference of, 125–29,
    126*n*81, 127*n*85, 127*n*87, 128*nn*91–92,
    130*n*95
*Interactive Coupon Mktg. Group, Inc. v.
    H.O.T.! Coupons, LLC,* 174*n*31, 175,
    176*n*38, 187*n*81, 193*n*108, 196*n*119

Interference proceedings, 16–17
Inter partes proceedings, 16–19, 19*n*46,
    107*n*17, 110*n*30, 161, 254–56
Invalidity, 75, 87–90, 116*n*57, 130,
    146, 155, 159–60, 201–6, 206*n*166,
    219, 303
Inventors
    client identity issues, 26–31, 26*n*1, 26*n*4,
        28*n*11, 29*nn*12–14
    representation, 30, 30*n*17
    as corporate employees, 26–31, 28*n*11,
        29*nn*12–14
    joint, 92–98, 94*n*53
    MPEP rules on inventorship, 156
    verification, 90–92, 91*n*47,
        92*n*49, 93*n*52
Investment Company Act (1940), 34*n*22

Japan, 83*n*17, 133, 166
Jepson claim format, 79
Joint inventorship, 92–98
    definition, 92–94
    evaluation of, 94–97
    property rights, 94, 94*n*53
    representation, 97

*Kingsdown Med. Consultants, Ltd. v.
    Hollister, Inc.,* 111*n*33, 112*n*41, 125–27,
    141*n*130

Laches, 99–100, 100*n*62
*Landmark Graphics Corp. v. Seismic Micro
    Tech., Inc.,* 200
Language. *See also* Foreign language
    translations
    in claims, 85–87, 85*n*24, 86*nn*26–27
    consistency, 62
LexisNexis Patent Optimizer program,
    62, 80
London Agreement, 85, 85*n*22

Maintenance fees, 163–66, 164*n*3, 165*n*6
    inequitable conduct doctrine, 158–59
    lapsed, 38, 38*n*31
    notification, 100–101
    reminders, 38–39, 38*nn*31–32
    small entity v. large entity, 158–59
Malpractice claims
    due to missed deadlines, 99, 99*n*61
    increase of, 2, 163, 163*n*1
Manoir-Electroalloys Corp. v. Amalloy Corp.,
    38*n*30, 44

Manual of Patent Examining Procedure
(MPEP)
amendments to, 74, 74n2
on best mode, 146
on burying references, 131–32
on changes of address, 165
on co-pending applications, 148
on duty of disclosure, 120–21, 127–28,
153, 189
on information from ongoing
litigation, 153
on knowledge of prior art, 129–31
on mischaracterization of references, 133
on patent sale, 153
on protective orders, 185–86
on rules of inventorship, 156
scope of, 13, 13n18, 164n2
Markman hearings, 57–58
Markush, Ex parte, 79
Markush claim format, 79
Material limitations, conflict of interest,
51–52, 52n18
*McKesson Info. Solutions, Inc. v. Bridge
Med., Inc.,* 151–53, 151n167, 153n170
Means-plus-function claim format, 79–80,
80n10
Model Code (ABA)
on corporate family conflicts, 32–35,
33n22
scope of, 1, 11–12, 12n15, 20n54
Model Rules (ABA)
on advocate-as-witness
disqualification, 196
on confidentiality, 70
conflict of interest, 48–50, 48n7,
50nn13–14, 51n17
on prospective consent, 41–42
scope of, 1, 11–12
Molins PLC v. Textron, Inc.,
113n44, 124n76, 131n99, 132n101, 149
MPEP. *See* Manual of Patent Examining
Procedure

National Institutes of Health (NIH), 67–70
*Nazomi Commc'ns, Inc. v. Arm Holdings
PLC,* 169n2, 174n31, 176,
186n78, 188n85
Ninth Circuit Court of Appeals, 21
Nonobviousness, 78, 82–83, 82n16,
104, 151
*Novartis Pharm. Corp. v. Eon Labs Mfg.,
Inc.,* 208–9
Novelty, 78, 82, 131, 133

*Novo Nordisk Pharm. Inc. v. Bio-Tech. Gen.
Corp.,* 90n43, 140–41, 141n126

Obviousness. *See* Nonobviousness
Office of Enrollment and Discipline (OED).
See also PTO Code
disciplinary rules, 1–2
discipline final decisions, 307–32
Abdallah, Iman A., 307
Barron, Harry W., 309
Bell, Curtis A., 309
Bode, George A., 309–10
Burmeister, Marshall Arthur, 310
Callaghan, John E., 310
Carroll, Leo R., 310
Cohen, Herbert, 310
Cohen, Jonathan M., 311
Cohen, Matthew J., 311
Colitz, Michael J., Jr., 311–12
Combs, E. Michael, 312
Cooper, Byron W., 312
Corbin, Charles C., 312–13
Dabney, Tami A., 313
Davis, F. Eugene, 313
Denenberg, David W., 313
DeSha, Michael J., 313
Dix, Brendan B., 314
Drake, Malik N., 314
Dunsmuir, George H., 314
Eslinger, Lewis, 314
Flagg, Rodger H., 314
Flynn, William C., 314–15
Frease, John B., 315
Frederiksen, Mark D., 315
Garmon, Judith E., 315
Gernstein, Terry M., 315
Gilliam, Steven Dale, 316
Goates, Gary B., 316
Gould, David F., 316
Greenburg, Alan G., 317
Halvonik, John P., 317
Herring, Joseph C., 317–18
Hilke, Charles N., 318
Hill, Kenneth E., 318
Hillman, Val Jean F., 318
Ho, Lawrence Y.D., 318
Hoffman, Bernard S., 318–19
Hurey, Michael, 319
Illich, Russell, 319
Jennings, Larry M., 319
Johnson, Larry D., 320
Kaardal, Ivar M., 320
Kearns, Jerry T., 321

Kersey, George E., 321
Krause, Dean Luca, 321
Kroll, Michael I., 321
Liniak, Thomas Paul, 321
Lobato, Emmanuel J., 322
Lynt, Christopher H., 322
Maiorino, Salvatore J., 322
Marinangeli, Michael G., 322
Marks, Andrew S., 323
Marzocco, Ralph L., 323
Maxwell, Michael D., 323
Morton, Richard F., 323–24
Mullen, Martin G., 324
Mybeck, Walter, R., II, 324
Osredkar, Peter J., 324
Peirce, Matthew J., 324–25
Reichmanis, Maria, 325
Reynolds, David Duncan, 325
Rivera, Chrispin M., 325
Rose, Stuart W., 326
Rosenberg, Marshall e., 326
Rostoker, Michael David, 326
Ryznic, John E., 326–27
Schaefer, Kenneth R., 327
Schwartz, Stanley D., 327
Sheinbein, Sol, 328
Spangler, Jeffrey Thomas, 328
Stanback, Clarence F., Jr., 328
Sturges, Hiram, 329
Sylvester, Bradley P., 329
Tassan, Bruce A., 329
Teplitz, Jerome M., 330
Uland, Larry L., 330
Van Der Wall, Robert J., 330
Vander Weit, John, Jr., 330
Volk, David L., 331
Wengrovsky, Todd, 331
Wittenberg, Malcolm B., 332
Ziegler, Thomas K., 332
preemption, 18n45
restatements, 164
scope of, 1–2, 15
Officials, 255–58
On-sale bar, 124–25, 147
Opinion and trial representations. *See under*
Prosecution, with other forms of
representation

Patent and Trademark Office Code of
Professional Conduct. *See* PTO Code
Patent and Trademark Tracking System
(PATTSY), 63–64
Patent Cooperation Treaty (PCT), 74

Patent infringement suits. *See* Prosecution,
with other forms of representation
Patents
design patents, 76, 77–78
as form of protection, 75–78
plant patents, 76, 77
utility patents, 77
PATTSY (Patent and Trademark Tracking
System), 63–64
*PerSeptive Biosystems, Inc. v. Pharmacia
Biotech, Inc.,* 155n178, 156–57
Petitions
for accelerated examination, 160
disqualification, 16–17, 16n37, 17n39
to make special, 160
to reinstate, 159–60, 159n195, 280–81
Pfaff case, 147, 147n154
Plant patents, 76, 77
Possession of confidences, 69–70, 69n10,
238–40
Power of Attorney
client identity, 26–28, 28n8
joint Declaration and, 26–27
maintenance fees, 165
revocation, 27
Prior art
foreign language document, 135
misleading foreign language translation,
135–39, 136nn111–113, 136n115
nondisclosure of, 129–31
novel subject matter, 82–83, 83n17, 84n18
translation requirement, 135–39
Priority, property rights, 52–59, 54n26,
56n29
Prior sales, inequitable conduct doctrine,
146–47, 147n151, 147n154, 154
Process claims, 81–83
Product-by-process claims, 81–83
Product claims, 81–83
Professional Conduct Code. *See* PTO Code
Property rights, conflict of interest, 52–59,
54n26, 56n29
Prophetic examples, 90, 90n43
Prosecution
choice of law
applicable standards, 14–17, 14n24,
17n39
disciplinary rules, 15
USPTO disqualification, 16–17, 17n39
competency, 73–102
amendments, avoidance of
unnecessary, 83–84, 84n18
appeals, 84–85

Prosecution (*cont.*)
    broad scope of claims, 81–83, 81*n*14,
        82*nn*15–16, 83*n*17
    claims, types of, 78–80, 80*n*10, 85–87,
        85*n*24, 86*nn*26–27
    compliance specifications, 87–90,
        88*nn*35–36, 89*n*39, 90*n*43
    definiteness, 80
    filing dates, 101–2, 101*n*66, 102*n*67
    forms of protection, 74*n*1, 75–78, 75*n*3,
        76*n*6
    inventors, 90–92, 91*n*47, 92*n*49, 93*n*52
    maintenance fees, 100
    meeting deadlines, 99–100, 99*nn*60–61
    Office Actions, 98–99
    PTO Code on, 220–21
Prosecution, combining with other forms
    of representation, 168–209. *See also*
    specific cases
    applicable standards, 168, 168*n*1
    conflicts and liability, 182–86, 182*n*62,
        183*nn*63–64, 184*n*170, 185*n*71
    depositions of prosecuting litigators,
        192–96, 192*nn*104–106, 193*nn*107–108
        advocate-as-witness disqualification,
            194–96, 194*nn*111–113,
            195*nn*115–118, 196*nn*119–120
    inequitable conduct as conflict, 191–92,
        191*n*100
    litigation, 169–82
        analysis, 180–82, 180*nn*54–55,
            181*nn*56–58
        misuse of discovery materials, 169–72,
            169*n*2, 170*n*3, 170*n*5, 170*n*6, 171*n*8,
            172*n*14
    opinion and trial representations,
        197–209, 197*n*123
        advocate-as-witness disqualification,
            197–201, 197*n*124, 198*nn*126–127,
            200*n*130
        work product, 201–9, 201*n*135,
            202*n*139, 202*n*144, 203*n*148,
            204*n*156, 206*n*166, 207*n*175,
            208*n*176
    protective orders, 186–90, 186*n*78,
        187*nn*80–82, 188*nn*83–85, 189*nn*90–92,
        190*nn*93–95
Prosecution history estoppel, 84
Prospective consent, standards, 40–44,
    40*n*34
Protective orders
    execution of, 186–90, 190*n*94

disqualification of prosecuting
    litigators, 190
seeking of, 169–78, 170*n*3, 174*n*31,
    177*n*43, 178*n*47, 182–86, 184*n*70,
    185*n*71
PTO Code, 211–83. *See also* Office of
Enrollment and Discipline
canon 1, 220
canon 2, 227
canon 3, 236
canon 4, 238
canon 5, 240
canon 6, 248–49
canon 7, 250
canon 8, 256
canon 9, 258
Committee on Discipline, 213–15
conflict of interest, 45*n*1, 47–48, 47*n*2
correspondence, 217–19
definitions, 211–13
disciplinary rules, 219–20
    acquisition of interest, avoidance of,
        243–45
    administrative law judges, 266–67,
        274–75
    advertising, 228–29
    aiding unauthorized practice of law,
        236–37
    appeals, 275–76
    burden of proof, 271
    client confidences and secrets,
        preservation of, 238–40
    client identity of funds and property,
        preservation of, 260–61
    clients, direct contact with
        prospective, 229
    clients, limitation of business relations
        with, 245–46
    clients, limiting liability to, 249–50
    clients, representation of, 250–52
    clients, settling similar claims of, 247
    Commissioner decisions, 276–77
    communication and adverse interests,
        252–53
    communication of fields of
        practice, 230
    communications on a practitioner's
        services, 227–28
    competency, 220–21
    complaints, 264–66
    contested cases, 266
    criminal prosecution, threats of, 253

depositions, 272–73
disciplinary proceedings, 262
disclosure of information, 226
discovery, 273–74
employment, acceptance of, 233
employment, refusing due to
    impairment, 241–42, 246–47
employment agreements,
    restrictive, 232–33
evidence, 271–72
failure to act competently, 249
fees, division of among practitioners,
    232
fees, sharing legal, 237
fees for legal services, 231
filing of papers, 268–69
firm names and letterhead, 230–31
hearings, 270
impropriety, avoidance of
    appearance of, 259
influence, avoidance of other, 248
investigations, 261–62
misconduct, 221–26
motions, 269
names and letterhead, 230–31
officials, contact with, 255–56
officials, statements concerning, 257–58
partnerships with non-
    practitioners, 238
petitions to reinstate, 280–81
pleading amendments, 271
practitioner candidates, 258
proceedings, conduct in, 253–55
proposed findings and conclusions, 274
public officials, action as, 257
reprimand, suspension or
    exclusion, 261
resignation, 262–64
respondents, representation of, 268
rule suspension, 281
savings clause, 281
suspension, exclusion or
    reprimand, 261
suspension or exclusion of
    practitioners, 277–81
withdrawal due to practitioner as
    witness, 242–43
withdrawal from employment,
    45n1, 233–36
witnesses, contact with, 255
establishment of, 12n8
forms, 121–22

non-patent cases, 216–17
preemption, 17–19, 18n42, 19nn46–47
refusal to recognize practitioners, 217
removal of registered names, 215
scope of, 1–3, 219–20
trademark cases, 216–17
unenforceability, 114, 114n49
Public information, 68, 70
Public officials, 255–58

Raffkind, Eliot, 43–44
RCE (Requesting continued examination),
    129, 131, 154
Reasonable examiner standard, 114
Red Eagle Res. Corp. v. Baker Hughes, 20–21,
    20n55
Reexamination proceedings,
    inequitable conduct doctrine,
    154–55, 160–61
Registration, 5–11
    grant of authority, 5–6
    unauthorized practice of law, 6–11
        opinions, 9–10
        patent agents, 5–9, 10n6
        patent attorneys, 5–7, 10n6
Reinstatement petitions, 159–60, 159n195,
    280–81
Reissue proceedings, 55, 153n174, 154–55,
    154n175, 189
Rembrandt Techs., LP v. Comcast Corp.,
    57–59
Representation. *See also* Prosecution, with
    other forms of representation
    client identity, 30, 30n17
    ending dates, 37–39, 38nn30–32, 39n33
    of joint inventors, 97
    PTO Code, 250–52, 268
    scope of, 39–40
*Representation of Others Before the Patent
    and Trademark Office. See* PTO Code
Requesting continued examination (RCE),
    129, 131, 154
Revival
    co-pending applications, 101–2, 102n67
    Japanese patents, 166
    lapsed maintenance fees, 163, 163n1
    petitions to reinstate, 159, 159n195
Right to exclude, conflict of interest, 59–60,
    60n33
Rule 1.56. *See under* inequitable conduct
Rules and codes. *See specific
    rules and codes*

Sale, patent
duty to investigate, 117, 117n61
MPEP, 153
on-sale bar, 124–25, 147
ownership verification, 55–56
prior sales, 146–47, 147n151,
147n154, 154
prosecution bar, 187, 187n82
prosecution conflicts, 61–62
representation, 31n20
validity opinion, 10
Seagate Tech., LLC., In re, 207–9
Section 112 requirements
competency
definiteness, 80
inequitable conduct doctrine
best mode, 87, 144, 144n139, 146
enablement, 144–45, 144n139,
146nn146–147
Wands Factors, 89–90
Securities and Exchange Commission (SEC),
33n22
*Semiconductor Energy Lab. Co. v. Samsung
Elec. Co.*, 130n95, 136n112, 136n115,
137–38, 137nn116–17
Sentinel Prods. Corp v. Platt, 53–54
*Sibia Neurosciences, Inc., v. Cadus Pharm.
Corp., In re*, 172–80, 173n23, 173n26,
174nn30–31, 175n32, 175n35, 175n37,
176n38, 176n41, 177n45, 177nn43–45,
178n47, 190n93
Signatures, 217–19
Small entity status, 158–59
Standards, 11–23. *See also* Choice of law
patent agents' special issues, 22–23,
23nn65–66
professional conduct code
preemption, 17–19, 19nn46–47
during prosecution, 14–17, 14n24
disciplinary rules, 15
USPTO disqualification, 16–17
prosecution with other forms of
representation, 168, 168n1
State law
on adversity, 50–51
on advocate-as-witness disqualification,
198–200
client identity issues, 30, 30n16
on competitive decision-making, 179–80,
179n52
conflict of interest, 47–48
ethical rules, 1–3, 6–9, 12–13, 15n30

former client conflicts, 70, 70n17, 71n18
preemption
inequitable conduct doctrine, 105–10,
105n9, 106n10, 106nn12–13,
108nn18–19, 108nn24–27,
109nn29–31
Stroock firm, 33n22
Subject matter, 1–3, 61–62, 82–83, 83n17.
See also aspects of prosecution
Substantial relationship test, 66–68, 66n1,
67n5, 68n8
*Sun Studs, Inc. v. Applied Theory Assocs.,
Inc.*, 20n53, 28–30, 28n10, 66n1
Supremacy, 114
Supreme Court (New Hampshire), 70–71
Supreme Court, U.S.
on claim amendments, 84–85
on federal objectives phrase, 107n17
Suspension, attorney/agent, 222, 261, 262,
275, 277–81

Terminology. *See* Language
Test data, inequitable conduct doctrine,
139–43, 140n123, 140n125,
141nn127–128, 141n130,
142n132, 143n133
35 U.S. Code. *See* Section 112 requirements;
specific aspects of prosecution
Trademarks, 75–78, 216–17
Trademark Trial and Appeal
Board (TTAB)
conflict of interest, 49–50
on prospective consent, 42–44
Trade secret, as form of protection, 75–78
Translation requirement, prior art. *See*
Foreign language translations

Union for the Protection of New Varieties of
Plants (UPOV), 76, 77
United States v. See name of opposing party
University of N.M. v. Fordham, 14n24, 17,
17n38, 18, 49, 49n9, 49n11
U.S. Patent and Trademark Office (USPTO).
See also PTO Code; specific divisions
amendments to (2008), 8–10
choice of law, 14
disqualification, 16–17, 17n39
professional conduct code preemption,
17–19, 19nn46–47
U.S. Steel Corp. v. United States, 171n8, 174,
179
Utility patents, 77

Wands, In re, 89–90
Washington Rules of Professional
    Conduct, 12
Willful blindness doctrine, 117–18, 121–23
Willful infringement, 201, 207
Withdrawal, attorney/agent, 19*n*46, 33*n*22,
    45–47, 45*n*1, 109, 109*n*29, 233–36,
    242–43, 251
Wiz Tech, Inc., 33*n*22

Work product
    challenging validity of, 70–71
    former clients, 70–71, 70*n*17, 71*n*18
    risk of waiver, 201–9, 201*n*135, 202*n*139,
        202*n*144, 203*n*148, 204*n*156, 206*n*166,
        207*n*175, 208*n*176
Written description of invention, 88,
    88*nn*35–36